PATERNOSTER BIBLICAL MONOGRAPHS

Healing, Weakness and Power

Perspectives on Healing in the Writings of Mark, Luke and Paul

PATERNOSTER BIBLICAL MONOGRAPHS

A full listing of all titles in this series and Paternoster Theological Monographs will be found at the close of this book.

PATERNOSTER BIBLICAL MONOGRAPHS

Healing, Weakness and Power

Perspectives on Healing in the Writings of Mark, Luke and Paul

Audrey Dawson

WIPF & STOCK · Eugene, Oregon

Wipf and Stock Publishers
199 W 8th Ave, Suite 3
Eugene, OR 97401

Healing, Weakness, and Power
Perspectives on Healing in the Writings of Mark, Luke, and Paul
By Dawson, Audrey

ISBN 13: 978-1-60608-313-0
Publication date 12/10/2008
Previously published by Paternoster, 2008

This Edition published by Wipf and Stock Publishers by arrangement with Paternoster

PATERNOSTER BIBLICAL MONOGRAPHS

Series Preface

One of the major objectives of Paternoster is to serve biblical scholarship by providing a channel for the publication of theses and other monographs of high quality at affordable prices. Paternoster stands within the broad evangelical tradition of Christianity. Our authors would describe themselves as Christians who recognise the authority of the Bible, maintain the centrality of the gospel message and assent to the classical credal statements of Christian belief. There is diversity within this constituency; advances in scholarship are possible only if there is freedom for frank debate on controversial issues and for the publication of new and sometimes provocative proposals. What is offered in this series is the best of writing by committed Christians who are concerned to develop well-founded biblical scholarship in a spirit of loyalty to the historic faith.

Series Editors

To my Patients

Contents

Preface and Acknowledgements

This book is a revision of a doctoral dissertation accepted by the University of Aberdeen in 2005. The work was conducted under the patient supervision of Dr. Andrew Clarke, Senior Lecturer in New Testament in the University of Aberdeen and incorporates further comments by the examiners, Dr. Steve Walton, London School of Theology and Dr. Peter Williams, then of the University of Aberdeen.

Jesus' healing ministry has been a source of inspiration and comfort for workers in the caring professions for centuries. The subject of healing in the New Testament has been of interest to me, as I spent forty years working as a physician, before retiring to undertake biblical studies as a *very* mature student. As a clinical haematologist, I witnessed and lived through a period of enormous change in the treatment and prognosis of people with conditions such as leukaemias and lymphomas. Many of the patients I cared for had diseases, which at the outset of my career were rapidly fatal, but where scientific advances meant that several of these illnesses became amenable to treatment. Thus, patients who developed these diseases in later times often survived, and many remain today in good health. This has been for me the unfolding of one of the miracles of healing.

I also cared for many, who, though not cured physically, reached spiritual peace, and who were of enormous influence on my life and the lives of other carers, as well as on their family and friends. My experience has been that a meaningful contract between patient and carer always involves a relationship where compassion/love is of great importance. Although it is recognised that advances in medicine are made only with great effort, it is less commonly emphasised that care of a seriously sick and dying person takes a toll from the carer, both lay and professional, as well as the patient. There is a positive side, however. There were times in my interaction with a patient (which was frequently over many years), when the patient or I, or more usually both, realised that what bound us was much more than what is called the 'doctor-patient relationship'. This was often unspoken communication, often religious, which had the power to give both of us peace. The gospel-writers, from their viewpoint of the healthy, seemed to sense this power when they were describing Jesus' healing, and I believe that Paul, unhealed of his 'thorn', recognised it, for instance, in Rom. 8:38, in his awareness that nothing separates us from the love of God in Christ. It seems to me that weakness and power in the healing 'transaction' are complex areas, which I wished to explore in depth, particularly as such exploration may contribute to the lamentably limited dialogue between New Testament scholars and medical workers or medical historians.

There is a Scottish saying, 'The langer you live, the mair fairlies you see' (the longer you live, the more wonders you see). There were many wonders in my professional life; there were many people who, according to the 'rules' of science and nature, should have died rapidly, but who survived, and others who had no clear physical reason to die, but did. Thus, I find it easier than many people trained in modern scientific method to accept the reality of Jesus' miracle healing.

I am greatly indebted to the people who have encouraged me in this project. First, and easily foremost, I would like to express my gratitude to Dr. Andrew Clarke, for his patient supervision of the production of the dissertation, for his encouragement in my seeking its publication, and for his practical help when my computer skills were inadequate. His good-natured support and encouragement, his expertise and mental dexterity in heading me away from the innumerable cul-de-sacs down which my work wandered, and his intellectual toughness, kept me going, even when I plumbed the depths of despair about the project. Throughout all these trials, he remained interested and helpful in all aspects of writing a thesis and a monograph, as a staunch ally and a friend.

I wish also to thank both my sisters; one, who supported my decision to undertake the project in spite of difficulties; the other, who, because of her life-long disabilities, has given me painful insights into the problems which severe disability brings. I thank also my friends, who, though they undoubtedly regarded me as mad, also accepted and encouraged me.

Many teachers and members of the New Testament seminar in the University of Aberdeen contributed to my knowledge of the wider issues of New Testament scholarship, and to the experience of modern postgraduate learning, including teaching me enough I.T. skill to stop my computer from terrifying me all the time.

I have written the book in honour of all the patients who put their trust in me, in allowing me to care for them.

Abbreviations

The New Revised Standard Version of the Bible has been used throughout.

Reference sources are cited by the author's name and the full title at the first occurrence, then by name and short title thereafter. The system of abbreviations generally follows that of the *Journal of Biblical Literature* 117 (1998) 555-79, with the following additions:

ANRW	*Aufstieg und Niedergang der Römischen Welt*
BECNT	Baker Exegetical Commentary on the New Testament
NCBC	New Century Bible Commentary
NIBC	New International Biblical Commentary
NIDNTT	*New International Dictionary of New Testament Theology*
PNTC	Pillar New Testament Commentary
TPI	Trinity Press International
ZNT	*Zeitschrift für Neues Testament*

Chapter 1

Introduction

1 Prolegomena

Healing is an important aspect of life; illnesses have been known and attempts at healing documented since pre-history, and the use of plants and herbs in healing attested throughout the world.[1] Methods of healing have changed radically over time and place, however, and explaining the rationale of ancient healing is not straightforward, for several reasons. First, healing was invested in antiquity with elements of miracle, magic and religion; sickness and religion were closely connected, as religion sought to explain the existence of illness, and the suffering produced.[2] There are great gaps in our knowledge of these areas in ancient society, especially how healing, miracle and religion were deeply embedded in each other, since our understanding is coloured by our present-day mind-set.[3] Second, since healing, miracle and religion roused strong reactions in antiquity, the evidence was particularly liable to destruction, so that, although they were so important in the ancient world, relatively few artefacts and collections of miracle stories are likely to have survived.[4] Third, there is the

---

1 E.g. D. Guthrie, *A History of Medicine* (London: Nelson, 1945) p.2, records that bone diseases have been identified in animals dating from Palaeolithic times, and, pp.5-7, describes the finding of trepanned skulls from prehistoric adult humans. H. Avalos, 'Disability and Liturgy in Ancient and Modern Religious Traditions', in N.L. Eiesland and D.E. Saliers (eds.), *Human Disability and the Service of God. Reassessing Religious Practice* (Nashville: Abingdon, 1998) p.48, notes that the medicinal use of plants can be traced to pre-history, and some of these remedies are still to be found world-wide.

2 Avalos, 'Disability and Liturgy', p.48, observes that medicinal plants and healing liturgies were used together in most ancient cultures. G.B. Ferngren and D.W. Amundsen, 'Medicine and Christianity in the Roman Empire: Compatibilities and Tensions', in *ANRW* II.37.3 (1996) 2957.

3 J. Goldin, 'The Magic of Magic and Superstition', in E.S. Fiorenza (ed.), *Aspects of Religious Propaganda in Judaism and Early Christianity* (Notre Dame: University of Notre Dame Press, 1976) p.119. J.M. Robinson and H. Koester, *Trajectories through Early Christianity* (Philadelphia: Fortress, 1971) p.2, note that nowadays we compartmentalise different parts of life. H.J. Cadbury, *The Peril of Modernizing Jesus* (orig. 1937; London: SPCK, 1962) pp.26-28, wrote that we fill the gaps in ancient history with modern content, like stitching a new patch on an old garment.

4 M. Smith, 'Prolegomena to a Discussion of Aretalogies, Divine Men, the Gospels and Jesus', *JBL* 90 (1971) 178.

opposite problem, that the miraculous element of any narrative may have been heightened and distorted, initially as a result of propaganda and apologetic, and later, by time and tradition.[5] Fourth, the difficulties for present-day historians studying attitudes and beliefs of a past era and a different part of the world are particularly great in the area of healing miracles or magic, because of our present-day presuppositions from a scientific age.[6]

The study considers how three of the writers of the New Testament (Mark, Luke and Paul) understood and presented miracles of healing performed by Jesus and his followers, and how their perspectives were related to their theological views, reflecting now on what the ancient biblical writers believed at the time of writing. One simple reason for Jesus and his followers healing might be that it attracted the crowds, who then heard and responded to Jesus' message.[7] The more profound theological and humanitarian reasons that the ancient writers saw for miracle healing will be studied in the work. 'Healing' in this study refers primarily to the recovery from illness and/or disability, together with the consequences that follow, such as rehabilitation into the community, rather than dealing in detail with other circumstances, such as forgiveness of sin, which are sometimes referred to as 'healing' (and which may have the same socio-religious effects).

As the combined writings of Mark, Luke and Paul amount to more than half the material in the New Testament, the intention is to present the general perspectives of these writers in the context of healing, rather than to undertake detailed exegeses of all the passages discussed.

1.1 Mission and Outline

There seems to be a gap in the modern perception of healing in the New Testament. Many scholars have avoided the area of healing; some have accepted Jesus' and apostolic healing as being merely illustration of the teaching of the gospel message, while others have studied only the

---

5 Cadbury, *Peril of Modernizing Jesus*, p.24. F.H. Borsch, *Power in Weakness. New Hearing for Gospel Stories of Healing and Discipleship* (Philadelphia: Fortress, 1983) pp.xiii-xiv.

6 A.F. Segal, 'On the Nature of Magic. A Report on a Dialogue between a Historian and a Sociologist', in L.M. White and O.L. Yarbrough (eds.), *The Social World of the First Christians: Essays in Honor of Wayne A. Meeks* (Minneapolis: Augsburg Fortress, 1995) pp.275-80, especially p.279, draws attention to the extent to which we impose our culture on ancient cultures.

7 E.g. E.P. Sanders, *Jesus and Judaism* (London: SCM, 1985) p.164.

theological content of healing narratives.[8] This has resulted in there being available very little work which concentrates on the differences between the writers of the New Testament in their perceptions of miracle healing, particularly in relation to its power and significance, in the early church's Christology and mission. The aim is to assess the early church's perhaps variable view of miracle healing then, in particular, to distinguish the views of the ancient writers, without attempting to establish Jesus' perception of his healing.[9]

This assessment will be made by investigating miracle healing as portrayed in two synoptic gospels, Mark and Luke, in Acts, and in the undisputed Pauline letters, after first considering the circumstances and background regarding illness and healing in the world in which these books and letters were written. The choice of biblical documents is related partly to their assumed dating in the early church, but it also recognises that the fledgling church was confronted with questions of illness, and had a tradition of the healings of Jesus and his disciples. Aspects of medical anthropology and sociology, as well as narrative and theological considerations, will be prominent.

Chapter 2 will describe the background, both social and religious,[10] to miracle healing as depicted in the New Testament. The Jewish background is available to us both in the Old Testament, and in the writings of the inter-testamental period. The world in which the New Testament was written was a maelstrom of religious pluralism.[11] By the first century BC and AD, the Jewish influence was widespread, both in Palestine and throughout the Jewish Diaspora (which corresponded roughly to the Eastern Roman Empire), and was further publicised by the works of Philo and Josephus. Older Greek religions had often been superseded by mystery religions from Oriental and Egyptian sources, and healing was sometimes an integral part of these cults. Roman religions had become important, especially the Imperial cult, which was

---

8 Unusually, J. Wilkinson, *The Bible and Healing. A Medical and Theological Commentary* (Edinburgh/Grand Rapids: Handsel/Eerdmans, 1998) has considered biblical healing from a mainly medical viewpoint, as well as the theological content.

9 This is unlike the aim of E. Eve, *The Jewish Context of Jesus' Miracles* (JSNTSup 231; Sheffield: Sheffield Academic Press, 2002) p.3, who is concerned also with this aspect.

10 A.D. Clarke, *Serve the Community of the Church. Christians as Leaders and Ministers* (Grand Rapids/Cambridge: Eerdmans, 2000) e.g. pp.95-96, notes that the religious element was integral to civic and family life.

11 H.-J. Klauck, *Magic and Paganism in Early Christianity. The World of the Acts of the Apostles* (ET; Edinburgh: T. & T. Clark, 2000) p.1, quotes a hypothetical picture of pluralism in the ancient Roman Empire.

imposed on, and often enthusiastically adopted by, cities of the Eastern Roman Empire. Religion and healthcare, including magic, were important areas of social life, as people were deeply concerned about illness and harm, their prevention and cure. This milieu forms the background from which the three biblical writers depicted miracle healing by Jesus and his followers.

In the following two chapters, how the final writers of two synoptic gospels viewed Jesus' healing will be considered. There will be no attempt to get back to the underlying sources of the gospels; only the canonical accounts of the gospels will be studied. Chapter 3 will deal with how Mark, the author of what is accepted here as the first written gospel, depicts miracle healing by Jesus, and how Jesus passed on the ability to heal to his disciples, enabling them for mission. In particular in this chapter, the aim is to study in detail Mark's narrative description of Jesus' healing, so that these features may be used in comparison in later chapters. This portrait of Jesus' healing will be considered in relation to Mark's theology, particularly his Christology.

In Chapter 4, Luke's gospel will be targeted, as the synoptic gospel to be compared with Mark's in relation to healing. This has the advantage that we can then move easily from his gospel account to Acts, accepting that both were written by the same author. Luke's portrayal of healing in the early church will be compared with his depiction of Jesus' healing in the gospel. Since it is assumed that these accounts of healing would be influenced by Luke being a physician (Col. 4:14), the evidence for this view will be assessed briefly.

In Chapter 5, Paul's undisputed letters will be studied for evidence of the significance that Paul attaches to healing in the life of the very early church. Only the seven letters accepted by all scholars are included (Romans, 1 and 2 Corinthians, Galatians, Philippians, Philemon, and 1 Thessalonians); it is assumed here that the letters to the Colossians and Ephesians, as well as the Pastoral letters, were not written by Paul. Elements of Paul's autobiography and ethics found in these seven letters will be considered, and possible reasons for differences in his emphasis on miracle healing reflected upon, compared with the picture of Paul in Acts.

In Chapter 6, the similarities and differences in divine healing, as described by the ancient writers, and studied in Chapters 3, 4 and 5, will be analysed, noting the theological, especially Christological, basis to their different emphases, as well as the practical consequences. The views of the writers about the continuation of healing in the church after apostolic times will be considered from a number of angles, for instance, from a sociological viewpoint, and from the writers' understandings of the overthrow of Satan, in relation to illness and healing. As it is recognised that Jesus' healing ministry had not banished the problems of illness, the developments in healing in the later New Testament and beyond, in the early post-New Testament church, will be mentioned briefly, to assess the impact on the care of the ill, both in and beyond the church, that Jesus' healing may have had. Finally, the significance of the power of healing in the New Testament is reflected upon.

1.2 Problems in Researching Jesus' Miracle Healing

Since the depictions of the healing miracles of Jesus and his followers are the primary materials of the study, critical questions must be considered about these miracles, in the contexts of both the first century and today. If we can acknowledge that Jesus performed miracles of healing, it is then easier to accept that his followers did so also; thus we use here Jesus' healing as the paradigm of healing in these ancient writings. The further question of whether or not Jesus' healing miracles were unique, or were similar to other practices of the time, is impossible to answer with complete certainty (but is discussed briefly in Chapter 6).

1.2.1 Problems with Evidence of Ancient Healing

It is difficult to envisage any form of objective and absolute proof of a healing miracle in the first century that would be acceptable now; as Sanders writes, 'The recording angel has not left us a list of all the miracles ever done in Palestine'.[12] There are no written contemporary reports of Jesus' healing activities,[13] and even his disciples would have told slightly different stories from one another. Modern psychological studies have demonstrated that witnesses to a dramatic event have widely different recall of the detail.[14] There is considerable material available also about the way in which factors such as emotion during

---

12 Sanders, *Jesus and Judaism,* p.162.

13 J.P. Meier, *A Marginal Jew. Rethinking the Historical Jesus.* Vol.II. *Mentor, Message and Miracles* (New York: Doubleday, 1994) p.709. J.D.G. Dunn, *Christianity in the Making.* Vol.1. *Jesus Remembered* (Grand Rapids/Cambridge: Eerdmans, 2003) p.672, notes that there is no 'original report' of a miracle.

14 D.L. Schacter, 'Memory Distortion: History and Current Status', in D.L. Schacter (ed.), *Memory Distortion. How Minds, Brains and Societies Reconstruct the Past* (Cambridge, Mass./London: Harvard University Press, 1995) pp.1-43. J.D. Crossan, *The Birth of Christianity* (New York: HarperSanFrancisco, 1998) pp.59-84. He points out, (p.84) that we recall only general contours and snippets of major events.

dramatic events skew one's recall further; and when a witness recounts the scene repeatedly, he becomes more confident about detail, even when his memory is incorrect.[15]

The ways in which the tradition of Jesus' healing survived are also important; Dunn points out that we have only 'Jesus remembered';[16] none of our biblical writers are considered to have been eyewitnesses of Jesus' healing. We are studying writings *circa* AD 45-90,[17] which may have taken on aspects from the Graeco-Roman world, and/or may have been written to express what the author intended to convey.[18] Turner notes that we would not expect to find stories of Jesus failing to heal, as they would have little or no survival value in the church's oral tradition, and Smith points out that the best evidence of Jesus performing miracles is their persistent attestation by his enemies.[19]

We have to acknowledge that we have an imperfect database and understanding of the exact circumstances of Jesus' ministry,[20] although the core tradition remains. The argument of Bultmann, for instance, that

---

15 Crossan, *Birth of Christianity*, pp.60-67.

16 Dunn, *Jesus Remembered*. J.D.G. Dunn, 'Altering the Default Setting: Re-Envisaging the Early Transmission of the Jesus Tradition', *NTS* 49 (2003) 139-75, draws attention to the different characteristics of oral tradition, which we miss in our modern over-reliance on the written tradition.

17 The dates are wide, to include both Paul's earliest letters and the completion of Acts.

18 C.F.D. Moule, 'Introduction', in C.F.D. Moule (ed.), *Miracles. Cambridge Studies in their Philosophy and History* (London: Mowbray & Co, 1965) p.13; G. Theissen, *The Miracle Stories of the Early Christian Tradition* (ET; Edinburgh: T. &. T. Clark, 1983) pp.279-85, thinks that the stories have enhanced Jesus' miracles, perhaps by the gospel writers realising the potential in the motifs of a particular story. R.H. Fuller, *Interpreting the Miracles* (orig. 1963; London: SCM, 1971) p.35, suggests that the miracle stories in most instances rest on a generalised memory of what Jesus did.

19 M. Turner, *The Holy Spirit and Spiritual Gifts Then and Now* (Carlisle: Paternoster, 1996) p.256. Celsus, in *Origen, Contra Celsum*, 8.47, considers that the miracles were the main influence in the beginning of Christianity. M. Smith, *Jesus the Magician* (London: Gollancz, 1978) p.95. Dunn, *Jesus Remembered*, pp.689-90, stresses that early opponents of Christianity consistently accused Jesus of sorcery. A. Fridrichsen, *The Problem of Miracle in Primitive Christianity* (orig. 1925; ET, Minneapolis: Augsburg, 1972) p.170, n.29, noting that Jews forbade the use of Jesus' name in healing, considers that this indicates that they viewed Jesus as a powerful healer.

20 E.g. J.J. Pilch, 'Sickness and Healing in Luke-Acts', in J.H. Neyrey (ed.), *The Social World of Luke-Acts: Models for Interpretation* (Peabody: Hendrickson, 1991) pp.181-209, discusses the medical anthropology of Jesus' healing miracles, but his argument is weakened because he accepts the Context Group's wide class of first-century Mediterranean peasants as a single entity. Eve, *Jewish Context*, e.g. pp.350-51, 354, makes more specific points of criticism of Pilch's work.

miracles were inserted into the Jesus tradition[21] because of the Hellenistic influence on the early church, as it competed with other religious traditions that valued miracle workers, begs the question of the occurrence of any miracles, and merely shifts the problem to a group roughly contemporary with the early church.[22] Lampe notes the 'tiresome tendency to assume that the truth of Christian doctrine can be proved by the ability of believers to perform apparently impossible feats' in the apostolic and early post-apostolic church,[23] and this may have been a secondary cause for much cynicism later.

1.2.2 Modern Presuppositions and Ancient Healing

The ancient authors studied wrote their compositions according to the beliefs of their time. History is, however, not objective,[24] but is shaped by the historian's values, worldview, prejudices and perspective. Stendahl writes that the modern biblical scholar's primary task is to distinguish what the text meant then from what it means now.[25] Hull writes that 'we read the Bible through the world in which we ourselves are embedded'.[26] For instance, I will be commenting on the work of J.C. Thomas on disease in the New Testament;[27] his interest is in the theological aetiology of disease, mine in the presentation and treatment of ill people by the ancient writers. I am very aware that our different understandings of disease and healing now (his, as a scholar from the

---

21 R. Bultmann, *Theology of the New Testament*, Vol.1 (ET; London: SCM, 1952) pp.3-32, 130; R. Bultmann, *The History of the Synoptic Tradition* (ET; 2nd edn.; Oxford: Blackwell, 1968) pp.240-41; Meier, *Marginal Jew*, II, p.536. B.L. Mack, *A Myth of Innocence: Mark and Christian Origins* (Philadelphia: Fortress, 1988) pp.208-45, argues that the miracle stories represent the myth of one form of primitive Christianity.

22 G.R. Habermas, 'Did Jesus Perform Miracles?', in M.J. Wilkins and J.P. Moreland (eds.), *Jesus under Fire* (Carlisle: Paternoster, 1996) p.123, notes that the genetic fallacy is to challenge the perceived *origin* of an idea, instead of addressing the concept itself.

23 G.W.H. Lampe, 'Miracles in the Acts of the Apostles', in Moule (ed.), *Miracles*, p.165; Theissen, *Miracle Stories*, pp.265-76, demonstrates that belief in miracles is historically conditioned, and (p.274) was most intense at the end of the first century BC.

24 F.J. Beckwith, 'History and Miracles', in R.D. Geivett and G.R. Habermas (eds.), *In Defence of Miracles. A Comprehensive Case for God's Action in History* (Leicester: Apollos, 1997) pp.88-91, argues, however, that objectivity is possible.

25 K. Stendahl, 'Biblical Theology, Contemporary', in G.A. Buttrick et al. (eds.), *IDB*, Vol.1 (Nashville: Abingdon, 1962) pp.419-22.

26 J.M. Hull, *In the Beginning there was Darkness. A Blind Person's Conversations with the Bible* (London: SCM, 2001) p.3.

27 J.C. Thomas, *The Devil, Disease and Deliverance. Origins of Illness in New Testament Thought* (JPTSup 13; London/New York: Sheffield Academic Press, 1998, reprint 2002).

Pentecostal tradition, mine, from my experience in the medical tradition), colour our assessments of the first-century world of disease and healing; neither of us can totally uproot ourselves from our traditions.

More generally, the New Testament miracles of healing have raised many problems in the modern world. There has been embarrassment since the European Enlightenment about them; Goethe wrote that the miracle was faith's dearest child, but modern theologians often consider it to be a troublesome bastard.[28] More elegantly, Theissen points out that 'the features that modern theology finds undesirable are blamed on the period; the positive features are assigned to the credit of Christian experience.'[29] Nineteenth-century liberal theology, with its wish to free Christianity from supernatural baggage, and its optimism about the goodness of humanity, tried to brush off the idea of miracles.[30]

The temptation to imagine that our way of thinking is complete and perfect has to be avoided.[31] This can be seen as a major problem with the Jesus Seminar work,[32] which generally considers that most of the gospel healings should be relocated in the realm of story and myth. A well-known example of what Meier has called the 'academic sneer factor' is Bultmann's dictum,

> It is impossible to use electric light and the wireless,[33] and to avail ourselves of modern medical and surgical discoveries, and at the same time to believe in the New Testament world of spirits and miracles.[34]

---

28 Goethe, quoted by H.E. Remus, 'Miracles (NT)', *ABD,* Vol.4, p.869. Eve, *Jewish Context*, p.4, notes that, until very recently, scholars regarded miracle as 'a faintly embarrassing irrelevance'.

29 Theissen, *Miracle Stories*, p.293. G. Theissen and A. Merz, *The Historical Jesus. A Comprehensive Guide* (ET; London: SCM, 1998) p.282, note that we cannot regard the objectively probable as historical and the objectively improbable as unhistorical.

30 E.g. A. von Harnack, *What is Christianity?* (ET; New York: Putnam, 1901). R.D. Geivett and G.R. Habermas, 'Introduction', in Geivett and Habermas (eds.), *In Defence of Miracles,* p.12, note that this form of liberal theology was destroyed by the events of the First World War.

31 J.P. Ross, 'Some Notes on Miracles in the Old Testament', in Moule (ed.), *Miracles*, p.60. Cadbury, *Peril of Modernizing Jesus,* especially pp.37-38.

32 E.g. R.W. Funk and the Jesus Seminar, *The Acts of Jesus* (New York: HarperCollins, 1998) p.534.

33 The word itself shows how quickly material bears the mark of its time.

34 Meier, *Marginal Jew*, II, p.520. R. Bultmann, 'New Testament and Mythology', in H.-W. Bartsch (ed.), *Kerygma and Myth. A Theological Debate*, Vol.1 (ET; edition with Vols.1 and 2 combined; London: SPCK, 1972) p.5.

Bultmann pointed out that myths give worldly objectivity to that which is unworldly;[35] it is ironic that theologians have accepted the concepts of the Kingdom of God and eschatology, which are 'mythical' (in the sense of unprovable), while often not accepting Jesus' healing miracles. Hemer makes the point, with which I agree, 'I am content to operate in a framework where the possibility of miracle is accepted, and its appearance is not an automatic cue for reinterpretation or special interpretation'.[36]

Miracle healing is depicted as continuing in the apostolic church, at least in the book of Acts, and in the Pauline letters, so many of the comments here apply to healing by apostles, and others, in these documents of the New Testament.

1.2.3 Modern Interpretations of Illnesses Healed

The worldview about sickness, healing and exorcism has changed; illnesses are not now considered to be due, for instance, to demons or spells, but, rather, to bacteria, viruses, and mechanisms leading to, for example, the breakdown or overactivity of the sufferer's autoimmune system. In the mid-twentieth century, various scholars tried to find a 'rational' explanation for the healing miracles; the rise of interest in psychology and psychosomatic medicine allowed some theologians to see cases of 'possession' (see *1.3.2*) in the gospels as mental illness, and other sickness as psychosomatic, so Jesus could be portrayed as a charismatic healer, treating hysterical conversion symptoms or psychosomatic problems.[37] It seems apparent, in a world where the occurrence of many major organic diseases has been amply demonstrated from the Hippocratic literature, from archaeology and from palaeopathology,[38] that those who approached Jesus in supplication would not *all* have had psychiatric or psychosomatic illnesses,[39] so the fashion to explain the miracles as purely triumphs of psychological

35 R. Bultmann, *Jesus Christ and Mythology* (ET, Brit. ed.; London: SCM, 1960) p.19.

36 C.J. Hemer, *The Book of Acts in the Setting of Hellenistic History,* C. Gempf (ed.) (WUNT 49; Tübingen: Mohr [Siebeck], 1989) p.443.

37 E.g. Smith, *Jesus the Magician,* pp.8, 106, regarded Jesus as healing people with hysteria; D.E. Aune, 'Magic in Early Christianity', in *ANRW* II.23.2 (1980) p.1525, believes that most of the healing was of psychosomatic conditions. J.K. Howard, *Disease and Healing in the New Testament: An Analysis and Interpretation* (New York/Oxford: University Press of America, 2001) has the same view.

38 E.g. R. Jackson, *Doctors and Diseases in the Roman Empire* (London: Brit. Mus. Pub., 1988) pp.175-86.

39 This is not to deny that psychological and social factors might be important in a person's sickness. (See Chapter 3, *1.5.2.*)

intervention has somewhat receded. In the synoptic gospels, all sorts of illnesses are included, limited in variety only by what is amenable to description in the gospel genre.

1.3 Definitions of Key Terms in Healing

Among the more thorny problems are the definitions, both then and now, of the terms used in describing ancient healing. Yet, an attempt has to be made to define miracle, magic, healing and exorcism, in order to provide some clarity, but without imposing an alien understanding on the biblical data. It should be noted that scholars since the Enlightenment have struggled to do this, without total success.

1.3.1 Miracle and Magic

It was particularly in Judaism and, later, Christianity, that magic was regarded as the natural enemy, while followers of these religions were themselves open to charges of practising magic.[40] In the context of the first century, we have to acknowledge the fact that both magic and miracle were deeply embedded in religion, so any attempt at a precise definition of, say, magic inevitably involves comparison with related areas, particularly with miracles and religion.[41] 'One man's magic is another's miracle', and 'one person's religion is another's magic', that is, one attributes the miracles of one's own healer to one's god, those of one's opponents to magic.[42] Attempts to highlight alleged differences between magic and miracles have been made frequently by Christian writers, as their view persisted that magic (which was decadent) was separable from miracle and religion.[43]

Alleged differences include suggestions that magic was mysterious,

---

40 P.J. Achtemeier, 'Jesus and the Disciples as Miracle Workers in the Apocryphal New Testament', in Fiorenza (ed.), *Aspects of Religious Propaganda*, 1976, p.153; A.F. Segal, 'Hellenistic Magic: Some Questions of Definition', in R. van den Broek and M.J. Vermaseren (eds.), *Studies on Gnosticism and Hellenistic Religions* (Leiden: Brill, 1981) p.370.

41 Aune, 'Magic', pp.1515-16, defines magic in relation to the dominant religion. Segal, 'Hellenistic Magic', p.349-50, considers that we try to distinguish magic too sharply from religion.

42 H.E. Remus, 'Miracle', in *ABD,* 4, p.859. H.D. Betz, 'Magic and Mystery in the Greek Magical Papyri', in C.A. Faraone and D. Obbink (eds.), *Magika Hiera: Ancient Greek Magic and Religion* (Oxford: Oxford University Press, 1991) p.245.

43 A.M. Reimer, *Miracle and Magic. A Study in the Acts of the Apostles and the Life of Apollonius of Tyana* (JSNTSup 235; London: Sheffield Academic Press, 2002) pp.3-14, describes the history of attempts at separation during the nineteenth and twentieth centuries.

miracles were usually public; magic was performed for a fee, unlike miracles, or was for social manipulation, not for moral benefit; magic often used materials and technical methods, both of which were rare in miracles;[44] magical 'tricks' compelled belief, whereas miracles occurred as an outcome in those with faith in God.[45] In comparing magical incantation and prayer, the attitude of the pray-er was considered important, thus, magic was regarded as combative, prayer submissive (although a magician might use both supplication and command).[46] These distinctions seem to be comparing miracle with the practice of black magic, or to be merely denigrating magic, often in order to maintain the purity of religion.[47] The proposition that one could differentiate by the way the story was told is also untenable, because the format of any healing narrative, with a description of the scene, the severity of affliction, the method of healing, the occurrence of cure, and the reaction of the crowd, is similar.[48]

In considering a definition of magic, we see that one such as Kee's; 'a technique, through word or act, by which a desired end is achieved, whether that end lies in the solution to the seeker's problem, or in damage to the enemy who caused the problem',[49] is too broad and imprecise. It becomes clear that efforts to pinpoint the essence of magic always entail compromise; as Garrett notes, the problem is that labels depend on the social and cultural presuppositions of both labeller and labelled.[50] Meanings change with the culture under discussion, so that

---

44 G.H. Twelftree, *Jesus the Exorcist: A Contribution to the Study of the Historical Jesus* (WUNT 2/54; Tübingen: Mohr [Siebeck], 1993) p.157.

45 C.C. Black, 'Christ Crucified in Paul and Mark: Reflections on an Intercanonical Conversation', in E.H. Lovering and J.L. Sumney (eds.), *Theology and Ethics in Paul and his Interpreters. Essays in Honour of Victor Paul Furnish* (Nashville: Abingdon, 1996) p.202.

46 F. Graf, 'Prayer in Magic and Religious Ritual', in Faraone & Obbink (eds.), *Magika Hiera*, p.188. Segal, 'Hellenistic Magic', p.352, says incantations were often hymns to Greek gods.

47 Aune, 'Magic', p.1510, says that the distinctions date from a time when belief in magic was regarded as decadent. Segal, 'Hellenistic Magic', p.351; Goldin, 'Magic of Magic', p.122.

48 Fuller, *Interpreting the Miracles*, p.33; H. Remus, *Jesus as Healer* (Cambridge: Cambridge University Press, 1997) p.10.

49 H.C. Kee, *Medicine, Miracle and Magic in New Testament Times* (SNTSMS 55; Cambridge: Cambridge University Press, 1986) p.3.

50 S.R. Garrett, *The Demise of the Devil. Magic and the Demonic in Luke's Writings.* (Minneapolis: Fortress, 1989) p.52; S.R. Garrett, 'Light on a Dark Subject and Vice Versa: Magic and Magicians in the New Testament', in J. Neusner, E.S. Frerichs,

we are misled by our own cultural assumptions. Segal notes that no definition of magic can be universally applied, because magic cannot be construed as a proper scientific term.[51]

Modern thought has shown that a miracle, too, is almost impossible to characterize. David Hume in 1748 defined it as a violation of the laws of nature; but the concept of 'laws of nature' is itself a slippery one, which defies definition, as these laws change when new scientific discoveries are made.[52] R.J. Berry, an eminent geneticist, notes that what are referred to as the 'laws of science' are only generalisations of our experience. 'It is not logically valid to use science as an argument against miracles. To believe that miracles cannot happen is as much an act of faith as to believe that they can happen.'[53]

In discussing Jesus' healing miracles, we are considering events which were regarded as unusual and extraordinary by his contemporaries, which were not normal in the realm of human abilities, and were inexplicable by empirical, rational deductions.[54] Meier's suggestion for a definition of miracle is:

> a) An unusual, startling or extraordinary event, that is in principle perceivable by any interested and fair-minded observer, b) an event that finds no reasonable explanation in human abilities or in known forces that operate in our world of time and space, and c) an event that is the result of a special act of God, doing what no human power could do.[55]

P.V.M. Flesher (eds.), *Religion, Science and Magic. In Concert and in Conflict* (New York/Oxford: OUP, 1989) pp.144, 148.

51 Segal, 'Hellenistic Magic', p.351. Graf, 'Prayer in Magic', p.188, suggests that magic is a term that should be removed from scientific, and therefore modern, vocabulary.

52 D. Hume, 'Of Miracles', in *Philosophical Essays Concerning the Human Understanding* (orig. 1748); reprinted in Geivett and Habermas (eds.), *In Defence of Miracles,* p.33. Meier, *Marginal Jew,* II, p.512, and p.526, n.9.

53 R.J. Berry, 'Miracle: Scepticism, Credulity or Reality?', in A. Walker (ed.), *Different Gospels. Christian Orthodoxy and Modern Theologies* (New ed.; London: SPCK, 1993) p.67, quoting a statement in *The Times* of 13th July 1984 by fourteen eminent scientists, including himself. The fact that there is no means of proving that Jesus did *not* perform healing miracles is cogently argued by W.L. Craig, 'The Problem of Miracles: A Historical and Philosophical Perspective', in D. Wenham and C. Blomberg (eds.), *Gospel Perspectives,* Vol. 6. *The Miracles of Jesus.* (Sheffield: JSOT Press, 1986) e.g. p.43. Habermas, 'Did Jesus Perform Miracles?', pp.126-27, p.132, urges against ruling out the supernatural. He considers that, if Jesus' resurrection is accepted, then his miracles are more likely. Remus, *Jesus as Healer*, pp.104-18, thinks that it is unprovable intellectually that Jesus was a healer.

54 Meier, *Marginal Jew*, II, p.511; Eve, *Jewish Context*, p.17.

55 Meier, *Marginal Jew*, II, p.512. He gives a history of the definition, p.514, n.5.

To a definition very similar to Meier's, Turner adds: d) 'it [miracle] is usually understood to have symbolic or sign value (e.g. pointing to God as redeemer or judge)'.[56] Kee offers a similar, though distinctive, view with regard to a healing miracle, 'a miracle embodies the claim that healing can be accomplished through appeal to, and subsequent action by, the gods, either directly, or through a chosen intermediary'.[57] It is noticeable that in all these definitions, the idea of deity is embedded.

The problem of defining and differentiating miracle from magic was made more urgent by the history-of-religion school portraying magic as an important influence on the gospel accounts of Jesus' ministry, which produced a sharp reaction from the early twentieth-century biblical theology movement.[58] Many modern scholars consider that healing magic and miracle are not separable, at least by the methods so far employed.[59] Nock, as long ago as 1955, considered that it was not helpful to draw a sharp line between magic, miracles and religion, and this corresponds with Aune's more recent suggestion that there was in the first century a continuum between white (healing) magic and religion.[60] On the other hand, Reimer, having confirmed that the difficulties of separating magic and miracles are insurmountable when they are defined too rigidly, either in absolute terms, or in terms derived from sociology (which itself contributed to the knowledge base of miracle versus magic, but was still polemical), suggests that one should abandon rigid definitions, and use a polythetic approach. In this, some, but not all, criteria would need to be fulfilled, in the decision as to whether magic or miracle had occurred.[61] This is an indication of the difficulty, but may be an acceptable present-day suggestion for the first-century situation. The problem is to reach modern agreement about the ancient writer's viewpoint; difficulties are at their most acute when we consider the situation in the Acts of the Apostles (see Chapter 4, *3.4.4*).

It is accepted that differentiating magic, miracle and religion clearly is practically impossible, partly because they all defy satisfactory definition, and partly because charge and counter-charge were probably

56 Turner, *Holy Spirit and Gifts*, p.272, n.31.

57 Kee, *Medicine, Miracle and Magic*, p.3.

58 Aune, 'Magic', pp.1509-10.

59 Meier, *Marginal Jew*, II, p.541, considers that medicine, magic and miracles overlapped; Segal, 'Hellenistic Magic', p.349, notes that there is too much overlap to distinguish miracles from magic.

60 A.D. Nock, 'Religious Symbols and Symbolism, I', in *Essays on Religion and the Ancient World*. Vol.2 (orig. 1955; republished Z. Stewart (ed.), [Oxford: Clarendon, 1972]) p.889. Aune, 'Magic', p.1512.

61 Reimer, *Miracle and Magic*, pp.8-12, 13-14.

more powerful in the area of magic and miracle than in any other area of life in the Ancient Near East. Although disputes about whether healing was miraculous or magical were commoner in Graeco-Roman than in earlier times,[62] it is salutary to realise that a discussion on differentiating magic and religion would have been incomprehensible to a first-century pagan, since magic was entrenched in all religions.[63]

These problems from the first century are more obvious now, since modern biblical scholars are products of a history where Christianity eventually overwhelmed the opposition in the pagan Roman Empire, and where scientific accuracy is a way of life.

1.3.2 Healing and Exorcism

There is also a problem in our modern interpretation of ancient writers' views of disease causation, where a considerable present-day superstructure has been built upon what is believed to be their first-century ideas. There is modern agreement that demons were seen then as causing at least some illnesses, though Yamauchi persuasively argues against the idea that ancients believed all disease was attributable to them.[64] His summary of what were assumed to be sources of illness in the Ancient Near East is both moderate and succinct. He considers four were significant; a) a divine source, as punishment for sin, b) possession *or* attack by demons, c) black magic by an enemy, and d) a 'natural' (as opposed to a supernatural) source; and he elaborates on these in the rest

---

62 Remus, 'Miracle', p.858; Theissen, *Miracle Stories*, pp.231-32, believes that this may be due to selective survival and destruction of material.

63 Aune, 'Magic', pp.1520, 1557; H.D. Betz, *The Greek Magical Papyri in Translation, Including the Demotic Spells*. Vol.1. *Texts* (Chicago: University of Chicago, 1986) p.xlviii, considers that magic met religious needs and expectations. Betz acknowledges that the material is based on the work of Karl Preisendanz (1883–1968), who, with others, produced the *Papyri Graecae Magicae. Die griechischen Zauberpapyri*, Vol.1, 1928, Vol.2, 1931.

64 E. Yamauchi, 'Magic or Miracle? Diseases, Demons and Exorcisms', in Wenham and Blomberg (eds.), *Gospel Perspectives*, 6, e.g. p.142. Yamauchi, pp.92-93, refutes the view that demonological aetiology of disease was general in antiquity. D.B. Martin, *The Corinthian Body* (New Haven: Yale University Press, 1995) p.156, reports that the 'superstitious' attributed disease to attacks by gods, or invasions by demons. This attribution is a measure of the fear of disease; for instance, J.G. Cook, 'In Defence of Ambiguity: Is There a Hidden Demon in Mark 1:29-31?', *NTS* 43 (1997), pp.184-208. He, p.198, notes the belief that gods of the Greek pantheon could send fever; the Romans had the goddess *Dea Febra,* where classifying an illness as a goddess, who needed placation, showed fear of the disease.

of his article.[65] Although Ferguson judges that in the ancient world demons were believed to cause most illness, he considers that demon-possession was often regarded as different from illness produced by their attack; Thomas, from a widely different perspective, also considers that demon attack was different from possession.[66]

The controversy in assessing now whether the ancient writers saw a divergence between sicknesses caused by *attack* by demons or other agents, and sicknesses due to *possession* by demons is important. Invasion by evil spirits, resulting in the body's captivity (which the church traditionally termed 'possession', as opposed to 'oppression', that is, the infliction of harm from outside agents, including demons) was considered to show Satan's reign in the individual, whereas oppression did not.[67] In the gospels, where there were apocalyptic expectations, and the Kingdom of God was seen in mortal combat with the Kingdom of the devil, the difference between possession and oppression affects the theological interpretations of healing and exorcism. Thus, an exorcism by Jesus (rather than a healing) might be interpreted as the (coming) defeat of Satan's control of the world and the in-breaking of the age to come, as Satan's minions possessed, and not merely harassed, the victim. This separation of attack by outside agents (including demons) from demon-possession also has huge repercussions on later understanding, for instance, that people with diseases regarded as due to demon-possession would be unacceptable in the church.[68]

The difference between demon *possession* of the victim and (possible) demon *attack* causing illness seemed to be based at least

---

65 Yamauchi, 'Magic or Miracle?', pp.99-149. See also Chapter 2, *2.2.4*. This is in contrast to the dictum of C.J. Singer and A. Wasserstein, 'Medicine', in N.G.L. Hammond and H.H. Scullard (eds.), *OCD* (2nd ed.; Oxford: Clarendon, 1970) p.660, that 'medicine in the New Testament is mainly that of opposition to evil spirits.'

66 E. Ferguson, *Demonology of the Early Christian World* (Symposium Series Vol.12; New York/Toronto: Mellen, 1984) pp.4-5. Thomas, *Devil, Disease*, e.g. pp.157, 200-202. His main thesis is that God, rather than the devil (or demons), was regarded by biblical writers as mainly responsible for diseases.

67 Turner, *Holy Spirit and Gifts*, p.255.

68 Thomas, *Devil, Disease*, pp.200-204, 227, seems there to offer special pleading for non-demon-possession for the 'righteous' in the gospels, for instance, Simon Peter's mother-in-law, and Paul. D.S. Cairns, *The Faith that Rebels* (London: SCM, 1928) p.19, noted that the church had an official exorcist for centuries; C. Strecker, 'Jesus and the Demoniacs', in W. Stegemann, B.J. Malina and G. Theissen (eds.), *The Social Setting of Jesus and the Gospels* (Minneapolis: Fortress, 2002) p.117, observes that in 1999, the regulation for the official Roman Catholic rite of exorcism was revised.

partly on the observed method of treatment;[69] a god was invoked to make the 'possessing' demon obey by exact words of command, using prepared formulae.[70] Since the verbs ἐπιτιμάω (order) and ἐκβάλλω (expel) are used in exorcisms in the gospels, it is assumed by modern writers that this signifies that the victim was not merely attacked, but possessed, by a demon, and many consider that the gospel writers separate clearly healings and exorcisms.[71] The circular argument is advanced that one can tell whether the evangelist considers an illness as due to possession, or merely attack, by an evil spirit or other agent, by the way that it was treated by Jesus; Jesus 'rebuked' demons, and ordered them to come out of the possessed person (exorcism) whereas he touched (perhaps laying his hands on) those considered to have other illnesses (healing).

Further, exorcisms have been characterised as violent, and healings as being achieved peacefully.[72] This seems to be a case of *post hoc, ergo propter hoc*; thus, if the healing of a person with epilepsy were accompanied by a *grand mal* attack (which is violent, due to electrical discharge in the motor area of the brain), then that would be seen as 'proof' that exorcism, rather than healing, had been used, and so evidence that the victim's epilepsy was due to demon-possession.

The point is of importance for all New Testament criticism concerned with healing, since there is often modern conformity with the idea that the gospel-writers saw that it was in Jesus' exorcisms, as opposed to his healings, that the battle between Satan and God was particularly manifest, so exorcisms offered the clearest evidence of Jesus'

---

69 Theissen, *Miracle Stories*, p.85.

70 Remus, *Jesus as Healer*, pp.23-24. B.L. Blackburn, *Theios Anēr and the Markan Miracle Traditions. A Critique of the Theios Anēr Concept as an Interpretative Background of the Miracle Traditions Used by Mark*. (WUNT 2/40; Tübingen: Mohr [Siebeck], 1991) p.185, notes that it was Graeco-Roman tradition that powerful evil spirits required a god's power to conquer them.

71 E.g. Wilkinson, *Bible and Healing*, p.69f; Aune, 'Magic', p.1524; R.T. France, *The Gospel of Mark. A Commentary on the Greek Text*. NIGTC (Grand Rapids/Carlisle: Eerdmans/Paternoster, 2002) p.108; R.A. Guelich, *Mark 1-8:26*. WBC, Vol.34A. (Dallas: Word Books, 1989) p.76; B. Witherington III, *The Gospel of Mark. A Socio-Rhetorical Commentary* (Grand Rapids/Cambridge: Eerdmans, 2001) p.91, n.14. O. Temkin, *Hippocrates in a World of Pagans and Christians*. (Baltimore/London: Johns Hopkins University Press, 1991) p.101, says, however, that the boundary between healing and exorcism was not fixed. F.E. Brenk, 'In the Light of the Moon: Demonology in the Early Imperial Period', in *ANRW* II.16.3 (1986) 2108, notes that John's gospel mentions no exorcisms, and considers that this is related to a different understanding of evil spirits there.

72 Theissen, *Miracle Stories*, pp.88-90.

eschatological defeat of Satan, and of Jesus' Christological identity.[73] Considerable caution has to be exercised in such an interpretation, and its theological significance. It seems to me that too much has been built on this separation of healing from exorcism, artificially widening the often vague division between them, in the belief that this is following faithfully the gospel stories.[74] It seems unproductive to search for alleged differences between healing and exorcism in an area so ill defined, and dependent on a world-view so different from our own.

The separation of healing and exorcism may be useful as a shorthand description, but is not fundamentally safe. It is not possible in this monograph, however, both to maintain clarity and to kick against the convention, so the term 'healing' is used throughout in *both* a generic, all-encompassing sense and *also* to indicate physical healing, while 'exorcism' is particular to casting out evil spirits that the gospel writer may see as possessing a person.

Since the difference affects the theological portrayal of healing and exorcism, the area will be discussed further in the gospel accounts.

1.4 Conclusion

The monograph is being written after more than two centuries of scepticism about miracles, so it is difficult to avoid appearing to be uncritically defensive of the historicity of miracles without complicating the text unnecessarily. In very recent mainstream biblical scholarship, there does seem to be an increasing, though not universal, inclination to take the miracles seriously.[75] Dunn and many other modern writers

73 E.g. G.H. Twelftree, 'ΕΙ ΔΕ —ΕΓΩ ΕΚΒΑΛΛΩ ΤΑ ΔΑΙΜΟΝΙΑ', in Wenham and Blomberg (eds.), *Gospel Perspectives,* 6, p.390, regards exorcism as the activity seen particularly as the battlefield with Satan. J.T. Carroll, 'Sickness and Healing in the New Testament Gospels', *Int* 49 (1995) pp.130-142; Witherington, *Gospel of Mark*, pp.90, 95. R.H. Gundry, *Mark. A Commentary on his Apology for the Cross* (Grand Rapids: Eerdmans, 1993) p.75; Sanders, *Jesus and Judaism*, pp.134-35. That exorcism was the key to Jesus' identity as Messiah seems to stem from the idea in Second Temple Judaism that the Messianic age would bring destruction to the demonic world (T. Levi 18, 1 En. 55:4).

74 E.g. M.J. Borg, *Jesus. A New Vision. Spirit, Culture and the Life of Discipleship* (New York: Harper & Row, 1987) p.61. As a physician, I am very conscious, like anyone who has tried to treat a patient with potentially fatal disease, of the presence of forces of darkness, both in the patient and the therapist.

75 Eve, *Jewish Context*, pp.6-7, indicates the trend by noting the increasing number of pages devoted to miracles in recent studies of the historical Jesus. Mack, *Myth of Innocence,* p.211, considers, of miracles, that the closer to the spectacular, the less the

affirm that Jesus' healings are among the unassailable facts about Jesus.[76]

In the world of the first century AD, where there was a huge interest in supernatural powers,[77] and also considerable illness and need, healing was an important power. Although considering healing in isolation limits the comparisons that can be made between the biblical writers, recognition of their differences in portraying healing is a potent way for us to gain some insight into this major area of life in the first century.

---

significance. He believes, p.208, that the stories are the source of the scholarly impression of something dramatic happening at the beginning of Christianity.

76 Dunn, *Jesus Remembered,* p.670; B.L. Blackburn, 'The Miracles of Jesus', in B. Chilton, and C.A. Evans, (eds.), *Studying the Historical Jesus. Evaluations of the State of Current Research* (NTTS 19; Leiden: Brill, 1994) pp.354-62; C.A. Evans, 'Authenticating the Activities of Jesus', in B. Chilton and C.A. Evans (eds.), *Authenticating the Activities of Jesus* (Leiden: Brill, 1999) pp.3-29; S.L. Davies, *Jesus the Healer. Possession, Trance, and the Origins of Christianity* (London: SCM, 1995) p.66. Eve, *Jewish Context,* p.17, notes that virtually all scholars agree that Jesus did healings and exorcisms that his contemporaries thought were remarkable.

77 E.g. C.E. Arnold, *Ephesians: Power and Magic. The Concept of Power in Ephesians in the Light of its Historical Setting* (SNTSMS 63; Cambridge: Cambridge University Press, 1989).

Chapter 2

The Background to Jesus' Healing Ministry

In this chapter, the background to Jesus' healing ministry is considered from Jewish and Graeco-Roman perspectives, while noting that, by the first century AD, there was considerable overlap between them. The chapter sketches the backdrop for the New Testament writings on healing.

1 Sickness and Healing in Judaism

Throughout their scriptures, Israel's writers sought to explain suffering, of which sickness was an important part, in religious terms. Their rationalisation had to be consistent with their covenant religion, where Yahweh cared for his special people. The intention in this brief review is to highlight some important landmarks, which show how the writers of the Old Testament and later Second Temple Judaism expressed the development of their religious understanding of sickness/suffering and healing/salvation. Sickness and healing in the Old Testament is first reviewed, developments in the later Second Temple period assessed, then figures of healing in Judaism, including especially the Messiah, but also other intermediary figures between God and man, are focused on. ('Man' is used throughout as the generic term representing all human beings).

1.1 Sickness and Healing in the Old Testament

Old Testament writers understood the election of Israel as signifying that God would both care for, and discipline, his people. The core of Hebrew covenant piety was the requirement for faith in God alone. Failure to worship Yahweh as the only god was seen as the source of Israel's misery; for instance, because of their corporate sin, apostasy and worship of idols, God was portrayed heaping disaster on his people, causing, among other afflictions, hunger, 'burning consumption' and bitter pestilence (Deut. 32:21-24). The writers also recognised that God would cause illness and death among Israel's enemies *qua* enemies of God's elected people; for instance, the Egyptians suffered plagues (Exodus 9, 12), and the Assyrians besieging Jerusalem died suddenly (2 Kgs. 19:35). Sickness as God's punishment of sinful individuals was also described frequently, for instance, Miriam developed 'leprosy' (Num. 12:10-15), and David was punished for his adultery by the death of his baby son (2 Sam. 12:15).[1] The element of education by discipline can also be found, where illness was accepted as part of the divine plan, as God refined by suffering (e.g. Job 5:17-18).

Diseases and disabilities were particularly important for the Israelites, because of the laws preventing many disabled people from taking part in religious ritual; they were 'outside the camp', according to the purity laws laid down in Leviticus 11–15. As Yahweh was perfect and pure, no imperfect or crippled animal was to be offered to him in sacrifice (Deut. 16:21), and, similarly, people with the disabilities listed in Leviticus 21:17-21, who were 'unclean', could not approach his altar and profane his sanctuary (Lev. 21:22-23). The dread of uncleanness pervaded the Old Testament and later Judaism; unclean things were contagious.[2] The food laws, which represented an important symbol of Israel's unique status with God (Lev. 11:24-40), were integrally bound with decrees about illness, and the relationship between ritual cleanness, table-fellowship and healing of disease remained close throughout Israel's history, being prominent in the New Testament.

'Leprosy' was especially feared because, as a condition with broken skin, it breached the boundaries of the sufferer's body, and so made others impure.[3] In the story of King Uzziah (2 Chr. 26:16-23), where leprosy followed immediately his unlawful act of sacrificing on the altar, he remained unhealed, lived the rest of his life isolated from his family, and his son reigned in his stead. The story illustrates both the perceived close relationship between sickness and sin, and the severe social consequences of disease.[4] A sinner who repented was acceptable to God, and could become again a full member of God's people, but the problem with sickness was that one was not fully acceptable before God *until* one was healed.[5]

---

1 It is usually accepted, e.g. Wilkinson, *Bible and Healing,* pp.46-48, that biblical 'leprosy', especially in the Old Testament, covers many conditions, not only, and perhaps rarely, the disease caused by the bacillus Mycobacterium leprae (but see Chapter 3, *1.5.2*). The baby seemed to be regarded as a sinner-by-proxy (Ps. 51:5), as his death was in punishment of his father, not of him.

2 B. Chilton, *Jesus' Baptism and Jesus' Healing* (Harrisburg: Trinity, 1998) p.68, notes that sacred things were not seen as spreading holiness (Hag. 2:12-13).

3 Broken skin is unusual as a primary problem in true leprosy. Chilton, *Jesus' Baptism,* p.59, discusses the concept of impurity.

4 Remus, *Jesus as Healer*, p.31.

5 The legacy of this belief in Judaeo-Christian tradition has produced difficulties in the church (see Chapter 6, *3*).

Healing by God was also stressed in the Old Testament, as part of his covenant with his people, for instance, 'I am Yahweh who heals you' (Ex. 15:26). God did not heal only corporately, and only the people of God; he also healed individuals, and foreigners. He restored to health Abimelech, a non-Israelite king, in response to Abraham's prayer (Gen. 20:17), and there are many accounts of God healing individuals.[6] The idea of being disciplined (by illness or disaster) before being healed, applied both to Israel, 'I kill and I make alive; I wound and I heal' (Deut. 32:39), and to other nations, for instance, Egypt, whom Yahweh struck, then saved (Isa. 19:1-22). The theme of divine healing is expanded especially in the psalms (e.g. Ps. 30:2; 147:3). In Psalm 103:3, it is Yahweh 'who forgives all your iniquity, who heals all your diseases'; sin and illness were closely related, as were divine forgiveness and healing. Yahweh was seen to be especially near sick people if the sufferer called, that is, recognised his need (Ps. 145:18-19).[7]

1.1.1 Sickness and Healing as a Metaphor

Both sickness and healing were also used frequently in a metaphorical sense in the Old Testament. Israel's faithlessness was referred to as a disease requiring God's healing (e.g. Hos. 5:13; 11:3), and Jeremiah portrayed the Babylonian exile resulting because Israel's 'sickness' (wickedness) was beyond healing (Jer. 8:15, 22).[8] Healing as a metaphor for salvation was established in Jewish thought long before Jesus' ministry, for instance, 'for you who revere my name, the sun of righteousness shall rise with healing in his wings' (Mal. 4:2). In these examples, the omnipotence and transcendence of God were stressed; the barrier to God saving Israel was her iniquity (Isa. 59:1-2), not God's inability. Deutero-Isaiah was instructed to bring to the oppressed, the broken-hearted and the captives (Isa. 61:1-2) the good news that, despite Israel's wickedness, God would heal her (57:18-19). This picture of God healing in spite of sin is found in some of the psalms (e.g. Ps. 107:17-20). God's transcendence was tempered by his immanence, which emphasised the element of concerned compassion for the sufferer, obvious in Ezekiel's imagery of God as the good shepherd, both caring and healing (Ezek. 34:15-16).

---

6 E.g. Jeroboam's withered arm (1 Kgs. 13:6) and Hezekiah's illness (2 Kgs. 20:5-8).

7 A. Oepke, 'νόσος', *TDNT*, 4, p.1094.

8 H.C. Kee, 'Medicine and Healing', *ABD*, 4, p.660.

1.1.2 Innocent and Vicarious Suffering

The oppression that Israel endured in the centuries before Christ's coming was probably responsible for the development of Jewish thought on suffering. Job puzzled over his undeserved personal suffering, when he knew himself to be innocent. Old Testament prophets, whose actions were governed by God's command, had borne the burden of Israel's sin, and had suffered (e.g. Ezek. 4:4-8). As an extension of ideas of undeserved suffering, the concept of vicarious suffering is found, whereby the sins of God's people might be expiated through the sufferings of an innocent person, instead of by sacrificing an animal as a sin-offering. Isaiah 53 is the key passage, where the unknown Suffering Servant, wounded by the will of God for the nation's sins, would be exalted, because 'he poured himself out to death' (v.12), that is, his innocent life was given voluntarily as an offering for sin. By taking the consequences of Israel's sins upon himself, the Servant's suffering allowed the nation to become whole, that is, God's people to be healed. 'He has borne our infirmities and carried our diseases (quoted in Mt. 8:17), we accounted him struck down by God' (Isa. 53:4-5), shows sickness regarded as an important form of suffering, and demonstrates again how vital and persistent was the association of disease and sin.

1.1.3 Intermediaries and Suffering

Israel wrestled with the conviction that her misfortunes were too great to be the result of purely human sin. While maintaining their faith in the one, transcendent, God, Israel's writers believed that there were beings between God and man, who acted as mediators. This perception was important in their theological explanation of national and individual suffering. The awareness of heavenly intermediaries was never allowed to interfere with the strict Judaic separation between God and man; 'God is not man' (Num. 23:19).[9] The concept of angels as messengers of God was, however, widespread especially in Genesis, e.g. 'the angel of Yahweh called to Hagar' (21:17), where 'angel' may have been used as a figure of speech, to avoid attributing courier duties to God. Jewish mysticism (e.g. Ezek. 1:4-28), with its interest in heavenly figures, also developed further in apocalyptic Jewish writings. Demons and evil spirits were uncommon in the Old Testament; although Saul suffered from the effects of an evil spirit, it was emphasised that it was sent by God (e.g. 1 Sam. 19:9), and the Nephilim in Genesis 6:1-4 were

---

9 As the tyrant Antiochus Epiphanes IV was dying, he also realised that 'mortals should not think that they were equal to God' (2 Macc. 9:8-12).

associated with wickedness, but were not called demons.[10]

Vermes believes that the source of Israel's belief that sickness and sin were the works of the devil came from Persia, brought back to Israel on return from the Babylonian exile.[11] This was part of the Persian idea of cosmic dualism, that good and evil existed in the world, and transcended humanity.[12] In the prologue to Job, where God allowed Satan to harm Job, God might not have been totally in control of Satan, although God's ultimate supremacy is confirmed in the book.[13] Before the end of the Old Testament, the view that God was solely responsible for sickness had been diluted occasionally by the suspicion that demonic power (e.g. the watcher of Dan. 4:13) might cause sickness (Nebuchadnezzar's illness), although it was God who healed him (v.34).

In summary, the Old Testament religious understanding of the causes of suffering and sickness, in the context of a covenant people disobedient to a transcendent God, is outlined briefly. Sin and disease were closely related; sickness might be as punishment, or pedagogical, the result of God's discipline, and might be actual or metaphorical, as might healing (salvation). Awareness developed of the possibility of an innocent person suffering, and that this may be vicarious, and the decision of the 'victim'. In the Old Testament, except perhaps in the book of Daniel, God was regarded generally as omnipotent, with power to impart suffering and healing to individual and nation, to Israel and foreigners. The development of the concept of an evil power, in the form of Satan, was not allowed to violate Israel's monotheism, but could explain the persistence of suffering, for instance, Job's story introduced the possibility of Yahweh not always being in absolute control of Satan, and by the end of the Old Testament, Satanic power was suspected of causing some illness.

---

10 Yamauchi, 'Magic or Miracle?', p.119. A.E. Harvey, *Jesus and the Constraints of History* (Bampton Lectures, 1980; London: Duckworth & Co., 1982) p.117. W. Cotter, *Miracles in Greco-Roman Antiquity* (London: Routledge, 1999) p.90, suggests that the idea of the Nephilim 'opened the door' to the idea of demons. The interest in fallen angels expanded greatly in later Second Temple Judaism.

11 G. Vermes, *Jesus the Jew. A Historian's Reading of the Gospels* (London: Collins, 1973) p.61.

12 E.P. Sanders, 'Paul', in J. Barclay and J. Sweet (eds.), *Early Christian Thought in its Jewish Context* (Cambridge: Cambridge University Press, 1996) p.121.

13 J.D.G. Dunn, *The Theology of Paul the Apostle* (Grand Rapids: Eerdmans, 1998) p.38, considers that Satan was seen there in an ambiguous relationship to God, as a force hostile to God, but permitted to act so, in order to serve God's will.

1.2 Developments in Later Second Temple Judaism

The concept that innocent suffering might occur, especially during religious persecution, was sharpened by the second-century BC Maccabean revolt against the Seleucid attempt to 'hellenise' Judaism, which threatened Israel's purity laws (e.g. 2 Maccabees 6, 7). Martyrdom was seen as drawing the 'wrath of God' on the few, instead of on all the people; that is, the few suffered in order to save Israel. The Old Testament prophets came to be regarded, especially after the Maccabean uprising, as the prototypes of martyrs.[14]

1.2.1 Eternal Life

The account of the Maccabean rebellion also depicted another development in Israel's understanding of the theology of suffering. Having described in horrific detail the destruction of the martyr's body, the writer of 2 Maccabees 7:9 indicated that the martyr's prize would be everlasting life, because he had died for God's law. Concern for the fate of the individual after death superseded earlier religious goals of longevity, health and success (e.g. Deut. 6:2; Jos. 1:8), although hope of a life after death had been expressed previously in the Old Testament (e.g. Pss. 49:16, 73:23-24; Isa. 26:19). The idea of salvation, therefore, included both healing and prosperity in this life, and a life to come, but gradually the concern with life after death grew in importance in some strands of Judaism.[15] Unlike the belief of Greek philosophy, body and soul were usually regarded as inseparable in Judaism (although this was not universal),[16] so that for an afterlife for both body and soul, resurrection was required.

In the Wisdom literature, a further development was that righteous men would reap the reward of eternal life only after testing by God (e.g. Wis. 3:1-9). In 1 Enoch 22:9-14, the belief is described that God would judge individuals after death.[17]

---

14 N.T. Wright, 'Jesus', in Barclay and Sweet (eds.), *Early Christian Thought,* p.54. J.L. Sumney, '"Paul's Weakness": An Integral Part of Apostleship', *JSNT* 52 (1993) p.76.

15 B. Witherington III, *The Acts of the Apostles. A Socio-Rhetorical Commentary* (Grand Rapids/Cambridge: Eerdmans, 1998) p.842.

16 In Wisdom of Solomon (e.g. Wis. 3:1-3), there is no mention of resurrection of the *body* after death.

17 L.P. Hogan, *Healing in the Second Tempel (sic) Period* (Freiburg/Göttingen: Universitätsverlag/Vandenhoeck & Ruprecht, 1992) pp.61-62, notes that the Book of Watchers (Parables of Enoch) i.e. Chs. 1-36, was the earliest part of 1 Enoch, probably from third century BC; the fragments found at Qumran, 4QEn[a] and [b], probably date to the first half of the second century BC.

1.2.2 Suffering and Satanic Forces

The idea that God did not have absolute power over Satan developed further in later Second Temple Judaism, and this was important in explaining people's suffering. The views of the relationship between God and angelic/demonic powers in cosmic struggle with him were variable, but the common idea was of a hierarchy of evil spirits, with Satan as the most powerful, and a battle between the righteous and elect people of God, and God's enemies.[18] Although most writers thought that God was more powerful than the forces of darkness, the influence of evil was great; the search for the power of evil in Jubilees and 1 Enoch (both based on Gen. 6:1-4) dominates these books.[19] By the first century AD, it was believed by many Jews that sickness was mainly caused by the powers of darkness, but in the end, these powers would be overcome, and God's work in renewing creation would be complete.[20]

1.2.3 Sick People as Religious Outcasts

Sick people were disadvantaged further in later Second Temple Judaism. Although by the first century, Israel was subject to Roman control, the Temple authorities still had great religious power, and were frequently corrupt. The Pharisees, aware of the corruption, and trying to live as pure lives as possible, treated everyday life, not just Temple worship, as sacred ritual. An important consequence of this was that, by Pharisaic rules, social intercourse with the pure, including table-fellowship, was denied to 'sinners', who included many sick and disabled people, who were regarded as unclean. They were also denied full membership of the community at Qumran, which had broken away completely from what they saw as corrupt Temple worship (for instance, in 1QSa 2.3-11, blind, sick and disabled people were excluded). These developments increased the problems of sick people, and the need for healing, by the first century (and also demonstrate the diversity within Judaism).

---

18 Cotter, *Miracles*, pp.117-19. N.T. Wright, *The Climax of the Covenant. Christ and the Law in Pauline Theology* (Minneapolis: Fortress, 1992) p.28. L.A. Jervis, 'Becoming like God through Christ. Discipleship in Romans', in R.N. Longenecker (ed.), *Patterns of Discipleship in the New Testament* (Grand Rapids: Eerdmans, 1996) p.148, notes that the righteous tried to imitate God.

19 E.g. in 1 En. 15:11-12; 16:1, as in Jub. 10.12-13, demons from the dead giants caused demon-oppression and demon-possession, and (1 En. 16.1) will continue to do so until the day of judgment. G.W.E. Nickelsburg, *1 Enoch 1. A Commentary on the Book of 1 Enoch, Chapters 1-36; 81-108.* (Hermeneia: Minneapolis: Augsburg Fortress, 2001) p.91, notes that Jubilees is a Jewish elaboration on 1 Enoch.

20 Kee, 'Medicine and Healing', p.661.

In summary, the idea of innocent suffering became more prominent in Second Temple Judaism, particularly during religious persecution in the second century BC. At that time, the possibility of an afterlife became more definite, as did a belief in God's judgement after death. Ideas of intermediaries between God and man as at least partly responsible for suffering developed further in Second Temple Judaism, and allowed Israel to see the powers of darkness, usually as a hierarchy of evil spirits with Satan in command, as mainly responsible for her misery. By Pharisaic times, sufferers from certain diseases were excluded from ordinary social intercourse, as well as from parts of the Temple worship, because of the concept that sickness was the result of sin, and because of fear of ritual uncleanness. It can be deduced, by the separation of the groups in Israel (e.g. Pharisees, the community at Qumran), that there were different theological emphases, seen here in the area of sickness and healing.

1.3 Messiah and Other Figures of Healing

In spite of Israel's tribulations, Jewish religion remained generally optimistic that disease and death, along with sin, would be banished from her people, and the restoration of Israel would mean reconciliation with God. For instance, sin would be forgiven in the new covenant, as forecast by Jeremiah (31:31-34, especially v.34) and by Isaiah (e.g. 35:5-6). As these prophecies remained unfulfilled over generations, however, they came to be understood to refer to a future, eschatological, time. The people began to look forward to this time, when God would defeat the powers of evil, and so healing, national and individual, physical and metaphorical, would take place. The idea of God using figures of healing (for instance, the prophets) as his intermediaries is found in the Old Testament, but developed greatly in later Second Temple Judaism, when apocalyptic ideas became stronger, and Graeco-Roman influences were incorporated into Jewish thinking. The most important concept of a healing intermediary was that of a Messiah.

1.3.1 Messiah as Eschatological Healer

The concept arose of a Messiah, anointed by God, and endowed with the Spirit of God, with power to release the people from their misery, heal their suffering, and save Israel. Old Testament prophets began to look forward to a Messianic day of healing. When this idea began is not clear, but it may have grown out of Israel's continuing suffering after the exile. Jewish eschatological literature, rooted in the struggle of an oppressed people for justice and liberty, expected that God would proclaim a time of healing and salvation, coinciding with the beginning of the Messianic age.[21]

In the prophecies of this eschatological 'day of healing', all the major human disabilities were to be healed (Isa. 35:5; 61:1-2, although in neither of these texts is healing of those with leprosy, or resurrection of the dead, mentioned). Neonatal death and premature ageing were to cease (Isa. 65:19-20). Blind people were to see; blindness was often used in both Old and New Testaments in the metaphorical sense of failure to know God, but sight was also regarded as the highest of the human senses (e.g. Deut. 32:10; Ps. 17:8; Zech. 2:8). Blind and other disabled people, who could not approach the inner courts of the house of God, would, once healed, be accepted there.[22] Although the Isaianic passages refer to individual healing, other prophecies considered national healing, and the 'day of healing', the time when disease and death would disappear, was for the whole faithful remnant of 'Israel', when, for instance, eunuchs, as well as Gentiles, would be accepted (e.g. Isa. 56:3-4).

Israel expected her redemption to be accompanied by much suffering,[23] possibly as part of God's discipline, before the hoped-for Messianic age; forgiveness would be granted to the faithful remnant who survived God's judgment. Apocalyptic Judaism envisaged God continuing to discipline his creation until the time came for him to triumph over evil, to renew creation, and to vindicate the faithful, who were suffering in the cosmic war between good and evil.[24]

The term, 'the Messiah', never occurs in the Old Testament, and Charlesworth emphasises that the so-called Messianic passages there (e.g. 2 Samuel 7; Isa. 7:14; 9:6-7; 11:1-3; Zech. 9:9) are merely

---

21 G.H. Wenham, 'Christ's Healing Ministry and his Attitude to the Law', in H.H. Rowdon (ed.), *Christ the Lord* (Leicester: InterVarsity Press, 1982) p.125. N.T. Wright, *Jesus and the Victory of God* (London: SPCK, 1996) p.xvii. Wright, 'Jesus', p.48.

22 H.C. Kee, 'Magic and Messiah', in J. Neusner, E.S. Frerichs and P.V.M. Flesher (eds.), *Religion, Science and Magic in Concert and Conflict* (Oxford: Oxford University Press, 1989) p.137.

23 M.J. Borg and N.T. Wright, *The Meaning of Jesus* (San Francisco: HarperSanFrancisco, 1999) p.98; Wright, *Jesus and Victory*, p.579, discusses the 'Messianic woes' in detail.

24 In 1 En. 91:14, 'the deeds of the sinners shall depart from upon the whole earth', whereas in 4QEn^{g}, 'the world shall be written for destruction'. W. Horbury, *Jewish Messianism and the Cult of Christ* (London: SCM, 1998) p.59, considers that the latter verse assumes that the world would be entirely dissolved before the new creation. J.H. Neyrey, *Paul, in Other Words: A Cultural Reading of his Letters* (Louisville: Westminster John Knox Press, 1990) pp.163-64, believes that evil always attacks good.

implicit.[25] Horbury, however, holds the opinion that Messianism grew up in Old Testament times, and formed a coherent set of expectations, which profoundly influenced ancient Judaism.[26]

A leader of Israel was expected, one appointed by God to guide the people on the 'day of the Lord', and there seemed to be two possible types of anointed leader. One was a powerful king, a greater David. In Israel, the king was chosen by God (e.g. 1 Sam. 16:12-13), and this was important if a Messiah was to re-establish kingship.[27] Ezekiel prophesied that God would set over his flock a compassionate shepherd, a king like David (Ezek. 34:23). In another prophetic tradition (Zechariah 8 and 9), the just, humble servant-king would be Israel's saviour, as a militaristic deliverer.

The alternative possible type of Messiah was a prophet like Moses. The life and work of Moses was intimately bound up with the first great salvation of Israel, from slavery in Egypt, and with the establishment of Israel as God's covenant people, when Moses received the Law. (His meeting on Sinai, and his special relationship with God, are referred to throughout Israel's history.) The promise that God would raise up a prophet like Moses (Deut. 18:15-19) led to the belief that Moses would return as Messiah.[28] A third possibility (Mal. 4:5) was of Elijah preceding the 'day of the Lord' (although in Mal. 3:1-2, Elijah heralded, not a Messiah, but Yahweh).

In the two centuries before the second Temple was destroyed, Messianic ideas strengthened and diversified (and this is mirrored in the diversity of opinions by modern scholars). Charlesworth points out that the term 'the Messiah' is not used in the Old Testament Apocrypha (although Sirach 48:1-11 enlarged on the idea of Elijah as Messianic forerunner), but Horbury notes that this is true only of the Apocrypha's prose and mainly narrative books.[29] The Pseudepigrapha have the most significant records of Jewish Messianism. The term, 'Messiah' is first found explicitly in the Psalms of Solomon (17:32), in the context of a Davidic ruler, who, it was envisaged, would maintain the purity of

---

25 J.H. Charlesworth, 'From Messianology to Christology: Problems and Prospects', in J.H. Charlesworth (ed.), *The Messiah. Developments in Earliest Judaism and Christianity* (Minneapolis: Fortress, 1992) p.12.

26 Horbury, *Jewish Messianism*, e.g. p.6.

27 D.E. Aune, 'Christian Prophecy and the Messianic Status of Jesus', in Charlesworth (ed.), *The Messiah,* p.411.

28 That 'no-one knows Moses' burial place' (Deut. 34:10-12) hinted at his ascension to heaven. Charlesworth, 'From Messianology', p.14; R.H. Fuller, *The Foundations of New Testament Christology* (New York: Scribner's Sons, 1965) p.46.

29 Charlesworth, 'From Messianology', p.16. Horbury, *Jewish Messianism*, p.53.

God's people; both 1 Enoch and the Psalms of Solomon expected that the work of the Messiah would be to deliver God's final word to Israel.[30] In the Qumran documents, an eschatological prophet like Moses was expected, as well as a High Priest (the Messiah of Aaron) and a Prince (the Messiah of Israel), roles filled, perhaps, by the teacher of Righteousness.[31]

There was also late Jewish expectation of a Mosaic eschatological prophet who was able to perform miracles.[32] In the Testaments of the Twelve Patriarchs, a Messiah was foretold who would bind Beliar on earth (e.g. T. Dan 5:10; T. Levi 18:12), and so bring Israel back to the New Jerusalem.[33]

The concept of a hidden Messiah is also found in second- and first-century BC material (e.g. 4 Ezra 13:52 and 1 En. 62:6-7), perhaps based on the story of David, who was not initially obvious as kingly material (1 Sam. 16:11-12). In the Wisdom literature, a Messiah (the Wisdom of God) would not be recognised by the ungodly (Wis. 2:12-22), who might test him, even by torture (2:19), but God would save him. There are two possible Old Testament references to the death of a Messiah; that the one they have 'pierced' shall be mourned (Zech. 12:10-12), and perhaps in Daniel 9:26, as 'an anointed one cut off', but a suffering Messiah was not generally expected,[34] and the idea of a crucified one

30 J.H. Charlesworth (ed.), *The Old Testament Pseudepigrapha*. 2 Vols. (London: Darton, Longman and Todd, 1983-85). J.D.G. Dunn, 'Messianic Ideas and their Influence on the Jesus of History', in Charlesworth (ed.), *The Messiah*, p.367. J.C. O'Neill, *Who Did Jesus Think He Was?* (Leiden/New York/Cologne: Brill, 1995) p.45, considers that there was substantial evidence in first-century Jewish documents that a Davidic Messiah was expected. Vermes, *Jesus the Jew*, p.94.

31 W.A. Meeks, *The Prophet-King: Moses Traditions and the Johannine Christology* (Leiden: Brill, 1965) p.165, e.g. 1QS 9.11. The Damascus Document (CD 12.23) has only one Messiah 'of Aaron,' and (14.19; 19.10-11; 20.1) 'of Aaron and Israel'. Horbury, *Jewish Messianism*, p.59, points out that the Qumran documents were mainly dated to the Hasmonaean period, and therefore antedate the more strongly Messianic texts of the Old Testament Apocrypha and Pseudepigrapha.

32 O. Betz, 'The Concept of the So-Called "Divine Man" in Mark's Christology', in D. Aune (ed.), *Studies in New Testament and Early Christian Literature* (NovT Sup 33; Leiden: Brill, 1972) pp.229-40.

33 It is accepted that the Testaments of the Twelve Patriarchs had major Christian interpolations; e.g. Twelftree, *Jesus the Exorcist*, p.185. A. Roberts and J. Donaldson, *The Ante-Nicene Fathers. The Writings of the Fathers down to AD 325*, Vol.8. (Edinburgh/Grand Rapids: T. & T. Clark/Eerdmans, 1989) pp.16-17, 26, place the Testaments at the end of the second century AD.

34 Charlesworth, 'From Messianology', p.8; Oepke,'νόσος', *TDNT*, 4, p.1097, notes that a Messiah bearing his people's sickness was not expected. There was one later

(who, according to Deuteronomy 21:23, would be cursed by God) was not considered. Vermes is emphatic that ideas of suffering, death and resurrection of a Messiah were not part of first-century Jewish faith.[35]

Finally, there were several popular movements in Palestine, some regarded as Messianic, before, during and after the time of Jesus, resulting in abortive uprisings against political oppression.[36] This type of Messianism saw military or revolutionary might as the way to Israel's salvation; it is easy to understand the fears of the Jewish religious establishment that such Messianic movements risked both incurring the wrath of the Roman Empire, and fragmenting Israel's loyalties.

Although Horbury considers that there is evidence of widespread Messianism from the time of Alexander the Great, and the silence in the second century BC books of the Apocrypha does not exclude Messianic hope, which is elaborated in the Qumran documents, Charlesworth and Dunn draw attention to the ill-defined nature of pre-Christian Jewish Messianic literature, and regard it as clear that Israel never had a common Messianology.[37] I would agree with this consensus, especially in view of the evidence of Luke 7:20-23. Specifically, most modern writers believe that there is no evidence that passages such as Isaiah 53 were applied to 'the Messiah' before the first century AD.[38] The concept of a united Israel expecting their Messiah, and accepting the prophecies of Deutero-Isaiah as to his nature, is now usually regarded as a development that took place in the early church.[39]

1.3.2 Kings and Prophets as Healers

However closely they held the relationship between sickness and sin, the Old Testament writers acknowledged that there was always a reservoir of sickness in the community, and they were aware that there was an ordinary human duty of care. Concern for those who were weak

---

Talmudic suggestion of an unrecognised Messiah as the beggar at the city gate, binding his sores (b. *Sanh.* II. 98a).

35 Vermes, *Jesus the Jew*, p.38.

36 Josephus, *Ant.* 20.167, noted that the people were encouraged to join, as they would be shown 'signs and wonders'. Charlesworth, 'From Messianology', p.15.

37 Horbury, *Jewish Messianism*, p.63. Charlesworth, 'From Messianology', p.6; Dunn, 'Messianic Ideas', pp.369-71.

38 E.g. B. Witherington III, *Paul's Narrative Thought World: The Tapestry of Tragedy and Triumph* (Louisville: Westminster John Knox, 1994) p.133; Wright, *Climax of Covenant*, p.60-61.

39 Charlesworth, 'From Messianology', p.11, poses the question as to whether the Isaiah 53 prophecy of the Suffering Servant became associated with Jesus' life in his own teaching, or if it was a *post eventum* belief, shaped by his death on the cross.

and sick was, and remained, a covenant responsibility, a sacred duty of all God's people throughout Israel's history. They were to care for individuals who were sick, crippled, and aged (Lev. 19:32), as well as the stranger, all subsumed in the command to love the neighbour (Lev. 19:18).[40] There is no suggestion that ordinary people were to attempt active healing. Even the priests were concerned only with assuring purity; their roles in, for instance, 'leprosy' seemed to be to confirm the diagnosis (Lev. 13:2-15), certify that healing had occurred (13:6-7, 16-17), and preside over guilt- and sin-offerings (14:2-32), rather than to heal.

As well as general 'neighbourly' care, the idea that men might be especially empowered by God to heal both individuals and Israel developed, and extended in later Second Temple Judaism. The leaders of God's people were to be particularly diligent in the care of the weak members, unlike those shepherds who neglected their sheep, and who were condemned (Ezek. 34:2-6; Zech. 11:15-17). In addition to having a general concern for the well-being of Israel, however, the leaders were expected also to strengthen the weak, restore sick people to health, tend the injured (Ezek. 34:4), and heal the maimed (Zech. 11:16). The language is metaphorical, but the writers were aware that the leaders should have taken an active role in both care and healing. One of the benchmarks of the zeal with which rulers exercised social justice was their care of lame individuals in their societies (e.g. Zeph. 3:19; Mic. 4:6-7). The writers, both in the Old Testament and later Jewish writings, believed that God had appointed kings, who were recognised as healers and who, at God's command, would perform miracles. Although Solomon's healings are not described in the Old Testament, his reputation as a healer was documented by the first century BC and AD.[41]

Prophets were also considered capable of works of healing. The most famous prophet-healer was Moses, 'unequalled for his signs and

40 D.J. Wiseman, 'Medicine and the Old Testament', in B. Palmer (ed.), *Medicine and the Bible* (Exeter: Paternoster, 1986), p.23. J.B. Adamson, *The Epistle of James,* NICNT (Grand Rapids: Eerdmans, 1976) p.199, believes that guilds for visiting the sick dated back at least to the Old Testament (see Chapter 6, *2.2*).

41 J.P.M. Sweet, 'The Theory of Miracles in the Wisdom of Solomon', in Moule (ed.), *Miracles*, p.119, considers that healing arts were included in God's gift to Solomon as part of the wisdom he prayed for (1 Kgs. 3:9), and are alluded to in Wisdom of Solomon (e.g. 7:20). Sweet, p.118, regards Wisdom of Solomon as written in Alexandria in the first century BC; others, e.g. Hogan, *Healing,* p.49, place it between 50 BC and 50 AD. Josephus, e.g. *Ant.* 8.44-45, emphasised Solomon's reputation as a healer. He noted, *Ant.* 8.46-49, that the Jewish Eliezer, using roots according to instructions in Solomon's book, exorcised a demon-possessed man in the presence of Vespasian.

wonders' (Deut. 34:11). There is an understanding in the Old Testament that the Spirit of God was given for one task,[42] but, by the first century, Philo portrayed Moses as having a permanent spirit of healing from God (e.g. *About Giants* 6.27). Other healer prophets, especially Elijah and Elisha, healed non-Israelites (1 Kgs. 17:24; 2 Kgs. 5:3), as well as Israelites. Prophecy and miracle healing were regarded as integral parts of the prophet's ministry, as they were endowed with what came to be known as the Spirit of prophecy; their prophecies pointed forward to the eschatological day of God's healing, and meantime their healings glorified God.[43]

The story in 2 Kings 20:1-11 gives us a glimpse of Old Testament understanding of sickness, healing, and the prophet's role. The prophet Isaiah told King Hezekiah (gravely ill with, presumably, bacteraemia) that God had decreed that he would die, but Hezekiah's prayers and tears prevailed on God (showing God's compassion). The means of healing was the application of a fig poultice to Hezekiah's abscess; that is, healing resulted from an action instigated by the prophet.[44] As well as this sign of God's power, Hezekiah requested, and was given, the sign of the shadow reversing on the sundial (2 Kgs. 20:8-11). The account, with its mixture of miracle, magic and prophecy, could easily have come from pagan writings, and suggests that there was, even in the historical writings of the Old Testament, some interaction with the views on healing of surrounding peoples.

1.3.3 Magic, and Miracle-Workers as Healers

Israel was forbidden to use the 'abhorrent practices' of other nations, including sorcery, divination and consultation with ghosts/spirits, oracles from the dead (Deut. 18:9-14), or mediums and wizards (Lev. 19:31). It seems highly probable that these strictures were necessary

---

42 In Num. 11:16-17, God takes some of the Spirit that is on Moses, and puts it on the 70 elders, so that they will share in the burden of care for the people. (This is relevant in Chapter 5, *1.4*.) W.R. Telford, 'Book Review of Carl H. Holladay, *"Theios Aner" in Hellenistic Judaism: A Critique of the Use of this Category in New Testament Christology* (1977)', *JTS* 30 (1979) 246-52.

43 Turner, *Holy Spirit and Gifts*, pp.5-13. A.B. Kolenkow, 'Relationships between Miracle and Prophecy in the Greco-Roman World and Early Christianity', in *ANRW* II.23.2 (1980) 1471-72. Also, p.1483, Kolenkow notes that for Moses, Elijah and Elisha, miracles were regarded as signs of a prophet; their prophecies were reinforced by their miracles (e.g. Ex. 4:1-9, 30-31). Wenham, 'Christ's Healing Ministry', p.125.

44 A healing manoeuvre is rarely mentioned in the Old Testament. This one represents good medicine, since any measure to facilitate drainage of the abscess would have encouraged the subsidence of the bacteraemia.

because many Israelites relied on them as protection against evil power, and for healing.[45] The narrative of the dead man revived through contact with the bones of Elisha (2 Kgs. 13:20-21) is unmistakably magical. Achtemeier states that, by the first century AD, Jews in both Palestine and the Diaspora believed in, and practised, magic, despite the direct commands of the scriptures and the rabbis; generally, there seems to be good evidence that magical practices flourished in Judaism.[46]

It was certainly acceptable in Judaism to be expelling demons from the demon-possessed; Jewish exorcists are mentioned in Matthew 12:29 (par. Lk. 11:19), and incantations against demons are recorded in the Talmud (e.g. *b. Ber.* 6a). In the Dead Sea Scrolls, the tradition of holy men who did healing and exorcism is found.[47] The two famous Jewish miracle workers of the first centuries BC and AD were, respectively, Honi the rainmaker and Hanina ben Dosa, both of whom seemed to be holy men, who might be regarded as heirs of the prophetic tradition.[48] (The debate as to whether or not prophecy in Israel had ceased by the first century has not been resolved finally.)[49] Although ben Dosa, a Galilean, may have been a Pharisee and rabbi, both men seem to have worked in the mode of charismatic healers, largely independently of institutional Judaism, and Vermes believes that they were resented by the orthodox.[50] As well as Honi's rainmaking (e.g. *m. Taan.* 3.8), both treated illnesses, such as fever. Ben Dosa was reputed to have healed the son of a famous rabbi from a distance, a feat regarded by the community

---

45 C.J. Roetzel, *The World that Shaped the New Testament* (Atlanta: John Knox, 1985) p.99.

46 Achtemeier, 'Jesus and Disciples', p.152. Witherington, *Acts of Apostles,* p.580, writes that pagans of the time regarded Jewish magic as especially powerful. Roetzel, *World that Shaped*, p.101, notes the line between magic and divinely sanctioned power was not always well defined.

47 E.g. 1QapGen. 20.28-9, where Abraham healed, and exorcised an evil spirit from, Pharaoh. Healing and exorcism were seen as one process there.

48 Aune, 'Magic', p.1539.

49 Vermes, *Jesus the Jew*, p.74, and B. Vawter, 'Introduction to Prophetic Literature', in *NJBC*, p.191, both regard it as absent at that time; most others, e.g. Sanders, *Jesus and Judaism*, p.271, p.402, n.6, and S.H. Polaski, *Paul and the Discourse of Power* (Sheffield: Sheffield Academic Press, 1999) p.79, consider that the idea of prophecy having ceased in Israel is not sustained by evidence. M.A. Hooker, *The Signs of a Prophet. The Prophetic Actions of Jesus* (Harrisburg: Trinity, 1997) pp.6-7, suggests that, with the establishment of the Old Testament canon, the only way that the written word would be accepted as authoritative was by attributing it to an earlier prophet.

50 Vermes, *Jesus the Jew*, pp.56, 74.

as evidence that a healer was a prophet,[51] and this was confirmed by his ability to tell during his prayers which of his 'patients' would live or die (*b. Ber.* 34b). Both relied on prayer, and their deeds were regarded as less important than their piety. A later Jewish holy man, Eliezar ben Hyrcanus, was also regarded as an important prophet and miracle worker in the Talmudic tradition.[52]

Many prominent Jews of the religious establishment appeared to attach little importance to healing, however; for instance, Hillel and Shammai did not perform miracles, although it was understood that great rabbis could heal.[53] Theissen points out that miracle stories were absent from Tannaitic literature, but became increasingly common by the beginning of the third century AD (e.g. *b. Ber.* 6a; *b. Shab.* 67a, 110b).[54] This increase in folk traditions of miracles is confirmed in the Sepher-ha-Razim, a Hebrew document of the third to fourth century AD, illustrating the ongoing interest in Jewish magic and miracles then.[55] According to the Talmud, members of the Sanhedrin had to know about sorcery, so that they could judge witches (e.g. *b. Sanh.* 17a; *b. Men.* 65a).

1.3.4 Physicians as Healers

The usual work of the physicians who embalmed the body of Jacob (Gen. 50:1-3) is not explained, but physicians were not held in high regard in the Old Testament. Job called those who offered conventional theological explanations of his misfortunes 'worthless physicians' (13:4), and Jeremiah scorned the (metaphorical) physicians who failed to restore his people (Jer. 8:22; 46:11), whose 'balm in Gilead' did not heal Israel's wound. King Asa died some time after he consulted physicians, instead of seeking help from God (2 Chr. 16:12).

Tobit (Tob. 2:10) noted that physicians increased the sufferings of sick people. However, Sirach affirmed the honourable status of physicians, who had been granted skill from God to care for their fellow

---

51 Fuller, *Interpreting the Miracles,* pp.21-22. The fact that he was not seeking benefit from healing is confirmed by the story of his poverty in *b. Taan.* 25a.

52 J. Neusner, *Eliezer ben Hyrcanus. The Tradition and the Man, Studies in Judaism in Late Antiquity*, Vol.1 (Leiden: Brill, 1973) e.g. pp.327-33.

53 Vermes, *Jesus the Jew*, p.93.

54 Theissen, *Miracle Stories,* p.273, n.31.

55 *Sepher-ha-Razim: The Book of Mysteries*, M. Margalioth (ed.), (orig. 1966; ET, SBLTT Series 25; Atlanta: Scholars' Press, 1983).

creatures (38:1-2), and were devout men of prayer (Sir. 38:13-14).[56] In the writings of the Qumran community, Charlesworth initially believed that a document fragment, 4Q Therapeia, described a 'ward round' of sick/wounded people.[57] Philo described a group near Alexandria, the Therapeutae, as people who had mastered the art of healing souls.[58]

Some Jewish writers commented on the medicines that physicians used. Herbs, many of which were considered to have magical elements, were seen as powerful therapeutic tools in both Jewish and Gentile healing practices. Perhaps because of Gentile approval, or since Babylonian medicine (which Israel had encountered at the exile) involved both herbs and astrology,[59] remedies based on herbs were regarded in different lights in different areas of Second Temple Judaism. In the Book of Watchers (1 Enoch 1-36, based on Gen. 6:1-4), healing herbs were regarded as dangerous (e.g. 1 En. 7:1), since the fallen angels had introduced knowledge of them. Sirach, Wisdom of Solomon, and Tobit were generally positive about the use of natural substances; for instance, medicines created from the God-given herbs of the ground were seen as good, and provided for healing (Sir. 38:4). In Wisdom 7:20, Pseudo-Solomon knew the varieties of plants and the virtues of roots;[60] and Tobias used natural medicines in healing (Tob. 11:10-13), and exorcism (Tob. 8:2-3). In the book of Jubilees, Noah was taught about herbal medicines by angels (Jub. 10:10, 12), so that, although the teaching of healing remedies was connected with the origin of evil in the world, the knowledge was acceptable.[61] In Tobit, however, it was the

56 Hogan, *Healing*, p.38, notes that Sirach, written in *c.* 180 BC, was translated into Greek in 132 BC, in Alexandria. There, the medical tradition of Hippocrates was active and respected.

57 Meeks, *The Prophet-King*, p.164, notes that the community is an important independent Jewish witness to healing, since the Dead Sea Scrolls were affected neither by the post-Jamnia consolidation of Judaism, nor by Christianity. J.H. Charlesworth, 'Appendix–4Q Therapeia', in Kee, *Medicine, Miracle and Magic*, pp.128-34, although he later reconsidered this. Both Hogan, *Healing*, p.167, n.88, and Martin, *Corinthian Body*, p.283, n.14, deny that the document is concerned with healing; it is now considered to be a scrap of material from a writing exercise. In view of the community's views on disabled people, it seems unlikely that the fragment is about healing.

58 Philo, *On the Contemplative Life*. 1.2. According to Hogan, *Healing*, p.173, Philo was interested in spiritual, rather than physical, healing.

59 Hogan, *Healing*, p.81.

60 Hogan, *Healing*, pp.50-51, believes that the writer may have had knowledge of medical theories and vocabulary.

61 Hogan, *Healing*, pp.91-92, notes that, since it was knowledge sanctioned by God, the people would not be, as in Babylonian medicine, contaminated by idolatry. He, pp.85-86, notes that, although the provenance is unclear, Jubilees was probably written in the

angel Raphael who was mediator of divine healing (the name means 'God heals'); in Jubilees 23:30 it was the Lord who healed, and in Wisdom 16:12, it was God's word, rather than 'herb and poultice', that healed.[62]

In summary, Jewish writers portrayed that the continuation of Israel's sufferings led her people to consider how God would relieve their plight, and the idea emerged that this evil age would end in a future, eschatological time set by God, where disease and suffering would disappear for Israel's faithful. As this healing/salvation was prophesied, the idea of a man anointed by God, a Messiah, who would lead the faithful remnant, emerged in Second Temple Judaism. There were various expectations, especially of a king like David, or a prophet like Moses. A dominant belief was that, in the Messianic age of eschatological prophecy, after a period of intense suffering, salvation would be given to those of Israel who remained faithful, and survived God's judgment. The apocalyptic literature portrayed a Messiah winning a battle against the forces of evil. Most modern authors, except Horbury, believe that that there was considerable diversity by the first century about the expectations of the nature of a Messiah, who would herald the time of healing.

In addition, while the people had a sacred duty to care for the weak members of their community, their rulers were charged with healing, under the command of God. The Old Testament prophets were also frequently able to heal, so that both their prophecies and their healing powers bore witness to the hand of God, and there was a significant healing miracle tradition in the Old Testament. In Second Temple Judaism, some charismatic holy men and miracle workers were acknowledged as effective healers. Although magic was officially forbidden in Judaism, there was evidence of recourse to it, just as there was in paganism. The standing of physicians was low in the Old Testament, but by the second century BC, both physicians and 'natural' herbal medicines were accepted in some strands of Judaism. Particularly by later Second Temple Judaism, widely different views with regard to healing are apparent.

---

early second century. J.C. VanderKam, *The Book of Jubilees*. Guides to Apocrypha and Pseudepigrapha Series (Sheffield: Sheffield Academic Press, 2001), pp.12, 17-22, suggests a mid-second-century BC date.

62 Philo, *On the Special Laws*. 1.252, points out that medicine does not benefit all people and may do great harm; God is the preserver.

1.4 Conclusion

A brief description of the progress of widely accepted Jewish thought about sickness and healing has been presented, to explain the Jewish background to Jesus' and apostolic healing, as depicted in the New Testament. The major developments have been traced, from the concept of an all-powerful Yahweh both causing and healing the illnesses and sufferings of his covenant people, through the writers' recognition of vicarious suffering for the benefit of the people, of the possibility of an afterlife, of the awareness of evil forces over which Yahweh might not be in full control, and of the need for an eschatological healer, as well as human intermediaries who could heal.

Non-Jews have been criticised for considering first-century Judaism as a monolithic, unchanging whole.[63] We have seen that there were various views on healing, and on intermediaries between God and man, in the period before Jesus' ministry, and this diversity will be important when we consider attitudes to healing within the New Testament. Israel viewed herself as profoundly weak, and in need of metaphorical healing and restoration, before she could fulfil her destiny to be a light to the nations (Isa. 49:6). The longing for a Messiah and the desire for an eschatological age of healing were elements that would inevitably meet. They met in the coming of Jesus, Messiah, healer, and Son of God.

2 Sickness and Healing in the Graeco-Roman World

Having considered the Jewish aspects, we now turn to pagan understanding of sickness and healing in the Eastern Mediterranean area, before and at the time of Jesus' ministry and the gospels.

There has been a long tradition of separating paganism[64] from Judaism, partly by later historians attempting to study the New Testament through the eyes of its writers, but, more fundamentally, by the very early (Jewish) church as it was beginning to evangelise Gentiles.[65] It is now accepted that Hellenistic and Roman influences

63 E.g. J.D.G. Dunn, 'Who Did Paul Think He Was? A Study of Jewish-Christian Identity', *NTS* 45 (1999) 183.

64 H.-J. Klauck, *The Religious Context of Early Christianity. A Guide to Graeco-Roman Religions* (ET; Edinburgh: T. & T. Clark, 2000) p.2, points out the negative connotations of the term, but dismisses as inaccurate alternative terms, such as polytheism, foreign religions, etc.

65 A.J.M. Wedderburn, 'Paul and Jesus: The Problem of Continuity', in A.J.M. Wedderburn (ed.), *Paul and Jesus. Collected Essays* (JSNTSup 37; Sheffield: JSOT Press, 1989) p.101.

were highly pervasive in Jewish life, both in the Diaspora and in Israel. Many Jews in Palestine were bilingual; many of their names had both Greek and Jewish components; inscriptions on tombstones in Beth She`arim were often in Hebrew, Latin and Greek; second- and first-century BC Jewish literature was often written in Greek, and some (e.g. 3 Maccabees) was modelled on Greek philosophical literature. Conversely, there was considerable pagan interest in Judaism.[66]

As with Judaism, whose roots were established in the Old Testament, so in the paganism of the first century AD, the epochs before the founding of the Roman Empire were significant in the background to Jesus' healing ministry. Experiences from classical Greece, through Hellenism and the Graeco-Roman period, played an essential part in the development of beliefs about suffering and healing.

In the Ancient Near East, what is referred to as Hellenism was a mixture of cultures, Greek and non-Greek, especially from Egypt, but also from Asia, by way of trade and conquests; so 'Hellenism' includes the 'orientalisation' of Greek ideas and practices.[67] The Hellenistic period, from the time of the conquests of Alexander the Great, ended with Roman take-over at different times in different parts of the East, and the struggle for political power extended from Hellenistic times into the first century AD. The Roman influence became progressively more dominant in both environment and thought from the beginning of the Empire, in the mid-first century BC, but it built on this prior culture. Thus, although 'Hellenistic' and 'Graeco-Roman' are used as shorthand, both are inadequate descriptions of the cultures, and especially give the erroneous impression that we are dealing with static entities. This is a similar point to the criticism levelled at New Testament scholars describing non-Christian religions, and is important in relation to healing in the New Testament.[68]

---

66 E.g. I.H. Marshall, 'Palestinian and Hellenistic Christianity: Some Critical Comments', *NTS* 19 (1973) p.274. L.V. Rutgers, *The Jews in Late Ancient Rome* (Leiden: Brill, 1995) p.100. E. Ferguson, *Backgrounds of Early Christianity* (2nd ed.; Grand Rapids: Eerdmans, 1993) p.512.

67 T. Engberg-Pedersen, 'Introduction', in T. Engberg-Pedersen (ed.), *Paul in his Hellenistic Context. Studies of the New Testament and its World* (Edinburgh: T. & T. Clark, 1994) p.xix. B. Blackburn, *Theios Anēr and the Markan Miracle Traditions: A Critique of the Theios Anēr Concept as an Interpretative Background of the Miracle Tradition used by Mark* (WUNT 2/40; Tübingen: Mohr [Siebeck], 1991) pp.10-11; M. Hengel, *Judaism and Hellenism*, Vol.1 (ET; London: SCM, 1974) pp.1-5.

68 E.P. Sanders, *Paul and Palestinian Judaism* (London: SCM, 1977) p.20; Robinson and Koester, *Trajectories*, p.12, say that we tend to assume that other religions were static, and that only Christianity was moving.

When the Greek city-states (which had had their own god or goddess), lost their supremacy, and the democracy of the classical era gradually changed to rule by an elite oligarchy by the first century BC,[69] the power of the ancient Olympian gods faded. The people felt a great need for their gods to be actively helpful to them; Sanders writes that there was evidence of Hellenistic pessimism, where citizens felt that they were enslaved by powers over which they had no control, regarding themselves as under the influence of τύχη (chance). [70] Even Pliny the Elder saw himself as under the power of the Roman goddess *Fortuna*, 'We are so much at the mercy of Chance, that Chance herself, by whom God is proved uncertain, takes the place of God'.[71]

In this milieu, it is not surprising that new religious cults (as well as magic) became important forces. Religious propaganda was aggressive, and was directed at influential members of society, normally in cities, which were most interested in 'foreign' cults.[72] Although Judaism was not an actively missionary religion, it expanded in the first century AD.[73] The Jewish Diaspora had many synagogues (for instance, Rome had nine), and people were attracted to their local communities because of their distinctive common life style,[74] which invited the interest of proselytes and 'God-fearers'. Also, Judaism appealed to the Graeco-Roman world because of the antiquity of its faith, and its great heroic figures, an appeal increased by the writings of Philo.[75]

---

69 Clarke, *Serve the Community*, p.18.

70 E.P. Sanders, *Paul, the Law, and the Jewish People* (Philadelphia: Fortress, 1983) p.152.

71 Pliny, *Natural History* 2.22-23.

72 E.S. Fiorenza, 'Miracles, Mission and Apologetics: An Introduction', in Fiorenza (ed.), *Aspects of Religious Propaganda*, p.16. D. Georgi, 'Socioeconomic Reasons for the "Divine Man" as a Propagandist Pattern', in Fiorenza (ed.), *Aspects of Religious Propaganda*, pp.35-36.

73 Ferguson, *Backgrounds of Early Christianity*, p.512. The view of Jewish missionary activity was based on Matt. 23:15, but that is a Christian interpretation. Fiorenza, 'Miracles, Mission', p.2.

74 A. Chester, 'The Jews of Judea and Galilee', in Barclay and Sweet (eds.), *Early Christian Thought,* p.20. J.L. Sumney, *Identifying Paul's Opponents. The Question of Method in 2 Corinthians*. (JSNTSup 40; Sheffield: Sheffield Academic Press, 1990) p.50; D. Georgi, The *Opponents of Paul in Second Corinthians* (ET; Edinburgh: T. & T. Clark, 1987) p.87, considers that the synagogue was Judaism's most important propaganda tool. J. Barclay, 'The Jews of the Diaspora', in Barclay and Sweet (eds.), *Early Christian Thought*, p.37.

75 R.A. Horsley and N.A. Silberman, *Message and Kingdom: How Jesus and Paul Ignited a Revolution and Transformed the Ancient World* (New York: Grosset/Putnam,

In summary, at the turn of the ages, Graeco-Roman ideas, with all their diversity, may be traced from the earlier history of classical Greece and Hellenism, but the notion of a neat division between Hellenistic and Jewish influences on Christianity on this basis alone cannot be sustained.[76] Separating the Graeco-Roman effect on the New Testament completely from Second Temple Judaism is mainly a modern editorial convenience rather than a historical fact, since there was considerable mingling of cultural influences.

2.1 Intermediaries in Paganism

The idea of intermediaries between gods and humans was widespread in the Graeco-Roman world, but it had developed in a very different way to the concept in Judaism, and this is crucial to understanding differences with respect to suffering, healing and power between paganism and Judaism.

Intermediaries were acceptable in classical, Hellenistic and Graeco-Roman cultures, because of the fluid relationship between humans and gods. Humanity was considered capable of achieving divine status and honour,[77] a concept not possible in Judaism, with an all-powerful, transcendent God. Since the human/divine division in Greek and Roman cultures was not inexorably fixed, it was accepted that there was a loose hierarchy of gods, demi-gods, and heroes, down to ordinary human beings at the bottom of the heap.

Hero cults date back to classical Greek times. Heroes were often rulers; they could become gods, sometimes after death (e.g. Aelius Aristides, *Herakles* 40.11) or by, for instance, a military victory, and they might be historical or mythical. Mythology was common; heroes, being greater than ordinary men, were often regarded as begotten by a god, so, although kinship was important in the ancient world, a hero was released from the necessity of being like his father.[78] A hero might be referred to by the term θεῖος ἀνήρ (TA), meaning a man either of divine descent, or god-like because of his deeds.[79] Since political and

1997) p.118; C.J. Roetzel, *The Letters of Paul. Conversations in Context* (2nd ed.; London: SCM, 1983) p.27. Philo, e.g. *Life of Moses,* II.50.279-91.

76 Aune, 'Magic', p.1538.

77 M. Hengel, *Christ and Power* (ET; Philadelphia: Fortress, 1977) p.7, suggests that this began in early Hellenism, but most scholars see it as dating back to classical Greece, e.g. Georgi, 'Socioeconomic Reasons', p.30.

78 Bultmann, *Theology of New Testament,* 1, p.130. Smith, *Jesus the Magician,* pp.18-19.

79 W. Von Martitz, 'υἱός, κτλ', *TDNT,* 8, p.338. (See *2.1.2.*)

religious powers were inextricable in Graeco-Roman times, worship of heroes and rulers was a logical corollary. The basic functions of a god were help and rescue, i.e. 'saving', so whoever provided these was seen as having divine power.[80] 'To save' did not usually have an otherworldly concept; salvation was concerned more with health and prosperity than an after-life. Compared with Judaism, expecting an eschatological Messiah, pagan thought was interested in divine help in the present.

2.1.1 Cults of the Powerful

Kings were connected to the divine world, either as superior human beings or by being divinely chosen,[81] for instance, Alexander the Great. Introduced in his reign, the Hellenistic ruler cult probably arose from Egypt, where the Pharaohs had long been regarded as gods.[82] With the beginning of the Roman Empire, Augustus ushered in a golden age of peace, after the civil wars and political weakness of the earlier first century BC. The *Pax Romana* brought material benefits to many (but not all), and it endured because of the administrative and political power of the Emperor. Augustus became regarded as a god in the eastern part of the empire, and as the gods appeared to favour Rome, the ruler cult and Roman power fused in the Imperial cult.[83] Witherington regards the Imperial cult as presenting Christianity with its stiffest opposition.[84]

In the Greek cities, by the first century AD, the benefactor cult was important; 'doing good', which in Judaism largely meant giving alms to those poor and sick in the community, in Greek paganism meant conferring benefits on the city, and this in turn resulted in honour and respect for the benefactor.[85] The cities were in competition with each other in their benefactions, as news of them might reach the attention of the emperor, the principal benefactor.[86]

These cults demonstrate the practical consequences of the underlying Greek idea that gods were like men, but with more 'virtue', and were endowed with immortality. Rulers and benefactors were to be honoured 'as a god', perhaps as θεῖος ἀνήρ. Emperors and rulers were often expected to be able to heal, and there was an important link between

---

80 E.g. Remus, *Jesus as Healer,* p.9, notes that a healer was often referred to as 'saviour'. Klauck, *Magic and Paganism,* pp.254-55.

81 Aune, 'Christian Prophecy', pp.411-12.

82 Klauck, *Religious Context*, p.260.

83 J.B. Green, 'The Death of Jesus and the Ways of God', *Int.* 52 (1998) p.28. Klauck, *Magic and Paganism*, p.43; Hengel, *Christ and Power*, p.9.

84 Witherington, *Acts of Apostles,* p.825.

85 Harvey, *Jesus and Constraints,* p.9.

86 Clarke, *Serve the Community*, pp.53-55, p.27.

authority and healing (see Chapter 6, *3*).[87]

2.1.2 θεῖος ἀνήρ (TA)

The study of intermediaries in pagan healing would be incomplete without mention of the concept of TA, 'divine man'. The origins of the term are not clear, but may well have arisen from the northern Indo-Germanic idea of a shaman, who combined the roles of seer, poet and wise man.[88] In classical times, a TA was probably a man, not a god (except by apotheosis or assumption into heaven), but, as we have seen, divine and human merged easily in pagan thought, and the TA, like the 'hero', encompassed both historical and mythical figures.[89] Features, such as miraculous birth, and acquiring divinity at death, were common. Holladay believes that philosophers were not often regarded as TAs, the exception being Pythagoras, as he was both philosopher and miracle-worker.[90] Empedocles, a disciple of Pythagoras in the sixth century BC, described himself in a way that sums up the idea of a TA:

> But I go about (among) you as an immortal god, no longer as a mortal, honoured by all. — They follow after me — some requiring sayings from the oracle, others seeking to experience a word that brings healing in their manifold sicknesses, having already long been riddled with severe pain.[91]

---

87 Smith, 'Prolegomena', pp.184, 182. Cotter, *Miracles*, p.8, and on p.36, she notes that the description of Vespasian's healings (e.g. Tacitus, *Histories* 4.81-2) fits well with the Imperial cult. W. Grundmann, 'δύναμαι/δύναμις', *TDNT*, 2, p.286, notes that healing miracles were often referred to as δυνάμεις in paganism.

88 M. Hengel, *The Charismatic Leader and his Followers* (ET; Edinburgh: T. & T. Clark, 1981) p.25.

89 D.L. Tiede, *The Charismatic Figure as Miracle Worker* (SBLDS 1; Missoula: University of Montana Press, 1972) p.1, notes the term was used rarely in classical times. B.L. Blackburn 'Miracle Working Theioi Andres in Hellenism (and Hellenistic Judaism)', in Wenham and Blomberg (eds.), *Gospel Perspectives*, 6, p.186. Blackburn, *Theios Anēr*, p.263.

90 Porphyry, *Life, Pythagoras* 29-30. C. Holladay, *Theios Aner in Hellenistic-Judaism: A Critique of the Use of this Category in New Testament Christology* (SBLDS 40; Missoula: Scholars' Press, 1977) p.23.

91 Empedocles, *Katharmoi* 1.112.1, from Diogenes Laertius, *Lives of Eminent Philosophers* 8.62. Diogenes Laertius had a low opinion of Empedocles, who he considered (8.66) was boasting. There is some doubt as to the authenticity of the piece, however; M.R. Wright (ed.), *Empedocles: The Extant Fragments* (New Haven/London: Yale University Press, 1981) p.19, considers that Diogenes Laertius' account of the epigrams attributed to Empedocles was almost certainly spurious; B. Inwood, *The Poem of Empedocles* (ET, rev. ed.; Toronto: University of Toronto Press, 2001) pp.11, 81,

The idea of a TA seems to have been fairly widely held in Hellenism, and extended into Graeco-Roman culture of the first century AD.[92] Corrington considers that the term changed over time, possibly as a response to changing concepts of power,[93] but it seems that, rather than developing in meaning, the definition was always nebulous in the ancient world. It might be used to describe divinity, and/or miracle working, and might include those with gifts such as prophecy, oracular and ecstatic utterances, wisdom and rhetorical ability.[94] TAs might enhance the reputation of a city, but they were often feared, and might suffer death (e.g. Socrates) or exile (e.g. Thucydides).[95]

The similarity of the careers of such divine men to that of Jesus was recognised by the early Christian apologists; for instance, Justin considered the divine man concept was a demonic imitation of Christianity (*Apologies* I. 21-27). Early twentieth-century scholars were enthusiastic about the role of the TA as the crucial link between Christian and pagan thought, for instance, Dibelius and Bultmann used the concept as evidence that the gospel miracle stories had their origins in the Hellenistic TA concept.[96] There has been a considerable body of literature on the TA since, as scholars (e.g. Otto Betz, Dieter Georgi, David Tiede, Carl Holladay, Morton Smith, Gail Corrington, Jack Kingsbury, Eugene Gallagher and Barry Blackburn)[97] debated whether

---

considers that the quotation may have been derived from Heracleides. It does, however, give the flavour of the TA concept.

92 Blackburn, *Theios Anēr,* p.94, notes that this is true especially in Neo-Pythagoreanism, in the renaissance of the teachings of Pythagoras (e.g. Apollonius of Tyana); J.D. Kingsbury, 'The "Divine Man" as the Key to Mark's Christology—The End of an Era?', *Int.* 35 (1981) p.248; Roetzel, *World that Shaped*, p.103, suggests that there was widespread belief that TAs existed and did mighty works.

93 G.P. Corrington, *The 'Divine Man': His Origin and Function in Hellenistic Popular Religion* (New York: Lang, 1986) pp.44-46, thinks the meaning of the term was on a trajectory.

94 Holladay, *Theios Aner*, p.15, but notes, p.241, that not every miracle worker was regarded as a TA.

95 Georgi, 'Socioeconomic Reasons', pp.28, 29, 34.

96 M. Dibelius, *From Tradition to Gospel* (orig. 1919, ET; New York: Scribner's Sons, 1935) pp.70-97; Bultmann, *History of the Synoptic Tradition,* pp.218-241, especially p.240. See Holladay, *Theios Aner*, p.103.

97 Betz, 'Concept of "Divine Man"', pp.229-40; Georgi, 'Socioeconomic Reasons', pp.27-42; Tiede, *Charismatic Figure* ; Holladay, *Theios Aner*, e.g. pp.38, 239-40, thinks that it was very liable to lead to heretical ideas in the early church; Smith, *Jesus the Magician*, e.g. pp.74-75; Corrington, *'Divine Man';* Kingsbury, 'Divine Man', p.248, regarded the role of TA to have been exaggerated; E.V. Gallagher, *Divine Man or*

the concept might provide a lead to understanding the Christology of the early church. Their consensus is that the idea was overplayed in the early twentieth century, and does not explain either New Testament Christology or the source of the New Testament miracle stories. My estimate, distilled from these opinions, is that the term TA was useful shorthand for a product of the Greek understanding of a person from a given kinship and society, who rose above the common herd to become a philosopher, a benefactor, and/or a miracle-worker. Although it was a highly ambiguous term, it illustrated the belief in intermediaries between gods and man, and so is useful now, to indicate the intellectual atmosphere in and before the first century. That does not mean that Jesus must be fitted into this category, and the suggestion that, *because* Jesus was reported as healing, *therefore* this part of his ministry must have been added from Hellenism, is neither logical nor warranted.

In summary, the concept of intermediaries between gods and men was widespread in Greek and Roman culture. It differed from that in Judaism, since in Graeco-Roman culture, the divine/human division was not fixed; rather, there was a loose hierarchy of gods, demi-gods, heroes and men. Heroes were often divine, and could be historical or mythical (or a mixture of these); one form was the TA, a term referring to the specially gifted, a great man, healer, or both. This was in line with the cult of worship of the powerful, for instance, the Imperial cult, but reactions to a TA might include fear, with the need to remove him. The concept of TA was alluded to fairly commonly in the Graeco-Roman period, but never defined. It became important to some twentieth-century biblical scholars, who suggested that it might have given the early church its understanding of Christology, and, in particular, the gospel accounts of Jesus' healings. It seems to me that the concept of TA, although ill defined, *has* some merit in helping us to understand the atmosphere in the eastern Roman Empire, but it does not follow that it must be the explanation for Jesus' healing ministry.

2.2 *Healing and Healers in the Graeco-Roman World*

Plato wrote that no worker had time in life to spend being ill and being cured, and this seemed to apply even more to the first centuries BC and AD, where the economic and social conditions in many cities were

Magician? Celsus and Origen on Jesus (SBLDS 64; Chico: Scholars Press, 1982); Blackburn, *Theios Anēr*, p.263, regards the term as a 'twentieth-century abstraction'.

probably appalling.[98] Illnesses were common, and the social consequences severe.[99] As well as being unable to continue one's livelihood, ἀσθένεια (weakness) of the body meant humiliation in the eyes of others; ill-health and disability were considered to be associated with inferior intelligence, and weakness of character.[100] In the world of Sophism and rhetoric, power, health, beauty and vigour were considered necessary in order to survive and thrive.[101] Also, there was often the suspicion that gods or demons were responsible for illness, and thus that ill-health was due to black magic, resulting in the ill person being shunned.[102]

The term 'health care system' today suggests an organised system, related closely to our biomedical ideas of health and disease; to the medical anthropologist, it is a conceptual model, arrived at by considering how people in a particular social setting think about health. Health care is the nexus of adaptive responses to the human problems created by sickness.[103] Pilch's scheme of three overlapping forms of ancient eastern Mediterranean health care (professional, popular and folk sectors) is a useful attempt to disentangle the scene,[104] but any system explaining care should be viewed with the following provisos:

a) The purpose of any separation is merely a means of following possible routes that people might take to deal with their ill-health.

---

98 Plato, *Republic* II.406C-E. J.J. Meggitt, *Paul, Poverty and Survival* (Edinburgh: T. & T. Clark, 1998) pp.62-63, and n.49, p.50. This may be an unduly pessimistic view; S.J. Friesen, 'Poverty in Pauline Studies', *JSNT* 26 (2004) pp.323-361, has reopened the discussion, which is joined by J. Barclay, 'Poverty in Pauline Studies: A Response to Steven Friesen', *JSNT* 26 (2004) 363-66, and by P. Oakes, 'Constructing Poverty Scales for Graeco-Roman Society', *JSNT* 26 (2004) 367-71. (See Chapter 5, *2.5*.)

99 Jackson, *Doctors and Diseases,* pp.185-86. C. Forbes, 'Comparison, Self-Praise and Irony: Paul's Boasting and the Conventions of Hellenistic Rhetoric', *NTS* 32 (1986) pp.19-20. P. Marshall, *Enmity in Corinth: Social Conventions in Paul's Relations with the Corinthians* (Tübingen: Mohr [Siebeck], 1987) pp.xiv, 52-54. (See Chapter 5, e.g. *2.4.1*.)

100 Plutarch, *Moralia* 88F; Plutarch, *Lives*; *Solon* 21.3, notes that 'deceit and affliction were in the same category, all perverting a man's reason'. Cicero, *De Oratore (About the Orator)* 2.58.235-37; 59.238-39.

101 Cicero, *De Oratore* 2.11.45-46; Plutarch, *Moralia* 90E; Martin, *Corinthian Body*; B.W. Winter, *Philo and Paul among the Sophists* (SNTSMS 96; Cambridge: CUP, 1997) pp.117-18. See Chapter 5, *2.4.2*.

102 J.H. Elliott, 'The Evil Eye and the Sermon on the Mount,' *Bib Int* 2 (1994) p.62.

103 A. Kleinman, *Patients and Healers in the Context of Culture. An Exploration of the Borderland between Anthropology, Medicine and Psychiatry* (Berkeley and Los Angeles: University of California Press, 1980) pp.24-27.

104 Pilch, 'Sickness and Healing in Luke-Acts,' pp.192-94.

b) The situations of ill people might be very different at various times and in diverse places in Hellenistic and Graeco-Roman times; I would regard as simplistic the belief of the American social anthropologists' Context Group, that first-century Eastern Mediterranean culture was monolithic, and to a large extent, static.[105]

c) The material that we work with is only what has survived, so it is easy to have a distorted view of the overall scene.

Kleinman makes the point that anthropologists often restrict their interest to the sacred forms of healing, and disregard its non-sacred aspects.[106] In this brief account of the health care available in the first-century eastern Roman Empire, the sacred may be dominant, but the non-sacred is given its place. The forms of health care can be separated into Hippocratic medicine, institutionalised cultic healing (for instance, the cult of Asclepius), healing by charismatic (usually itinerant) healers, and the use of magic, but it is recognised that these are artificial separations; there is a great deal of overlap between them, as there is between health care, related arts (e.g. astrology and divination) and religions. Health care often depends also on extraneous factors, such as availability and cost, in particular circumstances.[107]

2.2.1 Medicine

The practice of observational medicine is attributed to Hippocrates, in the fifth century BC, beginning from the island of Cos. Most of the original documents have been lost, and the so-called 'Hippocratic Corpus' may have been an assortment of works, perhaps compiled by Galen.[108] The reason for the careful observations made was mainly to establish the prognosis of an illness, but treatments with both drugs and surgery were described, often by non-medical writers.[109] Hippocratic medicine recognised and used nature and natural substances as having major preventative and healing powers, although details of healing were

---

105 J.H. Elliott, *What is Social-Scientific Criticism?,* (Minneapolis: Fortress, 1993) p.19.

106 Kleinman, *Patients and Healers*, pp.28-29.

107 Cotter, *Miracles*, p.206, notes that some Greek cities had 'public physicians', ἀρχιάτροι, to give free services to citizens, in order to avert disease and epidemics.

108 Jackson, *Doctors and Diseases,* p.20, notes that Galen wrote prodigiously in the second century AD, especially commentaries on the Hippocratic treatises.

109 E.g. Pliny, *Natural History* 20-32; Celsus, *De Medicina (On Medicine)*, 2.10.1-17. Jackson, *Doctors and Diseases*, e.g. pp.23-24. He describes, p.66, 'the house of the Surgeon' in Pompeii, which contained many medical and surgical instruments when Pompeii was excavated.

often relatively scanty.[110] Several famous physicians of the first and second centuries AD followed Hippocrates' method of accurate observation, especially Aretaeus of Cappadocia.[111] Aulus Cornelius Celsus, a Roman patrician, writing in the period AD 14 to 37, was probably not trained as a physician, but described accurately medical conditions that are easily recognisable today (e.g. *De Medicina* 2.7.5-38). This was possible, because technical terms were not commonly used in Hippocratic medicine.

Hippocratic medicine also attempted to understand the *causes* of diseases. The view was that illnesses were primarily due to an upset of the body's harmony (e.g. Hippocrates, *Diseases* 4.51.1-7). Much (but by no means all) of this crude 'physiological' aetiology has been disproved. The medical school at Alexandria, famous for its interest in anatomy (see Chapter 4, *4*), was particularly active in seeking understanding of human physiology. The 'physiological' was the opposite of the 'ontological' view of the causation of disease, where the body was seen as attacked from outside (not by e.g. bacteria, but by e.g. evil spirits). These two views of aetiology represented, respectively and approximately, the beliefs of the elites and the lower classes.[112] By the early Roman Empire, the balance had swung in favour of the second view, which in turn influenced the treatment considered appropriate for healing. Although medical schools flourished, 'popular' medicine swamped medical 'science'. Astrology blossomed, and medicine became so involved with it, that medical technique became distinctly more magical.[113] For instance, Pliny the Elder described many folk remedies, some of which seemed to combine medicine with magic.[114] Galen, although usually portrayed as a traditional physician of the second century AD, was an example of this phenomenon of medical syncretism. Sceptical of magic, and considering both medical and philosophical schools to be teaching superstition, he used dreams and

---

110 Hippocrates, *Airs, Waters, Places* 7.1-100, discusses in detail the importance of a clean water supply. A.E. Harvey, *Renewal through Suffering. A Study of Second Corinthians* (Edinburgh: T. & T. Clark, 1996) p.32, comments that this was a culture less interested in *how* a person recovered than *that* they did.

111 F. Adams, *The Extant Works of Aretaeus the Cappadocian* (London: Sydenham Society Pub., 1856).

112 Martin, *Corinthian Body*, p.150.

113 J. Scarborough, 'The Pharmacology of Sacred Plants, Herbs and Roots', in Faraone and Obbink (eds.) *Magika Hiera,* p.155. Kee, 'Magic and Messiah', pp.125-26.

114 E.g. Pliny, *Natural History* 26.68, describes herbal remedies for consumption (what we would now describe as pulmonary tuberculosis); in 28.48, he describes cures for ear afflictions using much more exotic, 'magical' ingredients.

auguries in new healing methods, or to change incurable diseases into curable ones. He became a devotee of Asclepius, and trained in the Asclepieion at Pergamum, after having been himself healed there.[115]

Hippocratic medicine was much criticised by Roman writers. It was relatively late in being adopted by Rome, their reservations being that it was a Greek tradition, and, so, foreign (Greek) physicians were employed in Rome.[116] Many people did not trust physicians; they sometimes used esoteric materials (possibly dangerous, and often expensive) rather than herbs and 'natural' cures; and they were greedy, as they usually charged fees.[117] For instance, Pliny portrayed Asclepiades, a physician of the first century BC, as a professor of rhetoric who became a physician because it was financially more rewarding (*Natural History* 26.15). Asclepiades, however, won acceptance for Greek doctors and medicine in the Roman Empire for (at least) two feats; he revived a man whom he recognised as still alive on his funeral bier (Celsus, *De Medicina* 2.6.16-18), and he healed Emperor Augustus of rheumatic disease.[118] Despite criticism, the emphasis in the Hippocratic tradition on accurate observation of patients has remained its important contribution to the present day.

---

115 C.A. Faraone 'The Agonistic Context of Early Greek Binding Spells', in Faraone and Obbink (eds.), *Magika Hiera*, p.15, notes that Galen scoffed at more overt forms of magic, such as binding spells; yet G. Sarton, *Galen of Pergamon* (Lawrence, Kansas: University of Kansas Press, 1954) p.16, records that Galen studied medicine because his father had a dream telling him to. L.C. Alexander, 'Paul and the Hellenistic Schools: The Evidence of Galen', in Engberg-Pedersen (ed.), *Paul in his Hellenistic Context*, pp.70-72, confirms this. Theissen, *Miracle Stories*, p.270; Martin, *Corinthian Body*, p.155. E.J. Edelstein and L. Edelstein, *Asclepius. A Collection and Interpretation of the Testimonies*. Vol. I. *Collection of the Testimonies* (Baltimore: Johns Hopkins University Press, 1945) T401.

116 E.g. Pliny, *Natural History* 29.7, is critical of Greeks in general, and their physicians in particular.

117 Martin, *Corinthian Body*, p.187; Yamauchi, 'Magic or Miracle?', p.113, reports that physicians were held liable for their failures. O. Temkin, *Hippocrates in a World of Pagans and Christians* (Baltimore/London: Johns Hopkins University Press, 1991) p.102, notes that physicians were taught not to undertake treatment if they considered the case hopeless. Celsus, *De Medicina* 2.5.21, emphasised this teaching; they would not then be accused of greed, by charging fees.

118 Celsus, *De Medicina*, Prooemium, 2. Jackson, *Doctors and Diseases*, p.31. M.J. Harris, '"The Dead are Restored to Life": Miracles of Revivication in the Gospels', in Wenham and Blomberg (eds.), *Gospel Perspectives*, 6, p.301, considers Pliny saw this as the cause of public opinion shifting to favour physicians.

2.2.2 Cult Healing

Emma and Ludwig Edelstein comment, 'To be liberated from disease was [man's] main concern', and MacMullen opines that the chief business of religion was to make sick people well.[119] Certainly, religious healing cults flourished in the first century BC and AD. From classical Greek times, two gods were especially renowned for healing, Herakles, a man who became a hero, then a god, and Asclepius. Later, the mystery cult of the Egyptian goddess, Isis, became very popular in Graeco-Roman culture, and healing was one of her many attributes (e.g. Plutarch, *Moralia* 351E-384C). Asclepius is used here to illustrate the healing cult figures, as he was the main representative of divine healing throughout pagan antiquity.

There were many mythological stories about Asclepius, of which this is a very simple summary.[120] The father of Asclepius was Apollo; his mother was killed before his birth, and Chiron, a centaur (mythical half-man, half-horse), brought him up and taught him healing skills. Zeus killed the adult Asclepius for raising at least one dead man to life,[121] but he was then deified and, so, was immortal.[122] The divine or heroic figure suffering on behalf of others was common in classical (e.g. Herakles), Hellenistic and Graeco-Roman cultures.[123]

Asclepius was regarded as displaying divine power in his healings, increasingly in Hellenistic times.[124] His fame and influence spread further at the time of the Roman Empire, where he was worshipped as a god well into late antiquity.[125] Sufferers from illnesses were treated in Asclepieia, where healing and worship facilities were adjacent. The first and most renowned temple was at Epidauros, where many of the

---

119 E.J. Edelstein and L. Edelstein, *Asclepius. A Collection and Interpretation of the Testimonies*. Vol. II, *Interpretation of the Testimonies* (Baltimore: Johns Hopkins University Press, 1945) p.224. R.M. MacMullen, *Paganism in the Roman Empire* (New Haven/London: Yale University Press, 1981) pp.49, 51. He notes also that Σωτήρ (Saviour) was often the word used for Asclepius without further definition.

120 Edelstein and Edelstein, *Asclepius*, I, pp.1-59.

121 This was not an uncommon feature; see Euripides, *Alcestis*, 122-9; also Edelstein and Edelstein, *Asclepius*, I, p.37.

122 B. Witherington III, *Conflict and Community in Corinth. A Socio-Rhetorical Commentary on 1 and 2 Corinthians* (Grand Rapids: Eerdmans, 1995) p.112. As MacMullen, *Paganism in the Roman Empire*, p.55, points out, the element of resurrection is not seen as applying to the god's followers.

123 Bultmann, *Theology of New Testament*, 1, p.129.

124 Edelstein and Edelstein, *Asclepius*, 1, e.g. T423, pp.221-37.

125 Edelstein and Edelstein, *Asclepius*, II, p.257, describe the cult as extant in the sixth century AD.

inscriptions, bearing witness to healings, and dating from the fourth century BC onwards, were found.[126] A second Asclepieion was set up at Pergamum in Asia Minor (where Galen later trained), and Asclepieia then became widespread. Of the more famous, there was one on the island of Cos (where Hippocrates was born, and where there was most evidence of the use of medical and cult healing together);[127] in Corinth,[128] Athens,[129] on Tiber Island at Rome[130] (where ill slaves were abandoned by their masters in the first century AD),[131] and in Aelia Capitolina (Jerusalem) in the early second century AD.[132]

Although the 'incubation' method (sleeping in the *abaton*, within the temple) was universal in Asclepieia, other techniques, such as the use of harmless snakes and dogs, and the ministrations of priests, who could both heal and deliver oracles, were employed variably.[133] In the Hellenistic tradition, miracles performed by charismatics resulted in immediate cure (see *2.2.3*), but this was not always so of treatment in Asclepieia, where documented healing was sometimes over several months, and was often in cooperation with the sufferer's physician.[134] Also, the importance of both a pure water supply and a healthy site for an Asclepieion was recognised as significant for recovery;[135] the commands to sufferers to lead a healthy life, the references to the use of herbs, and some descriptions of operations in Asclepieia, all indicate that medical and cult healings were often combined.[136]

Asclepius was believed to heal even those who were doubtful, or sceptical, of his healing powers, that is, prior faith was not a prerequisite

---

126 Edelstein and Edelstein, *Asclepius*, I, e.g. T382-5, T422-24. Many had disappeared by the first century AD.

127 Ferguson, *Backgrounds of Early Christianity*, p.211.

128 Harvey, *Jesus and Constraints*, p.115. R.F. Collins, *First Corinthians*. SacPag Series, Vol.7 (Collegeville: Liturgical Press, 1999) p.454. (See Chapter 5, *1.4*).

129 Edelstein and Edelstein, *Asclepius*, I, T427.

130 Yamauchi, 'Magic or Miracle?' p.113, notes that it was set up after a plague in Rome in 293 BC.

131 Edelstein and Edelstein, *Asclepius*, I, T858; Suetonius, *Divus Claudius* 25.2.

132 Blackburn, *Theios Anēr*, p.231, n.233.

133 Kolenkow, 'Relationships', p.1477.

134 Edelstein and Edelstein, *Asclepius*, I, e.g. T404.

135 T409, T707, in Edelstein and Edelstein, *Asclepius*, I. Also, H. Avalos, *Illness and Health Care in the Ancient Near East. The Role of the Temple in Greece, Mesopotamia and Israel* (HSM 54; Atlanta: Scholars' Press, 1995) pp.48-49; A.T. Cheung, *Idol Food in Corinth. Jewish Background and Pauline Legacy* (JSNTSup 176; Sheffield: Sheffield Academic Press, 1999) p.29.

136 Edelstein and Edelstein, *Asclepius*, I, T397, T410-1, T367, T412; Achtemeier, 'Jesus and Disciples', p.154.

of healing, but rather its consequence.[137] It seems that those with deafness, speech problems, blindness and lameness were healed, as well as sufferers from the broad spectrum of major illnesses that afflict humankind; people from all social classes were treated at Asclepieia, and Asclepius was seen as the friend of the poor and humble, in pain and in fear of death.[138] Illness did not prevent the sufferer from entering the shrine to worship (very different from Judaism).[139] The evidence of the widespread use of Asclepieia over a millennium points to the importance of this means of healing, and it is not surprising that the healing cults were initially important competitors to Christianity. Justin and Origen, for instance, regarded Asclepius' healing cult as Christianity's major rival.[140]

2.2.3 Charismatic Healers

There were holy men in the eastern Roman Empire throughout antiquity, who were thought to control their bodies by their asceticism, and communities by their power over, for instance, demons and diseases. They were apparently more common in outlying areas, and few detailed stories of their healings have survived. They were external to the patron-client system, and the establishment; Brown believes that healings were a secondary concern to them, their first being to prove their authority.[141] Common themes were that the charismatic healer was able to cure where a physician had failed; or that people might go to such a healer to avoid, or recover from the effects of, the physician's treatment.[142] It appears that some holy men were peripatetic, while others worked in pagan temples.[143] Smith suggested that New Testament miracles were considered different from those performed by the holy men of the Graeco-Roman world, because the latter were reported by

137 Blackburn, *Theios Anēr*, p.205; Remus, *Jesus as Healer*, p.31. Theissen, *Miracle Stories*, p.132.

138 Harvey, *Jesus and Constraints*, p.115. Remus, *Jesus as Healer*, p.9; Theissen, *Miracle Stories*, pp.236-37. However, he notes, p.270, that by the second century AD, the clientele seemed to be from the higher social classes.

139 Avalos, *Illness and Health Care*, p.75.

140 Justin, *Apologies* 1.54.10, *Dialogue with Trypho* 69.3, and Origen, *Contra Celsum (Against Celsus)* 3.25. L. Wells, *The Greek Language of Healing from Homer to New Testament Times* (Berlin/New York: W. de Gruyter, 1998) p.14. See Chapter 6, *2.2.3*.

141 P. Brown, 'The Rise and Function of the Holy Man in Late Antiquity', *JRS* 61 (1971) 88.

142 Harvey, *Jesus and Constraints*, p.108; Remus, *Jesus as Healer*, p.9; Cotter, *Miracles*, p.201. See Mk. 5:26.

143 Vermes, *Jesus the Jew*, p.42; Twelftree, *Jesus the Exorcist*, p.27.

the upper-class literary tradition of antiquity, whereas the New Testament is a lower-middle-class product.[144] This is unproven, and too sweeping a rationalisation, but it highlights a possible difficulty in making comparisons now between healing by different means in ancient society.

The most famous pagan itinerant holy man was Apollonius of Tyana, in Cappadocia, a later near-contemporary of Jesus. There were earlier traditions about Apollonius, but his definitive biography was not available till more than a century after his ascension/disappearance in AD 96-98.[145] In this romantic biography, he is presented as a Neo-Pythagorean who adopted the poverty, asceticism, and life-style of Pythagoras.[146] As a peripatetic teacher, philosopher and wonder-worker, he was the first-century epitome of a TA. The circumstances of his birth were miraculous; he treated people who were lame, blind and paralysed, as well as, *inter alia*, a young man with demon-possession (Philostratus, *The Life of Apollonius* 4.20), and a young woman whom he raised from her funeral bier.[147] The *Life*, recalling features found in Jesus' miracle tradition, may have been written as a polemic against Christianity, but seems more likely to have been an *apologia* to refute Apollonius' opponents, who were reviling him as a magician.[148] The value of his biography to us now is that it documents a pagan miracle-healer recognised in the Ancient Near East at about the time of Jesus.

---

144 Smith, 'Prolegomena', p.179, especially n.38.

145 *The Life of Apollonius,* by Flavius Philostratus, commissioned by Julia Domna, wife of the Emperor Alexander Severus. Cotter, *Miracles,* p.38, notes that this delay was not unusual. For instance, many of the traditions about Pythagoras come from biographies of him in third and fourth centuries AD by Porphyry and Iamblichus; Pyrrhus lived in the third century BC, but Plutarch's *Lives*, containing his story, was written in the first century AD.

146 Roetzel, *Letters of Paul*, pp.23-25, notes that there had been a Pythagorean revival, beginning in the first century BC, and the combination of religious piety, philosophy, and astrology was important in Neo-Pythagoreanism.

147 Fuller, *Interpreting the Miracles*, p.64, points out that the story parallels Lk. 7:11-17, unique in Jesus' miracle stories, but a common feature of pagan miracle stories, in that healing occurred unbidden. Philostratus, *Life of Apollonius* 4.45, suggests that the woman was not quite dead, and Martin, *Corinthian Body*, p.113, sees that Philostratus' caution/scepticism reveals Apollonius as a good diagnostician in detecting life.

148 Blackburn, *Theios Anēr*, pp.74-75. Opponents included Origen, *Contra Celsum* 6.41.Hengel, *Charismatic Healer*, p.27. Ferguson, *Backgrounds of Early Christianity*, pp.362-63, notes that earlier accounts had presented him as a magician and charlatan, but Ferguson sees him as like the apostles in the Apocryphal Acts.

2.2.4 Healing and Magic

As has been noted, the Hellenistic world had a great interest in healing wonders and wonder-workers. Magic, closely interwoven with all forms of healing in the Graeco-Roman world, was ubiquitous throughout the ancient Near East in the first centuries BC and AD, because it was regarded as efficacious.[149] People understood that the powers that threatened them and their world were political, cosmic and personal, such as war, famine and disease, but they invested these forces with mythological significance. Magic was important in any society that both recognised the spirit world in all areas of life, and also took seriously the forces of evil.[150] Brown describes the situation that persisted into late antiquity:

> To sin was no longer merely to err; it was to be overcome by unseen forces. To err was to be unconsciously manipulated by some invisible malign power.[151]

The early Roman emperors, alarmed about the increasing interest in astrology, proscribed magic. Books of magic were burned, and magicians and astrologers expelled from Italy at different times, so magic was often 'underground', although enough material has survived to refute large-scale or effective repression.[152] Since mainly literary material was lost thus, while some non-literary artefacts survived, historians may have a distorted idea of the significance of magic, compared with other areas of Graeco-Roman life. In fact, it seems that, although magical practices were supposed to be illegal in the first-century Roman Empire, they were regarded as criminal only if they were harmful, that is, as black magic.[153] By the late first century AD, emperors, although still officially opposed to magic, were becoming increasingly interested in it.

The social system in the Roman Empire was highly ordered, and

---

149 Achtemeier, 'Jesus and Disciples', p.152. Segal, 'Hellenistic Magic', pp.357-58.

150 Roetzel, *World that Shaped*, p.99; Smith, *Jesus the Magician*, p.4. Witherington, *Acts of Apostles*, p.577; Klauck, *Religious Context*, p.214, considers that the conditions for faith in magic, that is, unshakeable convictions in intermediaries between men and gods, and the interconnectedness of all things, were both present.

151 P.R.L. Brown, *The World of Late Antiquity from Marcus Aurelius to Muhammad* (London: Thames & Hudson, 1971) pp.53-54.

152 Georgi, *Opponents*, p.94. Segal, 'Hellenistic Magic', p.357; Aune, 'Magic', p.1521. C.R. Phillips III, '"*Nullum Crimen sine Lege*": Socio-Religious Sanctions on Magic', in Faraone and Obbink (eds.), *Magika Hiera*, p.263.

153 Aune, 'Magic', p.1518; Segal, 'Hellenistic Magic', p.358.

society extremely conformist.[154] Sociologists consider that magic was especially common where there was distress, and so it was overt in the lower classes, as evidence of social alienation, and as a device for survival.[155] People from the upper classes risked losing face if they went to a magician for healing.[156] The *literati*[157] were apparently either critical or sceptical of magic (e.g. Plutarch, *Moralia* 164B), but, for instance, Pliny, though disapproving officially (*Natural History* 30.1-2), seemed to have half-believed in it, judging by the folk remedies he collected (e.g. *Natural History* 28.48). The situation seems to have been that belief in the power of magic was practically universal in the Graeco-Roman world, while *acknowledging* that belief was dependent on class.

The Roman establishment may have resented magicians because they worked mainly independently of regulated society. Even though they might have been capable of healing, they were regarded as inferior to TAs, and this might have been related to their origin;[158] the word μάγος (magician) was Hellenised from the Persian, Persia was the enemy of the Roman Empire, so a pejorative meaning was attached to the name.[159]

Knowledge of the subject has been much improved by the finding of many of the *Papyri Graecae Magicae*, and their subsequent translations. The papyri recorded material over several epochs, from Hellenistic times to late antiquity, but, although they were mainly from the second to sixth centuries AD, the material was probably used unchanged over long periods.[160] They were regarded as non-elite writings, but many scholars have remarked on the higher literary quality of the prayer-like incantations, which were heavily syncretistic. Elements were taken from different religious cults, and sometimes it seemed that the writer had

---

154 R. MacMullen, *Roman Social Relations 50 BC to AD 284* (New Haven/London: Yale University, 1974) p.105, says that verticality was the key to understanding the social scale; J.W. Aageson, '"Control" in Pauline Language and Culture. A Study of Romans 6.' *NTS* 42 (1996) p.86.

155 Theissen, *Miracle Stories*, p.240.

156 Martin, *Corinthian Body*, p.156.

157 K. Hopkins, *A World Full of Gods. Pagans, Jews and Christians in the Roman Empire* (London: Phoenix/Weidenfeld & Nicolson, 1999) points out that the percentage of literate people in the first century was tiny. His educated guess, pp.84-85, is that less than 2% of adult males in the Roman world were literate by AD 100.

158 Goldin, 'Magic of Magic', p.123. Segal, 'Hellenistic Magic', p.356. Witherington, *Acts of Apostles*, p.576. Achtemeier, 'Jesus and Disciples', p.155, notes that one popular belief was that they came from Egypt. Arnold, *Ephesians: Power and Magic*, pp.14-15, points out that Ephesus was regarded as the magical capital of Asia Minor.

159 A γοής indicated a purveyor of magic even lower on the social scale; it was the term Celsus applied to describe Jesus, in Origen, *Contra Celsum* 1.71.

160 Betz, *Greek Magical Papyri*, I, pp.ix, xliv.

little idea of the meaning of the religious texts.[161] Only some papyri have survived, but they demonstrate the imprecise relationships between magic and healing, and magic and religion.

Surviving non-literary magic is mainly in the form of amulets (charms), lead tablets, and similar artefacts. In some situations, these might represent self-help, 'DIY' magic, but in most, a magician would have acted as facilitator. Amulets seem to have been used originally by the poor, and were made from materials such as wood and papyrus, most of which have perished. The use of amulets grew in the first century AD, when the materials on which messages were written became more durable, sometimes of precious substances e.g. gold, silver and jewels, indicating their use by rich people.[162]

In relation to healing, magic was found both in prevention and cure. Prevention of disease (e.g. plague) was sought by applying magical spells and protective amulets (phylacteries).[163] Magic was employed in treating most illnesses, and the surviving material allows us to make some deductions about the significant illnesses of the times. For instance, spells concerning fever were common,[164] and details of the fever's periodicity indicate that malaria was present (and feared) in many parts of the eastern Roman Empire; nightly, quartan, and semi-tertian fevers are mentioned in *PGM* LXXXIII.5 and LXXXVII.5-6 (see Chapter 3, *1.5.2* and Chapter 5, *2.3.2*).[165] Magic to cure blindness was often sought (e.g. *PGM* XCIV.22-26; XCVII.1-6), and magic spells to deal with demon possession, tumours, migraine and epilepsy are found. Pleas for raising someone from the dead occurred occasionally, sometimes sceptically or guardedly, perhaps because Asclepius was killed for doing so.

Methods of magical healing were common to most forms of ancient

---

161 Segal, 'Hellenistic Magic', p.352. E.g. *PGM* XCIX.1-3 states 'God is one who heals every sickness'. *PGM* LXXXIII.1-20, to relieve fever, contains jumbled phrases from the Old Testament and New Testament, including part of the Lord's Prayer.

162 Theissen, *Miracle Stories*, p.271.

163 E.g. *PGM* VII.579-90. K. Hopkins (with M. Letts), 'Death in Rome', in K. Hopkins, *Death and Renewal,* Vol.2 (Cambridge: CUP, 1983) p.208, note that 'plague' could mean any type of infectious disease. R. Kotansky, 'Incantations and Prayers for Salvation on Inscribed Greek Amulets', in Faraone and Obbink (eds.), *Magika Hiera*, p.107.

164 E.g. *PGM* LXXXIII.1-20 through to XC.14-18 are all concerned with treatment of fever. Cook, 'In Defence of Ambiguity,' pp.184-208. P.G. Bolt, *Jesus' Defeat of Death. Persuading Mark's Early Readers* (SNTSMS 125; Cambridge: CUP, 2003) pp.76-87.

165 W.M. Ramsay, *The Church in the Roman Empire before AD 170* (2nd ed.; London: Hodder & Stoughton, 1893) p.63.

'health care', and usually involved a rite, sometimes rudimentary.[166] Touch was important in cultic healing in Asclepieia, by rulers, and by charismatic healers (e.g. Philostratus, *Life of Apollonius* 4.45), as well as by magicians. It might be light touch, massage, or as laying-on of hands, and it was thought to impart power from the healer to the patient.[167] Lalleman and Aune both draw attention to the fact that healing by touch alone was highly unusual in the Graeco-Roman culture of the time (although others do not fully corroborate this).[168] It is clear, however, that in many pagan accounts of healing, 'touch' involved a major manoeuvre, and this may explain the discrepancy.[169] Various other acts of healing were described, like the use of saliva applied to the subject's affected part, as well as more complex and overtly magical manoeuvres.[170] Not all magicians worked in the same way,[171] but exactitude in each magical rite was important, so that healing would be achieved only if a spell or incantation was followed to the letter.

Written words (e.g. on lead tablets) were also employed. Cursing others could be seen as an extension of caring for one's own kinship, in an environment where poor people were competing for what they regarded as scarce, finite material resources in the Eastern Mediterranean world.[172] Many lead tablets, inscribed with curses or binding spells, *defixiones,* have been found, dated over centuries, from

---

166 Vermes, *Jesus the Jew*, p.24.

167 Edelstein and Edelstein, *Asclepius* I, T438. Touch might be by animals, priests or the god. Theissen, *Miracle Stories*, pp.92-93, and Remus, *Jesus as Healer*, p.21, note that there was a widespread idea that power resides and emanates from certain individuals or objects.

168 P.J. Lalleman, 'Healing by a Mere Touch as a Christian Concept,' *TynBul* 48 (1997) 355-61; Aune, 'Magic', p.1533, reports that touch was by the gods and was common, while touch by human workers was rare, in Hellenistic magic. Cotter, *Miracles,* p.203, notes the physician Herophilus (*c.* 300 BC) saw medicaments as 'the hands of the gods', effective by doing what divine touch could do. Blackburn, *Theios Anēr,* p.113; Bultmann, *History of Synoptic Tradition*, p.22; Theissen, *Miracle Stories*, pp.92-93.

169 E.g. Plutarch, *Lives*, *Pyrrhus* 3.4, described how King Pyrrhus healed sufferers from a 'splenetic condition' (presumably malaria), by pressing his right foot on the sufferer's splenic area. Tacitus, *Histories* 4.81, described Vespasian healing a man with a useless hand by trampling on it to exert healing pressure.

170 Remus, *Jesus as Healer*, p.20; Twelftree, *Jesus the Exorcist*, p.158. Kee, 'Magic and Messiah', p.138, however, maintains that applying saliva therapeutically was not found in the Hellenistic or Roman periods.

171 Theissen, *Miracle Stories*, p.233, has categorised miraculous activity according to the methods used.

172 Faraone, 'Agonistic Context', p.20; B.J. Malina, *The Social World of Jesus and the Gospels* (New York/London: Routledge, 1996) p.81.

the fifth century BC; the content of curses was initially brief, but later became more complex.[173]

With magicians seen as at least intermittently possessed of divine powers,[174] there was reason to be in awe of them. Magic was seen as dangerous (e.g. *PGM* VII.579-90; 429-58); victims of a curse might die, and if one could see the future by divination, one might cause it.[175] Flourishing in situations of distress, magic itself often produced social conflict, and accusations of magic were used in social definition and control.[176]

The literature on demonology in paganism is a sub-division of that on magic and religion. While apocalyptic Judaism saw the stark contrast between the divine and demonic, Greek culture, relaxed about the hierarchy of the divine/human world, perceived no gulf between them. Greeks and Romans accepted that demons might be good or bad influences, and Plutarch wrote widely on them (*Moralia* 415A-417F).[177] Pliny was sceptical about demons, but this was unusual. A magician manipulating poorly-understood psychic forces, was effectively acting as a god or demon, with power to ward off, or mobilise, dark forces. Demon-possession is important in modern biblical scholarship, with respect to the theological understanding of exorcism in Jesus' ministry.[178]

In summary, illness was a catastrophe in the first century BC and AD, both intrinsically to the sufferer, and to his honour and standing in the community, so healing was very important. There were several types of healthcare; only broad categories are outlined here, and it is recognised

---

173 Faraone, 'Agonistic Context', pp.5-6, 18.

174 Grundmann, 'δύναμαι/δύναμις', p.284; Smith, *Jesus the Magician*, p.74.

175 H.C. Kee, *Miracle in the Early Christian World. A Study in Sociohistorical Method* (New Haven/London: Yale University Press, 1983) p.213. Kolenkow, 'Relationships', p.1474.

176 Theissen, *Miracle Stories*, p.243. M. Douglas, *Purity and Danger. An Analysis of the Concepts of Pollution and Taboo* (London/New York: Routledge, 1966, reprint 1993) p.102, notes that charges and counter-charges of magic were common.

177 J.Z. Smith, 'Towards Interpreting Demonic Powers in Hellenistic and Roman Antiquity', *ANRW* II.16.1 (1978) 431. D. Newton, *Deity and Diet. The Dilemma of Sacrificial Food at Corinth.* (JSNTSup169; Sheffield: Sheffield Academic Press, 1998) p.356; Kolenkow, 'Relationships', p.1478, notes that Pythagoreanism allowed movement from having a daimon to becoming one. Brenk, 'In the Light of the Moon', p.2075, notes that Plato presented Socrates as possessing a δαίμονιον, his inner voice or divine monitor, guiding his actions throughout his life.

178 See Chapter 1, *1.3.2.* Pliny, *Natural History* 28.4-9; Plutarch, *Moralia* 168B, considered that the superstitious attributed disease to attack by gods or invasion by demons. Harvey, *Jesus and Constraints*, p.104. Dunn, *Theology of Paul*, p.104.

that overlaps in these categories were large, and that standards and availability of care were variable within the eastern Roman Empire.

Greek medicine, regarded as dating from Hippocrates, was radically mixed with folk medicine, astrology and magic, especially from the first century BC onwards, but the emphasis on careful observation of patients remained. The most widespread and long-lasting of the healing cults was that of Asclepius; healing in Asclepieia combined religion, magic and medical principles, and was regarded as successful. Other healers were charismatic itinerants, apparently widespread in the eastern Roman Empire, the most famous being first-century AD Apollonius of Tyana, whose biography, written much later, illustrates many of the features. Magicians were regarded as having significant healing powers, even though magic was officially proscribed, and magical books sometimes destroyed. In a world with a rigid social scale and a low level of literacy, this meant that much of the material surviving is *either* the sceptical view of Roman elites, *or* non-literary artefacts, amulets and curse tablets, used mostly by the lower classes. The *Papyri Graecae Magicae*, although they were written mainly at a later period, have enlarged our knowledge of the ancient practice of magic in the first century. Magic was an important source of power, as well as of fear and social conflict. Demonology was perhaps a particular area of magic, since illness was thought to be due often to demon activity or possession.

2.3 *The Power of Healing in the First Century*

Healing was, thus, a very important part of life in the eastern Roman Empire before Jesus' ministry, and was bound up with power and authority, with magic and religion.

All miraculous/magical healers had some power, which in Graeco-Roman culture was an important form of currency. Blackburn considers that Hellenistic miracle stories were told mainly in order to show that the healer was in some way divine (often as a TA).[179] The elite (especially emperors) might be healers, that is, their authority could *include* miracle working. The non-elite, with no financial, political or military influence, could have authority *because* of their ability to perform 'mighty works', δυνάμεις; healing sick people was one of the few ways for a plebeian to gain power in the first-century Roman Empire. Although in multi-cultural pluralism, ancients were fairly tolerant of others' religious activities, religions were in competition with one another. In the eastern Roman Empire, there was a preoccupation

179 Blackburn, *Theios Anēr*, pp.6-7.

with the power of magic and miracles as advertisement for a religion; δυνάμεις were important, both as signs of the god's presence, and of his supremacy.[180]

The two worlds, of Judaism, and of Graeco-Roman culture, both had subtle perceptions of abstract concepts, such as power. Political and religious powers were closely related, both in Graeco-Roman life and in Judaism, and were represented, respectively, by the administration of the Roman Empire, and by the Temple authorities. In these cultures, many forms of sickness or disability were major threats to the sufferers, apart from obvious personal and social considerations, because of the loss of honour and standing in Graeco-Roman society, and the loss of acceptance in Temple worship and societal fellowship in Judaism. Thus, healing from illness was particularly significant in both cultures, and healers were important authorities, not only for themselves, but also for their god.

In summary, it is apparent that healing miracles and magic were regarded as vital, in an era when religions (and philosophy) were struggling for supremacy, because they conferred power on the individual healer, and, therefore, on his religion.

3 Conclusion

The religious, historical and cultural factors that lay as backdrop to healing by Jesus and in the early church have been described. These include the developments depicted in Old Testament Judaism, where, initially, Yahweh alone was believed to both cause and heal illnesses, but later, healing occurred under his direction by intermediaries, prophets (especially Moses, Elijah and Elisha) or kings (especially Solomon). As well as the suspicion that some ills might be the result of Satan's influence, the belief grew that Israel's ills would be solved only by the coming of an anointed one from God, a Messiah, who would herald the eschatological day of the Lord, an age of healing. Ideas of vicarious suffering by an innocent person, of martyrdom, and of the possibility of an afterlife were spurred on by the extent of Jewish oppression and suffering in Second Temple Judaism.

180 Phillips, "*Nullum Crimen sine Lege*", p.261; Smith, 'Towards Interpreting', pp.425-26, notes that others' beliefs were regarded, not as dangerous, but rather to be ridiculed. Tiede, 'Aretalogy', p.372. Corrington, *'Divine Man'*, e.g. p.111, sees power as at the root of belief, and is manifested by active means, such as δυνάμεις. Theissen, *Miracle Stories*, p.259; C.J. Roetzel, *Paul: The Man and the Myth* (Edinburgh: T. & T. Clark, 1999) p.163.

It is clear that, in at least one strand of Judaism, represented by Sirach, it was accepted that healing might involve the use of herbs and medicines from the earth, and that physicians might heal, with God's sanction. Although some differences may have been due to cultural mingling, so that Greek healing practices had influenced Jewish beliefs, both in the Diaspora and in Palestine, it is important that there was not one form of Judaism with regard to healing, certainly by the first century BC and AD.

The much less rigid division between the gods and man in paganism meant that attitudes to healing developed in a different way from those in Judaism. Demons were not regarded as part of an evil force under the control of Satan, as in Judaism, although they were responsible for some illness, and sometimes required to be expelled with magic. There were differences in views of sickness and healing within the Graeco-Roman world, as is obvious from the several forms of health care available. These included cultic healing (especially in Asclepieia), the practice of the charismatic holy man, magic, and Hippocratic medicine, based on rigorous clinical observation, and there was considerable overlap between them. Healing magic was ubiquitous, but the elite of the Graeco-Roman world were officially sceptical of both miracle and divination.

Although the chapter has been written as if Judaism and Graeco-Roman cultures were distinct entities, it is clear that they were neither completely distinct from one another, nor was either an entity. There was widespread syncretism, with respect to healing, with evidence of Graeco-Roman cultural influences on Judaism, and the effects of Judaism on the eastern Roman Empire. The two traditions came closer together, especially in the first centuries BC and AD, at least partly aided by the writings of Philo and Josephus, as Diaspora Jewish apologists, who advanced Jewish propaganda in their writings for Graeco-Roman readers, to persuade them of the greatness of the God of Judaism.[181] The overall picture was of a world interested, and actively involved, in healing, which was recognised as a form of power, often as religious power.

The chapter sets the scene for the narratives of Jesus' healing miracles, and helps to explain the background from which emerged the emphases and beliefs of the New Testament writers presenting and interpreting the stories.

---

181 Meeks, *The Prophet-King*, pp.100-46. For instance, Philo, *Life of Moses* 2.50.279-91, reinterpreted Moses so that he conformed to the picture of what pagans might recognise as a hero, a TA, with major healing skills.

Chapter 3

Mark and Healing

1 Mark's Portrayal of Healing

1.1 Introduction

As was discussed in Chapter 1, scholars since the European Enlightenment, because of their reserve about the supernatural, and their search for objectivity, have often sought to disprove the possibility that Jesus performed miracles. At the least, however, Jesus' healing was recognised as something which his observers, friend or foe, saw as different from the norm.[1] During most of the twentieth century, Jesus' healing miracles were given minor attention, compared with the emphasis on his teaching.[2] Many factors contributed to this, including the popularity of Bultmann's work on demythologising the New Testament, but this is a declining influence on today's quest for the historical Jesus, which includes his miracles.[3] Interest in the New Testament writers' presentations of healing, both by Jesus and the apostles, has increased; in the last ten to twenty years there has been evidence of less resistance and more curiosity about supernatural powers of good and evil than there had been in the previous forty years,[4] and many recent scholars accept that Jesus performed healing miracles.[5]

By the mid-twentieth century, it was apparent that the efforts of form criticism to get back to the sources of the gospels were not revealing the detail of Jesus' historical ministry, and other disciplines became more prominent.[6] It is assumed that the gospels' contents were composed

---

1 Horsley and Silberman, *Message and Kingdom,* pp.49-50. Bultmann, *Theology of New Testament,* 1, p.7, agreed that Jesus did deeds that were regarded as miracles in the minds of both Jesus and his contemporaries, that is, deeds that were attributed to a divine cause.

2 There were, of course, exceptions, e.g. Fuller, *Interpreting the Miracles*; Moule (ed.), *Miracles*; H. van der Loos, *The Miracles of Jesus* (Leiden: Brill, 1965).

3 Bultmann, *Jesus Christ and Mythology.* Evans, 'Authenticating the Activities', p.12.

4 Theissen, *Miracle Stories,* p.277; Meier, *Marginal Jew*, II. B. Witherington III, *The Gospel of Mark. A Socio-Rhetorical Commentary* (Grand Rapids/Cambridge: Eerdmans, 2001) p.196.

5 The evidence has been summarised by Blackburn, 'Miracles of Jesus', pp.353-94.

6 For instance, the social and historical aspects of life in the eastern Roman Empire became regarded as important background to the events of Jesus' ministry and the early

from the oral traditions, which were likely to atrophy as the writings became regarded as authoritative.[7] In this and subsequent chapters, we will consider only the canonical version of the gospels. Since the final writer of this gospel is anonymous, we shall refer to the author as Mark throughout. As it is accepted here that Mark's gospel was the earliest to be written, it is assumed that it would be a source book of Jesus' ministry, life and death, so Mark's story of Jesus' healing would have influenced the position adopted by later writers.[8]

What Mark wanted to teach his readers, and his effects on later Christian writers are, then, of great importance in considering whether, a) there was a uniform understanding of the significance of Jesus' and apostolic healing in the early church, which changed gradually with time during the first and subsequent centuries (in line with the theory of a general 'trajectory' of the church),[9] or b) there were different views in different churches about divine healing, at least from the middle years of the first century.

The dating of Mark's gospel might help to 'place' within the early church Mark's views on Jesus' healing. The date is uncertain, but the consensus is that it was written somewhere between AD 65 and 75.[10] I am assuming that it was written fairly soon before AD 70 (since Mk. 13:2 seems compatible with the description, later in Mark 13, of the

church recounted in the New Testament; also narrative criticism became important. R.A. Guelich, *Mark 1-8:26,* WBC, Vol.34A (Dallas: Word, 1989) p.xxxiv, writes of the 'excesses of form criticism'; G. Theissen, *The Gospels in Context. Social and Political History in the Synoptic Tradition* (ET; Edinburgh: T. & T. Clark, 1992) p.1, considers that classical form criticism has taken on an aura of false certainty. See B. Holmberg, *Paul and Power. The Structure of Authority in the Primitive Church as Reflected in the Pauline Epistles* (ConBNT II; Lund: C.W.K. Gleerup, 1978) p.2; Fiorenza, 'Miracles, Mission', p.19.

7 C.L. Blomberg, 'Concluding Reflections on Miracles and Gospel Perspectives', in Wenham and Blomberg (eds.), *Gospel Perspectives,* 6, p.452.

8 W.R. Telford, 'Introduction: The Interpretation of Mark. A History of Developments and Issues', in W.R. Telford (ed.), *The Interpretation of Mark* (2nd ed.; Edinburgh: T. & T. Clark, 1995) pp.2-3, notes that interest in Mark's identity has waned in recent years, but that, for over 100 years, Mark's gospel has been accepted as the first to be written. N. Perrin, 'The Christology of Mark. A Study in Methodology', in Telford (ed.), *Interpretation of Mark,* p.126, points out that redaction criticism is especially difficult in Mark, where we have less knowledge of his sources, compared with the later gospels.

9 Robinson and Koester, *Trajectories.*

10 M.D. Hooker, *The Gospel according to St. Mark,* BNTC (London: A. & C. Black, 1991) p.8; D. Rhoads and D. Michie, *Mark as Story. An Introduction to the Narrative of a Gospel* (Philadelphia: Fortress, 1982) p.4; Witherington, *Gospel of Mark*, pp.31, 66-70. Theissen, *Gospels in Context,* p.235, suggests it was post AD 70. L.W. Hurtado, *Mark,* NIBC (Peabody: Hendrickson, 1989) p.8, dates it between AD 50 and 75.

coming woes, rather than being specific to the temple destruction), and that it was written for a mixed readership (or audience) of Jewish and Gentile Christians,[11] and, probably, God-fearers. Since the experiences of the churches for which Mark was writing may be reflected in the gospel, to a lesser extent knowledge of the recipients would have been useful, but is not available.[12]

The gospel's literary genre is of significance, as we compare later the emphasis on healing in the gospels with that in Paul's letters. In spite of other proposals (for instance, that the word gospel, εὐαγγέλιον, in the first verse refers to its genre), it is widely accepted that, in a narrative about Jesus in a loose chronological framework, the genre could be called biography.[13] Witherington, accepting it as biography, draws attention to the fact that an ancient biography written about a man not of the privileged classes is remarkable; Mark signals in the first verse that he is writing about Jesus, the Christ, and so this is theological, rather than social, narrative.[14]

There is considerable controversy as to whether or not the gospel originally ended at 16:8. There are proponents of this as the original ending.[15] Many commentators are doubtful, for instance, Edwards

---

11 D.R. Catchpole, 'Mark', in Barclay and Sweet (eds.), *Early Christian Thought,* p.74, note that Mark does explain Jewish customs (e.g. 7:3-5), so he was accommodating Gentile readers.

12 Hooker, *Gospel According to Mark,* pp.7-8, says that the earliest tradition was that the gospel was written in Rome, although she is agnostic on the subject; Theissen, *Gospels in Context*, p.236, suggests a locus in Syria, which might explain the early presence of churches in Damascus and Antioch in the description of Paul's life in Acts.

13 Some scholars have referred to its genre as gospel; France, *Gospel of Mark*, pp.4-6, points out that 'gospel' does not designate a literary genre, but indicates the subject matter; he regards Mark as biography. W.R. Telford, *Mark* (Sheffield: Sheffield Academic Press, 1995) p.34, describes Mark's gospel as 'a product of literary artifice and faith-inspired imagination'. R.A. Burridge, *What are the Gospels? A Comparison with Graeco-Roman Biography* (SNTSMS 70; Cambridge: CUP, 1992) pp.217-19, draws attention also to the fact that biography was a common form of writing in Graeco-Roman life. T.H. Weeden, *Mark: Traditions in Conflict* (Philadelphia: Fortress, 1971). Witherington, *Gospel of Mark*, pp.1-9, regards it as most likely to be a biography. J.D.G. Dunn, 'Messianic Ideas and their Influence on the Jesus of History', in Charlesworth (ed.), *The Messiah,* p.371, considers all the synoptic gospels are in the form of biography.

14 Witherington, *Gospel of Mark,* p.32. See *1.2,* the discussion on 'Son of God' in Mk. 1:1.

15 Hooker, *Gospel According to Mark*, pp.393-94; E. Best, *Mark. The Gospel as Story* (Edinburgh: T. & T. Clark, 1983) p.132; J. Camery-Hoggatt, *Irony in Mark's Gospel. Text and Subtext* (SNTSMS 72; Cambridge: CUP, 1992) p.177; Rhoads and Michie, *Mark as Story,* throughout.

believes that the idea of the intended ending being at 16:8 'owes more to modern literary theory than to the nature of ancient texts', and several other writers consider that some accident befell Mark, or, more probably, the original manuscript (which appears to end in mid-sentence), so that 16:8 was not Mark's intended ending.[16] Modern writers are agreed that both the shorter and longer endings are very different in style from the gospel to that point, and have come from a later time.[17] In the absence of the finding of an authentic ending, we are here working on the principle that the ending is at 16:8.

Finally, this chapter considers Mark's presentation of Jesus' (and the disciples') healing miracles only; Jesus' other miracles are not discussed, although, for instance, the feeding miracles impinge on the healing narratives, both by their character and their positions in the gospel.

In summary, the reductionism in the importance of Jesus' healing miracles in the gospel stories, which arose with the Enlightenment, and persisted well into the twentieth century, is beginning to be redressed. Mark's gospel is accepted here as the first one written, and thus is of great significance in determining how Jesus' healing was viewed in at least one part of the early church, and how it probably influenced later writing. The purpose of this chapter is to consider how Mark depicts Jesus' healing, and uses it to present his theological understanding of the Jesus event. Mark's technique of narrating Jesus' healing, and its importance, will be considered first, and then Mark's theological interests, to show how he used Jesus' healing, in particular in relation to the crucifixion.

---

16 J.R. Edwards, *The Gospel according to Mark*, PNTC (Grand Rapids/Cambridge: Eerdmans, 2002) pp.500-03, [501] who points out that the gospel starts with the announcement of divine sonship, and ends in fear and panic. J.R. Donahue and D.J. Harrington, *The Gospel of Mark*, SacPag Series, Vol.2 (Collegeville: Liturgical, 2002) p.460. Witherington, *Gospel of Mark*, pp.40-49; France, *Gospel of Mark*, p.28, n.57.; he notes, pp.670-73, that accepting 16:8 as the end stems from Lightfoot, and France, p.684, states also that 16:8 makes it difficult to envisage the follow-up.

17 R.H. Gundry, *Mark. A Commentary on his Apology for the Cross* (Grand Rapids: Eerdmans, 1993) notes, pp.1009, 1012, that the longer endings are not accepted by the important uncials; both Sinaiticus and Vaticanus omit 16:9-20. C.G. Kruse, *New Testament Models for Ministry. Jesus and Paul* (London: Marshall, Morgan & Scott, 1983) p.67, notes the likely origin of the longer endings as in the early second century.

1.2 Mark as a Theological Narrator

Mark's gospel is written from an apocalyptic world-view, where evil forces are very active, but where God is about to defeat Satan, and bring about the 'day of the Lord' (the Kingdom of God).[18] Narrative critics comment on Mark's skills as a storyteller, and point out that he writes as the omniscient narrator, whose characters did not know what he knows.[19] Mark reveals to the reader at the outset (1:1) Jesus' Christological identity, (although the words υἱοῦ θεοῦ 'of the Son of God' are missing from some important uncials). Most commentators point to the likelihood that 'of the Son of God' was omitted in error there, because of the occurrence together of six words ending in οῦ.[20] A good reason for considering that Mark would have intended the term to be present at the beginning of the gospel is his repeated emphasis on Jesus as Son of God. It occurs in 1:11 and 9:7 (as God's words), in 3:11 and 5:7 (spoken by demons), and in 15:39, when the Roman centurion recognised him as a Son of God. France sees 'Son of God' as a central part of Mark's Christology.[21] The narrative is thus an elaborate inclusion between 1:1 and 15:39, with humans failing to identify Jesus as the Messiah, although unclean spirits identified Jesus correctly.

This is one strategy to keep the tension high throughout the gospel, and Mark uses several other means to do so, for instance, highlighting Jesus' conflicts, with the religious authorities, the disciples, and his own family, until the final conflict resolution in his death. Again, tension is maintained by the intercalation, 'framing', of one story by another (e.g. 5:22-45), and by a motif of secrecy about Jesus' Messiahship, with the failure of the disciples to understand completely, but with occasional glimpses of revelation. Many of these literary devices are seen most clearly in relation to healing.

Mark's story-telling produces some improbabilities, for instance, in his depiction of Jesus ordering silence from demons, who in a crowded place, screamed that they recognised him as Son of God (1:23-24),[22] and

---

18 Wells, *Language of Healing,* p.127, emphasises the difference from the Old Testament, where it is assumed that evil was created by God; by the time of the gospels, evil 'assumes an almost ontological nature'.

19 E.g. Rhoads and Michie, *Mark as Story*.

20 Aland *et al.*, *Novum Testamentum Graece,* notably Sinaiticus*, B, D, L, and W. Gundry, *Mark*, p.33; France, *Gospel of Mark*, p.49; Edwards, *Gospel of Mark*, p.25; Hooker, *Gospel According to Mark*, p.34; Guelich, *Mark 1-8:26*, pp.6-10.

21 France, *Gospel of Mark*, p.50; Gundry, *Mark*, p.34.

22 H.J. Nielsen, *Heilung und Verkündigung. Das Verständnis der Heilung und ihres Verhältnisses zur Verkündigung bei Jesus und in der ältesten Kirche* (Leiden/New York/Köln: Brill, 1987) p.111, notes that the demons were forbidden to make Jesus'

in the injunctions to people who were healed of major diseases or brought back from death (e.g. 5:43; 7:36; 8:26) to tell nobody.[23] Other aspects of his healing narrative also show 'poetic licence'. For instance, one might expect the synagogue ruler to object to both the presence of the man with the unclean spirit, and Jesus' exorcism in the synagogue on the Sabbath (1:21-27), yet this is not mentioned. The sequel to Jesus healing the Gerasene man, when the demons were transferred to pigs (5:11-13), is not easily understandable to the modern Western mind. In general, however, Mark's accounts are presented in a 'true-to-life' form.[24]

Mark's gospel has often been called a passion narrative with a long introduction.[25] No healing is described after Mk. 10:52, although miraculous happenings did not cease then (for instance, the tearing of the temple veil, and the empty tomb). Mark's confining of Jesus' healings to the pre-passion narrative signals to the reader that events more momentous even than Jesus healing occurred during the passion. It may be that Mark wishes to portray Jesus' resurrection as the great healing miracle by God, of which the other healings were merely the prelude. In accepting the ending of Mark at 16:8, it seems to me that Mark wants to demonstrate Jesus' crucifixion, abandoned, the epitome of weakness, as the theological climax of the story,[26] and the abrupt ending helps to emphasise Mark's Christology. (See *2.5*).

In summary, Mark presents the theological biography of Jesus from the viewpoint of an omniscient narrator, who maintains dramatic tension throughout, and who has shaped his gospel so that Jesus the healer is depicted in the pre-passion narrative, while the crucifixion emphasises his weakness.

---

theological identity, not his healing, known; H. Räisänen, *The 'Messianic Secret' in Mark* (ET; Edinburgh: T. & T. Clark, 1990) p.173, makes the same point.

23 Räisänen, *'Messianic Secret'*, e.g. pp.168, 248, argues that the secrecy motif in Mark does not have a unitary explanation; in particular, the secrecy with regard to healing may have practical purposes, as well as theological ones (see *1.3.1*).

24 Remus, *Jesus as Healer,* p.29.

25 M. Kähler, *The So-Called Historical Jesus and the Historic Biblical Christ* (orig. 1892; Philadelphia: Fortress, 1964) p.80, n.11, applied his description to all the synoptic gospels; J. Marcus, 'Mark–Interpreter of Paul', *NTS* 46 (2000) p.479, considers that it is most appropriately applied to Mark. Witherington, *Gospel of Mark*, p.5, points out that 19% of Mark's narrative verses are passion narrative, compared with 15% in Matthew and Luke.

26 Marcus, 'Mark–Interpreter of Paul', p.475.

1.3 The Importance of Jesus' Healing to Mark

There are several methods that a gospel writer could use to show that he regards Jesus' healing as important. These include making healing stories prominent in the narrative, indicating that healing was not merely an appendage to another activity (such as teaching) which established Jesus' authority, and demonstrating that it was his healing that attracted crowds (and opposition). Mark uses all these three.

1.3.1 Prominence of Jesus' Healing

The prominence Mark gives to Jesus' healing miracles is one indication of how significant he considers them. Wilkinson analyses the number of verses that each gospel writer devotes to Jesus' healing activity. In Mark's gospel, of a total 678 verses, 139 (20%) are devoted to healing, a much higher percentage than in the other gospels. However, Mark has proportionately more narrative in his gospel than the others, and, of Mark's total narrative verses, 40% are healing stories, similar to Matthew (40%), Luke (35%) and John (33%). Although conceding that this is a crude indication, Wilkinson regards it as evidence of the significance of Jesus' healing to all the gospel-writers.[27]

Mark seems committed to showing that Jesus devoted much time and energy to healing, and that it was a very prominent part of the ministry.[28] He depicts that healing sometimes threatened to swamp other parts of Jesus' ministry (e.g. 1:35-38, 45; 3:7-12, 13), when he was so sought after that he had to take avoiding action. Mark's healing summaries (e.g. 1:32-34, 39; 3:10-12; 6:5, 54-56) also highlight that the individual healings were a small part of Jesus' healing ministry. The summaries function in the same way as do the statements in John 20:30-31 and 21:25, which demonstrate that only a tiny part of Jesus' work was recorded. In the summaries, Mark uses hyperbole to great effect; 'they brought to him all who were sick or possessed with demons', 'and the whole city was gathered around the door' (1:32-33); 'all who touched' the fringe of his cloak 'were healed' (6:55-56), and this gives a vivid picture of the pressure put on Jesus to heal. Healings are also depicted in

27 Wilkinson, *Bible and Healing*, pp.64-65, 67, and Blackburn, 'Miracles of Jesus', p.356, also point to the frequency of multiple attestations of many of the healings in the synoptic gospels, as proof of their acceptance by the evangelists.

28 In Borg and Wright, *Meaning of Jesus,* p.222, Wright emphasises that miraculous healing occupied a major part of Jesus' public ministry. Eve, *Jewish Context*, p.352, points out that Jesus is never presented in the gospels as addressing suppliants' problems other than sickness; thus, in Luke's gospel, Jesus refuses to be judge in an inheritance dispute (12:13-15).

different geographical areas, including Gentile territory (e.g. 5:1-20; 7:24-30, 31-37; 8:22-26). Again, Jesus' opponents are portrayed as accepting that Jesus healed and exorcised (see Chapter 1, *1.2.1*); in Mark, the Beelzebub controversy (3:22) did not follow a specific exorcism by Jesus, as in the other Synoptic gospels. This seems to point to his enemies' recognition that he had performed exorcisms previously, and it fits also with their comment at the crucifixion, 'he saved others' (15:31).

These devices serve to highlight the prominence that Mark gives to Jesus' healing.

1.3.2 Jesus' Healing versus his Teaching

Sanders notes twentieth-century scholars' almost exclusive concentration on Jesus as a teacher; many, but not all, these scholars stress Jesus' teaching, especially in Mark, and thus play down emphasis on his healing in the gospels.[29] The healing stories have frequently been regarded as merely illustration of his teaching about the Kingdom of God; healing is subsumed in teaching. Mark's programmatic statement (1:14-15) *is* of Jesus' proclamation, but the modern emphasis on Jesus' teaching, to the detriment of his healing, is being redressed.[30] Chilton observes, rightly, that teaching in Mark highlights Jesus as a teacher, rather than emphasising the content of his teaching,[31] and, as Mark usually provides some detail of his healing, this seems to be evidence of Mark's interest in Jesus' healing.

---

29 Teaching and preaching are regarded here as synonymous. Sanders, *Jesus and Judaism*, p.356, n.1. E.g. Best, *Mark. Gospel as Story*, p.62; K. Warrington, *Jesus the Healer. Paradigm or Unique Phenomenon?* (Carlisle/Waynesboro: Paternoster, 2000) p.1, considers healings in the gospels were secondary to the message; Hogan, *Healing*, p.260, thinks that Mark, especially, sees teaching as Jesus' priority; J.D.G. Dunn, *Unity and Diversity in the New Testament. An Inquiry into the Character of Earliest Christianity* (London: SCM, 1977) p.186, notes that teaching is a very important part of Jesus' ministry in Mark. E. Schweizer, 'Mark's Theological Achievement', in Telford (ed.), *Interpretation of Mark,* p.69, regards Jesus' teaching and miracles to be in parallel. Guelich, *Mark 1-8:26*, p.315, judges Jesus' teaching to be in word and deed.

30 For instance, Davies, *Jesus the Healer*, p.10, disagrees with the view that Jesus was primarily a teacher, and suggests provocatively that this has arisen because most New Testament scholars are university teachers. Remus, *Jesus as Healer*, p.13, notes that the gospel of Mark gives less space to Jesus' teaching, and more to his deeds, than the other gospel writers.

31 B. Chilton, 'An Exorcism of History: Mark 1:21-28', in Chilton and Evans (eds.), *Authenticating the Activities,* p.219.

Various scholars draw attention to the fact that Mark particularly emphasises Jesus' authority.[32] The episode which Mark depicts as the beginning of Jesus' public ministry, his teaching and healing in the synagogue (1:21-27), established Jesus as a teacher 'with authority', but Mark omits any mention of the content of the teaching there.[33] Rather, he directs our attention to his account of Jesus healing, where even the *scope* of Jesus' authority in healing was greater than that of his teaching.[34] Again, Jesus was teaching (2:2) when the paralysed man was lowered through the roof, but we are not told the content of the teaching.

There are pericopae where it is difficult to separate teaching and healing, for instance, in the description of the reaction of his own townspeople (6:2), and when Jesus empowered his disciples both to proclaim and to cast out demons (3:14-15; 6:7-13). But Mark does not always link closely Jesus' preaching and healing. In 3:8-11 and 6:53-56, the crowd gathered to be healed, while in 6:34, the crowd is depicted assembling for teaching only. Mark also portrays Jesus avoiding the crowds, who were asking for healing, in order to proclaim over a wider geographical area (1:38),[35] so the two activities are often separated.

Thus, Mark seems to demonstrate that Jesus' healing is not merely an illustration of his teaching, but is itself significant in establishing Jesus' authority.

1.3.3 Jesus' Healing Attracting Crowds and Opposition

This partial separation by Mark of Jesus' healing and teaching makes it easier to see which of Jesus' activities Mark portrays as attracting the crowds. Although Hengel judges that in all the Synoptics, the two activities probably attracted equal attention, several scholars consider that the attraction was Jesus' healing; the fact that Mark rarely tells us *what* Jesus taught, but describes his healings, is support for the view that

32 Guelich, *Mark 1-8:26*, pp.47, 56, 60. Gundry, *Mark,* p.302, believes that Mark was more interested in the *authority* of Jesus' teaching, than in his words. Dunn, *Unity and Diversity*, p.186, suggests that Jesus' authority rests upon the content of his teaching. Remus, *Jesus as Healer,* p.42, considers that Jesus' healing power bestows authority on his teaching.

33 Mack, *Myth of Innocence*, p.234. He thinks, p.238, that Mark spells out Jesus' authority later (9:7), when God said, 'He is my son; listen to him'.

34 H. Anderson, 'Jesus: Aspects of the Question of his Authority', in J. Neusner, P. Borgen, E.S. Frerichs and R. Horsley (eds.), *The Social World of Formative Christianity and Judaism* (Philadelphia: Fortress, 1988) p.292, notes that Jesus' influence in healing extended to the unclean spirits, as well as the worshippers.

35 Remus, *Jesus as Healer*, p.59. Guelich, *Mark 1-8:26*, pp.70-71.

Mark considers Jesus' healing to be the main attraction for the crowds.[36] Smith goes so far as to suggest that Jesus was remembered primarily as a holy man doing miracles, and it was on that basis that his sayings and teachings were recalled,[37] but most would disagree with that view, on the evidence from Mark's gospel.

A crowd was not always present in healing stories. Peter's mother-in-law was healed in the privacy of her home (1:30-31), and the Syrophoenician woman was also in a house during her verbal exchange with Jesus (7:25-30). The man with leprosy (1:40) would have been isolated from the crowd by his condition, and Jesus sometimes led the sufferer away from the crowd (7:33; 8:23). Crowds *are,* however, important in much of Mark's portrayal. He describes two general responses by the crowd after a healing; amazement (e.g. 1:27; 5:20, 37), which might result in greater crowds (e.g. 1:32), or fear (e.g. 5:15), which might lead to a request for Jesus to leave (5:17). The crowd reaction is significant to Mark's healing narrative, although Theissen suggests that wonder was a stereotyped closing motif in synoptic miracle stories, and Witherington considers that the crowd's amazement and wonder were inadequate reactions, demonstrating an imperfect faith.[38] Dwyer, however, draws attention to the importance in Mark's gospel of the motif of wonder, as it suggests both the element of mystery, and evidence of the crowd's awareness of the breaking-in of the Kingdom of God.[39]

It seems to me that Mark often portrays accurately the reactions of a crowd to healing, and it is sometimes a significant part of his narrative. He manages to convey that, on occasion, the crowd were sceptical of Jesus' healing power, for instance, that they believed that Jairus' daughter was beyond help by Jesus (5:40), and again, perhaps they thought that the boy with epilepsy had died as the result of Jesus'

---

36 M. Hengel, *The Charismatic Leader and his Followers* (ET; Edinburgh: T. & T. Clark, 1981) p.66. Borg and Wright, *Meaning of Jesus*, p.73; Sanders, *Jesus and Judaism,* pp.164-65. Räisänen, *'Messianic Secret',* p.246, suggests that the Messianic secret as applied to healings was a means for Mark to stress the great publicity aroused. Theissen and Merz, *Historical Jesus*, p.281, consider that Jesus impressed (and provoked) his contemporaries supremely by his miracles.

37 Smith, *Jesus the Magician,* pp.12, 16. This is related to Smith's view that Jesus was a healer in the mould of the Hellenistic TA.

38 Twelftree, *Jesus the Exorcist,* p.176. Theissen, *Miracle Stories*, pp.69-71. Witherington, *Gospel of Mark*, p.92. Remus, *Jesus as Healer*, p.29, comments on Mark's depiction of the crowd reaction as that which a charismatic figure would arouse.

39 T. Dwyer, 'The Motif of Wonder in the Gospel of Mark', *JSNT* 57 (1995) 49-59, [52].

ministrations (9:26). The crowd there had been keenly interested; 'a crowd came running' (9:15, 25), and Mark describes accurately the communal response to an unusual happening, and the fickleness of mass opinion; he later depicts a crowd who behaved in the same way when Pilate invited them to have him release Jesus (15:6-14), whom they had recently welcomed into Jerusalem (11:8-10).

Mark also depicts the attraction of the crowds as a major reason for Jesus being in conflict with the authorities. Some of the conflict might have been expected to be political, in an occupied country with previous uprisings, where the presence of crowds risked clampdown by the authorities,[40] but early in the gospel, Mark describes the opposition as specifically religious, and much of it was related to Jesus healing. Mark demonstrates this by making an episode of healing (2:1-12) the first occasion when Jesus had a brush with the religious establishment, and another healing (on the Sabbath, of the man with the withered hand, 3:1-6) the incident precipitating the organisation of the first plot by the religious and civil authorities to kill Jesus.[41] Throughout the gospel (e.g. 2:5-6, 24-28; 3:1-6; 7:1-13; 10:2-9; 11:15-18, 27-33; 14:61-64), Mark portrays the root of the conflict as Jesus' claim to authority, which clashed with the power of the Temple and the religious leaders.[42] It was this aspect of Jesus' healing that brought him into confrontation with the religious establishment.

Along with most of his Jewish contemporaries, Mark would consider that sin was a significant cause of sickness. He presents the opposition in 2:1-12 as being to Jesus' words of forgiveness, rather than to the physical healing; the theological controversy was over who could forgive sin. Guelich points out that the statement in 2:5, 'your sins are forgiven' could not be accepted as a divine passive, as the scribes would not have acknowledged Jesus' right to forgive sin in God's name; Hooker believes that not even a Messiah would be considered in Judaism to have authority to forgive sins.[43]

The story is odd as a healing narrative; divine forgiveness itself should have enabled the man to recover; however, in the altercation between Jesus and the scribes, the man was still lying on the mat,

---

40 Horsley and Silberman, *Message and Kingdom*, p.59.

41 The alliance of the Pharisees with Herodians (again in 12:13) seems unlikely, in spite of the explanation offered by France, *Gospel of Mark,* p.149, who notes that the Herods controlled the appointment of the High Priest before AD 6 and after AD 37. Rather, it seems to demonstrate the strength of the opposition arrayed against Jesus.

42 Guelich, *Mark 1-8:26*, p.133.

43 Guelich, *Mark 1-8:26*, p.87. Hooker, *Gospel According to Mark*, p.88; Thomas, *Devil, Disease,* p.145, accepts her view.

although he was able to walk immediately when Jesus told him to do so (vv.11-12). Sanders suggests that Jesus always offered inclusion in the Kingdom, even when the suppliants were still sinners, i.e. had not fulfilled the cultic repentance required by the temple authorities.[44] This seems the probable explanation for the opposition; Jesus had granted unconditional forgiveness while the man was still suffering from his illness.[45] The crowd recognised his recovery as God's work (unusually for Mark, see Chapter 4, *2.1.4*). This story is followed immediately by criticism of Jesus for dining with 'tax-collectors and sinners' (2:14-17); healing and forgiveness of sin were linked, both by their position in Mark's narrative, and by Jesus' reply to criticism there, indicating that his purpose in coming was as a 'physician', presumably to both sinners and sick people (2:17).[46]

We can conclude that Mark stresses that Jesus' healing was significant in attracting both the crowds and religious opposition.

1.3.4 Summary of the Importance of Healing to Mark

Mark makes clear in many ways his view of the importance of Jesus' healing ministry. By the large volume of material devoted to Jesus' healing, the depiction of crowds seeking healing, and the recognition of his healing power by both the crowds and his enemies, Mark emphasises Jesus' healing in his ministry. He also indicates its prominence by his hyperbole in the summaries, and by mentioning repeatedly that Jesus risked being overwhelmed by the healing task. Although scholars anxious to play down Jesus' healing have seen his preaching as being pre-eminent and establishing his authority, and his healing as merely illustrative, Mark's account does not support this view. Mark describes Jesus' authority as being manifest in both his teaching and his healing, but frequently omits the *content* of Jesus' teaching, while being more specific about his healing, and in this way, also, indicates the importance he attaches to Jesus' healing. This is not, of course, to suggest that Jesus' healing and teaching were unrelated, but that it is often possible to separate them sufficiently to allow us to study Mark's view of healing. The partial separation of Jesus' teaching and healing allows the conclusion that Mark portrays Jesus' healing as a major

44 Sanders, *Jesus and Judaism,* p.206. W. Wink, 'Mark 2:1-12', *Int* 36 (1982) 60; Gundry, *Mark*, p.112.

45 Sanders, *Jesus and Judaism,* pp.44-45, sees this as the main objection by the Pharisees to Jesus healing 'sinners'.

46 Remus, *Jesus as Healer*, p.33, notes that the comment means that there was no general antipathy to physicians in the gospel.

factor in both his attracting the crowds, and in provoking religious opposition.

It is clear that in Mark's gospel, the miracles are depicted as occupying a fundamental position, with no hint of them being 'pasted on' from the Hellenistic world.

1.4 Mark's Description of Jesus as a Healer

Mark makes it clear that Jesus' ability to heal carried with it the imperative that he would use his power. The picture Mark presents is that Jesus would heal anyone who recognised their need for healing, and appealed to him; he told nobody that they must bear their disease.[47] Healing was sometimes an onerous duty, and Mark demonstrates Jesus' healing responsibilities beautifully, in his account of Jesus' encounter with the woman with a chronic condition (5:25-34), while he was on his way urgently to a dying child. The story is usually considered an example of Mark's narrative device of intercalation, and much is also made of the common theological themes of healing a female, of uncleanness (of uterine blood, and death), and of the 12 years (the length of time of the woman's illness and the age of the girl, often related to her menarche).[48] All three synoptists relate the story, and Gundry's suggestion that such a situation may have actually happened in Jesus' ministry seems possible; for our purpose, it illustrates Mark's recognition of the burden that Jesus' healing power laid on him.[49]

We have mentioned that Mark does show awareness of the ease with which Jesus' healing might engulf the time available to him for preaching, and so he did have to avoid the crowds who were preventing him doing other work (1:35-38; 3:7-12). Gundry suggests that Jesus ordered the parents to maintain silence about their daughter being raised from death (5:43), in order that he could escape the crowds who wanted

---

47 Sanders, *Jesus and Judaism*, p.159, notes we are given no indication as to how Jesus discovered that he could heal. Harvey, *Jesus and Constraints,* p.105. Warrington, *Jesus the Healer*, p.161, notes that Jesus is never portrayed as seeing sickness as of pedagogical value to the sufferer.

48 E.g. Hurtado, *Mark*, p.88, sees the number as symbolising the tribes of Israel. C. Myers, *Binding the Strong Man. A Political Reading of Mark's Story of Jesus* (Maryknoll, New York: Orbis, 1988) pp.202-203, sees it as the time of the contrast between the child's life of privilege and the destitution of the woman. Gundry, *Mark*, pp.284-85, regards the allegorical aspects as having been over-emphasised. I would agree.

49 France, *Gospel of Mark*, p.234. Gundry, *Mark,* p.268. The dilemma that Jesus faced in the intercalated story would be familiar to any clinician.

to be healed.[50] There is no real evidence in Mark that Jesus was a reluctant healer, although in the conversation with the Syrophoenician woman (7:27), Jesus is portrayed as initially reserving healing for the benefit of Israel.[51] The idea of reluctance was possibly based on his refusal to give a sign to the Pharisees (8:11-12), or perhaps related to the secrecy motif.[52] Hurtado suggests that Jesus showed some aversion to crowds (in 7:36; 8:23),[53] but it seems to me more likely that these particular situations illustrate how Mark depicts Jesus' action, in true-to-life fashion.

Mark never suggests that Jesus asked a sufferer if, or in what way, he had sinned, before healing him, nor did Jesus mention the cause of the illness; his concern was healing the sick person.[54] The immediate reason for Jesus to heal in Mark's gospel seemed to be straightforward; in individual cases, he was asked to do so, by the sufferer (1:40), a relative (5:22-23; 9:17, 22), or friends (2:3), and this is implicit also in the summaries, where sick people were brought to Jesus for healing. Mark's Jesus never healed without being asked, as occurred in pagan healing narratives.[55]

Suetonius considered that Vespasian's healings were important in conferring on the new Emperor prestige and divinity, and Bultmann

---

50 Gundry, *Mark*, pp.276-77; Meier, *Marginal Jew*, II, p.844, ns.27, 28, critiques the suggestion, but Cairns, *Faith That Rebels*, p.77, considered that secrecy was sometimes a device to allow Jesus to leave without the crowd following. So also Räisänen, *'Messianic Secret'*, p.160, n.62.

51 Harvey, *Jesus and Constraints*, p.105, hints at this reluctance. Witherington, *Gospel of Mark*, p.107, regards this idea as unfounded, but maintains that healing was not the focus of Jesus' mission. W. Loader, 'Challenged at the Boundaries: A Conservative Jesus in Mark's Tradition', *JSNT 63* (1996), 45-61, considers that Jesus *was* cautious in his attitude to healing (1:40-45; 5:25-34; 7:24-30). B.J. Malina, *The Social Gospel of Jesus. The Kingdom of God in Mediterranean Perspective* (Minneapolis: Fortress, 2001) pp.104-105, notes that valuable resources, including health-care, were regarded as limited, so could be increased only at the expense of others. Perhaps Mark regarded them as finite. Gundry, *Mark*, pp.373-74, suggests that healing Gentiles was depriving the disciples of Jesus' *teaching* time.

52 Guelich, *Mark 1-8:26*, pp.70-71. Räisänen, *'Messianic Secret'*, pp.246, 250, points out, in relation to secrecy about healing, that the presence of the crowds caused some inconvenience to Jesus. Carroll, 'Sickness and Healing', p.132, considers that the secrecy was at least partly a means of crowd control.

53 Hurtado, *Mark*, p.119.

54 M. Kelsey, *Healing and Christianity: A Classic Study* (2nd ed.; Minneapolis: Augsburg Fortress, 1995) p.51. Eve, *Jewish Context*, p.352, defines Jesus' practice as 'naturalistic', not 'personalistic', i.e., he concentrates on healing, not on the cause of the sickness.

55 E.g. Philostratus, *Life of Apollonius* 4.45.

opined that, since Jesus' healings were recorded in order to show Messianic authority or divine power, evangelists (and modern theologians) were unimpressed with the idea of compassion as a motive for Jesus.[56] In Mark's gospel, this seems to me to be wrong. In 9:22, the father of the epileptic boy asked Jesus to have compassion, while Bartimaeus in 10:47 requested Jesus to have mercy; these pleas indicate that both the suppliants and Mark recognised that compassion was a *sine qua non* in Jesus' healing. That Jesus was moved by compassion, σπλαγχνισθείς, is mentioned only once with respect to healing in Mark's gospel, presumably because it was recognised as a given. In that encounter (1:41), Jesus' emotion is rendered ὀργισθείς (anger) in Codex Bezae, and, as the harder reading, many modern writers believe it is more likely to be original.[57] Anger (at the ravages of the disease, at the social consequences of the man being excluded from normal life [Lev. 13:45-46], or at the implication that he would not be prepared to help the man) seems a likely reaction for Mark to impute to Jesus, and verse 43 continues the idea of Jesus' anger. Mark also describes Jesus' anger with the Pharisees, and grief at the hardness of their hearts, in the story of the man with the withered hand (3:5). Anger is implied in Jesus' question about whether it was lawful to do good or do harm on the Sabbath (3:4), and also when the Pharisees asked for a sign (8:11-12). This fits with a gospel-writer who does not feel the need to spell out Jesus' compassion in healing, but is prepared to portray Jesus' anger.

Indeed, Mark makes a point of depicting Jesus' humanity. His accounts of his mental agony in Gethsemane (14:34), and on the cross, 'Why have you forsaken me?'(15:34) underline this. Of all the gospel-

---

56 Suetonius, *Divine Vespasian, The Lives of the Caesars* 7.2; Bultmann, *History of Synoptic Tradition,* p.219; Sanders, *Jesus and Judaism*, p.160, mocks such an understanding, but Schweizer, 'Mark's Theological Achievement', p.69, maintains that Jesus' deeds were never understood by Mark as an expression of compassion.

57 W. Bauer, F.W. Danker, W.F. Arndt, and F.W. Gingrich (eds.), *A Greek-English Lexicon of the New Testament and Other Early Christian Literature* (3rd ed.; Chicago: University of Chicago Press, 2000) p309, mention, but do not consider it. France, *Gospel of Mark*, p.115, notes that ὀργισθείς is not widely attested, only in D of the uncials. He notes the comment that scribes did not find it necessary to remove 'anger' in 3:5 and 10:14, but regards this as ignoring the fact that there was an obvious cause of anger in that context. France notes also that the lack of mention of σπλαγχνισθείς in Matthew and Luke suggests that they found ὀργισθείς there, and so they omitted any word for emotion. See discussion in Wilkinson, *Bible and Healing*, p.99, and in Guelich, *Mark 1-8:26*, pp.74-75. Schweizer, 'Mark's Theological Achievement', sees it as anger, p.83, n.22. M.J.J. Menken, 'The Position of Σπλαγχνίζεσθαι and Σπλάγχνα in the Gospel of Luke', *NovT* 30 (1988) p.113, thinks that the attestation of D, 'being angry', is correct.

writers, Mark portrays most vividly Jesus' sense of total rejection on the cross.[58] If, as I believe, Mark sees Jesus' crucifixion as the climax of his gospel,[59] then, in portraying the emotions of Jesus in the healing stories, he is rehearsing Jesus' humanity and vulnerability. Alternatively, if Mark considers Jesus' resurrection as the great miracle, with the healing miracles merely a foretaste, then we would expect Mark's Jesus, the innocent sufferer for mankind, to experience keenly on the cross, his rejection by society and apparently by God, before the divine healing of vindication and resurrection, in the same way that those whom Jesus healed had often been rejected from normal society, before being restored.

In summary, Mark describes Jesus as healing those presented to him, and not avoiding this activity, except when it threatened to interfere with the other commitments of his ministry. Compassion, implicitly, and anger, overtly, are both emotions Mark portrays Jesus showing in the healing narratives, the latter especially when he was opposed in his work by the religious establishment. Mark emphasises the humanity of Jesus, showing him as one who felt and acted as a caring healer, who did not see the sufferer merely as the object of miraculous cure, or as useful evidence of his message. This picture matches Mark's account of Jesus on the cross.

1.5 Mark's Account of Illnesses Healed

It seems to me that, in portraying theologically the spectrum of sicknesses healed by Jesus within the gospel genre, Mark had several options. He could describe Jesus fulfilling the Old Testament (especially Isaianic) prophecies as the eschatological Messiah; represent Jesus healing conditions which were regarded as intractable by other healers, and so raising his status above other miracle-workers, both pagan and Jewish; portray sickness in such general terms that illnesses were unidentifiable (then or now); or depict, in a way that his readers would recognise, conditions known and feared in first-century Palestine. The alternative(s) Mark adopts will help to establish what he wants his readers to grasp of the significance of Jesus' healing ministry.

---

58 N.A. Dahl, 'The Purpose of Mark's Gospel', in C. Tuckett (ed.), *The Messianic Secret* (Philadelphia: Fortress, 1983) p.30.
59 E.g. Marcus, 'Mark – Interpreter of Paul', p.475.

1.5.1 Fulfilling Prophecy

The range of illnesses in Mark's gospel were more varied than in Isaiah 35:5-6, where sufferers were blind, deaf, lame or dumb,[60] conditions particularly suited to theological interpretation, whereas Isaiah 61:1 prophesied liberation of all who were oppressed and captive, and this might include all those suffering 'oppressive' illnesses.[61] Jesus' healings in Mark were also broader in scope than those of Elijah and Elisha, but there is some resemblance to the circumstances of two healings. Jairus' daughter's healing can be compared with 1 Kings 17:17-24, where a boy appeared to be dead, but was revived by Elijah, and 2 Kings 4:18-37, where a boy was raised from death by Elisha;[62] also, the healing of the man with leprosy (Mk. 1:40-44), can be compared with Elisha treating Naaman's leprosy (2 Kgs. 5:1-19). One of Jesus' healings, of a deaf and speech-impaired man (Mk. 7:31-37), is a more distinct example of Mark portraying Jesus as fulfilling prophecy.[63] It is notable that, even there, and in the story of the blind man of Bethsaida (8:22-26), both placed in Mark's gospel in close proximity to his account of disciples who did not 'hear' or 'see' spiritually Jesus as Messiah, yet, where the inference is most obviously theological, Mark describes the conditions and healing in factual terms.[64]

Thus, there *is* a little evidence of Mark demonstrating Jesus fulfilling prophecy, and perfecting the healings of the Old Testament.

1.5.2 'True to Life' Descriptions of Illnesses

Before discussing the illnesses that Jesus encountered, there are some preliminary points to be made. Patients do not come for healing of a disease, but with symptoms of how they feel, or what they are unable to do, and, sometimes, because of how others view them.[65] Sicknesses are

---

60 Those who are blind, deaf and dumb are all to be healed on the Day of the Lord, in Isa. 29:18. Witherington, *Gospel of Mark*, p.239, points out that blindness is never actually treated in the Old Testament.

61 Sanders, *Jesus and Judaism*, p.161, notes that, since demon-possession was not part of Isaiah's world-view, exorcisms were not mentioned there.

62 The efforts of Elijah and Elisha in raising the dead child were much more strenuous than Jesus' in raising Jairus' daughter.

63 The word used of his speech is μογιλάλος 'could hardly speak', found only in 7:32 and in LXX Isa. 35:6.

64 Black, 'Christ Crucified', p.204, notes that Mark embeds his theology in realistic narrative.

65 A.C. Twaddle, 'Sickness and the Sickness Career: Some Implications', in L. Eisenberg and A. Kleinman (eds.), *The Relevance of Social Science for Medicine* (Dordrecht: D. Reidel, 1981) p.112.

defined differently in every society, as they occur in specific settings, and in interaction with other people, so ideas about illness, and what people do when they are ill, vary with the culture.[66] Medical anthropologists, being culturally orientated, are opposed to ethnocentrism and its medical offspring, medicocentrism.[67] Anthropological terms for illness include a) 'disease', as the biological dimension of non-health, which is objective (and is now the focus of medicine); b) 'illness,' which refers to the more subjective dimensions of non-health, for instance, the symptoms, the difficulties in coping, perhaps the social problems resulting; c) 'sickness', which is the term for the social dimension, the inability to meet the social obligations defined by others (usually those who define the person as unhealthy).[68] Thus, illness does not exist in isolation; it affects the afflicted, but often also his family, and his social standing. This is true of all cultures, but was especially true in the first-century world, with both the Graeco-Roman context of the honour and shame system, and with the Jewish belief in the relationship between sickness and sin.

Human beings react to reality as they perceive and understand it in a concrete historical period,[69] and Mark's descriptions of the people whom Jesus healed are told in a factual way; Myers considers that Mark chooses realistic narrative rather than highly fabricated fictions of apocalyptic to tell the healing stories.[70] This makes his healing narratives seem the most accessible of the ancient writers being studied. It is recognised that this is a danger, and any modern comment on the conditions healed by Jesus invites a charge of medicocentrism.[71] The warnings of medical anthropologists about 'diagnosing' in these circumstances are well founded, and many modern examples of 'hyper-diagnostic' approaches to biblical illnesses can be found.[72] Mark usually

---

66 Theissen and Merz, *Historical Jesus*, p.311. G. Lewis, 'Cultural Influences on Illness Behavior: A Medical Anthropological Approach', in Eisenberg and Kleinman (eds.), *Relevance*, p.151.

67 Pilch, 'Sickness and Healing in Luke-Acts', p.182. Medicocentrism can be defined as a belief that scientific Western medicine has the only truth in questions of health and sickness.

68 Twaddle, 'Sickness', pp.111-12.

69 P.J. Achtemeier, 'Miracles and the Historical Jesus: A Study of Mark 9:14-29', *CBQ* 37 (1975) 488.

70 Myers, *Binding*, p.104. Black, 'Christ Crucified', p.204, writes that Mark is 'anthropologically animated'.

71 Bolt, *Jesus' Defeat of Death*, p.26. Davies, *Jesus the Healer*, pp.5-13, thinks that there is a risk of assuming a Jesus with whom we are in substantial agreement.

72 Avalos, *Illness and Health Care*, pp.18-20. E.g. E. Davis, 'The Illness of Miriam, Sister of Moses', *Koroth* 9, 1-2 (1985) pp.99-100; M. Sussman, 'Sickness and Disease',

gives enough information in his narrative to allow an educated guess, albeit 'etic',[73] as to the nature of many of the illnesses, even in an environment so different in time and place.[74] Thus, 'converting' Mark's descriptions of illnesses tentatively into terms that are more familiar to us may make them more relevant to modern readers, although it is recognised that this will be a gross approximation.

I offer general footnote comments on the illnesses in Mark's gospel, without quoting references from medical textbooks, since the comments are uncontroversial medically. Jesus healed Peter's mother-in-law with fever (1:30-31);[75] a man with leprosy (1:40-45);[76] a paralysed man (2:1-12);[77] a man with a withered hand (3:1-6);[78] a woman with menorrhagia

---

ABD, 6, p.10, suggesting that the 'serpents' of Num. 21:6-9 were guinea-worms; J.D.M. Derrett, 'Mark's Technique: The Haemorrhaging Woman and Jairus' Daughter', *Bib* 63 (1982) 474-505.

73 Myers, *Binding*, pp.142, 148, defines the term as cultural outsider perspective.

74 Kelsey, *Healing and Christianity*, p.58, maintains that we cannot attach modern labels to the illnesses; he then proceeds to divide the illnesses into organic disease, functional disorders and psychic illness. R. Bennett, *The Diseases of the Bible* (London: Religious Tract Society, 1887), p.11, points out that diseases may change in severity or character with time and circumstances.

75 Wilkinson, *Bible and Healing*, p.222, notes that one of the common causes of high fever in Northern Palestine was malaria. See P.F. Burke, 'Malaria in the Greco-Roman World: A Historical and Epidemiological Survey', in *ANRW* II.37.3 (1996) 2252-79. See also Chapter 2, *2.2.4*. A.E. Harvey, *Renewal through Suffering. A Study of 2 Corinthians* (Edinburgh: T. & T. Clark, 1996) p.23, and p.23 n.53, notes that malaria was referred to as πυρέτος (fever).

76 Although 'leprosy' was a biblical term used for many skin diseases (see Chapter 2, *1.1*), there were religious taboos and fear of contracting disease from sufferers, so the effects of isolation and exclusion were present as in true leprosy. Temkin, *Hippocrates*, p.101, considers that true leprosy, which was widespread in the Orient, *did* occur in the world of the New Testament. Meier, *Marginal Jew*, II, p.700, reports that Hansen's disease (the old eponymous name for true leprosy) was found in the area that became the Eastern Roman Empire from 330 BC.

77 This might have been due to upper or lower motor neurone involvement of his legs, so cerebral palsy with spastic diplegia, paraplegia, ascending (Landry's) paralysis, or poliomyelitis, were all possibilities, in the absence of any clue from Mark as to the length of time he had been paralysed.

78 Withering of the hand suggests long-term neurological damage, by e.g. cerebral palsy, or poliomyelitis. Poliomyelitis would be common in the crowded cities of the Roman Empire, and cerebral palsy likely where only primitive midwifery was available in poor rural and urban communities, where women were likely to suffer from malnutrition, osteomalacia, and consequent pelvic contraction.

(5:25-34);[79] a girl probably dead (5:22-24, 35-43);[80] a deaf man with a speech impediment (7:31-37);[81] a blind man from Bethsaida (8:22-26);[82] and blind Bartimaeus (10:46-52). The exorcisms were performed on a man in the synagogue (1:21-28);[83] a man in the Gadarene tombs (5:1-20);[84] a Syrophoenician girl (7:24-30);[85] and a boy with epilepsy (9:14-29).[86]

These observations are made to substantiate the point that Mark portrays Jesus healing conditions that could be recognised then, and, so his readers could identify with the sufferers. There is no evidence that Mark depicts Jesus as treating *only* conditions (such as deafness, lameness and blindness) which were not treated by contemporary pagan or Jewish charismatics, or healing *only* diseases which were congenital, or especially difficult to treat.[87] It is recognised that, in cultures where living conditions are intolerable, or where stigma attaches to anyone with mental illness, sufferers tend to 'somatise' their problems,[88] and it is accepted that attitudes and emotions affect health and healing (both

---

79 As her condition was long-standing, hormonal imbalance or uterine fibroids would be two probable diagnoses. Howard, *Disease and Healing*, p.94, suggests, however, that it was psychologically-generated dysfunctional uterine bleeding.

80 Likely to be due to an infectious disease, especially bacterial meningitis, judging by the rapidity of her deterioration, and the urgency described.

81 Witherington, *Gospel of Mark*, p.234, sees the man's deafness as a later development, but speech difficulty is not a major problem if a child has learned to speak before becoming deaf, so I would assume that his deafness was profound from birth or soon after, and the difficulty with speech secondary to it.

82 Despite its similarity to the narrative of 7:31-37, the man can be assumed to have had sight previously, and so recognised that Jesus' first attempt at healing was not totally successful. (This ignores the nuances of theological blindness and imperfect perception.)

83 The picture fits that of *grand mal* epilepsy, with post-ictal automatism (v.24), which would explain the man's cry.

84 He had features compatible with a psychosis, perhaps paranoid schizophrenia, or bipolar affective disorder (manic-depression).

85 Not enough information is given to hazard an educated guess; 'second hand' accounts of symptoms are notoriously difficult to assess; it is an example of Mark being a careful narrator of Jesus' healings.

86 The two descriptions of *grand mal* fits are unmistakeable. The inability to speak (9:17) and hear (9:25) would be due to the seizure described in v.20, *pace* France, *Gospel of Mark*, p.365.

87 Vermes, *Jesus the Jew*, p.42, considers Jesus could be regarded as a charismatic healer. Harvey, *Jesus and Constraints*, pp. 115, 117.

88 Eve, *Jewish Context*, pp.354-6. Kleinman, *Patients and Healers*, p.149, defines somatisation as the 'substitution of somatic preoccupation for dysphoric affect and affective disorders into complaints of physical symptoms and illness'. Remus, *Jesus as Healer*, p.111.

positively and negatively), but I consider that those writers who believed that Jesus treated *only* people with neuroses or psychosomatic disorders[89] seem to have missed the picture that Mark paints of Jesus healing.

In summary, it seems clear that Mark does not select illnesses exclusively to align with scriptural prophecies (or, at least, with those that were possible to describe in his narrative genre),[90] although at least one episode did fit. Rather, his narrative depicts a wide range of sicknesses that were common, recognisable, and burdensome in first-century Palestine. He presents these vignettes as true to life, expecting that his readers would recognise the illnesses, and identify with the sufferers. This does not impede Mark's theological use of these conditions, but, rather, reinforces the point that Mark is showing Jesus' healing ministry as being an important part of the message of the nearness of the Kingdom of God.

1.6 Mark's Terms for Illness and Healing

The terms used for illness in Mark are mostly standard words and phrases of his time, and serve to demonstrate that his understanding of illness is like that of the majority of his contemporaries, rather than that of Hippocratic physicians. Terms include μάστιξ (3:10), a scourge, suggesting an outside agency (e.g. divine affliction or unclean spirits); although often used to describe an acute condition, it can be applied to a chronic one (5:29, 34). In 6:5, ἄρρωστος is used and, like the commoner term ἀσθένεια, denotes weakness or disability. The phrase, κακῶς ἔχειν (literally 'to have badly', e.g.1:34) is common in Mark. He employs the terms unclean spirits and demons synonymously, though demons, rather than unclean spirits, are reported as being expelled.[91]

Usually, Mark utilizes factual terms for healing. The verb most commonly used for healing, both by Jesus and his disciples (e.g. 6:13), is θεραπεύω.[92] There is only one occasion when the alternative verb to heal, ἰάομαι, is used (5:29). Also, the verb to restore, ἀποκαθίστημι, is

89 E.g. Smith, *Jesus the Magician*, p.8; Meier, *Marginal Jew*, II, p.661; L.D. Weatherhead, *Psychology, Religion and Healing* (London: Hodder & Stoughton, 1951).

90 It would, for instance, be difficult in Mark's narrative format to enact the prophecy of Isa. 65:20, where neonatal death and premature ageing were both to disappear.

91 Guelich, *Mark 1-8:26*, p.56. Witherington, *Gospel of Mark*, e.g. p.34, n.102, sees Mark's use of the phrase 'unclean spirits' as part of his apocalyptic worldview.

92 Wells, *Language of Healing*, pp.134-55, demonstrates that, in the Synoptics, it involves working and caring, and includes healing the soul as well as the body.

employed once (3:5), as is καθαρίζω, to cleanse (of leprosy, 1:40), and ὁρκιζω (to exorcise, uttered by a demon, 5:7). The term ὑγιής (being made sound, 5:34) occurs in the sense of restoring health. Σῴζω (to save) is found, frequently in the passive voice (e.g. 5:23; 6:56), but also in the phrase, 'your faith has saved you' (5:34; 10:52), sometimes as rescue, rather than in its full theological meaning. However, Mark does portray healing as an important form of saving, not only as rescue from exclusion from society, but more positively, to new life in the true Israel and its worship. He does not always clarify if salvation is for this life only, but Jesus in the 'little apocalypse' (Mark 13), warning of the woes ahead, pointed out that the one who endured to the end would be saved (13:13), implying eternal life.

Of the more theological terms for healing in the New Testament, Mark applies σημεῖα καὶ τέρατα (signs and wonders) only to the deeds of false Christs and prophets, deeds which were designed to lead astray (13:22), not, as in the LXX and Acts, for healing in relation to Messianic and apostolic claims.[93] Σημεῖον is used alone in 8:11, and not in the context of healing, when the Pharisees asked for, and were refused, a sign from Jesus to validate his claims. The other term found in Acts for miracles, δυνάμεις, ('mighty works' or 'powers') is used mainly in somewhat negative contexts in Mark. He mentions it twice in the story of his rejection, once used by the people (6:2), and again when Jesus could do no δυνάμεις in Nazareth (6:5); soon after, he uses it when Herod considered Jesus' δυνάμεις were due to John the Baptist *redivivus* (6:14), and again, when the disciples discussed the man using Jesus' name to expel demons (9:39). In 5:30, Jesus felt δύναμις going out of him as the woman touched his clothes. In 1:40 and 9:22-3, the cognate verb is used, first by the man with leprosy, confident of Jesus' ability to heal him, and later, when the father of the boy with epilepsy appealed for help to Jesus tentatively, 'if you can', and Jesus echoed his words, adding 'all things are possible to one who believes'.

In summary, Mark shows evidence of his common worldview of illness, in the use of terms such as 'scourge', and 'unclean spirits', that is, he assumes that unclean spirits were responsible for many conditions that Jesus healed. He utilises mainly matter-of-fact words for healing. Although he does include 'salvation' in the healing narratives, this is often in the sense of rescue from the present predicament. Words with more specifically Messianic implications, such as 'signs and wonders' and 'deeds of power', are mainly reserved for situations other than Jesus

93 Blackburn, *Theios Anēr,* p.251; T.J. Weeden, 'The Heresy that Necessitated Mark's Gospel', in Telford (ed.), *Interpretation of Mark,* p.95.

healing. I would regard these findings as supporting the view that Mark depicts Jesus healing real people with significant illnesses in the world of his time.

1.6.1 Healing and Exorcism in Mark

As was discussed in Chapter 1 (*1.3.2*), gospel writers' portrayal of healing and exorcism is often difficult to assess with certainty. Mark, in keeping with most writers of the first century, is aware of the presence and threat from demons. It seems to me that Mark does not make a point of distinguishing sharply between those sick (and possibly attacked by demons) and those demon-possessed, and so, between healing and exorcism. For instance, the healing summaries are a mixture of healing and exorcisms; 1:32 refers to 'sick and demonised' people; in 1:34, 'he healed those ill with many diseases and cast out many demons, and told the demons not to re-enter'; 1:39, 'he cast out demons'; 3:10-12, 'he healed many, so that all who had diseases pressed on him in order to touch him; whenever the unclean spirits saw him, they fell before him, calling him Son of God, and he warned them not to make that known'; 6:5, 'he healed a few sick (people) by laying his hands on them'; 6:54-56 'all (the sick people) who touched the fringe of his cloak were healed'. In 3:15 and 6:7, his disciples were to have authority to expel demons, while in 6:13, they expelled demons and healed on their mission. Thus, it seems that, while Mark does mention that he thinks demonic power is at work, and believes that demonic influences can produce symptoms, he is less concerned than some modern writers are as to whether there is, first, a sharp difference between demonic and other illness, or, second, between demon attack and demon possession.[94] Perhaps using Mark's term in 1:32 and 5:15, δαιμονιζόμενεν (demonised), rather than the term 'demoniac' favoured by many modern theologians, would at least allow Mark's perspective to be preserved.[95]

In the four texts where specific exorcisms are recounted by Mark (1:21-28; 5:1-20; 7:24-30; 9:14-29), Thomas believes that only in the last (9:14-29) does Mark attribute an illness directly to demon possession;[96] but he does not define what Mark depicts that Jesus

---

94 Specifically, my view on Mark's outlook here is at variance with Thomas, *Devil, Disease*, pp.159-60, who considers that the same evidence shows that Mark separates clearly healings and exorcisms.

95 Describing a person as a 'demoniac', like 'leper' or epileptic', is also diminishing to the sufferer, and ought to be avoided in descriptions nowadays.

96 Thomas, *Devil, Disease,* p.157. By p.160, Thomas considers that the demon there 'has brought on an illness'. He sees that a demon capable of inflicting deafness, dumbness and convulsions is in a special demon category, but makes no comment on

achieved by exorcism. Mark seems to me to be more interested in showing that Jesus (or his disciples) healed the person, than on the cause of the person's problem or the mode of their recovery.

In summary, although some separation of healing from exorcism is found in Mark's gospel, and may reflect common first-century concepts of illness (and possibly the Jewish apocalyptic outlook), I consider that Mark's demarcation of illnesses resulting from demon affliction, demon possession, or other causes is indefinite, or, at the most, betrays only a passing interest in differentiating them.

1.7 Mark's Account of Jesus' Methods of Healing

Mark is not nowadays regarded as himself recalling the detail of Jesus' miracles; he was not an eyewitness of Jesus' miracles, which were already in the tradition when Mark was writing his gospel. I would argue, however, that he has fashioned the earlier and oral material according to his own acute observation of first-century life.

There has been considerable debate as to whether Jesus healed in a way different from other miracle healers of the time. Jesus' methods are depicted as generally simple, involving no magical materials or formulae. Although there may have been fewer sensational elements to the gospel healing narratives than are found in contemporary non-Christian writings, some are present. For instance, in stories of miracle healing by charismatic healers of the time, cure was often instantaneous, and Mark frequently uses 'immediately'.(e.g. 5:29).[97] He does, however, employ the term in other situations (e.g. 1:12; 4:5) as a means of joining narrative events, in the same way as he uses, 'as soon as (they had left the synagogue)' (1:29), 'that evening' (1:32), 'from there he set out' (7:24). Narrative critics consider that it is a reflection of his literary style, to add pace and urgency to his account.[98]

As with other accounts of miracles in the ancient world, Mark often emphasises the difficulty of the task of healing. For instance, others had tried to control the Gadarene man with psychosis (5:3-4), and failed. Physicians had failed to heal the woman with menorrhagia (5:25-26); Mark's comments about the unpleasantness of their treatment and about

---

what Mark may have considered the cause of the man's disability in 7:32. Thomas' comments seem indirectly to support my view of Mark's ambivalence about the demonic aetiology of disease, and, particularly, about possession versus attack.

97 In that particular example, the word 'immediately' would be inappropriate in a medical account. Corrington, *'Divine Man'*, p.223.

98 Rhoads and Michie, *Mark as Story*, p.44.

their fees, may represent the practices of the times, and reflect what Mark's contemporary society believed of physicians.[99]

1.7.1 Touch

Although simple touch was regarded as rare in Hellenistic healing, the verb ἅπτομαι (to touch) is used on many occasions in Mark's gospel. It may reflect the widespread belief that healing ability resided in certain objects and people, and was activated by touch, power being conveyed from the healer to the sick person. The idea that Jesus was aware of power draining from him when the woman touched his clothes (5:30) is also common in pagan healing descriptions of the time.[100]

But Mark does not always mention touch by Jesus. Bartimaeus' sight was restored without reference to Jesus touching him (10:52). The man with the withered hand (3:5) was told to stretch out the hand, and healing was apparently performed by word only; it has been suggested that perhaps Mark depicts the healing without touch, so that, technically, no *work* was performed on the Sabbath.[101] In the episode 2:5-11, Mark may imagine it having been difficult in an overcrowded house for Jesus to touch the paralysed man, or may not feel it necessary to comment on it, in the high-context milieu in which Mark's gospel was written, where not all detail required to be supplied.[102] As the man's sins were forgiven by a word from Jesus, however, it may be that Mark is depicting the man being healed physically also by a word.

Mark makes no comment about the religious implications of Jesus touching the man with leprosy (1:41) and thereby becoming unclean himself (Lev. 13:45-46). Perhaps Mark's readers were to understand that Jesus would not be rendered unclean by touching leprous skin, as cure would be instantaneous, but more probably, Mark is depicting Jesus' mercy and holiness as being more powerful than the uncleanness

---

99 Tob. 2:10 and Sir. 38:15. Eve, *Jewish Context*, p.357, suggests that the 'physicians' in Mark may have been folk-healers. See Chapter 2, *2.2.1*.

100 Lalleman, 'Healing by Mere Touch', pp.355-61. Aune 'Magic', p.1536. Gundry, *Mark*, p.280, points to 2 Kgs. 13:20-1, where a dead man revives on touching Elisha's buried bones. Guelich, *Mark 1-8:26*, pp.62, 147.

101 Witherington, *Gospel of Mark*, p.98. It seems to me highly unlikely that Mark would portray Jesus putting that consideration before the need to heal the man.

102 B.J. Malina, 'Reading Theory Perspective: Reading Luke-Acts', in Neyrey (ed.), *Social World of Luke/Acts*, pp.19-20. High-context societies are ones where people have been socialised into shared ways of perceiving and acting; therefore much can be assumed, and texts are sketchy and impressionistic. The Bible, and other writings from ancient Mediterranean peoples, fit this high-context profile.

from disease.[103] There is considerable evidence of Jesus crossing boundaries in healing, here, by touching the unclean man, and also by condoning the actions of the woman with menorrhagia touching his clothes. Theissen draws attention to more profound boundary crossing in Jesus' healings.[104]

Mark also uses the word ἐπιτίθημι 'to lay hands on' in healing (e.g. 6:5). One request for Jesus to lay his hands on a sick person came from Jairus, who asked Jesus to do so in order to save his daughter (5:22). Mark also portrays Jesus taking sufferers by the hand to help them up (Peter's mother-in-law, 1:31, Jairus' daughter, 5:41, the boy with epilepsy, 9:27). Again, Jesus is depicted taking in his arms, and laying his hands on, the children brought to him (10:13-16), so Jesus' touch was, at least in that instance, a form of blessing, and may have been on the other occasions. It was his disciples, not Jesus, whom Mark portrays healing by anointing with oil (6:13), a recognised technique in healing in the ancient world, and found elsewhere in the New Testament (e.g. Lk. 10:34; Jas. 5:14).[105] Perhaps this is a subtle reminder by Mark that only Jesus' power of healing was such that he required minimal touch only.

There is more significant healing activity by Jesus in Mark's two pericopae, 7:32-35 and 8:23-25, which are similar to each other in their detail, different to the other healing narratives in Mark, and not recorded in Matthew or Luke. In healing the deaf-mute man (7:32-35), Jesus put his fingers in the man's ears, spat, and touched the man's tongue with his saliva. He looked up to heaven, 'sighed', presumably in prayer, and then used the Aramaic word '*ephphatha*'. This account is sometimes cited as close to the spells found in the *Papyri Graecae Magicae*.[106] The

---

103 M.J. Borg, *Conflict, Holiness and Politics in the Teachings of Jesus* (New York: Mellen, 1984) e.g. p.135.

104 Theissen, *Miracle Stories*, p.111. The boundaries crossed included rule-breaking of taboos about healing, e.g. on the Sabbath. Loader, 'Challenged at the Boundaries', p.45, asserts that Mark is radical in his presentation of Jesus' setting aside tradition and Law, but that he portrays Jesus as more conservative in healing.

105 Wells, *Language of Healing*, p.75, mentions its use in the Asclepieon at Cos, as a physical treatment. She notes, p.128, that the disciples would not have used methods of which Jesus did not approve.

106 So J.M. Hull, *Hellenistic Magic and the Synoptic Tradition* (London: SCM, 1974) pp.76, 82-83. Guelich, *Mark 1-8:26*, pp.395-96, rightly emphasises that the important point is that Mark translates the word, so that it is not to be seen as a magical incantation. In support of 'magical' overtones, Sanders, *Jesus and Judaism*, pp.166-67, suggests that Mark's account of Jesus 'losing his senses', when his family wanted to take him home (3:20-30), might refer to an altered state of consciousness, a 'magical state' which healers used in imitation of the madness they were trying to heal. I believe

two-stage healing of the blind man (8:23-25) involved Jesus putting saliva on the man's eyes, and touching the eyes.[107] The two narratives form a block of material, commonly interpreted as Mark using physical healing to highlight the spiritual blindness and deafness of his disciples; the stories are followed immediately by Peter's confession at Caesarea Philippi, Jesus' transfiguration and theophany, and, later, the complete and immediate healing of blind Bartimaeus. Even in the two healings of blindness, however, we note that Mark keeps the narrative credible.

Also, it is important that only in Mark's gospel is an initially incomplete healing by Jesus described; Guelich suggests that this indicates a physician's cure rather than a miracle, i.e. that Mark wishes to portray Jesus as the 'Great Physician' here.[108] It seems to me more significant that Mark is not averse to showing Jesus' failure to achieve immediate success in healing, in keeping with his portrayal of a fully human Jesus.

In summary, Mark portrays Jesus touching, or laying his hands on, suppliants, in a way that seems the natural action of a healer who was not using magical means; in only two healings did Jesus undertake more complex actions, in one of which he was not initially successful.

1.7.2 Words

In a world where the power of words was very important (e.g. in Graeco-Roman rhetoric, and in the incantations of magical formulae), Mark depicts Jesus speaking to the suppliant (e.g. 1:41; 2:5; 3:5; 5:34, 41; 8:22-26); that is, he emphasises Jesus' awareness of the need for communication between the healer and the suppliant. The words were often to integrate the healed person back into society, from which he had been excluded by the disease.[109] Thus, the man whose leprosy was

---

that a more natural reading of that episode would be that his family misunderstood Jesus' mission, and thought that they were acting pastorally.

107 The use of saliva is common in Graeco-Roman descriptions, e.g. Tacitus, *Histories* 4.81, where Vespasian healed a blind man; Pliny, *Natural History* 28.37-8, records its healing properties. Guelich, *Mark 1-8:26*, p.395, notes that it was considered therapeutic in both Graeco-Roman and Jewish worlds, although Kee, 'Magic and Messiah', p.137, who notes that it is not mentioned as an agent of healing in Hellenistic or Roman periods, or in Jewish literature, believes that Jesus was here using saliva as a challenge to the Jewish purity laws. In other circumstances, spitting in the other's face would have been interpreted as an insult. See Chapter 5, *2.4.1*.

108 Guelich, *Mark 1-8:26*, p.433.

109 Myers, *Binding*, p.146; Wright, *Jesus and Victory*, pp.191-96; Wenham, 'Christ's Healing Ministry', pp.122-23, all stress Jesus' healing as primarily restoring social wholeness, which had been denied to the sick. Eve, *Jewish Context*, p.352, notes that Jesus told the healed person to 'network' with others.

cleansed was commanded to show himself to the priest (1: 44); several healed people were sent home (2:11; 8:26); the man from Gadara was to tell his people of the mercy of the Lord (5:19-20). Also, Jesus told the woman with menorrhagia in front of the crowd that her faith had made her well, so that it was clear to the crowd that she was no longer unclean (5:34); and the parents of the dead girl were told to feed her (5:43), presumably as a sign of her return to normality. The interchange with the father of the epileptic boy (9:23-24) demonstrates Jesus' compassion and help to the man, as well as to his son. These words in Mark's accounts of Jesus' healings are often overlooked, but are extremely important in the overall restoration of the person to normal life in society. They make all the more poignant Mark's account of Jesus' cry of dereliction on the cross (15:34), where Jesus is portrayed as experiencing alienation from God.

In exorcisms, Jesus rebuked the demons in a manner that was exceptional only in that he used his own words of command (1:25; 5:8; 9:25), rather than using incantations based on famous powers from the past.[110] The expelled spirits, as in pagan descriptions, often made their presence felt; both the victims of epilepsy suffered *grand mal* seizures as the unclean spirits departed (1:26; 9:26), while in 5:13, the spirits had a devastating effect on the swine.[111] The spirits addressed Jesus as the 'Holy One of God' (1:24, in the Jewish synagogue), and 'Son of the Most High God' (5:7, in Gentile territory, and in keeping with the Gentiles' polytheism). To know one's opponent's name and identity was understood to give one an advantage over him, but Guelich points out that a demon's use of the exorcist's name was rare in pagan stories, and suggests that it was, rather, acknowledgement of Jesus' deity.[112] In the healing of the Syrophoenician woman's daughter (7:25-30), the exorcism was at a distance, so Mark reports only the end result, and instead, focuses on Jesus' discussion with the woman (7:27), showing

---

110 Twelftree, *Jesus the Exorcist*, p.386, says that Jesus was not unique in his praxis of exorcisms; and Aune, 'Magic', 1532-37, rejects the idea of a gulf between the 'powerful words' of Jesus and the magical incantations of others.

111 Twelftree, *Jesus the Exorcist*, p.96, suggests that both Mark and Luke dumb down the violent departure of a demon, a common theme both in Jewish exorcisms, and pagan ones, e.g. Josephus, *Ant.* 8.46-49, describing Eleazar's exorcism in the name of Solomon, and Philostratus, *Life of. Apollonius* 4.20, describing the throwing down of a statue by an exorcised demon. There seems no evidence of Mark trying to reduce the violence of the expelled demon.

112 Twelftree, 'EKBALLW TA DAIMONIA', p.374; Yamauchi, 'Magic or Miracle?', pp.134-35. Only in 5:1-20, did Jesus reply by asking the name of the spirits (5:9). Guelich, *Mark 1-8:26*, p.57.

that healing (and, so, salvation), which in the Old Testament was to be first for Israel, and then for the Gentiles, would be for all people together (v.29).[113]

So, Mark depicts Jesus speaking to the suppliants, often with words that help reintegrate the healed person back into society, and in exorcism, using his own words of command.

1.7.3 Prayer

Although Mark makes it clear that Jesus did take his prayer life seriously (1:35; 6:46; 14:22, 32, 36), and pointed out to his disciples the value of prayer in healing (9:29), Mark portrays Jesus as confident of his powers of healing when these were required. In the healing situation, he did not need to come before God as suppliant in order to heal. It is noticeable that Mark only once mentions Jesus possibly praying at the moment of healing (7:34), in contrast to the Jewish miracle workers, who were exceptional men of prayer (e.g. Hanina ben Dosa, *b. Ber.* 34b).

Kahl, whose interest is in the structural analysis of miracle narrative, has suggested a scheme for classifying the role of miracle healers. His analysis is helpful, particularly when we come to compare what the different biblical writers consider took place at miracle healings. Kahl describes three possible ways in which the divine power to heal may be applied; the healer may be a bearer of numinous power, when he can engage successfully in healing directly in his own power; he may be a mediator of numinous power, when he mediates the bearer's power to heal; or he may be a petitioner of numinous power, when he activates the bearer's power through prayer. In Mark's gospel, Jesus is depicted clearly as the bearer of this power in healing.[114] In subsequent chapters, we will see how the other ancient writers view the numinous power of healing.

1.7.4 Healing at a Distance, and Healing Gentiles

Healing from afar was recognised in the ancient world as being a relatively rare feat, and usually evidence that the healer was a prophet.[115] In addition to distance, the Syrophoenician child's healing (7:25-30) is one of probably four examples of healing outside the boundaries of

---

113 Hurtado, *Mark*, pp.115-16.

114 W. Kahl, *New Testament Miracle Stories in their Religious-Historical Setting. A Religiongeschichtliche Comparison from a Structural Perspective* (Göttingen: Vandenhoeck & Ruprecht, 1994) pp.76-79, 222.

115 Kolenkow, 'Relationships', p.1484.

Israel in Mark's gospel, the others being of the psychotic man from Gadara (5:1-20) where much of the narrative imagery of the swine is related to non-Jewishness,[116] the deaf man in the region of the Decapolis (7:31-37), and the blind man in Bethsaida (8:22-26).[117] Mark, in highlighting these occasions when Jesus was in Gentile territory, or in contact with Gentiles, shows healing as an important activity by which Jesus bridged the divide between Jew and Gentile, another form of boundary crossing (see *1.7.1*).

1.8 Conclusion

Although to read what lies on the surface may be to misread a gospel, it is as important to read the lines as to read between the lines, especially with regard to healing. Mark's healing narratives portray Jesus using the simplest methods found in pagan and Jewish healing stories. By demonstrating this simplicity, Mark emphasises Jesus' great power in healing; it needed no magical devices, and could heal all the diseases with which Jesus was confronted, in Gentiles as well as Jews. Although the authority shown in the healings is portrayed as unique, Mark seems to regard Jesus' healing techniques as unusually simple, rather than themselves unique. He depicts Jesus speaking to the sick people he healed, seeking to restore them to social life, as well as to health. I am aware, that in considering the miracle stories from this realistic perspective, I have read my own (medical) understanding into Mark's narrative. This puts an unusual slant on Jesus' healing miracles. In defence, I would point out that there is no reading of ancient documents that is without presuppositions.[118]

2 Mark as a Theologian, and his Use of Jesus' Healing

Until the beginning of the twentieth century, it was believed that Mark's gospel was simply an account of the historical Jesus' ministry, with little theological profundity. In 1901, Wrede opined that Mark's gospel was an early Christian apology to explain why Jesus was recognised as

116 Guelich, *Mark 1-8:26*, p.288; Witherington, *Gospel of Mark*, p.178.

117 Thomas, *Devil, Disease*, p.149, points out that Jesus performed this miracle in the vicinity of Caesarea Philippi (8:27), and returned to Galilee only later (9:30). France, *Mark*, p.301, notes that, whether or not Sidon is omitted from both 7:24, 31, Jesus was in Gentile territory for both of these healings. M. Bockmuehl, 'Halakhah and Ethics in the Jesus Tradition', in Barclay and Sweet (eds.), *Early Christian Thought*, p.270.

118 E.g. Hemer, *Book of Acts*, p.443, draws attention to the post-Enlightenment presuppositions about miracles.

Messiah only *after* Easter, and his work has been hugely influential in reinstating Mark as a theologian.[119] Eschatology, Christology, and discipleship are considered Mark's main theological interests,[120] but his concerns about faith are also important in healing.

We have seen that Mark portrays Jesus' healing as much more than an illustration for religious instruction, and certainly he does not regard it as romantic fiction, as is found frequently in writings about healing in the world of the time.[121] Although the various form-critical categories that have been suggested for the healing stories are not relevant to this study, it is notable that there is considerable variation in the central point of the narratives, many being Christ-centred (e.g. 2:1-12), others opposition-centred (3:1-6), and some suppliant-centred (10:46-52). There are also many theological purposes to which Mark puts the healing stories; different narratives emphasise different points, for instance, healing on the Sabbath, healing and forgiveness, and the importance of faith. The stories may be commonplace, but not their Christological and eschatological context and interpretation.[122]

In this section, Mark's theological themes of eschatology, discipleship, faith and Christology will be considered in relation to healing.

2.1 *Eschatology*

Mark's eschatology is related to his apocalyptic view that God's supremacy on earth will be established over the forces of evil, led by Satan. His gospel is about the fulfilment within history of the promises of God; through Jesus' death on behalf of many, a new covenant is established (14:22-24). Most theologians have regarded Jesus' healings as unique *because* of their eschatological message.[123] Mark's emphasis is on the Kingdom of God, which is glimpsed by the healed and the crowd in the healing narratives, so something of Mark's eschatological view can be seen in these stories. This will be discussed further when

---

119 Witherington, *Gospel of Mark*, p.49. W. Wrede, *The Messianic Secret* (orig.1901; ET; Cambridge/London: J. Clarke & Co., 1971); Tuckett (ed.), *Messianic Secret.*

120 E.g. Guelich, *Mark 1-8:26*, p.xxxviii.

121 E.g. Kee, *Miracle in Early Christian World*, pp.252-89.

122 C.K. Barrett, *The Holy Spirit and the Gospel Tradition* (Philadelphia: Fortress, 1947) p.57.

123 C.L. Blomberg, 'The Miracles as Parables', in Wenham and Blomberg (eds.), *Gospel Perspectives,* 6, p.348, concludes that they are evidence of 'God's sovereignty breaking in upon the confusion of this world'.

comparison is made between Mark and Luke with respect to eschatology and healing (see Chapter 6, *1.3*).

There were major developments between Jesus' ministry and the writing of Mark's gospel, of which the most important was the growth of awareness that Jesus was both Messiah and Lord, an integral part of the Godhead. The apparent delay in the Parousia may also have influenced Mark's view of the Kingdom of God, so that God's reign was to remain partly hidden until the eschaton. A factor that has been suggested as having affected Mark's perspective was that he had a knowledge of the letters of Paul; for instance, Martin considers that, by dramatising Jesus' life (particularly with respect to healing), Mark is addressing Paul's over-emphasis on the heavenly Christ at the expense of Jesus' earthly reality and history.[124] There are similarities between Mark and Paul's eschatological views (see Chapter 6, *1.5*), but the objection to the idea of Mark interpreting Paul is that there is no clear evidence in Mark's gospel that he had any knowledge of Paul and his letters.[125]

2.2 *Discipleship*

Mark's concern about discipleship has an important effect on his account of the gospel. Although it is unclear whom he considers as Jesus' disciples, the Twelve, or a wider group of followers, including Bartimaeus and the women at the cross (whom he depicts in a more positive light), Mark describes Jesus, in commissioning the Twelve both to preach and to heal (3:14-15), laying the foundation for apostolic healing. The usual theological view of the sequence of Jesus healing a blind man before and after Peter's confession is accepted as demonstrating the imperfect nature of the disciples' understanding of Jesus as Messiah.

The reason for the Twelve being portrayed by Mark as stupid has been debated. One theory is that it is polemical, so that the disciples act as a foil to believers such as Bartimaeus.[126] Other scholars have considered that it is pastoral, that Mark may be warning of the

---

124 R.P. Martin, *Mark: Evangelist and Theologian* (Grand Rapids: Zondervan, 1973) pp.160-61. W.R. Telford, *The Theology of the Gospel of Mark* (Cambridge: CUP, 1999) pp.164-69.

125 Marcus, 'Mark–Interpreter of Paul', pp.473-87. C.G. Kruse, *New Testament Models for Ministry. Jesus and Paul* (Nashville: Nelson, 1983) p.42.

126 Weeden, 'Heresy that Necessitated Mark's Gospel', pp.89-91. Witherington, *Gospel of Mark*, pp.54-56, considers that the picture of the disciples *is* polemical, but that the polemic seems to be at least partly a consequence of the apparent motif of secrecy.

difficulties and pitfalls of discipleship to the early church,[127] or to encourage others that even the disciples could become followers. It seems, from our knowledge of Mark's presentation of Jesus' healing, that the last idea is most likely; that Mark is depicting the disciples being 'healed' gradually by Jesus. Thus, the Twelve, 'blind' to the full meaning of Jesus as Messiah, were initially able to preach and heal (6:13), subsequently failed as followers (e.g. 9:19; 14:27-29), but recognised and regretted their failures (e.g. 14:72), and Mark implies in 14:28 and 16:7, that Jesus' faith in them would allow them to succeed as his trusted followers.

In view of Mark's presentation of Jesus' healing, it is considered that Mark's depiction of the Twelve is more likely to be pastoral than polemical, with Jesus continuing to trust them (and, so, other followers) in spite of their failures.

2.3 Faith

Marshall points out that faith is one of Mark's basic theological concerns;[128] it appears in Jesus' programmatic command (1:15), and Mark highlights it throughout the gospel (e.g. 4:40; 6:6; 10:52; 11:22-25).

The importance of faith is particularly clear in the healing narratives.[129] Often, faith is assumed, for instance, in the healing summaries where sick people were brought to Jesus (e.g. 1:32). Sometimes it is overt, e.g. 'if you choose, you can make me clean' (1:40); 'if I touch him, I will be made well' (5:28). Witherington understands the faith of the woman there is defective, involving belief in magical power, but this perception is challenged, and appears to me to be overcritical.[130] In the story of the boy with epilepsy, whom the disciples failed to heal, Mark indicates Jesus castigating the lack of faith of both the disciples and the boy's father, as the father was part of the

---

127 Telford, *Interpretation of Mark*, pp.35-36.

128 C.D. Marshall, *Faith as a Theme in Mark's Narrative* (SNTSMS 64; Cambridge: CUP, 1989), p.1.

129 Telford, *Theology of Mark*, p.100. Cairns, *Faith that Rebels*, p.16, emphasises that the faith of the suppliant is essential for Jesus to heal. Theissen, *Miracle Stories*, pp.129-32, and Guelich, *Mark 1-8:26*, p.85, consider that faith that preceded miracles separated the miracles of Jesus from the miracles of his contemporaries. Dunn, *Jesus Remembered*, p.692, notes that most references to faith in the synoptic gospels are in relation to miracles, and believes that synergism between the faith of the suppliant and Jesus' healing power was envisaged.

130 Witherington, *Gospel of Mark*, p.187. E.g. Warrington, *Jesus the Healer*, p.65.

crowd (9:19). It seems that Mark portrays Jesus then offering the father a second chance of faith (v.23), which the father accepted (v.24). In 6:3-6, the faithless were apparently not healed (and Mark's negative opinion of them is indicated by his off-hand comment about what was a significant miracle, that is, that Jesus did heal a few sick people by laying his hands on them). Theologians from the time of Fridrichsen have interpreted Mark's comment here as meaning that Jesus was unable to help people who did not recognise their need for help.[131]

Very often in Mark's gospel, the actual object of faith is not defined. Sometimes, it might be faith in Jesus' ability to heal. Marshall distinguishes between belief, which he defines as involuntary, and trust, which he understands as voluntary, but in practice they are inseparable, as belief depends on a modicum of trust.[132] Harvey considers that Mark uses many of the healing narratives as lessons in faith in a broader theological sense;[133] for instance, Bartimaeus (10:46-52) showed theological faith, as the physically blind man who 'saw' Jesus as Messiah, when he pleaded 'Jesus, Son of David, have mercy on me', *before* he made his request for physical sight. This story is placed soon after the overtly Christological material of Peter's confession and Jesus' transfiguration. Again, the children on whom Jesus laid hands in blessing (10:13-16) were brought because of their parents' faith, Jesus being recognised as God's emissary or representative. As the children were paradigmatic of the humble in society, this indicated considerable faith; the weak could only receive the benefits of the Kingdom of God as an unmerited gift from God.[134]

Redaction critics have regarded the significance of faith in Mark's gospel as paraenetic for the early church community for whom Mark is writing, but the faith depicted in Mark's account of the healing stories, and also in Jesus' teaching (e.g. 13:13), has a universal application.

Thus, faith, often not finely delineated, is important to Mark, and can be seen clearly in the healing narratives.

---

131 Fridrichsen, *Problem of Miracle*, p.79. (See Chapter 4, *2.1.7.*)

132 Marshall, *Faith as Theme*, p.55. Any physician is aware that, if a severely ill patient does not have trust in the physician's ability and willingness to struggle to heal, there is no chance of that physician treating him successfully.

133 Harvey, *Jesus and Constraints*, p.101. Telford, *Theology of Mark*, p.101, suggests that the faith was in Jesus' mission and person.

134 Hengel, *Charismatic Leader*, p.66, points out that this pericope fits well with Paul's justification by faith.

2.4 *Christology*

It is generally agreed that Christology is Mark's major theological concern. We have noted Mark's emphasis on Jesus as Son of God, (see *1.2*). In the healing stories, he reveals aspects of Jesus' identity, in the Christological titles (Son of God, Son of David), in Jesus' authority to forgive sin, and in his triumphs over sufferers' exclusion and death, but keeps Jesus' full identity veiled from the crowd (partly by the secrecy in the healing stories) until a complete understanding of his life and mission becomes possible.

There are several aspects of Mark's Christology, which are related specifically to healing. The most significant is Mark's presentation of Jesus as the bearer of numinous power, and recognised as such by the crowds, in the healing narratives, but there are other, related considerations.

2.4.1 Prophecy, Apocalyptic and Healing

Theologians have long been interested in the link between healing and prophecy in the gospels, and found in Old Testament Judaism (Chapter 2, *1.3*). Sanders and Aune both believe that the gospel-writers saw Jesus as a prophet; prophecy and miracles were closely associated in both Graeco-Roman and Jewish literature, and Kee demonstrates the continuity of Jesus' healing miracles with the Old Testament prophetic tradition.[135] Aune also regards the miracles, Jesus' prophetic actions (such as the entry into Jerusalem, and the Temple cleansing) and his proclamation of the imminent coming of the Kingdom of God, as all presented by Mark to legitimate Jesus' kingship, Messiahship, divinity.[136] It seems to me that Mark does not portray Jesus as *aiming* to legitimate his role as Messiah and Son of God; rather, the narrative (especially 1:11 and 9:7) allows the reader to draw his own conclusion.

Kolenkow emphasises the connection between the performance of miracles and the tradition of suffering, both of which were common among prophets; forecasting one's own untimely death was regarded as the greatest of all prophetic powers, and proof of not seeking benefit for oneself.[137] This fits with Mark's portrayal of Jesus (who predicted his

135 Kolenkow, 'Relationships', p.1471. Sanders, *Jesus and Judaism*, p.170. Aune, 'Christian Prophecy', p.406, regards Mark, along with other early Christians, as accepting Jesus as the definitive eschatological Mosaic prophet. Kee, *Miracle in Early Christian World*, pp.147-54.

136 Aune, 'Christian Prophecy', p.413.

137 A.B. Kolenkow, 'Paul and his Opponents in 2 Corinthians 10-13. *Theioi Andres* and Spiritual Guides', in L. Bormann, K. del Tredici and A. Standhartinger (eds.), *Religious*

violent death on several occasions, e.g. 8:31; 9:12; 10:45; 12:8; 14:8) as both a healer and a sufferer for the world's sins; the gospel, after the major emphasis on Jesus' healing, reaches its climax with his suffering and death.

Kee believes that, particularly in Mark, Jesus' healing follows Second Temple Judaism's apocalyptic tradition.[138] Although the story of Jesus' temptations is vestigial in Mark (1:12-13), the reader is to suppose that Jesus had divine power stronger than Satan's. Again, in the account of the Beelzebul controversy, Mark presents Jesus as working by the power of the Holy Spirit, which was more powerful than the power of Satan (3:29).[139] The *Papyri Graecae Magicae* demonstrate that the binding of the demon, then the plunder of his property, was a common motif in dealing with demons in antiquity; this weakens Twelftree's suggestion that Jesus was the first to make the connection between exorcism and the eschatological battle against Satan.[140]

Thus, Mark's awareness of, and subscription to, apocalyptic tradition, and his understanding of the healing and suffering roles of a prophet are means of his demonstrating Jesus as the eschatological prophet-Messiah.

2.4.2 'Divine Man' Christology, Corrective Christology and Healing

The concept of θεῖος ἀνήρ (TA) as applied to Jesus in his miracle working, was debated intermittently during much of the twentieth century (see Chapter 2, *2.1.2*). Bultmann regarded Mark's Christology as having developed from the TA concept (summarised as unusual lineage, miracles, eloquence, suffering, and, sometimes, escaping death).[141] The evidence in Mark's gospel of unusual lineage was

---

Propaganda and Missionary Competition in the New Testament World (NovTSup 74; Leiden: Brill, 1994) p.352. Kolenkow, 'Relationships', p.1494.

138 Kee, *Miracle in Early Christian World*, p.159-63.

139 Twelftree, *Jesus the Exorcist*, p.107, thinks that Mark portrays both Jesus and the Jewish exorcists as sharing the same source of power. C.C. Caragounis, 'Kingdom of God, Son of Man, and Jesus' Self-Understanding, Part 2', *TynBul* 40 (1989) 230, and Harvey, *Jesus and Constraints*, p.109, both disagree with that view.

140 E.g. *PGM* IV.3007-86. A. Deissmann, *Light from the Ancient East. The New Testament Illustrated by Recently Discovered Texts of the Graeco-Roman World* (ET; London: Hodder & Stoughton, 1910) pp.306, 370, n.5. Twelftree, *Jesus the Exorcist*, pp.227-28, considers that the battle had two stages; Satan bound at the beginning of the eschaton, and destroyed finally at the end. (See Chapter 6, *2.1.*)

141 Bultmann, *Theology of New Testament*, 1, pp.130-31, designated this divine-man (TA) Christology, regarded as mainly a *theologia gloriae*.

provided by God's affirmation of Jesus as his son at baptism (1:9-11)[142] and at transfiguration (9:7), both referring back to *Jewish* sources (Ps. 2:7; Isa. 42:1), as well as by the *pagan* centurion's words at his crucifixion, 'Truly this man was a Son of God' (15:39). It was a common early-twentieth-century idea that Mark presented Jesus largely as a healing Messiah, Son of God (that is, TA Christology), and some theologians have continued this perception.[143]

Most scholars, from the 1960s onwards, have considered that this was too simple a representation of Mark's Christology.[144] Many have believed, rather, that Mark allows the disciples and crowds to understand that Jesus was a TA, then demonstrates subtly that Jesus was a suffering Messiah, who had to die before God's Kingdom could be realised on earth. This is 'corrective Christology'; that is, the gospel has been written to correct the *theologia gloriae* Christology of the first half of Mark (and particularly related to Jesus' healing activities), in order to show the Messiah as the suffering Son of Man, the *theologia crucis*, particularly in the second half, but hinted at throughout.[145] This is considered to explain why miracles were not recorded in the second part of the gospel, since Mark is correcting the TA Christology of the miracle stories, and reshaping Christology to focus on the cross, where the Son of Man in weakness defeated Satan.

The 'corrective Christology' concept has been built upon from various angles. Redaction critics who regard the canonical gospel as reflecting the Markan community for which it was written, have considered that Mark's Christology is presented as corrective *for that community*, that is, that Mark's *theologia crucis* was at odds with the community's *theologia gloriae*, so this is a specific form of corrective Christology.[146] For instance, Weeden, who accepts this, combines it with the secrecy motif in Mark's accounts of Jesus' healings, to explain that the disciples' and others' blindness to the idea of a suffering Messiah was a teaching tool, to allow Mark's readers a full understanding of

142 Wrede, *Messianic Secret*, pp.72-81, regarded Mark depicting Jesus as *becoming* Son of God at his baptism.

143 E.g. Georgi, *Opponents of Paul,* pp.210, 213, 216.

144 Kingsbury, 'Divine Man', pp.245-46. Also E. Schweizer, *The Good News According to Mark* (ET; Atlanta: John Knox, 1970) pp.380-86.

145 C.M. Tuckett, *Christology and the New Testament. Jesus and his Earliest Followers* (Louisville: Westminster John Knox, 2001) pp.112-13, notes that the Son of *Man* figure, from Dan. 7, though not explicitly a suffering figure, is presented in the context of triumph after suffering; p.114, in Wis. 2-5, the Son of *God* is a righteous sufferer, so the two terms, Son of Man and Son of God, are somewhat ambiguous.

146 Telford, *Theology of Mark*, p.29.

Jesus as Messiah, which was not possible until after his death.[147] However, although redaction criticism has done much to draw attention to Mark as a theologian in his own right, I would agree with Burridge, who considers that it does not do full justice to Mark's account of Jesus' ministry.[148]

As discussed earlier, there is no evidence that the θεῖος ἀνήρ was a fixed concept in the ancient world. Boring makes the points that Mark's 'emphatic monotheism' would prevent him making use of a θεῖος ἀνήρ concept in his Christology, and that Mark thinks concretely and practically, with no abstract categories of 'divine' and 'human'.[149] I hope to have demonstrated the latter point by drawing attention to the way in which Mark's healing narratives are presented as true-to-life situations.

Nowadays, most disclaim the whole notion of corrective Christology. Telford points out that the miracles are not depicted in a negative light, as the theory suggests, but are used positively, and Theissen comments that for Mark to include sixteen miracle stories would be a clumsy way of warning his readers against belief in miracles.[150] Also, we have shown that Mark's miracle stories are not presented in a stylised way, which one would expect if their only purpose were later correction. Kingsbury rejects 'corrective' Christology, in favour of a positive view of Mark focussing on the whole meaning of Messiah, Son of God, which includes preaching, teaching and healing, but also includes his willing death on the cross, that is, 'Son of God' and 'Son of Man' complement one another throughout the gospel;[151] Mark emphasises that Jesus' death is 'as a ransom for many' (10:45). Most theologians consider that the theology of the cross is central to Mark's gospel.[152] Broadhead, who gives a succinct account of the twentieth-century history of the Christology of the miracle tradition in Mark, highlights that, although there were no miracle *stories* in the passion narrative, there were

---

147 Weeden, 'Heresy that Necessitated Mark's Gospel', e.g. p.91. Weeden, *Mark: Traditions in Conflict*, pp.159-68.

148 Burridge, *What Are the Gospels?*, pp.214-17.

149 M.E. Boring, 'Markan Christology. God-Language for Jesus?', *NTS 45* (1999) 457-59.

150 Telford, *Theology of Mark*, p.50. Theissen, *Miracle Stories*, p.294; Wells, *Language of Healing*, p.126, counts 19 healings in Mark. Guelich, *Mark 1-8:26*, p.151, rejects 'corrective Christology' on the grounds that Mark's portrait of Jesus in the miracle stories does not support it.

151 J.D. Kingsbury, *The Christology of Mark's Gospel* (Philadelphia: Fortress, 1983) pp.157-179, especially p.174.

152 E.g. Hooker, *Mark*, p.379; Räisänen, *'Messianic Secret'*, p.248. Edwards, *Gospel of Mark*, p.16. France, *Gospel of Mark*, p.660.

miraculous elements, indicating the presence of divine power associated with Jesus' death. This insight avoids a dichotomy between the Jesus of the miracles and the Jesus of the cross;[153] particularly, Mark's description of the tearing of the veil in the Temple (15:33) at the time of Jesus' crucifixion has the same effect as the healing miracles, in that it opens worship, and the Kingdom of God, to all.[154]

Thus, Mark portrays throughout his gospel that the Christ is both powerful and willingly weak for the sake of the world.

In summary, Mark is regarded today as a significant theologian, whose main concern is Christology. He uses both the healing stories and the passion narrative to present his subtle and comprehensive picture of a Christ, who possessed enormous power, but had to die in weakness to save the world.

3 Conclusion

Mark uses his considerable narrative powers to emphasise Jesus' authority in both healing and teaching, but the two activities are often separable in his gospel. This makes it easier to see that Mark portrays Jesus' healing itself as important, attracting the crowds, and antagonising the authorities. The healing stories are told in a matter-of-fact way, with attention to detail, by a writer with a good eye for both the suffering person and the reactions of the crowd. He demonstrates, though rarely mentions, Jesus' compassion in his healing, for instance, in the restoration of both father and son (9:22-24). Mark also shows Jesus himself as having human emotions (such as anger) in the course of these sharply-drawn narratives. By making the climax of his gospel Jesus dying, forsaken and in weakness,[155] Mark complements his picture of Jesus the miracle-worker; he portrays a Christ who was given all authority on earth, and yet came to suffer and die as ransom for the world's sins, in order to establish the Kingdom for all people, a goal greater than the glimpses of the Kingdom offered by his healings.

A distinct picture is created throughout Mark's gospel, of Jesus as *both* healer with authority, *and* as a willing victim/sufferer, as Mark

153 E.K. Broadhead, *Teaching with Authority. Miracles and Christology in the Gospel of Mark* (JSNTSup 74; Sheffield: Sheffield Academic Press, 1992) pp.13-21, 180-81, 184.

154 Broadhead, *Teaching with Authority*, p.181; Tuckett, *Christology and the New Testament*, p.115.

155 Hooker, *Mark*, p.379. France, *Gospel of Mark*, pp.610, 659, sees the Christological high point as 14:62, Jesus' reply 'I am' as marking Jesus' authority over those who presume to judge him.

depicts that both Jesus' authority and his undeserved suffering are required for his mission to succeed. He has shaped his gospel, so that Jesus' death in apparent failure, with only the pagan centurion understanding who he is, is the climax. If, as I accept, the ending of the gospel is at 16:8, then Mark leaves what follows to the imagination of believers.

Mark is the pioneer in gospel writing. His gospel is a deceptively simple, but very profound, statement of the material he wants to present. I have emphasised that Mark does not regard healings as merely illustrations of Jesus' teaching, although teaching is often by example, rather than by homily. There is no Sermon on the Mount/Plain, as in Matthew and Luke, yet Mark tells Jesus' message fully. He has assimilated the great findings of the very early church, that Jesus is not only Messiah, but also Lord, Son of God, an integral part of the Godhead, and Mark is grappling with the problem of explaining a mystery, which has been played out in the recent history of the first century, in a manner that his readers will understand. The healing stories from the tradition help to make his task possible. These stories, which illustrate both the faith and longing of sick suppliants, and the blindness and opposition of the authorities to Jesus, are used to bridge the complexity, in ways acceptable to his readers, of God sending his Son, fully human and fully divine, to live alongside his chosen people, who rejected him.

In the passion story, Mark may be portraying Jesus himself as the suppliant (as in the earlier healing stories), who undergoes unmerited suffering as the result of attack by evil. In this sense, Jesus' healing miracles lead us forward to God's great healing miracle, where Jesus, the suppliant on the cross, felt alienated from God, and cried in desperation to him, before his death and before the very early evidence of his resurrection. What is more certain is that, before the end of the narrative, Mark shows us that Jesus *had* accomplished his mission, to open the Kingdom of God to the whole world, signalled by the tearing of the temple veil, and the centurion's words. In these crucifixion vignettes, Mark demonstrates a subtle understanding of divine power, contrasted with the strength of Jesus' healing ministry, and seen at its most striking in Jesus' weakness at crucifixion. It is only after Jesus' death, raised by God and vindicated, that that power would eventually overcome even the supremacy of Rome.

Chapter 4

Luke and Healing

1 Luke's Portrayal of Healing

In this chapter, the portrayal of healing in Luke's gospel and in Acts will be studied, in an attempt to judge whether Luke's depiction of divine healing was significantly different from that of Mark. This is an important consideration in the debate as to whether views about healing diverged from the earliest days of the Jesus tradition, or whether there was a gradual systematic change during the first centuries after Jesus' ministry (see Chapter 6, *2.3*). Divergence in opinions about healing might be related to issues within the churches (for instance, cultural and social factors), to extraneous factors in the Graeco-Roman world, to different theological viewpoints (or personalities) of the writers, or even to changing beliefs of one writer.

1.1 Introduction

Luke's gospel is appropriate to consider after Mark's; it is accepted that Luke incorporated Markan material into his gospel, so comparison of Mark's gospel with Luke's should allow us to note change and/or progression of ideas. It is also accepted that the gospel of Luke and the book of Acts were written by one author,[1] that both books were planned as a unit,[2] and that the gospel was probably written before Acts (although this last is not a unanimous view).[3] The genre of the gospel seems to be similar to Mark's, and, less certainly, to Acts, where biography, history and theology occur in different proportions (see Chapter 6, *1.2.1*).[4]

---

1 R.C. Tannehill, *The Narrative Unity of Luke-Acts. A Literary Interpretation.* Vol.1. *The Gospel According to Luke* (Philadelphia: Fortress, 1986); I.H. Marshall, *The Acts of the Apostles. An Introduction and Commentary* (Leicester/Grand Rapids: InterVarsity/Eerdmans, 1980) p.19, n.1. He notes, p.44, that, from the second century, Luke was considered to be writer of both books.

2 E.g. R.H. Stein, *Luke.* The New American Commentary, Vol.24 (Nashville: Broadman, 1992) p.35.

3 Hemer, *Book of Acts,* p.405, thinks that the question is open.

4 F.W. Danker, *Jesus and the New Age. A Commentary on St. Luke's Gospel* (Philadelphia: Fortress, 1988) p.4, considers that there is a strong aretalogical ingredient in Luke's gospel.

A base to be established from which to study Luke's depiction of healing is with respect to the final writer of the gospel, the time of writing, his readership, and the gospel's relationship with the book of Acts. As with Mark's gospel, only the canonical version of Luke's gospel is being considered, and 'Luke' is accepted as the writer. Like the situation in Mark's gospel, the writer of Luke's gospel is anonymous, although he does refer to himself in the prologue. In addition to a version of Mark's gospel, he had access to other materials, that is, the putative 'Q' (which Matthew also had) and 'L' (material which has survived only in Luke's gospel). It is acknowledged that these assumptions are being made without reference to the vast scholarship that lies behind them. Luke's considerable literary skills are clear; for instance, the classical Greek technique of the gospel prologue (Lk. 1:1-4) contrasts with the Septuagint style of much of the rest of his writing.[5] He uses historical signposts (e.g. Lk. 2:1-3; 3:1), although sometimes not entirely accurately (Acts 5:35-37); it is accepted, however, that he is writing theologically, and his historical detail may have been adapted to this purpose.

'Luke' is mentioned in Philemon 24 and 2 Timothy 4:11, and also in Colossians 4, where he is noted to be a Gentile (v.11), and styled 'the beloved physician' (v.14).[6] The early church assumed this to be Luke the writer, or, at the least, accepted that the 'we sections' of Acts were from the pen of Luke, a companion of Paul.[7] This has been much debated, but it is generally assumed that the writer Luke was at least a second-generation Christian, and certainly not an eyewitness of Jesus' ministry.[8] He may have been a Jewish or Gentile Christian, but the consensus is that he expected his readers (e.g. Lk. 1:3; Acts 1:1) to be

5 Marshall, *Acts*, p.18.

6 E.g. J.A. Fitzmyer, *The Gospel According to Luke (I-IX),* AB (New York: Doubleday, 1981) pp.8, 40, thought that the writer was the traditional Luke of Phlm. 24 *et al.*, but is less certain later, in J.A. Fitzmyer, *Acts of the Apostles. A New Translation with Introduction and Commentary,* AB (New York: Doubleday, 1997) p.50. Whether or not Luke was a physician will be discussed later.

7 F.F. Bruce, *The Acts of the Apostles. The Greek Text with Introduction and Commentary* (3rd ed.; Grand Rapids/Leicester: Eerdmans/Apollos, 1990) p.18, proposes that Luke wrote Acts in his later years, about events in which he was involved in his youth. Stein, *Luke*, p.23, suggests that Luke may have been with Paul for only a short time, and not written his books until 20 years later. R. Maddox, *The Purpose of Luke-Acts* (Göttingen: Vandenhoeck & Ruprecht, 1982) p.7, considers that Luke may have been, from time to time in his youth, a junior member of Paul's circle. There seems to be too much detail in the 'we passages' for these suggestions.

8 E.g. R.C. Tannehill, *Luke,* ANTC (Nashville: Abingdon, 1996) p.21.

mainly Gentile Christians,[9] or God-fearers converted to Christianity.[10] The targeted readership is significant, as Luke seemed to encourage and support Gentile readers, particularly in Acts (e.g. 13:46; 18:6; 28:28), although he was writing the story of Jesus' ministry and the subsequent church development as part of the history of God's covenant with the people of Israel.[11]

The date of writing is also of some importance, in the attempt to establish whether the early church had a uniform, evolving view of Christian healing, or if there were divergent outlooks on its significance from the beginning. Both Bock and Hemer believe that the gospel was written in the 60s, but it is more commonly accepted that Luke–Acts was written after AD 70, although Paul died around AD 61-65 (before the end of Nero's reign), and Luke does not comment on Paul's death.[12] The consensus dating, between AD 75-90,[13] which I accept, means that there was more than a decade between Mark and Luke's gospels, during at least part of which it is presumed that Luke had access to a version of Mark's gospel. If it is accepted that Luke planned the entire work from the beginning, then one can view as a whole his portrayal of Jesus' ministry, life, death and resurrection, the effects of Jesus' ascension and gift of the Holy Spirit to the early church, and his (Luke's) concern to show that the church, as the new Israel, came through God's grace to both Jew and Gentile.

In summary, Luke-Acts is presumed for this study to have been written by one final writer as two volumes of a planned work, some time after the destruction of the Temple, so ten years, at least, after a version

---

9 D.L. Bock, *Luke 1:1-9:50*, BECNT (Grand Rapids: Baker, 1994) p.6; Fitzmyer, *Luke I-IX*, p.42, thinks that Luke was a Gentile Christian, but not a Greek. L.T. Johnson, *The Writings of the New Testament: An Interpretation* (Rev. ed.; London: SCM, 1999) pp.59, 214; Stein, *Luke*, p.26, points out that Luke avoids Semitic expressions, and explains Jewish customs. Tuckett, *Luke*, p.148, refers to the gospel as the Gospel for Gentiles. Tannehill, *Luke*, p.25, however, considers that Luke writes for a mixed Jewish and Gentile church.

10 H.C. Kee, *Good News to the Ends of the Earth. The Theology of Acts* (London: SCM, 1990) p.51, points to the significantly large group of Gentiles attracted to the Jewish understanding of God as one, who became Christian 'God-fearers'. Tuckett, *Luke*, p.62, suggests that Luke himself was a God-fearer, though he admits that the category may not have formally existed at the time.

11 Johnson, *Writings of New Testament*, p.219.

12 Bock, *Luke*, 1, p.16; Hemer, *Book of Acts*, pp.403-404.

13 Danker, *Jesus and the New Age*, p.18; Fitzmyer, *Luke I-IX*, p.57; Tuckett, *Luke*, p.37. C.K. Barrett, *The Acts of the Apostles. A Shorter Commentary* (Edinburgh/New York: T. & T. Clark, 2002) pp.xxxvii-xxxviii, considers that Acts was written between AD 80 and 90.

of Mark's gospel, with which Luke was familiar. The work was probably written for Gentile Christians, and presents Luke's portrayal of salvation-history, in which such readers had an honoured place.

2 Luke's Gospel and Healing

Some of the underlying theological themes that influenced Luke's portrayal of Jesus' healing will be considered, and the essentials of Luke's account compared with those of Mark, to assess how Mark and Luke understood the significance of Jesus' healing ministry. This will be followed by Luke's portrayal of apostolic healings in the book of Acts, and a comparison with his gospel account.

2.1 Luke's Theological Concerns in Jesus' Healing

Certain of Luke's major theological concerns lie as background to his account of the themes of suffering and Jesus' healing, and highlighting these initially may give us more ready access to his perspective. It is recognised that concentrating on healing skews the perspective of Luke's theological emphases; also that, in concentrating on what is particular to him, it is easy to miss his total message, and so some of the theological points mentioned below are not unique to Luke, or to healing, but are emphasised by him in that situation.

2.1.1 Salvation History

Conzelmann first drew attention to the prominence in Luke's presentation of the idea of salvation history.[14] He considered that Luke portrays Israel seeking an eschatological Messiah up to, and including, the time of John the Baptist, that Jesus' ministry was the important middle time, and the church became the continuation of the true, believing Israel for both Jews and Gentiles. His hypothesis has been modified with respect to the exact phases of the history, and his further belief, that Luke substituted salvation history to deal with the delay in the Parousia, has been critiqued.[15] The concept of salvation history and

---

14 H. Conzelmann, *Die Mitte der Zeit* (orig. 1925; ET as *The Theology of St. Luke*; New York: Harper & Row, 1960).

15 C.M. Tuckett, *Luke* (Sheffield: Sheffield Academic Press, 1996) pp.35-36, p.48, suggests that there were only two divisions, that is, pre-Jesus, and Jesus plus the time of the church. J. Nolland, 'Salvation-History and Eschatology', in I.H. Marshall and D. Peterson (eds.), *Witness to the Gospel. The Theology of Acts* (Grand Rapids/Cambridge: Eerdmans, 1998) pp.64-67, considers that Conzelmann overplayed the delay in the

the recognition of Luke's acute awareness of the purpose of God were, however, major advances in understanding Luke-Acts. It allowed the perception that Luke was reassuring his readers, mainly Gentiles, that God, always reliable in keeping his promises, included them in salvation, while also demonstrating that Christianity was in continuity with Judaism.[16] The concept of salvation history also allows the idea that Luke is aware that Conzelmann's 'middle time', the time of Jesus' ministry, is in the past, as Luke is writing from the third epoch, so the Kingdom of God had already been proclaimed (Lk. 16:16). Tuckett puts it that for Luke, Jesus' healing brings the sinner into the Kingdom of God as a present, not a future, reality (e.g. 19:9).[17]

Salvation history is a very important theme in Luke's gospel.

2.1.2 Prophecy

The concept of salvation history helps to explain Luke's stress on the fulfilment of Old Testament prophecy. The healing of Elizabeth's barrenness (Lk. 1:7-25) is told as an echo of 1 Samuel 1:2-20; the raising of the widow's son at Nain (7:11-16) recalls Elijah and Elisha's miracles (1 Kgs. 17:17-24; 2 Kgs. 4:18-37), and was recognised by the crowd as confirming the rise of a new, great prophet; and the two disciples on the Emmaus road summed up Jesus as a prophet (24:19). Minear believes that Luke perceives Jesus as one prophet in a succession of prophets, and Luke has Jesus himself making clear that he was a prophet, in 4:18-19 (quoting Isa. 61:1-2 and 58:6), 4:24, and 13:34.[18] Luke uses the evidence of fulfilment of prophecy from the Old Testament to defend God's work in history, and to convince followers of the truth of the Christian faith.[19]

There has been considerable debate about how Luke uses the Jewish concept of the 'Spirit of prophecy', particularly in relation to works of power in healing. Turner's conclusion is that the Spirit of prophecy was not regarded as dissociated from works of power in Jewish thought before Jesus' ministry; the 'Messianic' passages, especially Isaiah 11:1-

---

Parousia as causing a crisis in Lukan thought; I.H. Marshall, *Luke: Historian and Theologian* (3rd ed.; Exeter: Paternoster, 1988) especially pp.77-79.

16 Tuckett, *Luke,* pp.63-64.

17 H. Conzelmann, *Acts of the Apostles. A Commentary on the Acts of the Apostles* (ET; Philadelphia: Fortress, 1987) p.xlv . Tuckett, *Luke*, pp.34-35,47.

18 P.S. Minear, *To Heal and to Reveal. The Prophetic Vocation According to Luke* (New York: Seabury, 1976) p.81. (See *3.5.*)

19 Johnson, *Writings of New Testament*, p.219. Stein, *Luke*, pp.37-38. Grundmann, 'δύναμαι, δύναμις', *TDNT,* 2, p.300, considers that Luke sees Jesus' Messiahship in terms of prophetic power.

4, tell of the Spirit of wisdom, understanding, counsel and might, so there is no separation of power from knowledge and prophecy there.[20] Also, importantly, 'fear of the Lord' (Isa. 11:2), envisages a strong ethical component in the Messianic Spirit of prophecy. To Luke, Jesus is the Messianic prophet, endowed with the Spirit of prophecy. Miracles are included in Luke 4:18-19, as part of Jesus' role as prophet–liberator, not merely announcing, but effecting, liberty.[21]

Related to the importance of prophecy is Luke's repeated use of δεῖ 'it is necessary' (18 times in the gospel, 24 times in Acts).[22] It indicates that certain unexpected events had to happen in order to fulfil scriptural prophecy, to allow God's salvation plan to be accomplished, and it demonstrates Jesus' perfect obedience to God. The risen Christ on the Emmaus road (24:26) summarised Luke's understanding of salvation history, 'Was it not necessary that the Messiah should suffer these things, then enter into his glory?'

Luke also emphasises that, in the scriptures, prophets were rejected by Israel, and suffered as a result, and he highlights the actions of the religious establishment in causing the rejection and suffering of the prophets (11:47-51), including Jesus, whose prophecies regarding his own rejection and death are frequent (e.g. 9:21-22; 12:49-50; 18:31-33; 20:13-15).[23] But Luke recognises that Jesus' healing might meet with doubt or rejection from others besides the religious establishment; for instance, when John the Baptist sent his messengers to ask Jesus if he were the Messiah (7:23), Jesus answered by pointing out his fulfilment of Isaianic prophecy (35:5-6) and of 1 Kings 5, and then commented on the likelihood of this not being acceptable.[24]

---

20 In the Old Testament, the Spirit of God acted as the channel of communication between God and Israel's leaders, and God was shown in acts of power and in revelation, Turner, *Holy Spirit and Gifts*, pp.3-4. M. Turner, *Power from on High: The Spirit in Israel's Restoration and Witness in Luke-Acts* (JPTSup 9; Sheffield: Sheffield Academic Press, 1996) p.118.

21 Turner, *Holy Spirit and Gifts*, pp.30-34. Turner, *Power from on High*, pp.132-33, p.224.

22 Stein, *Luke*, p.46; Tuckett, *Luke*, p.34.

23 Minear, *To Heal and to Reveal,* p.90. Johnson, *Writings of New Testament*, pp.224-25, believes that Luke depicts Jesus as a prophet like Moses, who was accepted, then rejected, by his people, and that the long central section of the gospel, the journey from Galilee to Jerusalem, recalls the wilderness journey of Moses and the Israelites.

24 Meier, *Marginal Jew*, II, pp.135-36, notes that this indicated John's doubts. Fridrichsen, *Problem of Miracle,* p.99, thinks that John may have been the mouthpiece of criticism of Jesus' healing. Stein, *Luke,* p.225, considers that Luke recognised that Messianic healing was unexpected to John.

2.1.3 Holy Spirit and Power

The term Spirit (or Holy Spirit) occurs seventeen times in Luke's gospel (although sometimes the 'spirit' mentioned is an evil spirit), compared with only six times in Mark.[25] This may indicate either Luke's special interest in the Holy Spirit, or merely his narrative style, but Luke is regarded as depicting that Jesus was endowed by God with the Holy Spirit at his baptism (3:22), and that this was the source of his power of healing.[26] The quotation of Isaiah 61:1-2 in Jesus' programmatic statement in Nazareth (4:18-19) allows us to assume Luke's perspective of the Messianic nature of Jesus' empowerment, which includes healing.[27]

Reference to the Spirit is much commoner in the birth narratives and Acts than in the main body of the gospel, however. It does occur as Jesus' promise to the disciples of the gift of inspired speech when they are persecuted after his death (12:12), and, again, at the crucifixion, he commits his Spirit back to the Father (23:46), but Luke rarely mentions the Spirit during Jesus' adult life.[28] So, while the view that Luke portrays Jesus working under the aegis of the Holy Spirit is accepted, the Holy Spirit does seem to be relatively understated during Jesus' ministry. This may be because Luke wishes to present the Holy Spirit as the most distinctive mark of the Christian in Acts, and the source of power for apostolic preaching and healing (perhaps this is an effect of Luke writing a second volume).

Teaching and healing are often regarded as inseparable in Luke's account of Jesus' ministry,[29] and these activities do seem to be closer in Luke's gospel than in Mark's. For instance, the crowd came both to hear Jesus' teaching and to be healed (5:15; 6:17-18),[30] and Luke reports the content of Jesus' teaching (e.g. 4:21-27; 6:20-49; 11:1-13) much more often than Mark (Chapter 3, *1.3.2*). Fridrichsen and Danker believe that

---

25 Stein, *Luke*, p.47.

26 J.B. Green, *The Gospel of Luke,* NICNT (Grand Rapids: Eerdmans, 1997) p.216; J.B. Shelton, *Mighty in Word and Deed. The Role of the Holy Spirit in Luke-Acts* (Peabody: Hendrickson, 1991) p.75.

27 Turner, *Holy Spirit and Gifts*, e.g. p.31.

28 Tuckett, *Luke*, p.36, believes that Luke regards the Spirit as covert in Jesus until his ascension, when he has physically departed from the earth. This would explain why it does not appear particularly in relation to healing.

29 Green, *Gospel of Luke,* pp.204, 263; Danker, *Jesus and the New Age*, p.111.

30 Stein, *Luke*, p.196. In Mark's reports of the same incidents, he either leaves vague why the crowds gathered (1:45), or portrays that they had come for healing (3:8-11).

Luke sees Jesus as the Great Benefactor.[31] Although 'doing' (good) is especially important to Luke (e.g. 8:21; 10:25, 28; 11:28), as will be seen from the reported prominence of Jesus' healing, Shelton considers that Luke sees Jesus' healing and inspired preaching as both wrought by the Holy Spirit, and both miraculous, so that it would be artificial to divide them. Fitzmyer believes that Luke's view of Jesus' God-given power is associated with the presence of the Holy Spirit, and it was under that guidance that Jesus taught, preached and healed.[32]

Kahl, from his structural analysis of miracle stories, notes that Luke attributes Jesus' healing ability to the Holy Spirit, the Power of the Most High (of 1:35), and although he sees the baptism story (3:22, 'this day I have begotten you') as at some tension with 1:35,[33] he considers both statements as serving, at one level, Luke's intention to emphasise that Jesus is less independent and self-sufficient in healing than he appears in Mark; the remark, 'the power of the Lord was with him to heal' (5:17), sums up Luke's view of the nature of Jesus' healing ability. During healing, Luke shows that God is the originator, and Jesus the mediator, of divine power.[34] These references to God as the source of Jesus' power are, Kahl believes, because Luke portrays Jesus as a (super-) prophet (e.g. 7:16; 24:19), more powerful than his Old Testament predecessors.[35] Both Fitzmyer and Kahl consider that this is different from Mark's understanding. Fitzmyer further suggests that, in Mark's gospel, the power given to Jesus refers only to the ability to perform miracles.[36] Although it seems to me unsafe to differentiate the nature of Jesus' power in Mark and Luke so definitely, it is true that Luke appears much more concerned with emphasising the power of God working in Jesus than Mark. This is not to underestimate the importance

---

31 Fridrichsen, *Problem of Miracle,* p.66. Danker, *Jesus and the New Age*, p.4, notes that Luke uses much of the cultural atmosphere of the Graeco-Roman benefactor, with Jesus as the Great Benefactor.

32 Green, *Gospel of Luke*, p.276; Shelton, *Mighty in Word,* p.78; Fitzmyer, *Luke I-IX*, p.523.

33 Kahl, *New Testament Miracle Stories*, p.80.

34 Fridrichsen, *Problem of Miracle*, p.79, opines that Luke considers Jesus had unlimited healing power from God, while J. Jervell, *The Theology of the Acts of the Apostles* (Cambridge: CUP, 1996) p.30-33, draws attention to Luke's emphasis, both in the gospel and in Acts, on Jesus' dependence on God, in healing and in all aspects of activity.

35 Kahl, *New Testament Miracle Stories*, pp.80-81, notes that the Old Testament prophets did not have their own numinous healing power, but had the ability to invoke God for help.

36 Fitzmyer, *Luke I-IX,* p.523.

of the power of the Holy Spirit to Luke (see *2.1.2*), but demonstrates a difference, noted also by these workers, between the two evangelists in respect of their theological ideas of Jesus' healing.

Achtemeier points to Luke's predilection for adding the crowd's reaction, which is usually to praise *God*; he considers that this reflects the Lukan reaction to miracles, to see God behind Jesus' activity, thereby acknowledging Jesus to be the one whom God has chosen.[37] Thus, the crowd gave glory to God (e.g. 5:26; 7:16; 13:17; 18:43).[38] The crowd are reported as being amazed at the 'majesty', μεγαλειότης, of God (a term unique to Luke in this context) when the boy with epilepsy was healed (9:43); and praising God for Jesus' δυνάμεις (19:37). The healed in Luke's gospel also praised God rather than Jesus (e.g. 5:25; 13:13; 17:15; 18:43), whereas in parallel stories in Mark's gospel (e.g. 2:12; 10:52), the person healed, and often the crowd, are not recorded as saying anything.

Luke does mention power in other healing situations. Although Luke and Mark both note that Jesus was aware of power emanating from him in the story of the woman with menorrhagia, only in Luke did Jesus comment on it (8:46), and Luke, but not Mark, mentions power going from Jesus when he was touched by sick people in one of the healing summaries (6:19).[39]

We see that the Holy Spirit is a term used frequently by Luke, but less during Jesus' ministry than before and after. It seems established that Luke sees Jesus' baptism, when he is anointed by God with the Holy Spirit, as the source of his healing power. Luke's concept of this power is somewhat different from Mark's, in that the power of God working through Jesus is emphasised in Luke's gospel. Thus, Luke has a different theological understanding of Jesus' power to heal, compared with that of Mark.

---

37 P.J. Achtemeier, 'The Lucan Perspective on the Miracles of Jesus: A Preliminary Sketch', in C.H. Talbert (ed.), *Perspectives on Luke-Acts* (Edinburgh: T. & T. Clark, 1978) pp.153-67.

38 Kahl, *New Testament Miracle Stories*, pp.80-83. Remus, *Jesus as Healer*, p.58, suggests that Jesus' healings are recorded as assurance of his identity and power as Son of God, and considers that the acclamation of God (rather than Jesus) by the healed and the crowd is evidence for this view.

39 V.K. Robbins, 'The Woman who Touched Jesus' Garment: Socio-Rhetorical Analysis of the Synoptic Accounts,' *NTS* 33 (1987) pp.509, 512; Theissen, *Miracle Stories*, p.135.

2.1.4 Jesus' Obedience to God

Luke, more than Mark, highlights the occasions when Jesus prays (though, as in Mark's gospel, Jesus does not pray during the performance of miracles). The teaching of the Lord's Prayer (Lk. 11:2-4) is not found in Mark, and on many occasions, Luke's Jesus withdrew to pray (4:42; 5:16; 6:12; 9:18, 28, 29; 10:21), mainly in solitude, often in the desert. This may be further evidence of Jesus' dependence on God, as his power has to be refreshed by prayer, so that Jesus is depicted as being subordinate, and obedient, to God.[40] Kahl suggests that this is part of Luke's understanding that Jesus was a great prophet, superior to Elijah and Elisha (who prayed at the time of their healing miracles).[41]

Tannehill considers that Jesus' perfect obedience to his father is a dominant theme in Luke's gospel. His obedience is obvious in the words from the cross, 'Father, into your hands I commend my spirit' (Lk. 23:46),[42] compared with Mark 15:34, 'My God, my God, why have you forsaken me?' A corollary is Luke's emphasis on Jesus' righteousness, and his innocence of the charges made against him; the thief stressed Jesus' innocence (23:41), and the centurion at the cross also identified this (23:47), and praised God.

Thus, Jesus' perfect obedience to God is more emphasised by Luke than by Mark.

2.1.5 Apocalyptic, Satan and Demons

The difference between the power of God and that of Jesus in healing in Luke's gospel, compared with Mark's, may be related to Luke's more acute awareness of the power of Satan. The Jewish apocalyptic worldview, of the struggle between good and evil, between God and Satan, is very clear in Luke's writings, where the cosmic power of evil is behind all opposition to God and his people.[43] Conzelmann suggests that Luke portrays Jesus' ministry as free from the influence of Satan,

---

40 Tannehill, *Luke,* p.104; C.M. Tuckett, *Christology and the New Testament. Jesus and His Earliest Followers* (Louisville, Kentucky: Westminster John Knox, 2001) p.143.

41 Kahl, *New Testament Miracle Stories*, p.83, considers that Luke sees Jesus in these prayer pericopae as the petitioner of numinous power.

42 Tannehill, *Luke,* p.347, considers that this episode is more theologically charged than Mark's. It reflects Wis. 2:12—3:9 (e.g. 3:1, 'the souls of the righteous are in the hands of God').

43 Garrett, *Demise of Devil,* p.37; Green, *Gospel of Luke*, p.198.

but although the name of Satan does not appear in the gospel until 10:18, a sense of evil surrounding Jesus is clearly depicted.[44]

Related to the apocalyptic outlook is Luke's concentration on demons. Demonic powers, as the devil or Satan, have a large role in illness in Luke's gospel, where healing is often regarded as 'release' from oppression or demons.[45] Garrett considers that Luke uses the idea of the demonised much more than Mark throughout his gospel.[46] This may explain why Mark mentions demons (or unclean spirits) only in the healing narratives, while Luke also depicts Jesus detailing the dangers of expelled demons (11:24-26).[47]

Danker suggests that Jesus is portrayed as having more mastery over demons in Luke's gospel than in Mark's,[48] for instance, Jesus exorcised a demon without it emitting a great cry (Lk. 4:35), as it did in Mark 1:26, and Luke comments that the convulsion accompanying that demon's expulsion did no harm to the man. Similarly, in Mark 9:26, the boy with epilepsy suffered a *grand mal* fit while Jesus was healing him, while Luke 9:42 only mentions a fit immediately *before* Jesus rebuked the demon. In the Beelzebub controversy, Luke, more than Mark (3:27), emphasises the strength and power of God against demons, with words such as 'armour', 'armed', 'castle', and 'overpowered' (11:21-22). The pericope also seems to demonstrate Luke more sharply opposed to a 'competing' miracle worker than Mark; 'Whoever is not with me is against me' (Lk. 11:23) may be directed at other competitors (a theme which is much more obvious in Acts). These examples relate to Luke's emphasis on the power of God, as well as on Luke's acute awareness of the opposing powers.

---

44 Conzelmann, *Theology of Luke*, e.g. p.16; Tuckett, *Luke*, p.35. Garrett, *Demise of Devil*, pp.57-59, considers that Satan plays a much more important role in Luke's writings than is commonly supposed.

45 Remus, *Jesus as Healer*, p.68. Meier, *Marginal Jew*, II, p.648, notes, however, that Luke mentions few exorcisms from his sources apart from those common to Luke and Mark.

46 Garrett, *Demise of Devil*, p.40, p.129, n.15. Bock, *Luke*, 1, p.430, n.11, however, thinks that Luke pays less attention to demons in the journey section, Lk. 9–19, than elsewhere.

47 J.A. Fitzmyer, *The Gospel According to Luke (X-XXIV)*, AB (New York: Doubleday, 1985) p.919, suggests that the risk of demons wandering (11:24), and re-inhabiting their victim, may be presented to caution Christians not to be over-confident of the defeat of evil. C.A. Evans, *Luke*, NIBC (Peabody: Hendrickson, 1991) p.185, suggests that the Jewish exorcists (11:19) might have cast out demons only temporarily.

48 Danker, *Jesus and the New Age*, p.112. (See Chapter 3, *1.7.2*.)

Angels feature in Luke's writings, especially in the birth stories, and in Acts (e.g. 5:19; 8:26); Tuckett comments that angels, indicating a heavenly hierarchy, may be another means of Luke emphasising God's power and authority.[49]

We can see that Luke considers that evil spirits play a more major role than they do in Mark's gospel.

2.1.6 Affliction and Possession

The debate as to whether the gospel writers distinguish demon-affliction from demon-possession was discussed in Chapters 1 and 3. With respect to Luke's views, the positions taken up by today's theologians are variable.[50] Bock believes that there is a difference between being sick and being possessed, and that it was important to Luke that Jesus' first healing miracle was an exorcism (4:33-37), to demonstrate at the beginning of his ministry Jesus' power over evil and Satan. Evans maintains that Luke's distinction between Jesus' healings and exorcisms is not sharp, since he (Luke) considers that demonic forces were behind most illnesses, and Green considers that Luke makes no difference between illness and possession, as both required liberation.[51] Fitzmyer believes that healing and exorcism are not always clearly distinguished in Luke (although they should be), but Luke merges them, because people, unable to ascribe a definite cause to any illness, attributed it to the spirit world.[52] He further suggests that, in discussing the subject now, it might be helpful to ascribe illnesses in the gospels to 'demon-sickness,' and so avoid a distinction.[53] I would accept the evidence of

---

49 An angel inflicted temporary dumbness on Zechariah (1:20), as discipline because of his disbelief. Whether or not the story of the angel strengthening Jesus in Gethsemane (Lk. 22:43-44) should be included will be discussed later (*2.3.5*). Tuckett, *Christology and New Testament*, p.27.

50 Some consider that Luke does distinguish between them, e.g. Stein, *Luke,* p.226; J. Nolland, *Luke 1-9:20,* WBC, Vol.35A (Dallas: Word, 1989) p.204. Others, e.g. Fitzmyer, *Luke I-IX,* p.545, think that Luke sometimes distinguishes between possession and illness (e.g. 7:21, 13:32), but relates the two closely. Thomas, *Devil, Disease*, e.g. p.227, considers that Luke, of all the New Testament writers, blurs most the lines of distinction between illness and demonic activity in general.

51 Bock, *Luke,* 1, p.430; C.A. Evans, *Luke,* p.77; Green, *Gospel of Luke*, pp.358, 521. Wells, *Language of Healing*, p.200, suggests that, in the accounts of Jesus healing the boy with epilepsy (Mk. 9:25-27; Lk. 9:42), Luke omits Mark's mention of Jesus taking the boy to lift him up, because Luke regards it as an exorcism.

52 Fitzmyer, *Luke I-IX,* pp.542-43; Bock, *Luke,* 1, p.416, points out that nowadays we have deliberately minimised the spirit world by the use of abstract terms, like 'fate'.

53 Fitzmyer, *Luke I-IX,* p.545. The gospel writers do not, however, regard all illness as due to demonic influence, see Yamauchi, 'Magic or Miracle?', pp.89-183.

several of the healing summaries (e.g. 4:40-41; 6:17-19; 7:18-23), that Luke, like Mark, does not differentiate healing and exorcism sharply.

This blurring would explain best the point that, in the treatment of the illness of Simon Peter's mother-in-law, whose fever was severe enough for her to be bed-ridden, Mark relates that, when Jesus took her by the hand, and lifted her up, the fever left her, and she served the disciples (1:29-31). In Luke's account (4:38-39), Jesus rebuked the fever, with the same therapeutic effect.[54] Mark's account is taken to indicate that Jesus healed her from a physical illness, by touch, while some writers consider that Luke shows Jesus exorcising the demon of fever, by rebuke.[55] Even if the two evangelists had different notions of what Jesus did (healing or exorcism) in this episode, their perceptions of what resulted from Jesus' actions were the same.

2.1.7 Binding, Release, Reversal

Perhaps related to Luke's emphasis on demons is his concept of binding, and the release that Jesus' ministry brought to suffering Israel. Bondage results from conditions other than disease and demon-possession; those requiring Jesus' care were extended in Luke's account to include all who were dependent on help beyond themselves. Sinners (7:37-50) and tax-collectors (19:1-10), as well as the poor, the captives, the blind and oppressed, were the dispossessed of Israel, and women had a high profile among them (e.g. 8:2).[56] 'Seeking and saving the lost' (19:10) sums up Jesus' healing and preaching activities in Luke; he portrays Jesus teaching that the ancients' assumption that sick and poor people were sinful, and the healthy and wealthy righteous, was wrong (e.g. 6:20-26), and that, rather, the reverse was true.[57] This theme of reversal is important to Luke (e.g. 1:46-53) where the outcasts, the poor and the ill responded to the good news of the Kingdom of God. They were most

---

54 Kee, *Miracle in Early Christian World,* p.204. Thomas, *Devil, Disease*, p.204, sees here a demon inflicting illness without implying demon possession.

55 Guelich, *Mark 1-8:26*, p.62.

56 I.H. Marshall, *The Gospel of Luke*, NIGTC (Exeter/Grand Rapids: Paternoster/Eerdmans, 1978) p.184, considers that Jesus' reading from Isaiah at the beginning of his ministry (4:18-19) refers to the release from debt in the Jubilee year (Deut. 15:1-18), 'the year of the Lord's favour' (v.19). Danker, *Jesus and the New Age*, p.106, notes that the theme of loosing the bonds is expanded in the Beatitudes. J.B. Green, 'Good News to Whom? Jesus and the Poor in the Gospel of Luke', in Green and Turner (eds.), *Jesus of Nazareth: Lord and Christ,* pp.59-74; C.A. Evans, *Luke,* p.168.

57 Tannehill, *Luke,* p.95, points out that the 'good news to the poor' was in tension with the belief in ancient Mediterranean society that the elite were those favoured by God and man.

aware of their needs, so they received God's mercy and forgiveness (e.g. 7:36-50). Jesus' saying (5:31-32), 'those who are well have no need of a physician. I have not come to call the righteous, but sinners to repentance', is paraphrased by C.S. Lewis, 'Christianity has nothing to say to people who do not know they have done anything to repent of, and who do not feel that they need any forgiveness'.[58]

We see Luke's stress on the concepts of binding, release and reversal in his descriptions of Jesus' care of sick people, and extended into the areas of social deprivation and sin.

2.1.8 Healing, Forgiving and Saving

Forgiving sins is part of Jesus' programme of release for prisoners (4:18), and is found in Luke's account both of healing (5:20) and in other situations (e.g. 7:48). Although Luke's Jesus specifically rejected the notion of relating sin to suffering (13:1-5), yet in the story (from Mark) of Jesus healing the paralysed man and forgiving his sins (5:17-26), illness and sin were closely linked. It may be significant that only here (v.26), Luke uses the word παράδοξα for miracles of healing.[59] Various writers point out that the sentence, 'Your sins are forgiven' (e.g. 5:20) is not meant by Luke as a divine passive form of speech (see Chapter 3, *1.3.3*); for instance, Stein maintains that Luke understands that God gave Jesus power to heal, so would also support Jesus' claim to forgive sins, and Jews would hardly object to God forgiving sins.[60] Priests could, and did, mediate God's forgiveness, by prescribing sacrifices and repentance with restitution; but at the least, their leaders would object to Jesus, not a priest, proclaiming forgiveness of sins simply by his words. The question, 'Who is this, who even forgives sins?' (7:49), confirms that Luke does not consider 'your sins are forgiven' (7:48) as a divine passive.

Although Luke in the gospel uses the word 'Saviour' for Jesus only in the birth stories (2:11), the concept of being saved occurs frequently.[61]

---

58 C.S. Lewis, *Mere Christianity* (London: Collins, 1956) p.37.

59 Warrington, *Jesus the Healer*, p.59, n.35, suggests that Luke may have recognised the incongruity in Jesus forgiving sin *before* physical healing.

60 Stein, *Luke,* pp.176-77; also, p.373, in Lk. 13:12b, 'you have been released'; if *God* had released the woman from her kyphosis, the synagogue ruler could not complain.

61 Tuckett, *Christology and New Testament*, p.139, regards the paucity of use of the title is because of the Imperial cult, as the Emperor is often called Saviour; B. Witherington III, 'Salvation and Health in Christian Antiquity: The Soteriology of Luke-Acts in its First Century Setting', in Marshall and Peterson (eds.), *Witness to the Gospel,* p.158, points out that the angels proclaimed Jesus Saviour (2:11), immediately after the reference to Emperor Augustus in 2:1. Fitzmyer, *Luke 1-IX*, p.204. Stein, *Luke*, pp.433-

Fitzmyer notes that in the gospel, salvation is often deliverance from sickness, or sin, and related to faith, whereas by Acts, it has a more comprehensive meaning.[62] The story of the Samaritan man cleansed of leprosy (17:12-19), who was saved (v.19), as well as healed (v.15), makes this an unsafe generalisation.

2.1.9 Universality

Luke demonstrates in the two volumes that, as part of God's plan, the Christ-event was to open the true Israel to all believers, both Jew and Gentile. Tuckett considers that Luke extends Mark's enactment of Isaiah 40:3 to include Isaiah 40:5, 'The glory of the Lord shall be revealed, and all people shall see it together', so stressing the universality of salvation.[63] Simeon's song (2:29-32, quoting Isa. 49:6), Jesus at the start of his ministry describing the saving and healing of non-Jews by the prophets (4:24-27), and his command to proclaim his message to all nations (24:47), serve to confirm this.

As a foretaste of universality, Luke comments frequently, after portraying Jesus healing, that 'all the crowd' rejoiced (e.g. 13:17), were amazed (e.g. 5:26; 9:43), glorified God (e.g. 5:26), or were afraid (8:37).[64] In one of the healing summaries, 'all' were healed (6:19), rather than the 'many' of Mk. 1:34 (but this may merely reflect Luke's more exact writing). Universality also figures in the missions in the gospel, where the Twelve (9:1-6) had power and authority over 'all' demons, and the 70(2) others (10:1-20) sent out had authority over 'all' the power of the enemy (10:19).

That universal authority, emphasised in the gospel, is depicted as beginning to achieve reality in the healing of Gentiles in Acts.

2.1.10 Jesus' Crucifixion and Resurrection

The saving of the thief on the cross (23:42-43) as well as Jesus' final words, seem to indicate Luke depicting Jesus as much less weak and helpless than in the crucifixion scene in Mark. The development of Luke's gospel after the events of Jesus' crucifixion and burial is very

---

35, notes that 'your faith has saved you' is found in 7:50; 8:48; 17:19; 18:42. Danker, *Jesus and the New Age*, p.13, considers that Luke sees salvation as freedom of access to God.

62 Fitzmyer, *Luke 1-IX*, p.223.

63 Tuckett, *Luke*, p.51. Healing of Gentiles, however, is almost totally confined to Acts.

64 Fitzmyer, *Luke I-IX,* p.659, likens the crowd to a chorus in a Greek play. Howard, *Disease and Healing*, p.59, points out that Luke seeks to increase the sense of awe and wonder of the onlookers, to focus on Jesus' power.

different from the abrupt ending we have extant of Mark's gospel, where, after the women found the empty tomb, and the angel spoke to them, they ran away. From the point in Luke's gospel where the angels spoke to the women (Lk. 24:5-8), the disciples confirmed the empty tomb, and there were several resurrection appearances before Jesus' ascension (see later re. Lk. 24:51b), and the disciples had begun their rehabilitation before the end of Luke's gospel. The existence of the last chapter of Luke highlights his perception of the importance of the resurrection, and allows a smooth transition to the beginnings of the church in Acts.

2.1.11 Conclusion on Luke's Theology

Luke has several dominant theological concepts, which we can see as significant in his narrative of Jesus' healing. His strong sense of Jesus' ministry being in the 'middle time' of salvation history, and his stress on Old Testament prophecy, are important factors in the presentation. His emphasis is on Jesus as Messianic prophet, acting with the Spirit of the Lord upon him, a Spirit of prophecy, which includes the power to perform healing miracles. Jesus' relationship with God is presented as that of the powerful, but obedient son, and Luke stresses that Jesus' power to heal is from God. The source of Jesus' power is emphasised by the crowds in the healing stories glorifying God, in the resurrection appearances, and in Jesus' ascension. Luke's apocalyptic view of Satan's importance, and his awareness of the presence of demons, are both obvious, and colour his language about binding and release with regard to healing.

This *résumé* of widely accepted views of some of Luke's theological perspective and interpretation has been set out to allow focus on key points in his presentation of Jesus' healing ministry. In Luke's day, 'the miraculous dominated the general conception of the world';[65] in modern times, it is often assumed that the evangelists used healing miracles mainly as pegs on which to hang theological arguments, such as forgiveness of sin, work on the Sabbath, and, more generally, religious opposition to Jesus. Scholarly concentration on the theological arguments, rather than on the healing itself, has undoubtedly been productive, but it is also a successful strategy to avoid the modern difficulty in accepting Jesus' miraculous healing. Such considerations should not allow us to assume that Luke himself regards the healings as merely vehicles for his theological message. Green's view that Luke's

---

65 Fridrichsen, *Problem of Miracle,* p.59.

compulsion is to give theological meaning to Jesus' healings rather than to prove their veracity is accepted,[66] but Luke also intends to proclaim the healings themselves as important in Jesus' ministry.

2.2 Prominence of Jesus' Healing in Luke's Gospel

Luke's gospel is constrained within a framework that he inherited from Mark, and, probably in order to present his material in an orderly way (1:1-4), and perhaps in respect for Mark, he follows remarkably closely the format of Mark's gospel with regard to healing, while holding different theological views. Like Mark, Luke emphasises this aspect of Jesus' ministry, so the healing narratives are very prominent. He records all but three of Mark's accounts, follows faithfully their order and pattern, and even incorporates occasionally Mark's 'secrecy' motif into his narrative.[67] As in Mark, there are summaries of healings and exorcisms (4:40-41; 5:15; 6:17-19; 7:21; 9:11; and 8:2, the last referring only to women). The picture is of an evangelist concerned to follow Mark's narrative lead in the healings.

In addition, Luke tells two stories found also in Matthew's gospel (so assumed to be 'Q' material), the healing of the centurion's slave (7:2-10) and the exorcism of a demon from a dumb man (11:14), the latter story in both gospels preceding the Beelzebul controversy. Four healings by Jesus that are unique to Luke's gospel are also recorded; of the woman with kyphosis (13:10-17), the man with generalised oedema (14:1-4), the ten men with leprosy (17:11-19), and the high priest's servant, whose ear was severed (22:51). Also, there is the restoring to life of the widow's son at Nain (7:11-17).

Luke (unlike Mark) also depicts Jesus speaking several times of healing as an important part of his ministry. In Jesus' programmatic statement (4:18), healing of blindness was one form of freedom from oppression. His response to John the Baptist's disciples (7:21-23) had a great emphasis on healing; there, Luke indicates that Jesus recognised healing as an unexpected attribute of 'the One to Come', as he declared blessed the person to whom healing was not a stumbling-block to faith in him as Messiah (v.23).[68] Luke's Jesus also spoke about δυνάμεις

---

66 Green, *Gospel of Luke*, p.18.

67 Danker, *Jesus and the New Age*, p.189.

68 Fitzmyer, *Luke X-XXIV*, p.1212, is unsure if a Messianic figure was expected to be associated with healing; B. Witherington III, *The Christology of Jesus* (Minneapolis: Fortress, 1990) p.44, notes that the evidence that the Messiah was expected to be a healer is slim. Vermes, *Jesus the Jew*, p.32, believes that John is pointing out that a

performed by him in Tyre and Sidon (10:13), and outlined his mission as 'casting out demons and performing cures', a mission that was to be completed before 'the third day' (13:32).

Thus, Jesus' healing seems even more prominent in Luke's than in Mark's gospel, with stories from other sources, and comments on healing by Jesus in the Lukan description.

2.3 Luke's Alterations to Healing Narratives in Mark

2.3.1 General Changes

Generally, Luke's accounts of Jesus' healing are less realistic and more obviously theological than Mark's. Although Hemer refers to Luke cutting out 'otiose' material from Mark's narrative, Mark's descriptions are often clearer than Luke's, especially in the story of healing the boy with epilepsy (Lk. 9:38-43).[69]

Also, Luke's narrative produces further improbabilities by modifying Mark's story. For instance, Simon Peter reacted dramatically to Jesus providing the miraculous catch of fish, 'Go away from me, Lord, for I am a sinful man' (5:8), before Simon became a disciple, but *after* he had witnessed Jesus' exorcism in the synagogue in Capernaum (4:33), and after his mother-in-law (4:38-39) had been healed. Again, Luke portrays the woman with menorrhagia proclaiming before all the people that she had been healed of her bleeding (8:47), whereas Mark 5:33 has the woman telling Jesus, who makes it clear to the crowd; most women would understand the unlikelihood of her announcing the situation to the crowd. Generally, the reaction of the crowds to healing miracles often seems less sensitively painted in Luke (except when he follows Mark's account, e.g. Lk. 8:52-53), and this is related to his emphasis on universality (e.g. 'all' were amazed, 'all' rejoiced), compared with Mark, who sometimes depicts a mixed response of acceptance and rejection (Mk. 5:40, 42; 9:14, 26; see Chapter 3, *1.3.3*).

2.3.2 Literary Changes

Writers of gospel commentaries have noted many minor variations between Mark and Luke in the healing narratives, much of literary interest, but not relevant to this study. The words for sickness and

---

Messiah is meant to do more than heal. Fitzmyer, *Luke I-IX*, p.668, and Stein, *Luke*, p.227, think the stumbling block would be because people had pre-conceived ideas.

69 Hemer, *Book of Acts*, p.432. Mark gives both an accurate clinical history (9:17-18, 21-22), and a succinct description of the clinical signs (9:20, 26).

healing have been exhaustively studied, by Hobart and von Harnack, and in more modern times by Wilkinson, as part of the argument for Luke being a physician; Wells has also made a special study of nomenclature in ancient healing.[70] None of this material is repeated here, except to note that, more often than Mark, Luke uses as the verb 'to heal', ἰάομαι, especially in the middle voice, and that θεραπεύω, as in Mark, is not always confined to healing.[71] Like Mark, Luke does not use the more theological phrase σημεῖα καὶ τέρατα (signs and wonders) of Jesus' healing;[72] 'sign', used alone, is a term employed about unbelievers, as in Mark, e.g. in Luke 11:16, 29, when opponents were asking for a sign from heaven, and in 23:8, when Herod hoped to see Jesus perform a sign. Unlike Mark, Luke occasionally uses the term δυνάμεις positively for Jesus' miracles, especially when uttered by Jesus (e.g. 10:13) or the crowd (19:37).

As well as a version of Mark's gospel, Luke had other material available, so it may be that, with limited space in costly scrolls, he felt constrained to shorten Mark's stories. He was also writing in more elegant Greek, and most commentators give examples of this. Three examples are significant to our topic: Mark 2:3 describes a paralytic man, παραλυτικός, while Luke 5:18 describes him as a man paralysed, παραλελυμένος. Mark 5:15 has a demonised man, δαιμονιζόμενος, while Luke 8:27 describes a man having demons, ἔχων δαιμόνια. Lastly, the man in Mark 1:40 is a leper, λεπρός, while Luke 5:12 describes a man full of leprosy, ἀνήρ πλήρης λέπρας. This last is usually interpreted as Luke dramatising the illness, or writing in a better idiom, but these examples are also consistent with Luke avoiding designation of a suppliant merely by his disease, and thus diminishing the person.

2.3.3 Increased Pathos

In spite of reducing the length of many of Mark's healing narratives, Luke does add detail that usually increases the drama of the healing.[73]

---

70 W.K. Hobart, *The Medical Language of St. Luke: A Proof that 'The Gospel According to St. Luke' and 'The Acts of the Apostles' were written by the same Person, and that the Writer was a Medical Man* (Dublin: Hodges, Figgis & Co., 1882); A. von Harnack, *Luke the Physician. The Author of the Third Gospel and the Acts of the Apostles* (ET; London: Williams & Norgate, 1907); Wilkinson, *Bible and Healing*, pp.74-78, 161-69; Wells, *Language of Healing*.

71 Wells, *Language of Healing*, e.g. pp.154-55, 159-72. (See Chapter 3, *1.6*.)

72 K.F. Rengstorf, 'σημεῖον', *TDNT*, 7, p.229.

73 E.g. Stein, *Luke*, pp.164, 189, 261; Green, *Gospel of Luke*, pp.225, 289, 342.

He may point up the severity of the illness; Peter's mother-in-law was seized by great fever (4:38-39),[74] and the man with leprosy was 'full of leprosy' (but see above). Luke sometimes enumerates the possessing demons expelled, a feature not found in Mark e.g. the seven demons of Mary Magdalene (Lk.8:2), the seven returning demons in 11:26. (Seven, the perfect number, would indicate the highest number of demons that could possess a person.) He increases pathos in other ways; Jairus' daughter was his only daughter (8:42), and the boy with epilepsy was the father's only child (9:38). The withered hand affected (6:6) was the right hand.[75] Although this last may be seen as evidence of good clinical observation (see *4*), it is more likely, in view of Luke's theological interests, to indicate his accentuating the emphasis on God's power manifest in Jesus' healing. His account of Jesus' resistance to other miracle-workers (11:23) in the Beelzebul controversy is probably due to Luke's wish to play down the skills of Jesus' opponents, as this increases, by comparison, the power of Jesus' healings (see *2.1.3*).

2.3.4 Word and Touch

Shelton suggests that Luke, more than Mark, portrays Jesus using word rather than touch in healing, for instance, Mark's Jesus took Peter's mother-in-law by the hand, whereas in Luke's gospel, he healed her by word only.[76] It is true that in Luke 17:14, Jesus cleansed the ten men with leprosy by word only, but in the equivalent story to Mark 1:41, healing of the man with leprosy was also depicted as being by touch (Lk. 5:13). In Luke's gospel, as in Mark's, ἅπτομαι (to touch) is used

74 This may indicate malaria; see Chapter 3, *1.5.2*. Hippocrates, *Epidemics* I, in *The Genuine Works of Hippocrates,* Vol.1 (ET, F. Adams; London: Sydenham Society, 1859) p.368, discusses varieties of fever.

75 Bock, *Luke*, 1, p.528. Schneemelcher, *New Testament Apocrypha*, 1, p.160, quotes the gospel which the Nazarenes and Ebionites used mentioning the healing of the man with the withered hand, where the man was a mason, who could not work because of the withered hand, and would have to beg. J.R. Edwards, 'The Gospel of the Ebionites and the Gospel of Luke', *NTS* 48 (2002) 568-86, considers that the origin of the Hebrew Gospel in the Gospel of the Ebionites may have been among the sources of Luke's gospel.

76 Shelton, *Mighty in Word*, p.80. From the theological point of view, one would expect Luke to portray Jesus healing in the most minimal way possible, as evidence of Jesus' power from God. There is also the argument that Luke might regard fever as possession by demons, and so this was an exorcism. Warrington, *Jesus the Healer*, p.43, notes that rabbinic teaching forbade touching a person with fever, and Ferguson, *Demonology of Early Christian World*, p.86, observes that, although rabbinic literature was written later than the New Testament, it often preserves teachings of an earlier time.

frequently as the means of healing,[77] and when children were brought to Jesus, he would touch them in blessing (18:15). The verb ἐπιτίθημι, (to lay hands on) which also occurs in Mark's accounts of Jesus healing, is found in healing twice in Luke's gospel (4:40 and 13:13), so there seems to be no significant difference in the two with regard to the manner of healing. It is notable that Luke's gospel account of the healing of the boy with epilepsy (Lk. 9:41) lacks Mark's account of Jesus' words of help given to the boy's father.

2.3.5 Is Luke's Jesus less Human than Mark's?

Some scholars have noted that Luke seems to attenuate the humanness of Mark's narrative portrayal of Jesus in the healing stories.[78] Neither ancient writer refers frequently to Jesus' compassion; it is mentioned with respect to healing in Luke's gospel only for the widow whose son had died (Lk. 7:13), but it is assumed that Luke, like Mark, realizes that his readers would understand compassion to underlie Jesus' actions. Luke's Jesus, however, is not reported as showing any negative emotion when the man with leprosy came to him (5:12-16), unlike Mark (1:40-43),[79] and when Jesus healed the man with the withered hand (Lk. 6:9), there is no mention of Jesus' anger at the attitude of the Jewish religious authorities (as in Mk. 3:5), although the authorities are reported to be furious. When children were brought for blessing, Luke's Jesus is not depicted (18:16), as in Mark (10:13-14), indignant with the disciples who tried to stop them.

Mark portrays Jesus taking the children in his arms (10:16), while Luke does not mention Jesus holding them (Lk. 18:15-17), although they are described as young infants (βρέφη). On a different occasion, Mark depicts Jesus taking a child in his arms (9:36), while Luke's Jesus put the child by his side (9:47).[80] Marshall notes the differences between the two gospels in this story, and notes this omission by Luke of Mark's 'rather human trait'. Marshall regards this as evidence of Luke's 'general avoidance of attributing human emotions to Jesus'.[81]

77 Green, *Gospel of Luke*, p.650. E.g. 5:13 (Jesus touching the man with leprosy); 6:19 (the crowd touching Jesus); 7:14 (Jesus touching the bier); 8:44-47 (the woman touching Jesus); 22:51-52 (Jesus touching the ear).

78 E.g. Fridrichsen, *Problem of Miracle*, p.39, and Tannehill, *Luke*, pp.102, 111, 128, both note Luke avoiding mentioning Jesus' emotions.

79 Menken, 'Position of Σπλαγχνίζεσθαι', p.113. (See Chapter 3, *1.4*)

80 Fitzmyer, *Luke I-IX*, pp.816-17, noting that Luke, unlike Mark, omits both Jesus' emotion, and his embrace of the child, considers that Luke sees Jesus giving the child, the smallest and weakest member of society, the place of honour next to him.

81 Marshall, *Gospel of Luke*, p.396.

Admittedly, this pericope may reflect Luke's interest in emphasising Jesus' teaching, rather than evidence of him presenting a less human Jesus, but it may be that Luke is anxious to correct some of Mark's 'loose cannons'.

Neyrey draws attention to the lack of emotion shown by the Lukan Jesus immediately before his arrest; he notes that, whereas Mark emphasises Jesus' anguish (λύπη) in Gethsemane (14:34), Luke (22:39f.) plays this down.[82] This suggestion depends on whether or not we accept the many manuscripts that do not recognize verses 43 and 44; and most commentators consider that the verses should be deleted.[83] Omission of the verses does fit with Luke not citing Psalm 22:1 at Jesus' crucifixion, as Mark does.

All this may suggest that Luke wishes to portray Jesus as above the thrall of human emotions. Yet Luke portrays Jesus entering Jerusalem (19:37), being praised for his δυνάμεις, and, immediately afterwards, weeping over the city (19:41).[84] Further, Jesus spoke emotionally about the plight of the people of Jerusalem earlier (13:34-35), but not about his imminent death. Again, in both Jesus' parables unique to Luke,[85] the heroes, the Good Samaritan (10:33) and the father of the Prodigal Son (15:20), were moved by compassion, ἐσπλαγχνίσθη. Thus, it seems possible that Luke wishes his readers to know that Jesus approved the emotion of compassion in human beings, yet did not openly show emotion in much of his healing work, and in his own trials.[86] The picture

---

82 J.H. Neyrey, 'The Absence of Jesus' Emotions—the Lucan Redaction of Luke 22:39-46', *Bib* 61 (1980) 153-71.

83 Aland et al., *Novum Testamentum Graece*, note that they are omitted by P 75, Sinaiticus[1], A, B, N, T and W, although present in Sinaiticus*. C.A. Evans, *Luke*, p.559, thinks that the verses were inserted by a scribe, to show an immediate, dramatic response to prayer. Nolland, *Luke 18:35-24:53* WBC, Vol.35C (Dallas: Word Books, 1993) pp.1080-81, notes that the two verses break up the (imperfect) chiastic structure of the Gethsemane scene, and that the material has an emotional tone absent from the rest of Luke's account of the Gethsemane event. C.F. Evans, *Saint Luke*, TPI New Testament Commentaries (London/Philadelphia: SCM/Trinity, 1990) pp.812-13, notes that it is the sole instance of an angelic appearance to Jesus, and considers the words used, including sweat and drops of blood, are non-Lukan. He states that 'if verses 43-44 are omitted, the conflict in the will of Jesus is minimal, and the contrast with Mark's account considerable'.

84 Tannehill, *Narrative Unity*, 1, p.155.

85 Fitzmyer, *Luke I-IX*, p.258, notes that these have been called the Lukan parables of mercy; Danker, *Jesus and the New Age*, p.211, says that they are based on divine compassion (Hos. 6:6) as the model for human love.

86 Neyrey, 'Absence of Emotions', p.155, suggests that Luke may have been influenced by Stoic philosophy. Johnson, *Writings of New Testament*, p.234, thinks that Luke

fits with Luke's focus on the power and will of Jesus, inspired by the Holy Spirit, in complete obedience to, and reflecting perfectly the greatness of, God.[87]

This possible reduction of reported emotion may be one of the ways in which Luke edits out from Mark's narratives areas that Luke regards as unacceptable for Jesus, whose power he depicts as from God. The point is not proven, but may be important when we consider if differences in the evangelists' portrayal of healing were related to the theology (or the personality) of the writer.

2.3.6 Luke's Jesus is more 'Politically Correct' than Mark's

Other areas where Luke alters Mark's accounts of Jesus healing can be found. Luke portrays the crowds as more accepting of Jesus' power to heal, particularly in the story of the boy with epilepsy (Lk. 9:43, c.f. Mk. 9:26). The statement that Jesus was unable to undertake deeds of power in his hometown of Nazareth (Mk. 6:5) is omitted (although perhaps implied in Lk. 4:22b-24). There is a long account in Mark's gospel, following this rejection of Jesus, and the successful mission of his disciples, of the death of John the Baptist at the hands of Herod (6:14-29). Mark 6:14-16 risks the interpretation that Jesus was healing *because* he had the spirit of John, recently killed violently, that is, he was open to a charge of necromancy, and Luke's version avoids this interpretation by much reducing the account (9:7-9). Similarly, Luke modifies (8:19-21) the Markan episode (3:21-22, 31-32) of Jesus' family assuming that Jesus has lost his mind, and so had made a pact with the devil.[88] Instead of Mark's account (3:30), where people said that Jesus had an unclean spirit, Luke reports that they thought John the Baptist had a demon (7:33). Again, Luke omits Mark's description of the man with leprosy ignoring Jesus' warning to tell nobody of his cure, which Achtemeier sees as evidence of Luke's Jesus having greater authority.[89]

---

portrays Jesus as the Sophos, where self-control, freedom from fear and courage were models for followers.

87 Stein, *Luke,* p.172. J.G. Williams, *The Bible, Violence and the Sacred. Liberation from the Myth of Sanctioned Violence* (New York/ San Francisco: HarperSanFrancisco, 1991) p.200.

88 Fridrichsen, *Problem of Miracle*, p.102. Sanders, *Jesus and Judaism*, p.167, thinks that magicians may imitate the madness they are trying to heal (Chapter 3, *1.7.1*).

89 Achtemeier, 'Lucan Perspective', pp.157-58, notes that in Luke's gospel (5:15), 'an account went out'.

As a final example (although there are many more) of Luke's editing Mark's less 'politically correct' material with regard to healing, we consider the 'Great Omission'; Luke omits the material in Mark 7:24–8:26. Among the narratives deleted, there is a doublet of the feeding miracle, and three healing stories.[90] Bultmann suggested that the first of the healing stories, Jesus healing the daughter of the Syrophoenician woman (7:24-30), where the woman seems to win a verbal victory over Jesus, is replaced by Luke's story of the healing of the centurion's slave; both suppliants were Gentiles, both had considerable faith in Jesus, and both involved people healed at a distance.[91] Bultmann's suggestion can be sustained only if one accepts, first, that the stories were fabrications of the early church, as part of religious propaganda, and, second, that the narratives were told purely to exploit them for these points; neither position seems acceptable.

The second (Mk. 7:31-37) and third (Mk. 8:22-26) of the Markan healing stories omitted in Luke involved the use of saliva, and Mark 7:34 mentions the sigh directed towards heaven, and the utterance of the word, *Ephphatha*. These features may have made Luke consider them to have some of the ingredients of magic (even although Mark translated the word, see Chapter 3, *1.7.1*). Again, Mark 8:22-26, where Jesus' first attempt at healing was only partially successful, does not fit with Luke's portrayal of the omnipotence of God in Jesus' healings.

In summary, there seem to be several reasons for Luke's alterations to Mark's healing narratives. These include possible pressure on space, and Luke's more elegant writing, but there are more important theological considerations. For instance, second-attempt healing is omitted, as is an account of Jesus being able to heal only a few people in Nazareth. Luke emphasises the great power of Jesus' healing, as a power from God, based on the Messianic gift of the Holy Spirit. Similarly, Luke's interest in showing Jesus not usually giving way to emotions, such as pity, anger or anguish, except on account of unbelieving Israel, is unlike Mark's emphasis, and seems to be related to Luke presenting a different Christology to Mark. Luke is careful to remove from Mark's accounts any risk of Jesus being accused of using magic; this may indicate that this was a live debate among his first readers, but may well reflect Luke's own views on Jesus' healing.

---

90 Remus, *Jesus as Healer,* p.57; Fitzmyer, *Luke I-IX,* p.67. Marshall, *Gospel of Luke,* p.413, notes that Luke usually avoids doublets.

91 Bultmann, *History of Synoptic Tradition,* pp.38-39, questions the historicity of 'telepathic healing'.

2.4 *Luke's Account of Healing Narratives Attributed to 'Q'*

The healing narratives in Luke's gospel attributed to 'Q' and found also in Matthew's gospel, may throw further light on Luke's representation of Jesus' healing.

There are two healing stories, traditionally regarded as having a common source, which are found only in Matthew and Luke. The shorter narrative (Lk. 11:14) is the casting out of the mute demon (it was standard practice to attribute to the demon the name of the sufferer's problem). Although Mark reports the healing of the deaf man with a speech difficulty (7:31), Luke's story is closer to that of the blind and mute man in Matthew 12:22, as both narratives introduce the Beelzebul controversy, which was sparked off by this specific exorcism in Matthew and Luke, but not in Mark (3:22-30). Controversy is usually over the use by Luke of the term 'finger of God' (11:20), from Exodus 8:15, compared with Matthew's 'Spirit of God' (12:28),[92] but it is intriguing that both Matthew and Luke have a problem, which Mark avoids, namely, why the Jewish exorcisms (Lk. 11:19) were not expected to herald the coming of the Kingdom of God, but Jesus' did.[93]

In the healing of the centurion's slave (Lk. 7:2-10) near to death[94] (in Mt. 8:6, the slave was paralysed and in great distress), Luke portrays the centurion not personally meeting Jesus (as he does in Matthew's gospel), but rather sending Jewish elders to Jesus, for him to speak the word that would produce healing, so Luke's version has the element of healing from a distance.[95] Jesus signalled amazement at the centurion's faith, but the absence of face-to-face engagement with him makes the story somewhat artificial, in that a conversation between Jesus and the centurion, as in Matthew's account, would have been more natural; while the picture of intermediaries relaying such a conversation weakens the story. The centurion, a Gentile, was a benefactor of Israel,

---

92 Fitzmyer, *Luke X-XXIV*, p.922, suggests that 'finger of God' indicates the absence of magical charms or incantations. Turner, *Holy Spirit and Gifts*, pp.30-31, argues that the difference from Matthew's version is unrelated to the argument about whether Luke accepted the Spirit of prophecy as including the power to heal, but, rather, is in the interest of Luke's prophet-like-Moses Christology.

93 Caragounis, 'Kingdom of God', p.229. C.A. Evans, *Luke*, p.185, suggests that the Jewish exorcists produced only temporary cures.

94 The episode brought into Jesus' ministry the fulfilment of the prophecy of the healing of non-Jews in the Old Testament, described in Lk. 4:25-27.

95 Bock, *Luke,* 1, p.636; Fitzmyer, *Luke I-IX,* p.652; Stein, *Luke,* p.220, all suggest that the centurion wanted to spare Jesus a problem, since entering a Gentile house would render him unclean.

paying for the building of a synagogue (this is not mentioned in Mt. 8:5-13). Green considers that the story is an example of the Jewish elders using the gift-obligation system, as they were indebted to the centurion.[96] The citing of the benefaction may be a way for Luke to show Jesus healing non-Jews usually in extenuating circumstances in the gospel, but laying a firm foundation for healing of Gentiles in Acts. It fits with the principle that Luke's gospel is shaped significantly by the fact of the following book of Acts.[97]

The centurion's recognition that both Jesus and he were under authority, while both had authority, is found in Matthew's and Luke's accounts, but fits well with Luke's emphasis on the power of God, the source of Jesus' healing power, and Jesus' perfect obedience.

Thus, in the two healing stories attributed to Q, Luke's portrayal of God's power, and Jesus' authority under God, are prominent. The healing of the mute man emphasises the source of Jesus' healing, from God, and in healing the centurion's slave, Jesus is depicted as well-disposed to Gentiles (although not here in direct contact with a Gentile).

2.5 Healing Narratives Specific to Luke

In those stories where there is no parallel in the other gospels, it would be expected that Luke had a freer rein, so his underlying theological views may be more obvious.

The account of the raising of the widow's son in Nain (7:11-17), as well as reflecting pagan tradition,[98] has clear echoes of healing narratives from the Old Testament (1 Kgs. 17:22; 2 Kgs. 4:35). The crowd's response shows that they recognised the re-enactment of these stories, as they hailed Jesus as a great prophet (7:16). Luke emphasises the great power of Jesus to heal, by his raising the man by word only,

---

96 Stein, *Luke*, p.219, suggests that he may even be a God-fearer, but there is no evidence of this in the story; F.W. Danker, *Benefactor: Epigraphic Study of a Graeco-Roman and New Testament Semantic Field* (St. Louis: Clayton, 1982) p.213, notes that benefactions by Roman citizens in occupied countries were not unusual. Green, *Gospel of Luke*, p.285.

97 Tuckett, *Luke*, p.53, suggests that Luke's Jesus did not have extensive contacts with Gentiles, *either* because Luke was an accurate historian, who knew that Jesus did not go into Gentile territory, *or* because Luke was anxious to keep the eras apart, so Gentile healing is depicted as particularly in the era of the church. Witherington, *Acts of Apostles*, p.226, n.126, considers that Luke held certain ideas and motifs back until he composed Acts. Stein, *Luke*, p.258.

98 The widow had not appealed for Jesus' help, a feature found in pagan miracle stories. (See Chapter 2, *2.2.3.*)

compared with the efforts required by Elijah and Elisha.[99] The young man being the widow's *only* son increased the pathos, and Luke mentions that Jesus showed compassion for her plight.[100] The crowd were all awed, then glorified God (v.16), so the scene further emphasises the Lukan themes of fulfilment of prophecy, and the power of God working through Jesus. In the next pericope, Luke reports Jesus' answer to the questions asked by John the Baptist's emissaries, and Luke seems to have 'placed' the narrative of raising a dead person immediately before, in order to complete his legitimation of Jesus as a healing Messiah (a purpose for healing never found in Mark's gospel).

In the account of the woman severely kyphotic for eighteen years (13:11-17), bound by a spirit of weakness (v.11),[101] Jesus healed by word and laying on his hands. Luke emphasises his theme of Jesus freeing those held captive, and also stresses 'doing good' on the Sabbath.[102] As in 7:11-17, Jesus was not asked to heal the woman, but showed his compassion implicitly, in calling her to him.[103] The healed woman praised God (not Jesus), that is, Luke again demonstrates that Jesus' power was from God. Luke shows his interest in universalism; *all* the opponents were shamed, while the *whole* crowd rejoiced.[104]

---

99 Bock, *Luke,* 1, p.652.

100 Green, *Gospel of Luke*, pp.281, 289. Tannehill, *Luke*, p.128, notes Jesus' reaction here as unusual.

101 The phrase seems to me to be an example of Luke, aware of the prevalence of demons, not defining the nature of the woman's illness. Thomas, *Devil, Disease*, pp.223-24, considers that she was demon-attacked, rather than demon-possessed, and he notes that Jesus spoke to the *woman*, not to the demon, so concludes that this was not an exorcism. Wilkinson, *Bible and Healing,* pp.133-36, suggests that the woman suffered from ankylosing spondylitis. There are very few diseases, which would produce severe fixed kyphosis, and with which she would survive long-term, so, although ankylosing spondylitis is relatively unusual in women, this does fit the description. Eighteen years seems to be a device for indicating the difficulty of healing, rather than being either a diagnostic clue or a semantic reference back to 13:4.

102 Danker, *Jesus and the New Age*, p.132, sees the Sabbath debate dealing with the question of whether humans were more important than the dictates of the religious establishment. Tannehill, *Luke,* p.111, notes also that failure to 'do good' immediately might result in harm, a point certainly true in modern medicine.

103 Stein, *Luke,* p.373. Green, *Gospel of Luke*, p.221, raises the question as to whether a disabled woman would be accepted in an area of the synagogue where Jesus would see her, and this seems a reasonable doubt.

104 J. Jervell, *Die Apostelgeschichte. Kritisch-exegetischer Kommentar über das Neue Testament* (Göttingen: Vandenhoeck & Ruprecht, 1998) p.274, draws attention to the fact that joy is emphasised throughout Luke's writings as a natural effect of salvation.

The next healing story (14:1-5) is usually regarded as indicating Luke's penchant for narrative parallelism, in that the sufferer was a man healed on the Sabbath (like the woman with kyphosis). Jesus 'took him, healed him, and released him', from the disease which bound him (v.4). There is no vivid imagery of his illness (which was regarded then, and would be considered nowadays, as highly sinister). Dropsy was well known in the ancient world, as judged by the clinical descriptions of it, and by the finding of medical instruments to drain body cavities.[105] Since sufferers often drank massive quantities of fluid without their thirst being satisfied (a symptom of chronic renal failure), it is easy to see why the term dropsy was applied to sinners, winebibbers and money-lovers, and it was often regarded as due to, or punishment for, sin.[106] It would be odd, therefore, if the man had been invited to attend a meal at the Pharisee's house. This healing was part of Jesus' controversy with the religious establishment, so Luke is using a poorly delineated situation on which to hang a theological message,[107] a circumstance not found in Mark.

The story of Jesus cleansing the ten men with leprosy (17:11-19) has some strange features. First, the cleansing was not immediately obvious, as was usual in Jesus' healings, but became apparent as the suppliants were on their way, presumably to show themselves to the priests. Then, the Samaritan who came back was also unusual, as in Luke's gospel, the 'correct' response for the healed was to praise God. This the man did, but he also thanked, and apparently worshipped, Jesus (v.16).[108] Stein opines that all the sufferers must have had some faith, as they were cleansed.[109] The difference between being cleansed and being saved is not spelled out, but the story suggests that the salvation given to the Samaritan was comprehensive, and not just for this life, when Jesus said 'Your faith has saved you'.

In the episode of the high priest's slave injured in the arrest of Jesus, Luke is the only gospel-writer who depicts Jesus restoring (22:51) the severed ear (see *4*). This seems to be another example of Jesus healing a

---

105 F. Adams, *The Extant Works of Aretaeus the Cappodocian* (London: Sydenham Society Pub., 1856) pp.309-11. Hippocrates, *Airs, Waters, Places* VII.22-23, notes that dropsy may be fatal. Fitzmyer, *Luke X-XXIV*, p.1041, underestimates the severity and poor prognosis of dropsy, which indicates the presence of a condition such as cardiac or respiratory failure, severe renal or hepatic disease.

106 Tannehill, *Narrative Unity*, 1, p.228. Van der Loos, *Miracles of Jesus*, p.505.

107 Here, of Jesus seeking out and saving the lost (19:10); Danker, *Jesus and the New Age*, p.377, points to Jesus' association with the lost as his characteristic mark.

108 It recalls the gratitude for Jesus of the woman in 7:36-50.

109 Stein, *Luke*, p.433.

slave, and also of Luke using healing as a theological lesson, a demonstration of loving one's enemies (6:27).

In summary, the healing narratives unique to Luke demonstrate most of the points already noted as Luke's special concerns, but with even more emphasis on the theological elements. These include Jesus releasing the bound, stress on the universality of the crowd's response in glorifying God (and so also recognising that the source of Jesus' healing power is God working through him), and the appreciation that salvation is more than physical healing.

2.6 Relationship of Luke's Gospel to Acts

The presence of a sequel to his gospel seems to influence Luke's portrayal of healing both by Jesus and his followers. At least partly in order to accommodate the unfolding story of Acts, Luke seems to have adapted his account from that in Mark's gospel, which contains all the elements of his narrative in the one book.[110]

There is a little evidence that Luke wishes to depict the mission to the Gentile world being mainly after the resurrection, although that evidence is admittedly slim. Neither Mark nor Luke depicts Jesus seeking out sick Gentiles. Luke does not mention that the man in the tombs (8:26-37) was from the Decapolis (as in Mk. 5:20), even though the presence of the pigs indicated that Jesus was in Gentile territory;[111] the story of healing the Syrophoenician woman's daughter (where Mark depicts Jesus speaking directly to the woman) is absent; the centurion, whose slave Jesus healed, although a friend of Israel, had no direct contact with Jesus, unlike the story in Matthew; and the healings of the deaf-mute man (Mk. 7:31-37) and the blind man (Mk. 8:22-26), both of whom were healed in Gentile territory outside Galilee, are missing. Even the ten men with leprosy, of whom at least one was a Samaritan (17:10), had no physical contact with Jesus. Tuckett, drawing attention to the lack of extensive contacts of Jesus with Gentiles, considers that this demonstrates Luke's intention to portray clearly different eras of salvation history.[112] In Acts, the apostles, empowered by the Holy Spirit, carried preaching and healing, first to the Jews, then to Samaritans, then

110 For instance, a minor omission in Luke's gospel, compared with Mark's account of Jesus raising Jairus' daughter, the removing of the bystanders (Mk. 5:40), appears in Acts in the account of Peter raising Tabitha (9:41).

111 Stein, *Luke*, p.258, believes that Luke omits mention of the Decapolis, because he conceives that the mission to the Gentiles begins in earnest only after the resurrection.

112 Tuckett, *Luke*, p.53, (see *2.4*).

to God-fearing Gentiles, and finally to all Gentiles, as the next part of God's plan.

2.6.1 The Gospel Missions

Luke's account of the mission of the Twelve (9:1-6) differs from Mark's (6:6b-13) in ways mostly unrelated to our focus on healing, for instance, Luke's disciples were to preach the Kingdom of God, while Mark's preached repentance (See Chapter 6, *1.3*). In both gospels, the disciples on mission healed,[113] but in Luke's they were given 'power and authority' over demons, while Mark's Jesus gave them 'authority' only over them (a difference seen also in Luke's description of Jesus' healing, see *2.1.4*).

More significantly in considering the relationship of the gospel to Acts, Luke refers in detail to a subsequent, bigger mission (10:1-20) of seventy (seventy-two) others (the arguments for both numbers are discussed in most commentaries on Luke's gospel). This is not mentioned in Mark, and is conflated into one mission in Matthew. Although this second mission was in Palestine, it seems to foreshadow the apostolic missions to the Gentiles in Acts. Bultmann asserts that this *was* the mission of the early church, written into Jesus' lifetime, and by that time, the role of the Twelve was insignificant.[114] Minear considers that Jesus' instructions to the seventy represent Luke's understanding of Jesus handing on his prophetic role, previously to the Twelve, now to this larger body of followers, recognising, particularly in the comment about lambs among wolves (10:3), that these 'prophets' would have to endure the hardships and sufferings of the Messianic age.[115]

The seventy, who were commissioned to heal those who were sick and preach the gospel (10:9), experienced great joy at the submission of demons 'in your name' (10:17). The term, 'in my [Jesus'] name', is found only twice earlier in the gospel, once in 9:48 (when the welcome of the child 'in my name' could be assumed to be 'on the basis of my name'), and once with respect to the 'strange' exorcist (9:49), but is used frequently in Acts (e.g. 2:21; 9:14, 21; 22:16).[116]

---

113 Stein, *Luke*, p.276, thinks that exorcism was less significant than preaching or healing in this mission. Although demons are not mentioned in Lk. 9:11, this seems to have no particular significance for the mission.

114 Bultmann, *History of Synoptic Tradition*, p.145, indicating that certain events in the gospels were a fabrication of the early church (see *2.3.6*).

115 Minear, *To Heal and to Reveal*, p.69.

116 Marshall, *Luke*, pp.396-97, considers that in Lk. 9:49, and elsewhere, it means power to do mighty works that stem from Jesus. Turner, *Power from on High*, pp.425-

The modern consensus is that Jesus seeing Satan fall was not an ecstatic vision; it may be a symbolic way of Luke summing-up the effects of the mission, particularly the exorcism of demons, or it was a prophecy, previewing the victory over Satan resulting from the death and resurrection of Jesus.[117] The pericope shows Luke's apocalyptic view of God's power being pitted against Satan's; the snakes and scorpions (Lk.10:19) were traditional symbols of evil, and were regarded as homes for demons and evil spirits.[118] The term (v.20) 'names written in heaven' and found in several parts of the Old Testament (e.g. Ex. 32:32; Ps. 69:28; Dan. 12:1), is assumed to stress Luke's view that spectacular achievements were not as important as obedience to God.[119] I believe the passage is significant, as it is the only place in Luke's writings, in which Jesus may be warning against too heavy reliance by his followers on the value of healing miracles in spreading the good news.

In summary, the presence of Luke's second volume, which moves on to the narrative of the early church and the missionary activities of Jesus' followers, has contributed to some of the alterations in Luke's gospel accounts of Jesus' healing, compared with Mark's. In particular, Luke's second account of a mission concentrates on a large group of followers, and this prefigures the subsequent missionary activity in Acts. The emphasis there on the fall of Satan may represent a prophecy, which was played out in the period after Easter, while Jesus' *caveat* that it was more important for the followers' names to be written in heaven is in keeping with Luke's concerns about obedience to God (although it might also represent a warning about over-reliance in the early church on healing).

27, considers that the term 'name of Jesus' in Acts often appears to be a circumlocution for Jesus, and, in particular, is *not* separating the power of the Spirit from the power of his name.

117 Tannehill, *Luke*, p.178, considers that in Lk. 10:18 (which recalls Isa. 14:12, the myth of the king of Babylon), Satan falling from heaven represents his power being defeated. Fitzmyer, *Luke X-XXIV*, p.860; Green, *Gospel of Luke*, p.419; Garrett, *Demise of Devil*, pp.49-52.

118 Garrett, *Demise of Devil*, p.37, considers that Luke envisages the authority that Jesus exerted and delegated as at Satan's expense. C.A. Evans, *Luke*, p.174.

119 Maddox, *Purpose of Luke-Acts*, p.143, considers that the 70 were being warned against claiming Satan's fall as their own achievement. Ferguson, *Demonology of Early Christian World*, p.16. Fuller, *Interpreting the Miracles*, p.86, thinks that the 70 returning from mission should rejoice more at having their names recorded in heaven than being powerful healers. See Chapter 6, *1.4*.

2.7 Conclusion: Healing in Luke's Gospel

Luke, like Mark, emphasises the prominence of Jesus' healings in his gospel. He reproduces faithfully most of the healing episodes found in Mark's gospel, and adds several others, both from Q and from a further source (L). His accounts are designed in a more obviously theological way than are Mark's, so sometimes they lose sharpness in the narration of healing, in order to highlight the picture Luke paints of Jesus as the powerful but obedient son of God. During the actual healing, Luke's Jesus is portrayed as having the Messianic Spirit of prophecy to heal, and the crowd's response, where God, not Jesus, is given the glory, reflects Luke's goal to show Jesus as the powerful, subordinate son of God. Luke's Jesus remains compliant, and usually in tight control of his emotions, even on the cross. Related to the importance of divine power, the resurrection appearances are detailed in Luke's account, so that the resurrection has a high profile, and Luke can end his gospel with the disciples marshalled for action, before Jesus' ascension.[120]

3 The Book of Acts and Healing

3.1 Introduction

Unlike the synoptic gospels, there is no extant canonical writing by another author comparable to the book of Acts, so we have no other writer's view against which to assess directly Luke's account of the development of the early church. A comparison of the two volumes of the same author may be second best, but, since the two volumes stress somewhat different perspectives, it should be rewarding, especially as Luke seems to be less controlled by his sources in Acts than in the gospel.[121] The study of Acts may thus allow more insight into Luke's viewpoint than we can glean from his gospel.

---

120 See *2.1.10*. Whether or not the phrase in Lk. 24:51, 'carried up into heaven', missing from several uncials, including Sinaiticus*, should be included is not of great significance in the context of healing, but removing it makes the authenticity of the ascension in Acts 1:9-12, easier. Nolland, *Luke 18:35-24:53*, pp.1224-26, C.A. Evans, *Luke*, p.362, and Stein, *Luke*, p.624, all think that the phrase should remain. C.F. Evans, *Saint Luke*, pp.926-27, is undecided.

121 J. Jervell, *The Theology of the Acts of the Apostles* (Cambridge: CUP, 1996) p.116, considers that Acts has no direct literary link with any other New Testament writing. Johnson, both in *Writings of New Testament*, p.214, and in L.T. Johnson, *The Acts of the Apostles*. SacPag Series, Vol.5 (Collegeville, Minnesota: Liturgical, 1992) p.4, suggests

Although events clearly follow from the narrative of the gospel, Luke creates a strong sense in Acts that he is writing of a later period of history.[122] There are several ways in which Luke indicates that the ground has shifted. The most significant narrative-linking device is the ascension of Jesus (an occurrence peculiar to Luke), possibly mentioned in the gospel (24:51), and affirmed at the beginning of Acts (1:10-11), so that Jesus is physically absent from the earthly events throughout the succeeding narrative. Similarly, Luke relates the promise of divine power to his followers in the gospel (24:49) to the promise of the power of the Holy Spirit in Acts 1:8. These two connections are themselves correlated; the absence of the earthly Jesus is linked with the presence of the Spirit, poured out on the believers by the risen Jesus at Pentecost (Acts 2:34). Luke confirms (Acts 10:38) his belief that Jesus was anointed with the Holy Spirit by God (at his baptism), and the story of Acts is concerned mainly with the effects of the Holy Spirit bestowed on the apostles and believers.

It has been noted previously that the Holy Spirit is mentioned much more often in Acts than in the main part of Luke's gospel (see *2.1.3*), and Acts is in some ways the narrative of how the Spirit was received.[123] Shepherd, noting that the argument about whether or not the Lukan conception of the Holy Spirit (as the Spirit of prophecy) includes miracles continues in Acts, also points out that to attribute theological consistency to Luke is a Procrustean bed; Luke-Acts resists this systemisation, since Acts, especially, is narrative, not pure theology.[124]

There are some general factors that make Luke's depiction of healing in Acts both similar to, and different from, his account of healing in the gospel. Fletcher-Louis notes that only after Jesus' resurrection does Luke adopt the high Christology found in Acts, where he frequently describes the risen, exalted Christ in Acts, like Yahweh of the LXX, as Lord, κύριος; Witherington believes that Luke is seeking to portray faithfully the developing significance of Christ in the early church.[125]

---

that Luke had less source material, especially for the first half of Acts, than he had for the gospel. Marshall, *Acts*, pp.37-38, notes that the sources of Acts remain unknown.

122 D. Wenham and S. Walton, *Exploring the New Testament*, Vol.1. *A Guide to the Gospels and Acts* (London: SPCK, 2001) pp.267-68.

123 Johnson, *Acts*, p.14, suggests Acts can be called the Book of the Holy Spirit.

124 W.H. Shepherd, Jr., *The Narrative Function of the Holy Spirit as a Character in Luke-Acts* (SBLDS 147; Atlanta: Scholars Press, 1994) pp.20-21.

125 C.H.T. Fletcher-Louis, *Luke-Acts: Angels, Christology and Soteriology* (WUNT 2:94; Tübingen: Mohr [Siebeck], 1997) pp.18-21. But see *3.2.* Witherington, 'Salvation and Health', p.154. Tuckett, *Luke*, p.76, notes that in the gospel, the term Lord is used mainly in the vocative by those addressing Jesus, in the same way as, nowadays, we

This continuity-with-progress can be observed with respect to the source of divine healing. As we have noted, the gospel has an emphasis on God as the source of Jesus' healing. In Acts, Luke emphasises Jesus as mediator of God's redemptive activity in healing, for instance, in the church's early prayer to God (4:29-30), 'you stretch out your hand to heal, and signs and wonders are performed through the name of your holy servant Jesus'.[126]

The story moving forward has other effects on Luke's account of healing. As has been noted, Jesus' apostles in Acts undertook missions involving divine healing mainly of Gentiles, whereas Luke in the gospel shows Jesus healing mainly Jews. Again, while none of Jesus' healings occurred in Jerusalem (even the restoration of the severed ear was on the Mount of Olives), the first apostolic healing was in Jerusalem, then most were in Gentile territory, that is, the geographical area of healing spread. Also, the deliverance offered has often included, as well as healing and rescue, more obvious eschatological salvation in Acts (e.g. 11:14, 18; 16:30-34).

The main narrative of Acts purports to describe how the earliest followers of Jesus set about bringing his gospel to all humankind. This is portrayed as causing tension, as Luke underlines the need to welcome Gentiles (e.g. 15:1-2), while recognising that the church had to remain pure in all essential features (e.g. 10:15). Jesus' words about the acceptance and rejection of his followers in the account of the second mission (Lk. 10:16) were fulfilled in subsequent missionary healing (and preaching) activities in Acts. Luke depicts that success in both healing and preaching in Acts was often followed by rejection of the healers and preachers by the religious authorities, and persecution of apostles and followers, predicted in the gospel (e.g. 12:1-12), was persistent.[127]

---

might use 'sir'. There is overlap between κύριος used of Jesus and of God in the gospel and Acts. Marshall, *Luke: Historian and Theologian*, p.101, maintains that Luke uses the term to denote that God was active in Jesus; Danker, *Jesus and the New Age*, p.6, considers Luke uses the terminology more often for God than for Jesus.

126 Kahl, *New Testament Miracle Stories*, pp.86, 114-18, see *3.4.3*; Tuckett, *Christology and New Testament*, p.139, notes that Christ is called σωτήρ (saviour) only occasionally in Acts (e.g. 5:31; 13:23), in spite of his major role as mediator in apostolic healing, since saviour was a term often used of pagan healers and emperors; Tannehill, *Narrative Unity,* 1, pp.86-87; Shelton, *Mighty in Word*, p.82.

127 Danker, *Jesus and the New Age*, p.106; Minear, *To Heal and to Reveal*, p.69, sees this as evidence that the 'prophets' that Jesus had appointed were sharing in his hardships. Witherington, 'Salvation and Health', p.165, considers that Luke uses this

Some of these considerations might lead us to expect that healing would occupy a less prominent place in Acts than in the gospel. There *are* fewer accounts of healing in Acts, compared with the gospel; Wilkinson notes that healing narratives account for only 4.5% of the total narrative of Acts, yet incidental references (e.g. 5:12; 8:6-7) indicate that many more healing miracles are recorded than are described in detail. Wilkinson maintains that healing in Acts did not need to be a primary means of evangelism, in order to impress spectators, but his conclusion, that physical healing was not a major concern in the apostolic church,[128] underestimates its importance as depicted in Acts. Turner considers that the miracles in Acts legitimate the church 'intrinsically', that is, the miracles exemplify the preaching of the word (e.g. 8:6, 12), and are important aspects of how God's salvation breaks through. Healing is portrayed in Luke's writings as an integral part of the mission of witness, and I would agree with Kee, who states that 'signs and wonders' are central for the Acts narrative.[129]

In summary, healing in Acts is described in a way that fits with Luke's sense of a narrative advancing, as the church was founded and had to meet new challenges, particularly of taking Christ's message to the Gentiles. Changes from his gospel include the absence of the earthly Jesus, and the presence (and repeated mention) of the power of the Holy Spirit, bestowed by the risen Christ upon the apostles;[130] and Luke presents Jesus' ascension to explain these changes. The risen Christ is often referred to as Lord, and the Christology of Acts is probably higher than in the gospel (see *3.2*). As the church wrestled with the tension between striving for universalism while maintaining its purity, Luke shows dramatically the opposition that followers faced. Although he portrays salvation as a much wider concept than healing, yet healing is presented as integral to the mission of the church.

How Luke portrays the place of healing in the early church, after his depiction of its high significance in the gospel, will be assessed. He

---

tension between the work of the leaders of the church, and their suffering through rejection, to advance his implicit message of a *theologia crucis*.

128 Wilkinson, *Bible and Healing*, pp.157, 178. Lampe, 'Miracles in Acts', pp.165-66, considers that Luke does not attempt to prove the truth of Christian doctrine by the performance of 'impossible' tasks.

129 Turner, *Holy Spirit and Gifts*, p.251; Lampe, 'Miracles in Acts', p.171; H.C. Kee, *To Every Nation Under Heaven. The Acts of the Apostles* (Harrisburg: Trinity, 1997) p.50.

130 It is recognised that Paul is referred to as apostle (with Barnabas) in Acts only in 14:4 and 14:14.

refers to divine healing in two ways in Acts; in brief mentions of Jesus' earthly healing ministry, and in more detailed narratives of healings performed by his followers, told in a way which allows parallels to be drawn to Jesus' healing.

3.2 References to Jesus' Healing in Acts

Considering how prominent healing is in the gospel, and taking into account the number of speeches in Acts which record Israel's ancient and recent history, there are remarkably few references to Jesus' healing. This accords with the relatively small number of references to Jesus' ministry, compared to his passion, death and resurrection.[131] Jesus' healing is implicit in the general summary of his ministry as, 'all that Jesus began to do (and to teach)', in Acts 1:1, and in Peter and John's answer to the Sanhedrin, 'what we have seen and heard' (4:20).

The only two specific references are found in Peter's speeches. The first is in his Pentecost sermon (2:14-36). The original prophecy of Joel (2:28-31), quoted in Acts 2:17-21, does not include 'signs' in the earth, but it seems that Peter added it in v.19, so that he could equate the prophecy with Jesus' miracles; 'Jesus of Nazareth, a man attested to you by God with deeds of power, wonders and signs that God did through him among you' (2:22). Peter was claiming that God did the deeds of power and signs and wonders 'through' Jesus, a pattern that fits with Luke's subordinate Christology in healing, which we saw in the gospel.[132] Peter was addressing Jews of Jerusalem and Judea, who would have previous knowledge of Jesus' reputation for healing, a fact which Peter used (v.22), 'as you yourselves know'.

The second reference to Jesus' healing occurs in Peter's speech in Joppa to the household of Cornelius, a God-fearing Roman centurion. Jesus was described as 'anointed by God with the Holy Spirit and with power' (a reference to Isa. 61:1), and 'how he went about doing good (εὐεργετῶν),[133] and healing all who were oppressed by the devil, for

---

131 W.A. Strange, 'The Jesus-Tradition in Acts', *NTS* 46 (2000), especially pp.59-65. R. Brucker, 'Die Wunder der Apostel Kontroverse Wunder in frühen Christentum–Wirklichkeit oder Propaganda?', *ZNT* 7 (2001) p.38, emphasises the constant references back to the central and greatest miracle, the raising of Jesus from the dead by God (e.g. Acts 2:24, 32; 3:15; 4:2; 10:40).

132 Kahl, *New Testament Miracle Stories*, p.82, notes that the earthly Jesus is portrayed here by Luke as working miracles like the apostles did (see *2.1.3* and *3.4.3*).

133 In this passage, Jesus' miracles were being described to people who were knowledgeable about the Graeco-Roman tradition of benefactors. Kee, *To Every Nation*, p.173, considers that this accords with Graeco-Roman belief that those who did

God was with him' (10:38). This also continues Luke's view from the gospel (5:17) that Jesus' healing power came directly from God, after his anointing with the Holy Spirit at his baptism. Dunn rightly points out that 10:38 is a very moderate description of Jesus' healing ministry, after the high Christological statement of 10:36, 'Jesus Christ—Lord of all'.[134] It seems just possible that 10:38 reflects Luke deliberately playing down the healing aspect of Jesus' ministry, in order to emphasise, rather, his exaltation in the post-Easter situation (see *2.6.1*).

It is notable that Paul did not mention Jesus' healing miracles in any of his sermons in Acts (see Chapter 5).

In summary, the reason for the paucity of references to Jesus' healing is not clear, but fits with the fact that the speeches in Acts do not record Jesus' ministry in any detail.

3.3 Healing by Jesus' Followers

3.3.1 Inspired Speech and Healing in Acts

We considered whether Jesus' teaching and healing activities in the gospel could be separated. In Acts, the similar question is whether Luke separates inspired speech and miracles by Jesus' followers. Shelton argues against this, and certainly, there are frequent references to apostolic preaching and healing together (e.g. 2:42-43; 6:8-10; 8:5-8; 14:3).[135] Turner also considers that Luke in Acts shows that the Spirit poured out by Jesus at Pentecost was associated with both preaching and healing, a view corroborated by Talbert.[136] This would be the logical follow-up to Luke's gospel view. The opposite opinion is that of Dunn, who considers that Luke separates speech and miracles in Acts, so that

extraordinary public good deeds were gods in human form. Danker, *Jesus and the New Age*, p.5, demonstrates that Luke presents Jesus as the Great Benefactor in the Graeco-Roman setting; as Green, *Gospel of Luke*, p.25, points out, God is the Great Benefactor in Jewish piety.

134 J.D.G. Dunn, *The Acts of the Apostles*, Epworth Commentaries (Peterborough: Epworth, 1996) p.143.

135 Shelton, *Mighty in Word*, p.78. He sees the Holy Spirit linked to both activities.

136 M. Turner, 'The Spirit and the Power of Jesus' Miracles in the Lucan Conception', *NovT* 33 (1991) 124-52. See also, Turner, *Power from on High*, pp.276-78, on the Spirit of prophecy and the power to heal. C.H. Talbert, *Reading Acts. A Literary and Theological Commentary on the Acts of the Apostles* (New York: Crossroad, 1997) pp.48-49, enumerates three major and five minor functions of the Spirit.

the Spirit is manifest as inspired speech only; miracles are not attributed to the Spirit.[137]

There are points in favour of both views. The coming of the Spirit at Pentecost manifested itself immediately as an emphasis on speech rather than on healing; followers from every country understood one another's language (2:4-13), then Peter spoke boldly in public (2:14-36). The relationship of inspired speech (as glossolalia) to the coming of the Spirit is also found in 10:46 and 19:6. In the church's first recorded prayer, the supplication was for God's servants to have ability to 'preach with boldness, and that God's hand be stretched out to heal' (4:29-30), so the two activities were related there, even though the Spirit was not mentioned specifically, and some separation is implied in the wording.[138] There is more separation than in the gospel between preaching and healing in other areas of Acts; in several healing episodes (e.g. 9:32-35, 36-42), preaching is not mentioned, and in the story of the conversion of Sergius Paulus and the blinding of Elymas (13:6-11), teaching is referred to specifically only at the end of the account (v.12). One major reason for the apparent dichotomy seems to be the more continuous narrative style of Acts, unlike the shorter pericope technique of the gospel. This means that an episode is followed through; for instance, the detail of Peter's first sermon after the coming of the Spirit is recorded (2:14-36), and the consequences of Peter healing the lame man at the Temple (3:1-10) continue to be reported up to 4:37.[139]

Dunn's view, separating inspired speech from healing, seems somewhat too radical. It appears, rather, that Luke envisages that apostles, and the leaders appointed by them (for instance, Philip, in the story of Simon Magus), responded to the Spirit with both preaching and healing, while the 'ordinary' believers responded to the Spirit with speech phenomena, but not healing (see Chapter 6, *2.1.1*).

3.3.2 Healing in the Gospel and in Acts: Similarities and Differences

Most modern scholars agree that the book of Acts is written in a style that consciously recalls the narrative of Luke's gospel, so some events of Jesus' ministry were echoed in those of his apostles, and, in turn, the activities of other prominent followers, especially Paul, had parallels

---

137 Dunn, *Acts of Apostles*, p.58.

138 Nielsen, *Heilung*, p.181, considers that the acts of healing are subordinate to the proclamation there.

139 Tannehill, *Narrative Unity,* 1, p.5, refers to Luke's narrative being like a rope with many strands, where it is difficult to follow one strand throughout.

with those of the first apostles, especially Peter (see Tables 1 and 2).[140] These are unlike the parallels in the synoptic gospels, where one author has used material from another as his source. Luke's narrative parallels serve to keep the story line moving on, and these parallels allow for both similarity and difference. This is particularly clear in the area of healing.

There are many similarities between Jesus' and apostolic healings. For example, Jesus' raising of Jairus' daughter has a narrative parallel with Peter's raising of Tabitha (Table 1),[141] and Peter healing the lame man in Jerusalem is paralleled by Paul healing the crippled man in Lystra (Table 2). The healing summaries (2:43; 5:12, 15-16; 6:8; 8:6-7, 13; 14:3; 15:12; 19:11-12; 28:9) serve the same function as in the gospel, of demonstrating the wide extent of healing activity, but they also depict the apostles following Jesus' example in responding to need. There were no cries for mercy from the sick, yet they were often implicit, and, as in the gospels, compassion is not specifically mentioned as a reason for healing. Luke continues to emphasise the difficulties that the healer faced; the lame man, aged over 40, had congenital lameness (Acts 3:2; 4:22), the man at Lystra was also crippled from birth (14:8), and Aeneas had been bed-ridden for 8 years (9:33).

But the similarities are often superficial, and the presentation of healing in Acts, compared with those in Jesus' ministry, shows obvious differences. The repetitive pattern often highlights change, and allows the differences to stand out (Tables 1 and 2). The struggle between good and evil, between the Holy Spirit and evil spirits, takes on a different form in Acts. Jesus' healings and exorcisms in the gospel demonstrated his dominance over evil spirits in helplessly ill or demon-possessed suppliants, but in Acts, some individuals were motivated by an 'evil spirit' over which they seemed to have some control. For instance, in the story of Simon Magus, trying to buy for his own use the power of the Holy Spirit, presumably for healing (8:9-24), both his magic (v.9) and his encouragement of the belief that he was the 'power of God' (v.10)

---

140 E.g. R.C. Tannehill, *The Narrative Unity of Luke-Acts. A Literary Interpretation.* Vol.2*: The Acts of the Apostles* (Minneapolis: Fortress, 1990). The history of thought about the Peter–Paul parallels since the mid-nineteenth century is set out in D.P. Moessner, '"The Christ Must Suffer." New Light on the Jesus–Peter, Stephen, Paul Parallels in Luke-Acts', *NovT* 28 (1986) pp.221-23.

141 Peter ejected the mourners (as Jesus did in Mk. 5:40, but not in Lk. 8:51). This seems to be in keeping with Luke holding some material back from the gospel, to use in Acts (see *2.6*).

imply for Luke his association with the devil.[142] Garrett considers that the emphasis in Acts was on the struggle with Satan's authority over not only those sick and demonised, but also over Gentiles and unrepentant Jews.[143] It seems that Luke portrays in Acts the more varied difficulties encountered in healing and proclamation by the apostles, compared to his presentation of the more uniform opposition by the religious establishment to Jesus' healing and preaching.

An important change is that Luke seems to be using healing stories for different purposes in Acts compared with the gospel. The sufferer is depicted in some ways as less important than in the gospel; in only one narrative did Paul note the faith of the crippled man before healing him (14:8), and the reactions of the healed are rarely reported; the only recorded reaction of joy was from the lame man in Jerusalem (3:8). There was no injunction to silence after healing as there was in the gospels, since healings in Acts were important in spreading the good news.

The pattern of illness was also different in Acts. Sufferers from the illnesses found in the gospel are not mentioned; there was nobody with leprosy, and no woman with menorrhagia. Although exorcisms of the demon-possessed are mentioned in some of the summary accounts (e.g. 5:16; 8:7; 19:11), only one individual exorcism is described (16:16-8). It is possible that the Philippian girl had *petit mal* or temporal lobe epilepsy, and 'prophesied' during episodes of altered consciousness, but no other person with epilepsy or psychosis was healed; the closest parallel to the Gadarene man in the gospel was the man whose evil spirit attacked the Jewish exorcists (19:16). Sufferers from all these conditions would have been excluded from the worshipping righteous Israel of the Pharisees, but they should have been accepted in the community of the church, where the apostles were likely to have encountered them.[144] There was nobody with a withered arm, kyphosis, or oedema; the problem these sufferers illuminated in the gospel, of healing on the Sabbath, is not found as a concern in the church in Acts.[145]

---

142 Barrett, *Acts*, pp.118-19, notes that practising as a magus indicates Simon's illicit dealings with evil spirits; Garrett, *Demise of Devil*, pp.62, 66, 67.

143 Garrett, *Demise of Devil*, p.40.

144 Brucker, 'Wunder der Apostel', p.39, considers that these omissions are to demonstrate the apostles as clearly subordinate to their Lord.

145 Jervell, *Die Apostelgeschichte*, pp.501-502, discusses the relationship between the time of Paul's sermon, the 'breaking of bread', and 'the first day of the week' in Acts 20:7, in trying to decide whether Luke is describing the Eucharistic meal, or a daily celebration, when Eutychus was restored to life by Paul. Jervell concludes that Luke is stressing the miracle, not the time. H. Avalos, *Health Care and the Rise of Christianity*

The only blindness healed in Acts was that of Saul by Ananias, and it did not resemble the healing of the blind man in Jericho (Lk. 18:35-43), except in creating disciples of both. Hamm demonstrates the increasing spiritualisation of Paul's blindness on the Damascus road as it is recounted repeatedly in Acts, with a physical healing in 9:17, a more muted miracle in 22:6-13, then, by 26:12-18, the blindness is transposed to the recipients of Paul's mission, the Gentiles and Israel, and becomes a metaphor in which Paul is to open their eyes to the power of God.[146] Although this particular healing is a special case, the wide reporting of Paul's conversion conforms to the evidence that Luke is concerned in Acts to report especially those healings that would result in most response. Paul being bitten by a viper without harm (Acts 28:3-6) is presented as legitimating evidence of Christianity to the natives of Malta.[147]

The mention of the healed person's name is commoner in Acts than in the gospel. Aeneas, Tabitha and Eutychus were identified, perhaps because they were more prominent citizens than most of the gospel suppliants.[148] The father of Publius (described as the chief man in Malta) might correspond in social importance with Jairus' daughter in the gospel. Paul is portrayed as acting in vexation to exorcise the demon of the slave-girl (16:18), the only slave healed; and children, the paradigm of the helpless in society, were not reported being either healed or blessed in the Acts narrative.[149] The difference from the emphasis on the poor in the gospel fits with the greater interest in Acts on the prosperous, a finding that has been noted in areas other than healing.

(Peabody: Hendrickson, 1999) p.114, points out that in very early Christianity, restoring human health took precedence over rules about time.

146 D. Hamm, 'Paul's Blindness and Its Healing: Clues to Symbolic Intent. (Acts 9, 22 and 26)', *Bib.* 71 (1990) pp.68-69, notes that Paul and Barnabas, not Jesus, were first identified as the 'light to the Gentiles,' (Acts 13:47). Theological blindness recalls the language of the Pentateuch (e.g. Deut. 28:28-29), where covenant disobedience was cursed with blindness.

147 The story brings to fruition the episode of the seventy in the gospel, given divine authority to tread on snakes and scorpions with impunity (Lk. 10:19), but not being put to the test. Conzelmann, *Acts,* p.223, points out that the irregularities of the miracle, e.g. that venomous snakes do not hang on, and that there were probably no poisonous snakes in Malta, are not relevant to the story, which he considers has magical overtones.

148 Conzelmann, *Acts*, p.76, notes that in ancient miracle stories, the names of the healed are almost entirely absent. In the gospel (8:2-3), the socially prominent women who were healed by Jesus and become followers were named, however, while Bartimaeus, the beggar named in Mark's gospel, was unnamed in Luke's gospel.

149 Children may have been among the household of e.g. Cornelius (10:48), and the jailer (16:33), when they were baptised.

Marshall points out that Luke reports very little about the inner life of the church, as he concentrates his energies on the essential task of the early church, mission, and considers that this would account for the 'little ones' not being mentioned. Luke in Acts does emphasise the church's social and political legitimacy.[150]

Although the major healing work of Jesus continued in apostolic healing, the more ruthless aspect of power is highlighted in Acts, and there is no stress on loving one's enemies, which is highlighted in the gospel (e.g. Lk. 6:27). Jesus is portrayed as performing no miracles which harmed people, but several opponents of the early church in Acts suffered,[151] many in miraculous ways, for instance, Ananias and Sapphira died (5:1-11), Paul (9:8; 22:11) and Elymas (13:11) were blinded temporarily, the latter because he was combating Paul's preaching to Sergius Paulus (13:12). Many modern writers have found the 'punitive' miracles, particularly the deaths of Ananias and Sapphira, difficult.[152] Reimer suggests that Peter's effective curse pronouncements equate with the miraculous speech of the intermediary between God and people (e.g. in the Old Testament). In Peter's words, which meant the sentence of death for Ananias and Sapphira, Jervell sees that it is God himself who passed judgment, and inspired fear in the community (v.11), and the fear emphasised the credibility of the kerygma. Reimer accepts here the criteria for these acts being miracles, that is, that they evoked faith in others, and produced no personal gain to the intermediary, while they demonstrated the importance of a united church (see *3.4.4*).[153]

---

150 Marshall, *Acts*, pp.49-50. Tuckett, *Christology and New Testament*, p.133. J.C. Beker, 'Christologies and Anthropologies of Paul, Luke-Acts and Marcion', in M.C. de Boer (ed.), *From Jesus to John. Essays on Jesus and New Testament Christology in Honour of Marinus de Jonge* (JSNTSup 84; Sheffield: Sheffield Academic Press, 1993) p.177. Tannehill, *Luke*, p.24, suggests that Luke was writing for a group of churches with different social components.

151 We do not know from Acts if Simon Magus was later rehabilitated in the church or not; Klauck, *Magic and Paganism*, pp.22-23, writes that Luke leaves this open to his readers (unlike the apocryphal *Acts of Peter*, in W. Schneemelcher (ed.), *New Testament Apocrypha*, Vol.2, *Writings Related to the Apostles, Apocalypses, and Related Subjects* [ET; Cambridge/Louisville: Clarke & Co./Westminster John Knox, 1992] p.272, where Simon Magus was killed). It illustrates that Luke's primary interest in Acts is in the church, not in individuals.

152 E.g. Marshall, *Acts*, pp.110-11. C.K. Barrett, '*Imitatio Christi* in Acts', in Green and Turner (eds.), *Jesus of Nazareth: Lord and Christ*, p.260, notes that there is no mention of regret over these events.

153 Reimer, *Miracle and Magic*, pp.12, 46, 102. It is possible that Peter's confrontation produced fatal cardiac arrhythmia in both, but the story is told, of course, for its

Luke's depiction of the building up of the church also seemed to leave several innocent 'dogs of war'. Friends of the church were damaged (e.g. Jason, 17:6-9; Sosthenes, 18:17), and minor characters were given less care in Acts than in the gospel. The fate of the slave girl (16:16-19) no longer able to prophesy, is not mentioned; Peter's prison guards were ordered to be killed (12:19) because Peter had escaped; and there is no mention of what happened to the other prisoners in 16:26, after Paul and Silas' miraculous release.[154]

To summarise, the importance of both Jesus' healing ministry and of apostolic healing is underlined by the presentation of the latter in ways that seem to be deliberately narrated in parallel with Jesus' healing in the gospel. Although it may not be Luke's primary objective to portray the church spreading by deeds of healing, he presents healing by Jesus' followers as of great significance to the advance of the church. Narrative parallels allow the forward movement of the story to be emphasised, with different challenges being highlighted as Christianity met non-Jewish cultures. The characteristic features of Jesus' ministry, his compassion and care for the oppressed, poor and ill, seem to be played down often in Luke's account of the advance of the infant church, where, instead, power, including the power of healing, is emphasised.

3.4 Luke's Portrayal of Apostolic Healing

The aim is to see what differences there are in healing miracles in Acts, compared with the gospel, and how Luke signals them. We will consider the terms and methods used, Luke's view of the theology of apostolic healing, and the function and importance of both miracle and magic in Acts. This might give some indication as to whether Luke perceives Jesus' healings as being unique in type, or as a model for apostolic healing.

3.4.1 Use of Terms

The terms, τέρατα and σημεῖα καὶ τέρατα (wonders, and signs and wonders) are found in the LXX (e.g. Ex. 3:20; 4:30; 7:3, 9; 11:9, 10; Deut. 4:34; 6:22; 7:19; 34:11; 1 Kgs. 13:1-5; Isa. 8:18; Jer. 32:20; Ezek. 12:1-16.), where they were performed by God on behalf of Israel. The

---

theological implications. Jervell, *Die Apostelgeschichte*, pp.197, 199, believes that the story must have had some historical basis; the couple being named is important.

154 Jervell, *Die Apostelgeschichte*, pp.335-36, considers that the guards (12:19) were executed. Barrett, '*Imitatio Christi*', pp.253-54, notes that, for instance, in Acts 16:16-18, Luke does not suggest that the apostles showed compassion

next biblical cluster of the terms is in the early church. By the New Testament period, the term 'wonders' alone had become rare, and was combined with 'signs' to designate miracles.[155] Luke uses 'signs and wonders' in Acts to describe apostolic healing, possibly to approximate it to prophetic healing in the name of Yahweh. Healing miracles as 'signs and wonders' in Christ's name are common, for instance, 2:43 and 5:12 (by apostles); 4:30 (in the church's prayer); 6:8 (by Stephen); 14:3 and 15:12 (by Paul and Barnabas). In the gospels, 'sign', used alone, refers to unbelievers, and it appears also in the Sanhedrin's discussion of Peter's healing of the lame man (Acts 4:16). It is also found occasionally in relation to apostles, e.g. 'a sign of healing' described the lame man's cure (4:22), and Philip's healing and preaching are called 'signs' (8:6). We have seen that the term δυνάμεις was used occasionally for Jesus' miracles in the gospel; in Acts, it is qualified, for instance, Philip performed signs and great wonders (8:13), and Paul did mighty works, which were extraordinary (19:11).

There is no significant difference in the words used for sickness between the gospel and Acts. As in the gospel, Luke describes a paralysed man (Acts 9:33) as having been paralysed. The commonest verbs for healing are θεραπεύω (4 times in Acts, 14 times in the gospel), and ἰάομαι (3 times in Acts, 12 times in the gospel), and Wells demonstrates that θεραπεύω is always used in the passive in Acts (4:14; 5:16; 8:7; 28:9), but almost always in its active voice in the gospel; she regards this as a measure of difference between Jesus' and apostolic healing.[156] Luke uses other words for healing in Acts, e.g. στερεόω, referring to the strengthening of the bones (3:7, 16), and ἀπαλλάσσω (19:12) as release from disease, but this seems to be in keeping with his extensive Greek vocabulary. The noun for healing, ἴασις, is used in 4:22 and 4:30. The cripple in Jerusalem is healed by εὐεργεσία ('a good deed', 4:9), although it is a term more usually found in a Greek context. The same verse has σῴζω, meaning physical healing, as is often found in the gospel (Lk. 8:48; 18:42; and possibly 17:19) in the sense of rescue, but only used again thus in Acts in 27:34; whereas in 4:12, and

155 P.H. Davids, 'Signs and Wonders', pp.1093-95, in R.P. Martin and P.H. Davids (eds.), *Dictionary of the Later New Testament and its Developments* (Downers Grove/Leicester: InterVarsity, 1997) p.1093; H.C. Kee, *The Community of the New Age. Studies in Mark's Gospel* (London: SCM, 1977) p.24; D.J. Moo, *The Epistle to the Romans,* NICNT (Grand Rapids/Cambridge: Eerdmans, 1996) p.893, notes that the 'sign' represents the purpose of the miracle, the 'wonder' its marvellous and unusual character.

156 Wells, *Language of Healing*, pp.406-13.

elsewhere in Acts, σῴζω and σωτήπιον (to save, and salvation) are used in the full eschatological sense; the best example being 28:27-28, where in Paul's speech, spiritual healing was equated with the salvation of God.

The use in Acts of the more theological 'signs and wonders', compared with the terms used in the gospel, may signal that Luke sees apostolic healing as more of a religious propaganda tool than was Jesus' healing in the gospel. The legitimating function of miracles in the early church can be seen in 15:12, demonstrating the concept that miracles show proclamation of the gospel authenticated by God.[157]

3.4.2 Methods of Apostolic Healing

The use of words in healing is as important in Acts as in the gospel, but there is even less obvious distinction between exorcism by command and physical healing by touch here; for instance, Peter healed the lame man at the Beautiful Gate by command 'in the name of Jesus', and the paralysed Aeneas by word (9:34). Separating word and touch in most healing situations is artificial, since a healer would naturally have physical contact with a person, if only in a gesture of care and concern; for instance, in Acts 3:7 and 9:41, Peter helped the afflicted person up after healing (an action common in Mark's, but not recorded in Luke's gospel). Sometimes the healer touched the individual (e.g. 28:8), at other times the sick person touched the healer (or some representation of him, 19:12).

Instead of ἅπτομαι (the verb used mostly in the gospel for touch in healing), ἐπιτίθημι τὰς χεῖρας (laid hands) is commoner in Acts (e.g. 9:12, 17; 28:8). As in the Old Testament,[158] there is considerable emphasis on hands in Acts. The hands of the opponents are mentioned in the arrest of the apostles (4:3; 5:18), but laying-on of hands by apostles, transmitting the power of God, occurred in healing e.g. 5:12 (through the hands of the apostles); 14:3 (through their hands, i.e. of Paul and Barnabas); 19:11 (through Paul's hands); as well as in blessing 11:21 (the 'hand of the Lord', which may be that of God or Jesus), 'ordination' (6:6; 13:3) and in receiving the Holy Spirit (8:17-18; 19:6).

---

157 Nielsen, *Heilung*, p.182. S. Schreiber, *Paulus als Wundertäter: Redaktionsgeschichtliche Untersuchungen zur Apostelgeschichte und den authentischen Paulusbriefen* (BZNW 79; Berlin/New York: de Gruyter, 1996) p.293.

158 In the Old Testament, Yahweh's hand often symbolised his power, e.g. 1 Chr. 29:12, 'in your hand are power and riches'; Job 5:18, 'his hands heal'. In Isa. 42:6, Yahweh takes Israel by the hand in protection.

Thus, apostolic healing generally followed the gospel description of Jesus' methods, and the healing, blessing touch of Jesus in the gospel is depicted as being carried on in the work of the apostles in Acts.

3.4.3 Theology of Apostolic Healing

The Spirit poured out by the ascended Jesus in Acts is understood as the fulfilment of the gift prophesied by Joel (2:28-32), the Spirit of prophecy 'for all flesh', but there is some variation in Luke's perception in Acts as to how divine healing power was transmitted to the apostles. This may be related partly to the ambiguity in Acts as to whether 'Lord' refers to God or the ascended Christ (see *3.1*). In 5:12, signs and wonders were done 'through the apostles,' perhaps a divine passive, since in 19:11, 'God did extraordinary miracles through Paul'; and in 15:12, 'the assembly listened to Paul and Barnabas as they told of all the signs and wonders that *God* had done'. In these instances, God is the bearer (source) of numinous power, using Kahl's nomenclature. More usually, Luke assumes that Jesus, at his ascension, became (2:36) the source of power, and through Christ, divine power was channelled to the apostles.[159] As petitioners, the apostles often healed (and preached) 'in the name of Jesus', where Jesus was the mediator with God for apostolic healing (3:6; 4:10, 17-18, 30; 9:27-28.). This was a concept familiar to the Jewish authorities, who questioned the 'name' of the apostles' healing power (4:7). On one occasion, Peter said 'Jesus Christ heals you' (9:34), on another (14:10) Paul spoke the healing word directly. Kahl comments that Luke is portraying the ascended Christ as God's agent of salvation, so when the apostles healed 'in his name', they were pointing to Christ as Saviour, encouraging witnesses to join the faith-community. The apostles thus correspond to the Old Testament prophets, whose work pointed to Yahweh.[160]

The wording used in healing indicates that Luke does not always follow a systematic scheme for apostolic healing, although he regards healing as resulting from power from either God or the ascended Christ, and was for the purpose of proclaiming Christ.

---

159 Kahl, *New Testament Miracle Stories*, p.83, (see Chapter 3, *1.8.3*). Jervell, *Theology of Acts*, p.32, is convincing in his view that Luke emphasises Christ, risen and ascended by the act of God, as still subordinate to God. Barrett, '*Imitatio Christi*', pp.259-61, regards healing in Acts as Luke's way of demonstrating the power of *God*, e.g. in 3:16; 4:7-10; 19:11.

160 Kahl, *New Testament Miracle Stories*, p.227.

3.4.4 Miracle-Workers and Magicians in Acts

The narrative world of Acts is 'one in which the membrane separating the natural and the numinous sphere is permeable',[161] and there are many episodes where this is obvious. Fridrichsen points out that, as πράξεις (acts) can mean miracles, Acts can be named the book of 'Miracles of the Apostles'.[162] Garrett, who remarks that 'magic is an everyday aspect of life in the first century', especially in Acts, believes that Luke capitalises on the superficial resemblance of the phrase 'name of Jesus' to a magical formula, particularly the idea of a magician using the power of a young and violently-killed person.[163] This does not seem to fit Luke's use of the phrase in apostolic healing in Acts, nor with the example that the apostles inherited from Jesus, and received with his gift of the Holy Spirit.

Acts is the only work in the New Testament where there is a continuing overt battle between miracle-workers and magicians. Reimer bases his definition of each mainly on distillation of his findings in Acts:

> When an individual performs an extraordinary event which is understood to be a mediation of some sort of divine power, it will be classed a miracle if it is not performed for some personal advantage by the miracle-worker, it is a particularly powerful display of mediated divine power, it is not overtly undermining the acceptable social and political structures of *a given community*, and/or can be understood to occur within an established religious framework. On the other hand, it will be classed as magic if it is performed for the personal advantage of the intermediary, it is carried out in such a way as to suggest a manipulation of divine beings, it is overtly undermining acceptable social and political structures within *a given community*, and/or it is understood to be an act of religious deviance.[164]

He points out that these definitions are not absolute, and their application is subjective. The definitions cover episodes happening to believers in Acts, for instance, Philip snatched away from the carriage of the Ethiopian eunuch (8:39), and some of the escapes from prison (5:18-26; 12:2-11), as well as some of the healing summaries (5:11-12, healing produced by Peter's shadow falling on sick people; 19:11, suppliants touching Paul's aprons and sweat-bands in order to be

---

161 Reimer, *Miracle and Magic*, p.50.

162 Fridrichsen, *Problem of Miracle*, pp.60-61. Conzelmann, *Acts,* p.163, notes that πράξεις is a term widely used for magic at the time.

163 Garrett, *Demise of Devil*, pp.3, 66, 76, 102, 113.

164 Reimer, *Miracle and Magic*, pp.249-50 (my italics).

healed).[165] The difficulty with Reimer's (or any such) definition is that it depends on the defined 'given community', so it appears that there is no way round seeing the church as right, in Luke's eyes, and therefore having miracle-workers, in contrast to the opposition as wrong, and therefore classified as performing magic.

Parts of Reimer's definition depend heavily on a value judgment of the powers behind the healings in Luke's narrative. The important issue is what the ancient writer understands, and wishes to portray, had occurred. The powers of the Holy Spirit and that of magic are in overt opposition in Acts,[166] and Luke portrays magicians as working for their own benefit, for instance, Simon Magus (8:9-13, 18-24) trying to buy the power of the Holy Spirit, and Elymas, a Jewish magician, in the employ of a Roman official. Their magic is less potent than Philip and Paul's miracles, so 'bigger is better'.[167] The punitive miracles, however, rule out the idea that the *nature* of the miracle is a key criterion for distinguishing legitimate miracle-workers from illegitimate magicians in Acts.[168] The gospel account of Jesus' temptations (Lk. 4:1-13), demonstrating that miracle-working would be demonic if it were not based on obedience to God, seems to be played out in Acts. Luke's concern is to demonstrate the failure and perils of attempts by the church's opponents at magical healing, since he depicts all healing power as 'God's gift' (8:20).[169] Garrett rightly emphasises that the encounters with magicians in Acts are less about magic than about Christ's victories over Satan, but she also notes that the stories give an important insight into Luke's worldview of magic.[170]

My (minority) view is that Luke condones magic as a weapon when it was used to safeguard the unity of the church, while he distances the

---

165 The magical power of the fringe of the Jewish holy man's garment is mentioned in *b. Taan.* 23b, although Judaism did not officially countenance magic or magicians (see Chapter 2, *1.3.2*).

166 Kee, *Medicine, Miracle and Magic*, pp.115-16. Conzelmann, *Acts,* p.xlvii, considers that Luke's distinction in Acts between miracles and magic is apologetic, and is related to power.

167 Jervell, *Die Apostelgeschichte,* pp.261-62; Brucker, 'Wunder der Apostel', p.34. In the case of Simon Magus, the whole city followed him, but Philip's sermon and his great signs and wonders caused the people to change, so Philip's victory over Simon was huge.

168 Reimer, *Miracle and Magic*, p.111. See Chapter 1, *1.3.1.* Remus, *Jesus as Healer*, p.101, notes that Acts demonstrates the sociological phenomenon that accusations of being a magician arise from judgements influenced by group loyalties.

169 Tannehill, *Luke*, p.90; Shelton, *Mighty in Word*, p.82.

170 Garrett, *Demise of Devil*, p.102.

church from the opposing magical culture. Clearly, however, this reflects my perspective, which is based on long experience in medicine.

3.4.5 Summary of Apostolic Healing

The depiction of miracle healings in Acts shows important changes from the gospel portrayal of Jesus' healings. The terms mainly employed about healing in Acts have changed from those in the gospel, so the term 'signs and wonders', previously associated particularly with Moses' miracles in the Exodus, is common, and draws attention to the theological intent and miraculous nature of apostolic healing. The change seems to indicate Luke's wish to emphasise the major religious effect produced by apostolic signs and wonders. The method of healing used by the apostles remained simple, as in the gospel. Punitive miracles are found in Acts, particularly to defeat those seen to oppose the strength and orthodoxy of the church, including its healing ministry, and, conversely, some of the church's opponents were charged with using magic, which was ineffectual.

There is a more obvious presentation in Acts of healing of the socially prominent, although there is also considerable evidence of the depiction, as in the gospel, of apostolic healing for all who sought it. Healing seems to become more clearly an activity that attracted believers, with less emphasis on care, and more on its value as religious advertisement, than Jesus' healing.

The main theological difference between the gospel and Acts with regard to healing is that Luke portrays Jesus healing by power from God, with whom he was in such a close relationship that he did not need to ask for God's help for each miracle, whereas Jesus' followers normally invoked Jesus' name (i.e. his power) at the moment of healing, that is, Jesus had, at his ascension, become the source of healing power. This understanding was not uniform, however, as sometimes power was directly from God (see *3.4.3*). Jesus' healings are portrayed by Luke as unique in respect of this closeness to God's power and kingship; apostles' healing was often the means of spreading the message, but the purpose of their healing was to show Christ as God's agent of salvation, that is, to point people away from the apostle towards Christ, as the power to heal and save.

All the changes from the gospel seem to demonstrate Luke's intention of presenting healing as an important means of showing the power of Christ, in order to spread his message.

3.5 Responses to Apostolic Healing in Acts

Healing in both the gospel and Acts produced a dichotomous effect, on the one hand, faith and thanksgiving from the crowd, and on the other, opposition from the Jewish religious authorities. It is easy to see that miraculous healing would produce followers, but there was something in the message and the healing that invited derision and rejection, and created danger.[171] Luke depicts persecution as following both healing and preaching in Acts, in both Jewish (e.g. 3:2–4:37) and Graeco-Roman (e.g. 14:8-18) settings, although the responses and types of opposition to healing were often different from those in the gospel.

In the gospel, the Jewish religious authorities did not accept that the power behind Jesus' healing came from God. In Acts, the high priests and Sadducees in Jerusalem conceded that the apostles had healed by some supernatural power (4:16-17), although their opposition to that power being mediated by Christ continued. Luke's attitude about who might legitimately heal and exorcise seems to change from the gospel (Lk. 9:49), where he portrays Jesus encouraging his disciples to accept the unknown exorcist (probably the influence of Mark's gospel), and where the 'sons' of Jesus' opponents were able to exorcise (11:19); in Acts, Luke's stance hardens towards opponents who tried to use the name of Jesus to exorcise; hence the spectacular failure of the sons of Sceva (19:13-16), which had a strongly positive effect in spreading the gospel, with the residents of Ephesus, some of them Christian, burning their books on magic.

In the Gentile setting, the question of who was in need of healing was also different; for instance, the slave-girl with the spirit of divination (16:16) was acceptable in Greek culture, but both Jews and Christians were opposed to divination, because of its association with false prophecy (Deut. 13:1-5).[172] The girl is assumed by Luke to have an evil spirit, which was exorcised by Paul (16:18). Paul's opponents there, the Gentile slave-owners, whose source of revenue had been removed, lied

---

171 Hemer, *Book of Acts*, p.85. Minear, *To Heal and To Reveal*, p.10. Tannehill, *Narrative Unity*, 1, p.2, emphasises that rejection, especially by the Jewish religious authorities, is highlighted repeatedly throughout Luke-Acts.

172 The girl was accurate in her recognition of Paul *et al.* (possibly Silas and Luke) as 'slaves of the Most High God, proclaiming a way of salvation'. Kee, *To Every Nation*, p.197, suggests that the girl had been forced to prostitute her divinatory gift. G.N. Stanton, 'Jesus of Nazareth: A Magician and False Prophet who Deceived God's People?', in Green and Turner (eds.), *Jesus of Nazareth*, pp.179-80, points out that an allegation of being a magician includes being a false prophet.

about the reason for their hostility,[173] so that healing produced a train of opposition different from anything found in the gospel. On at least one occasion, Gentile reaction to healing is depicted as misunderstanding, rather than opposition; the response to Paul's healing at Lystra (14:8-10) was the attempt to offer sacrifices to Paul and Barnabas as gods. In that incident, Luke portrays that it was Jewish intervention that turned the Gentile crowd against Paul, who was stoned (v.19), but survived; Luke is intent on demonstrating particularly Jewish opposition to the church.

Persecution of Jesus' followers is often depicted as resulting in a successful outcome in Acts. Although there are several stories of believers' flights, for instance from prison, not all escaped. Stephen was stoned to death, James was executed, and Peter, Paul and others were imprisoned. The persecution in Jerusalem after Stephen's death, however, caused a dispersion of followers to e.g. Antioch, where the church flourished (11:26). Luke also portrays the repeated maltreatment, and even the final imprisonment in Rome, of Paul, as helping to spread the gospel (e.g. 28:30-31). Many scholars believe that Luke presents, first Jesus, then Peter, Stephen and Paul, as prophets like Moses, and so destined to rejection by Israel.[174] Moessner considers that in Acts, redemption was offered (by the apostles) for a second time to Israel, after she had rejected Jesus as Messiah, and her further rejection then led to the apostle-prophets being persecuted, but the Deuteronomistic pattern of Israel's disobedience→prophets urging repentance→rejection of prophets→God's punishment of Israel, was *broken* by Jesus, as the unique prophet, with the decisive saving action of his suffering, death and resurrection.[175] His message *would* spread, so that his prophecy of the Kingdom of God being for all *would* be fulfilled. The Holy Spirit's essential work was transforming Jesus' followers, so that they not only performed miracles, but also were able to endure the suffering resulting from rejection. Thus, Luke's view of the success of the gospel, as salvation, the forgiveness of sins and healing for eternal life, was often accomplished *because* of the suffering of the prophet-apostles.[176]

---

173 C.S. de Vos, 'Finding a Charge that Fits: The Accusation against Paul and Silas at Philippi (Acts 16:19-21)', *JSNT* 74 (1999) pp.51-63.

174 D.L. Tiede, *Prophecy and History in Luke-Acts* (Philadelphia: Fortress, 1980) pp.33-63; Minear, *To Heal and to Reveal*, especially pp.105-11. Johnson, *Writings of New Testament*, pp.224-25, considers the evidence for Luke seeing Jesus as the prophet like Moses is clearest in Stephen's sermon (7:17-44).

175 Moessner, 'Christ Must Suffer', pp.223, 226.

176 C. K. Barrett, 'Theologia Crucis–in Acts?' in C. Andresen and G. Klein (eds.), *Theologia Crucis–Signum Crucis* (Tübingen: Mohr [Siebeck], 1979) e.g. p.79, notes that

In summary, acts of healing, as well as proclamation, led to considerable maltreatment of the apostles, and Luke emphasises in Acts his theological awareness that the spread of Christianity would be achieved at least partly as the result of persecution of its missionaries, as essential to salvation history.

4 Luke as Physician

Lastly in this chapter, the claims are assessed briefly that the author of Luke-Acts was a physician, since this would have some bearing on Luke's portrayal and theological use of the healing miracles of Jesus and his followers.

Mainly as a result of the mention of 'Luke' in Colossians 4:14 as 'the beloved physician', the identity of the author of Luke-Acts as a physician has been generally accepted (e.g. the Muratorian Canon, perhaps dated *circa* 170-180, attributed the gospel to Luke, a doctor). The medical analogies in the gospels indicate that the evangelists did not show significant antipathy to the physician's work; both Mark and Luke note Jesus comparing himself to a physician (Mk. 2:17, par. Lk. 5:31), and in Luke's gospel (4:23) also saying 'Physician, heal yourself'.[177] At the least, the early existence of the tradition that Luke was a physician meant that, in the church of the late first century, there was a strand of opinion with no serious opposition to the efforts of physicians.[178] This was probably a major factor in protecting the practice of medicine in the church subsequently.

However, the evidence to substantiate Luke as a physician, or, at least, that he was writing from the viewpoint of a physician, is not compelling. Later support rested mainly on the allegedly medical terms used in Luke-Acts (assuming that Luke wrote both), or, alternatively, that the 'we-passages' in Acts contained less miraculous and more medical language than the rest of the work.[179] The literary data were

---

Acts does contain a *theologia crucis* in this connection, since the triumph of God's word often went hand in hand with the persecution of the messengers. See also *3.1.*

177 Marshall, *Gospel of Luke*, p.187, observes that this was a proverb found in other situations of the time. Kee, *Medicine, Miracle and Magic*, p.65, notes that the saying was a challenge to the one who points out a problem, that he must cure the problem. It is also an important indication of the contemporary atmosphere, that those who heal would be expected to be physically whole. (See Chapter 5, *2.4.1* and *2.4.2.*)

178 Hemer, *Book of Acts*, p.41.

179 The alternative assumes that these passages only were contributed by Luke the physician, and were grafted in to the book of Acts, e.g. S.E. Porter, *The Paul of Acts.*

dissected by Hobart and von Harnack, both of whom considered that Luke was a physician, but this conclusion was refuted by the work of Cadbury.[180]

Modern writers are divided in their opinions; Bock and Wilkinson believe that the writer of Luke-Acts was a physician, and Marshall agrees guardedly; Fitzmyer, convinced initially that Luke was a physician, is more uncertain in later work; Pilch is doubtful, and Johnson and Kee both regard Luke's language as merely educated Greek, with his description of healings influenced by Graeco-Roman medical tradition.[181] With regard to semantic issues, a feature favouring Luke being a physician is his use of descriptions of suppliants not solely by their disease, so he uses, for instance, 'a man having demons' (Lk. 8:27), but this is an 'etic', and modern, distinction, which has been prominent only for the last few decades. There is no description of any medical technique, or any language in Luke's writings like that found in the writings of Galen, but both genre and purpose of their writings were very different. We have to accept, also, that Luke was not writing for biblical critics searching for minutiae twenty centuries later, and that focussing exclusively on literary details may obscure other points in the debate.

From a medical perspective, other factors are more significant. Physicians have been trained since Hippocrates to be precise about the side involved, in any condition where right or left may be affected (e.g. Hippocrates, *Epidemics* I, Case VII; *Prognostics* VII; *On Wounds of the Head* XIX). There is also considerable evidence that Hippocratic training included knowledge of anatomy, especially of the limbs,[182]

Essays in Literary Criticism, Rhetoric, and Theology (WUNT 115; Tübingen: Mohr [Siebeck], 1999) p.60.

180 Hobart, *Medical Language of St. Luke,* and Von Harnack, *Luke the Physician,* both recognised that the memory/belief that Luke was a physician protected science and medicine in the Church, according to Van der Loos, *Miracles of Jesus*, p.86. H. J. Cadbury, *The Style and Literary Method of Luke.* Vol.1. *The Diction of Luke and Acts* (HTS 6; Cambridge, Mass.: Harvard University, 1919) especially pp.39-72, showed to his satisfaction that there was no literary evidence that Luke was a physician.

181 Bock, *Luke*, 1, pp.5, 7. Wilkinson, *Bible and Healing*, pp.79, 132, 162; Marshall, *Gospel of Luke*, p.34; Fitzmyer, *Luke I-IX,* pp.8, 40, c.f. Fitzmyer, *Acts*, p.50; Pilch, 'Sickness and Healing in Luke-Acts', p.182; Johnson, *Writings of New Testament*, p.214; Kee, *Medicine, Miracle and Magic*, p.79.

182 E.g. Hippocrates, *On Fractures* XIII; Galen, *On Anatomical Procedures* I.2.226, 243-53; II.3.287-91; III.1.340-42, notes that physicians must have accurate knowledge of the anatomy and function of all parts of arms and legs, before turning to inner

because the information was essential in treating injuries inflicted in battle.

Luke *is* specific (for instance, about which hand is withered, Lk. 6:6), but he mentions only the right hand throughout his writings. Right-handedness is, of course, much more common than left-handedness, and the right hand denotes theological power; when Yahweh's hand is specified, it is the right hand (e.g. the phrase in Ps. 110:1, 'sat at the right hand of God', is applied repeatedly to Jesus, e.g. Lk. 22:69). Luke is unique among the gospel-writers in stating that Jesus healed the severed ear of the high priest's servant (22:51). He notes that it was the right ear that was damaged (Mark does not state which ear). Luke reports Jesus earlier that evening, telling the disciples of impending persecution, and the need (metaphorically) to have a sword in defence (22:36-37). The disciples took the advice literally, producing two swords (v.38). Luke depicts a disciple[183] using a sword to sever the ear (22:49-50), and from the earlier pericope, he would be defending himself from an approaching attacker.

This raises the point, which I have not seen commented upon, that a right-handed swordsman would naturally attack his facing opponent's *left* ear. The muscle–tendon groups of the forearm and hand mainly involved in gripping an object (e.g. a sword handle) are *flexor digitorum profundus* and *flexor pollicis longus* (detail that would have been known to a first-century physician). These muscles are put at a mechanical disadvantage by anatomical extension of the wrist, which would happen if a swordsman attempted to strike the far side of the attacker, i.e. the right side. His grip would be weak, and it would be almost impossible, with poor control of grip, to attack an organ parallel with and close to the skull. I appreciate that there would have been both darkness and confusion at the arrest, but then there was no reason, other than a theological one, for Luke to specify which ear was damaged and repaired. The episode fits theologically both with Jesus' words in Luke 6:27 and 23:34, about loving and forgiving one's enemies, and also with Jesus healing a slave (7:1-10). Thus, I believe that Luke is portraying Jesus' healing theologically here, rather than considering clinical

---

structures. Celsus, *De Medicina* I. Book VI, *Wounds and Broken Bones,* shows awareness of anatomy; and he was writing before Luke.

183 Meier, *Marginal Jew*, II, pp.714-15, notes that in Mark (14:47), one of the bystanders, rather than a disciple, cut off the ear. In Jn. 18:10, Simon Peter delivered the sword blow to the slave's right ear. Nothing in the gospels suggests that Peter (or any of the disciples) was left-handed; it would be unlikely. Kee, *To Every Nation*, p.231, notes that one translation of the Latin 'Scaeva' is 'left-handed'.

accuracy, which a physician would do, even in making a theological point.

There are other, lesser, 'straws in the wind' against Luke being a physician. His description in the gospel of the boy with epilepsy is inferior to Mark's in important points of the clinical history, where Mark portrays the condition dating from childhood, resulting in the boy falling in to fire and water (important in differentiating hysteria from *grand mal*), and his inability to speak during the fit. Also, in the description of the fit witnessed, Mark, unlike Luke, differentiates the tonic (v.18), clonic (v.20) and post-ictal (v.26) phases. Luke also omits Mark's description of Jesus' conversation with the boy's father, an important part of healing in the particular therapeutic situation.

In Acts, Luke reports without comment the temporary blinding of Elymas, apparently at the behest of Paul (Acts 13:9-11), and this goes against all Hippocratic teachings about doing no harm. In the 'we-passages', Luke, if present with Paul in Troas, would naturally have gone to help when Eutychus fell from the window (20:9-12); similarly, in Malta, he would have offered aid to Paul, bitten by a snake, and perhaps also to Publius' father (28:3, 8-9).[184] Kee says that the author of Acts does not look to physicians, but to God, who acts directly on behalf of the needy,[185] but one would have expected that his trained reaction would have still resulted in his offering help. These points seem to outweigh the possibility that Luke did not criticise physicians (8:43b) as Mark did (5:26), in the story of the woman with menorrhagia, but the text of Luke 8:43 is uncertain, being omitted in B, D and other early versions, and so is a finding not even from proven silence.

To summarise, the early suggestion that Luke was a physician did a great deal to allow medicine to develop in the church over the first centuries of Christianity. The view that Luke was not a physician is important for this study; it allows us to regard Luke as a reporter of the significance of Jesus' and apostolic healing without considering the bias which would have been introduced, had he been trained in Hippocratic medicine. He can, therefore, be regarded legitimately as an acceptable example of one strand of tradition about healing in the early church, and, in undertaking the huge labour of recording his portrayal of both the Jesus-event and the subsequent development of the Christian mission, a very worthy example of his tradition. He demonstrates vividly how the new church was set up, and spread to most of the

184 Conzelmann, *Acts*, p.223, refutes the suggestion by von Harnack, *Luke the Physician,* pp.15-16, 61-62, that Luke gave medical assistance in 28:8-9.
185 Kee, *Medicine, Miracle and Magic*, p.65.

eastern Roman Empire, as far as Rome, to begin 'the healing of the nations' (Rev. 22:2).

5 Conclusion

Luke's gospel emphasises Jesus' healing even more than Mark's, and adds examples from his other sources. He follows Mark's layout of the healing narratives closely, while trying to correct what he regards as Mark's loose ends, to avoid the pitfalls of transmitting false impressions. Although he shows that healing was highly important to Jesus' ministry, Luke, unlike Mark, sometimes portrays healing as merely illustrative of his message (e.g. Lk. 11:14; 14:2-6). Also, he sometimes records healings as if they were for the purpose of justification of Jesus as Messiah, especially in Luke 7:11-23, which seems to be presented to show John the Baptist's disciples that healing was a Messianic sign. These features are not found in Mark's gospel.

Luke often increases the pathos of the healing situation, but he does not present Jesus the healer in the same way as Mark, who underlines Jesus' humanity; Luke's Jesus is depicted at all times as the powerful, obedient Son of God. In general, Luke seems to have much more interest in making theological points in each of the healing narratives, while Mark describes authentic details of healing, then reaches his theological conclusion by the way he relates the whole gospel, subtly allowing his readers to see the contrast between the power of Jesus, the healer, and the weakness of Jesus, the willing sacrificial victim. In Luke's writings, Jesus' crucifixion *is* emphasised, so a *theologia crucis* is apparent, both in the gospel and in the speeches in Acts, then God's actions, in Jesus' resurrection and ascension, sweep the reader forward into the story of the church triumphant against heavy odds, and the healings of both Jesus and the apostles are part of that narrative. Healings are not in counterbalance to the crucifixion, but are part of the story, and they continue in Acts.

The existence of two volumes of Luke's writings results in other important findings with respect to healing. It makes it clear that Luke does not see Jesus' miracles of healing as unique in their variety, as opposed to their power and purpose; the way in which Luke fashions the parallels in Acts seems to confirm that. He stresses, however, that Jesus' life, death, resurrection and ascension *are* unique; the followers' task is to use the power of the Holy Spirit conferred on them in whatever way they can (for instance, in healing) to bring all the nations to worship Jesus as Lord. In Acts, Luke sees the spread of the gospel as the primary purpose of the apostles (especially of Paul) and his tendency to use healing miracles as religious tools is more obvious than in the gospel, for instance, in the Council in Jerusalem, the story of miracles by Barnabas and Paul (15:12) 'turned the tide' in their favour.

Luke subscribes to first-century beliefs of the immanence and importance of the supernatural, especially with regard to demons, and the concept of magic (and he exploits these, in order to demonstrate the defeat of opposition to the church). Healing is portrayed as an activity that helps to spread the gospel message to the whole world, often by attracting people, but also by the persecution aroused. Luke uses healing as demonstrating God's power in both Jesus' and apostolic healing, but, as in the gospel, there is, in the Acts narrative of rejection and persecution of apostles, considerable evidence that Luke also has a *theologia crucis*.

Table 1. Jesus, Peter and Paul raising a person from dead			
Features	**Luke 8:41-56**	**Acts 9:36-42**	**Acts 20:7-11**
Healer	Jesus	Peter	Paul
Healed	Jairus' daughter	Tabitha	Eutychus
Place	House	Upper room	Upper room to ground
Healer absent at death	Yes	Yes	No
People weeping	Yes	Yes	No
Crowd expelled	No	Yes	No
Prayer	No	Yes	Not mentioned
Command to rise	Yes	Yes	No
Action	Takes hand	Takes hand	Falls upon
Reported	Yes	Yes	Not mentioned
Similar to gospel story		Yes	No

Table 2. Parallel Features of Healing of Lame/Paralysed				
Features	**Jesus**	**Peter**	**Peter**	**Paul**
	Luke 5:17-26	Acts 3:1-10	Acts 9:33-35	Acts 14:8-11
Unable to walk	Yes	Lame from birth	Paralysed 8 years	Lame from birth
Leapt*	Yes	Yes (twice)	No	Yes
Faith important	Yes	Mentioned	No	Yes
Start of mission	Yes	Yes	No	Yes
Jesus' power important	Yes	Yes	Yes	No
Crowd confusion	Corrected	Corrected	No	Corrected
Jewish opposition	Yes	Yes	No	Later
Similar to gospel story		Similar	Different	Similar

*Isaiah 35:6

Chapter 5

Paul and Healing

1 Healing in Paul's Letters

The importance that Paul in his letters attaches to healing, in Jesus' ministry, in the lives of people in the churches, and in his own ministry, is considered. Only the seven letters (Romans, 1 and 2 Corinthians, Galatians, Philippians, 1 Thessalonians, and Philemon) which are undisputed by all scholars are taken into account here.

1.1 Introduction

Our information about the earliest church is extremely limited. The first thirty years after the resurrection is the period of which we have least literary information.[1] Thus, Paul's letters are particularly important in the search for views on healing, being unique in the New Testament as a direct record over several years of an early follower of Jesus, and as the earliest extant canonical Christian documents. Compared with any other leader of early Christianity, we have most information about Paul. He was *not* the sole representative of early Christianity, of course. Just as there were several first-century Judaisms,[2] there were probably several different emphases and praxes in the first-century churches. Our knowledge of 'the early church' is based on the literary products of situations in which first and second generations of Christians found themselves, and those situations determined what writers chose to save, which was later preserved in the canon. There were probably other contemporary letters, no longer extant, with information about church practices, but the witness of minority groups, and probably of all the poor and illiterate, has vanished. What have survived may be the

---

1 M. Hengel, *Between Jesus and Paul* (London: SCM, 1983) p.46; I.H. Marshall, 'A New Understanding of the Present and the Future: Paul and Eschatology', in R.N. Longenecker (ed.), *The Road from Damascus. The Impact of Paul's Conversion on his Life, Thought and Ministry* (Grand Rapids: Eerdmans, 1997) p.44. Both consider that the first twenty years were the most decisive for the theology of the church.

2 J. Neusner, 'Science and Magic, Miracle and Magic in Formative Judaism', in Frerichs, Borgen, and Horsley (eds.), *Social World of Formative Christianity and Judaism,* e.g. p.64; J. Neusner (ed.), *The Modern Study of the Mishnah* (Leiden: Brill, 1973), pp.xii-xiii; Roetzel, *Paul,* p.7.

writings of the victors in first-century Christianity, and the material that was in the domain of the elites, or at least the literate.

As with the gospels of Mark and Luke, we have no conclusive dating of Paul's life or letters. His chronology is relevant in considering how early his influence might have been on major areas of the church. Murphy-O'Connor works back from Paul's mention in Philemon 9 that he was πρεσβύτης (old) at the time of the letter.[3] It was written from prison, but it is not clear which imprisonment is referred to (see 2 Cor. 11:23); if it were in Rome, we know from Acts that Felix had been replaced as governor by Festus, probably in AD 59-60, so it may have been written up to AD 60-62.[4] It is widely accepted that Paul's conversion/call was *circa* AD 33-34,[5] within a short time of Jesus' crucifixion, and he was executed around AD 60-62, but perhaps as late as AD 67.[6] The chronology of his letters is also imprecise; most, but not all, scholars agree that 1 Thessalonians was written first, and that they were written within 10 to 15 years, up to about AD 56-58.[7] As was mentioned previously, only the seven undisputed letters are being considered.

There are two different accounts of Paul's life and work, in the letters and in Acts. Jervell and others now regard Acts as considerably more accurate historically than F.C. Baur's estimate, but it is still necessary to accept some limitations of Acts with regard to the study of Paul's

---

3 J. Murphy-O'Connor, *Paul: A Critical Life* (Oxford: Clarendon, 1996) pp.1-8, notes that πρεσβύτης means that he was between 50 and 60 years of age, and suggests that he was born *circa* 6 BC; J.A. Fitzmyer, *Paul and his Theology. A Brief Sketch* (2nd ed.; Englewood Cliffs: Prentice Hall, 1989) p.9, suggests his birth was in the first decade AD. It seems likely that Paul was roughly contemporary with Jesus.

4 Murphy-O'Connor, *Paul*, pp.175-79.

5 D.G. Horrell, *An Introduction to the Study of Paul* (London/New York: Continuum, 2000) p.34, deduced this by working back from Paul's enforced departure from Damascus (2 Cor. 11:32-33), dated from extra-biblical data (the reign of King Aretas IV) to AD 37. Fitzmyer, *Paul and his Theology*, p.6, suggests the conversion was in AD 36.

6 Murphy-O'Connor, *Paul*, p.31, estimates his death as AD 67.

7 E.g. Marshall, 'A New Understanding', p.44, considers that Galatians is the first letter; S. Walton, *Leadership and Lifestyle. The Portrait of Paul in the Miletus Speech and 1 Thessalonians* (SNTSMS 108; Cambridge: Cambridge University Press, 2000) pp.144-47, considers that 1 Thessalonians was written early in the sequence of letters. Horrell, *Introduction to Paul*, p.42, notes that it is dated some time between AD 41 and (a more common estimate) 50-51. Dunn, *Theology of Paul*, p.731, n.16, believes that the letter to the Galatians was written soon after the Thessalonian letters R.J. Cassidy, *Paul in Chains. Roman Imprisonment and the Letters of Paul* (New York: Crossroad, 2001), p.236; Fitzmyer, *Paul and his Theology*, pp.2-15; Horrell, *Introduction to Paul*, pp.6, 45.

perspectives on healing (see *2.4*).[8] The nature of the letters is also important in considering Paul's attitude to healing. They are everyday letters, concerned with the problems of local churches, and since they are often in response to situations or questions, they may not give the full balance of Paul's view. Also, it is not safe to rely entirely on a person's self-analysis in his letters, particularly as we have imperfect knowledge of the world in which he lived, and have to acknowledge the huge gulf between ancient and present-day world-views.[9] Again, since biblical scholars have often concentrated on small areas of Paul's letters, the broader sweep of his ideas, and particularly how the difficulties he encountered might have developed his views, have frequently been ignored. Apart from the work of scholars such as C.H. Dodd, only relatively recently has it been acceptable to derive something of the development of the mind, personality, and character of the historical Paul from his letters.[10]

Much recent work has concentrated on the social background to Paul's letters, but relatively little attention has been paid to his miracle working, and this may obscure a gap in our understanding of Paul from his letters.[11]

---

8 J. Jervell, *The Unknown Paul. Essays on Luke-Acts and Early Christian History* (Minneapolis: Augsburg, 1984) p.9; also p.159, n.15, where F.C. Baur is quoted, 'the portrait of Paul in Acts is so different from the letters that one trusts in the historical reliability of Luke in Acts at the cost of the moral character of the apostle'. Holmberg, *Paul and Power,* pp.12-13. (See also Chapter 6, *1.5.*)

9 Deissmann, *Light from the Ancient East,* p.225 pointed out that they were not ancient philosophical/theological documents. Horsley and Silberman, *Message and Kingdom,* p.147, note that in polemical discourse Paul would include only those arguments that he believed would be most effective. Also, Paul may have been falsely modest, or arrogant, or mistaken, without it being apparent to us today. Polaski, *Paul and the Discourse of Power,* p.130, thinks that he had selective recollection and reporting; the letters were not dispassionate chronicles of events.

10 C.H. Dodd, 'The Mind of Paul: II', orig. 1934, reproduced in *New Testament Studies* (Manchester: Manchester University Press, 1953) pp.83-128. Roetzel, *Paul,* p.2; Murphy-O'Connor, *Paul*; B.J. Malina and J.H. Neyrey, *Portraits of Paul. An Archaeology of Ancient Personality* (Louisville: Westminster John Knox, 1996); B. Witherington III, *The Paul Quest: The Renewed Search for the Man of Tarsus* (Leicester: InterVarsity, 1998) p.75, points out that ancients did not regard responsive change as good.

11 E.g. G. Theissen, *The Social Setting of Pauline Christianity: Essays on Corinth* (ET; Edinburgh: T. & T. Clark, 1982); Meggitt, *Paul, Poverty and Survival*; B. Winter, *After Paul Left Corinth. The Influence of Secular Ethics and Social Change* (Grand Rapids/Cambridge: Eerdmans, 2001); Friesen, 'Poverty in Pauline Studies', pp.323-61. Roetzel, *Paul*, p.165, regards discussion of Paul's healing has been under-emphasised by many modern writers; he sees this, p.224, n.52, as due to embarrassment with miracles

In summary, the Pauline letters give us the only direct canonical glimpses we have of mid-first-century Christianity, and, also, of how Paul views miraculous healing. Twentieth-century discomfiture with miracles, combined with our incomplete knowledge of the times and culture, has meant that the significance that Paul attaches to healing in his letters has not been intensively explored.

1.2 Paul's Portrayal of Healing in the Letters

In considering Paul's portrayal of healing in his letters, we find that the references are somewhat ambiguous, since at no point does Paul describe concrete examples of supernatural healing.[12] The terms mentioned below *may* designate miraculous healing, or may merely be indicating something of the 'Pentecostal' excitement and sense of wonder that accompanied followers' acceptance of the gospel and receipt of the Holy Spirit, described in detail in Acts (e.g. 2:43; 4:31; 10:45-46), and which Paul observed in people in the churches that he planted.

Twelftree considers that the application of the term 'σημεῖα καὶ τέρατα' (signs and wonders) by Paul is meant to link the history of Israel with the new 'Exodus' in Christ, and Moo thinks that Paul uses the term, as in Acts, to emphasise the salvation-historical significance of his ministry.[13] As in the synoptic gospels and sometimes in Acts, Paul writes occasionally of 'signs' alone, with respect to unbelievers, for instance, 'Jews demand signs' (1 Cor. 1:22),[14] and when, in Paul's opinion, 'speaking in tongues' was a sign for unbelievers (1 Cor. 14:22).

In the synoptic gospels, miracles are rarely described as δυνάμεις, a term used sometimes in Acts. Paul uses δύναμις/δυνάμεις (power and powers are interchangeable in Paul) frequently in contexts other than healing, for instance, in challenging the Corinthians' power, comparing it unfavourably with God's power (1 Cor. 4:19-21). Where the term

---

in a modern age. Witherington, *Paul Quest*, devotes only one paragraph, p.81, to Paul's account of healing in the letters. Schreiber, *Paulus*, in analysing Paul's miracles, may be setting a trend in renewing interest in this area.

12 Ferngren and Amundsen, 'Medicine and Christianity', p.2962.

13 G.H. Twelftree, 'Signs, Wonders, Miracles', in G.F. Hawthorne, R.P. Martin, D.G. Reid (eds.), *Dictionary of Paul and his Letters* (Downers Grove/Leicester: InterVarsity, 1993) p.876. (See Chapter 4, *3.4.1.*). Moo, *Romans,* p.893.

14 This is usually regarded as referring to Jesus refusing to perform a 'sign' after a feeding miracle (Mk. 8:11-12). M.G. Goulder, *Paul and the Competing Mission in Corinth* (Peabody: Hendrickson, 2001) p.250, considers that, in 1 Cor. 1:22, Paul was unable to meet the Jewish demand for signs.

probably represents miracles[15] (Rom. 15:19; 2 Cor. 12:12, see below) Paul adds 'signs and wonders' as well, so the intention is to emphasise the divine nature of the healing. This combination of 'signs and wonders and powers' is found elsewhere, in the Old Testament (e.g. Deut. 34:10-12), and also in Hebrews 2:3-4.[16]

Δύναμις and πνεῦμα (spirit) are often found together in various forms, e.g. 1 Thessalonians 1:5, 'in power and in the Holy Spirit'; 1 Corinthians 2:4, 'Spirit and power'; Romans 15:13, 'the power of the Holy Spirit'; Romans 15:19, 'power of the Spirit of God'. The coming of the Spirit in the earliest days of the Christian mission made an impact, emotional as well as rational, on the lives of those who received it.[17] Paul uses the expression, 'manifestations of the Spirit' (1 Cor. 12:7) to refer to signs of its coming. Fee believes that the Corinthians who opposed Paul (1 Cor. 4:18) understood the Spirit to refer *only* to gifts (especially 'tongues'), which they regarded as evidence that they had reached perfection.[18] Paul does not deny signs of the Spirit, in both himself and his congregations, but, although these signs included gifts, his emphasis is rather on the Spirit's influence to transform lives, to reveal God's wisdom, and to lead to service, that is, on the fruit of the Spirit (Gal. 5:22-23), rather than the gifts. In Paul's letters, the term Spirit is never used alone to designate healing miracles.

Paul does draw on different phrases for 'doing good' (e.g. Rom. 2:7, 10; 7:21; Gal. 6:9, 10), but the activities do not, as in Acts 10:38, include healing. He never employs the verbs of healing, which are abundant in the synoptic gospels and Acts.[19]

In summary, Paul uses the terms 'powers' and 'signs and wonders' in his letters, sometimes together, in passages that may indicate healing.

---

15 Brucker, 'Wunder der Apostel', pp.33-34, considers that δυνάμεις means something like 'effects/proofs of the underlying power'. Schreiber, *Paulus*, pp.191-92, suggests that it may have been a recognised term for miracles among the new congregations.

16 W. Wink, *Naming the Powers. The Language of Power in the New Testament. The Powers*, Vol.1, (Philadelphia: Fortress, 1984) p.8, draws attention to the use of multiple words to identify the type of power, since power seems to be so complex a phenomenon that it needs many words.

17 J.D.G. Dunn, *A Commentary on the Epistle to the Galatians*, BNTC (London: A. & C. Black, 1993) p.153; W.A. Meeks, *The First Urban Christians; The Social World of the Apostle Paul* (New Haven: Yale University, 1983) p.138, comments that the Spirit had great authority in Paul's communities.

18 G.D. Fee, *The First Epistle to the Corinthians,* NICNT (Grand Rapids: Eerdmans, 1987) p.96.

19 A.C. Thiselton, *The First Epistle to the Corinthians,* NIGTC (Grand Rapids/Carlisle: Eerdmans/Paternoster, 2000) p.946.

To Paul, the Spirit is the important source of God's power to transform, but he does not apply it alone as a term for healing.

1.3 Possible Healing by Paul

Passages regarded as at least possibly referring to healing miracles performed by Paul, through the agency of Christ and the Holy Spirit, are assessed. There are five references in the undisputed letters where Paul might be the human agent, and they are presented in an accepted order of their writing.

1.3.1 1 Thessalonians 1:5

> Because our message of the gospel came to you not in word only, but also in power and in the Holy Spirit and with full conviction;

The authors of the letter are Paul, 'Sylvanus' and Timothy, to all of whom 'our message of the gospel' might apply, especially as v.2 has 'εὐχαριστοῦμεν–*we* give thanks', compared with 1 Corinthians 1:4 and Philippians 1:3, where, though there are other authorial names in 1:1, only Paul is giving thanks, εὐχαριστέω. Verse 5 comes in the middle of thanksgiving to God for the faith and steadfastness of the Thessalonian church. God had chosen them, brothers beloved by God (v.4), and the message came to them in power and in the Holy Spirit and in full conviction. This suggests that both converts and messengers were affected by the power and Holy Spirit. Effects of the Spirit (v.6) included joy despite persecution, in imitation of the apostles and the Lord, so they had become an example to all the believers in Greece.

Some scholars regard verse 5 as indicating that Paul was performing miracles; Wanamaker, reluctantly, and only on the basis of the other passages (discussed below), accepts this; Horsley and Silberman accept that the terms here describe some form of healing; Schreiber is definite that this is not a reference to Paul or the other authors performing miracles, but sees it as meaning that the power of the Holy Spirit was behind the apostles' preaching.[20]

---

20 Jervell, *Unknown Paul,* p.91; E.P. Sanders, *Paul* (Oxford: OUP, 1991) p.24; C.A. Wanamaker, *The Epistles to the Thessalonians. A Commentary on the Greek Text,* NIGTC (Grand Rapids/Exeter: Eerdmans/Paternoster, 1990) p.79; Horsley and Silberman, *Message and Kingdom,* p.160; Schreiber, *Paulus,* p.266.

On the grounds that the emphasis of the passage is on the power of the Spirit to change believers' lives, and on the converts' faith, love and joy, verse 5 does not appear to me to be highlighting Paul healing.

1.3.2 Galatians 3:5

> Does [God] supply you with the Spirit and work mighty works among you by your doing the works of the law, or by your believing what you heard?

Although there is no definite subject, it is assumed to be God. The rhetorical question is preceded by a very similar one in 3:2b, 'Did you receive the Spirit by doing works of the Law, or by believing what you have heard?' Again, there, it is assumed that the Galatians 'received' the Spirit from God. There is controversy over the phrase ἐξ ἀκοῆς πίστεως 'hearing of faith'. Williams regards the 'hearing' as passive only, while Witherington sees it as active, 'a believing hearing'. Dunn argues that 'hearing' indicated the Galatians' personal transformation as a result of the proclamation.[21] At the simplest level, it seems to me that the language of sight, not hearing, would be used for miracles, and that hearing implies preaching.

The whole passage has been widely debated. Witherington points out that the term 'receiving the Spirit' (v.2) was almost a technical one for conversion in the early church, so probably referred to the conversion experience of the Galatians.[22] The term might indicate receiving other benefits of the Spirit (e.g. Gal. 4:6-7, where God sent the Spirit of his son, so that the Galatians were no longer slaves, but children and heirs) and so the 'powers' in verse 5 could refer to miracles *or* to these other benefits. Many writers consider that the passage means that when the Galatians were converted, performing miracles was among their spiritual experiences.[23] Schreiber thinks that the power was ascribed to

---

21 R.B. Hays, *The Faith of Jesus Christ. An Investigation of the Narrative Substructure of Galatians 3:1-4:11* (SBLDS 56; Chico: Scholars Press, 1983) pp.143-49. S.K. Williams, 'The Hearing of Faith: "ἀκοή πίστεως" in Galatians 3', *NTS* 35 (1989) p.90, suggests 'the hearing which Christians call faith'. Witherington III, *Grace in Galatia. A Commentary on Paul's Letter to the Galatians* (Grand Rapids: Eerdmans, 1998) pp.212-13, sees it as meaning 'hearing and obeying'. Dunn, *Commentary on Galatians,* p.154.

22 Witherington, *Grace in Galatia*, p.210.

23 Witherington, *Grace in Galatia*, p.215; F.F. Bruce, *The Epistle of Paul to the Galatians,* NIGTC (Exeter: Paternoster, 1982) p.151; Fuller, *Interpreting the Miracles,* pp.20-21; G.D. Fee, 'Gifts of the Spirit', in *Dictionary of Paul and his Letters,* p.345; Horsley and Silberman, *Message and Kingdom,* p.150; E.P. Sanders, *Paul and*

Christ, with the power of the Spirit activating the apostles' preaching, and that Paul is mentioning miracles, but not referring to himself.[24]

I would accept the view that some converts had been enabled to perform deeds, which were regarded as miracles. The context is that Paul's energies were directed to rebuking the Galatians for being persuaded to revert to 'works of the law', in particular, to circumcision, after experiencing evidence of God's grace as a supply of the Spirit and miracles. Even if it were accepted (and this would be at variance with Gal. 4:13-14) that Paul is writing of God working miracles through him, then he is certainly not *highlighting* his own healing ability.

1.3.3 1 Corinthians 2:4

> My speech and my proclamation were not with plausible words of wisdom, but with a demonstration of the Spirit and of power.

The reason is given in verse 5, 'so that your faith might rest, not on human wisdom, but on the power of God'. As in Galatians 3:5, the 'Spirit and power' might mean that the Corinthians were aware of works of power occurring among them; however here the 'power' is the power of God, and these verses accord with Paul's argument from 1:18, where he contrasts the wisdom of men with the superior power of God. Fee considers that, although the phrase 'demonstration of Spirit and of power' *might* refer to miracles, it is more likely to mean the Corinthians' conversion, with concomitant gifts of the Spirit; while Twelftree thinks that the verse means both the Corinthians' encounter with God's power (which transformed their lives at conversion), and miracles, as proof of the gospel.[25] Several authors accept the verse as

---

Palestinian Judaism (London: SCM, 1977) p.450; Kruse, *New Testament Models for Ministry*, p.84. Goulder, *Paul and Competing Mission*, p.250, points out that, in a community convinced that the Spirit was at work in a dramatically new way, healings attempted would often be accepted as having been achieved.

24 Schreiber, *Paulus*, p.269. Nielsen, *Heilung*, p.204, considers that uncertainty remains as to who, the Galatians or Paul, performed the miracles.

25 Fee, *First Corinthians*, p.95, and n.28, considers that the term 'demonstration', ἀπόδειξις, has the meaning of 'proof'. R.A. Horsley, *1 Corinthians*, ANTC (Nashville: Abingdon, 1998) p.54; Schreiber, *Paulus*, p.234, sees the 'demonstration' as meaning a revelation from God. Brucker, 'Wunder der Apostel', p.33, considers that the term is an allusion in which Paul is referring to the 'collective memory' shared by him and his congregations, which we can no longer decipher. Twelftree, 'Signs', p.876.

evidence of Paul, through the agency of the Holy Spirit, performing healings or exorcisms.[26]

The 'demonstration' seems to suggest legitimation of the proclamation, which *could* be by miracles among the believers. In 2:3, Paul wrote of his own fear and trembling, and declared (v.2) his determination to preach 'only Christ, and him crucified'. This seems to make it unlikely, though not impossible, that Paul was boasting here of miracles performed by him through the agency of the Spirit; rather, it suggests that he was referring to the demonstration of the Corinthians' conversion.

1.3.4 2 Corinthians 12:12

> The signs of a true apostle were performed among you with utmost patience, with signs and wonders and mighty works.

The background to the verse is Paul defending his apostleship against fierce opposition in 2 Corinthians 10–13. Paul's opponents regarded spiritual gifts highly, and Barnett and Wolff both argue that they were boasting about their spiritual gifts, which legitimated them, and underestimating Paul's supernatural abilities, which they considered he lacked (11:13; 12:11-12), although that is not stated explicitly.[27] It seems to have been an early Christian idea that miracles identified a true apostle, and perhaps Paul believed this.[28] Some scholars consider that, as the opponents saw miracles as valid signs of an apostle of Christ, the term 'signs of an apostle' might have come from them, while others see it as a term already established in the early church.[29] Savage thinks the

---

26 Roetzel, *Paul,* p.164; Horsley and Silberman, *Message and Kingdom,* p.160; Sanders, *Paul*, p.24; J. Murphy-O'Connor, *The Theology of the Second Letter to the Corinthians* (Cambridge: Cambridge University Press, 1991) p.123.

27 P.W. Barnett, 'Opposition in Corinth', *JSNT* 22 (1984) pp.5, 11, 13; C. Wolff, 'True Apostolic Knowledge of Christ: Exegetical Reflections on 2 Corinthians 5:14ff.', in Wedderburn (ed.), *Paul and Jesus,* p.90. Holmberg, *Paul and Power*, p.125, points out that one of the important sociological motives for obeying is belief in the legitimacy of the leader.

28 Achtemeier, 'Jesus and Disciples', p.151. Schreiber, *Paulus,* p.293, considers that perhaps it was a concept that Paul had to accept.

29 Twelftree, 'Signs', p.876; R.P. Martin, *2 Corinthians*, WBC, Vol.40 (Waco: Word Books, 1986) p.435. R. Bultmann, *The Second Letter to the Corinthians* (ET; Minneapolis: Augsburg, 1985) p.231, argues that it was a fixed term, a slogan. C.K. Barrett, *A Commentary on the Second Epistle to Corinthians,* BNTC (London: A. & C. Black, 1973) p.321, considers it was a term used by the Corinthians, rather than by a group of opponents; M. Thrall, *A Critical and Exegetical Commentary on the Second*

idea that Paul used his opponents' words is overdone, while Hafemann believes that the primary 'sign of an apostle' was the outpouring of the Spirit on the Corinthian church, which was attested further by, but was different from, 'signs and wonders and mighty works.'[30]

Most writers accept that here Paul is writing of miracles that he performed, through the power of the Spirit,[31] although Goulder dissents, suggesting that Paul's 'signs of an apostle' were his tribulations, produced 'with utmost endurance' (ἐν πάσῃ ὑπομονῇ), a phrase Paul uses also in 2 Corinthians 6:4, in one of the peristasis catalogues; Goulder points out that healings are not performed 'in all endurance',[32] but with power, and that the opposition would not have raised the issue if Paul were known to perform healings.

The situation in 2 Corinthians 11-12 is important, as being the only occasion recorded in the letters when healing might have been an overt cause of discord. Georgi suggests that Paul's opponents might have been Hellenistic Jewish Christians, who saw Jesus, and perhaps themselves, as θεῖοι ἄνδρες, (TAs) and so, healers (11:13-14).[33] The identity of the opponents of 2 Corinthians 10-13, still debated, is only

---

Epistle to the Corinthians, ICC, Vol.II (2nd ed.; London/New York: T. & T. Clark/Continuum, 2004) pp.837-38, considers that the phrase had been coined prior to its use here, and would have been familiar to the Corinthians; Schreiber, *Paulus*, pp.217-18, also suggests it was a phrase in general usage by the early congregations.

30 T.B. Savage, *Power through Weakness. Paul's Understanding of the Christian Ministry in 2 Corinthians* (SNTSMS 86; Cambridge: Cambridge University Press, 1996) p.11. S.J. Hafemann, *2 Corinthians*, The NIV Application Commentary (Grand Rapids: Zondervan, 2000) p.467.

31 Bultmann, *Second Corinthians*, pp.231-32; Jervell, *Unknown Paul*, p.91; Sanders, *Paul*, p.24; Barrett, *Second Corinthians*, pp.320-22, cautiously; P.W. Barnett, *The Second Epistle to the Corinthians*, NICNT (Grand Rapids/Cambridge: Eerdmans, 1997) pp.579-81; Schreiber, *Paulus*, p.269. Murphy-O'Connor, *Theology of Second Corinthians*, p.123, considers that, in Paul's perspective, miracles were an unnecessary by-product. He considers that Paul indicated his miracle working here as a fact that could not be overlooked, but saw it of no central value.

32 Goulder, *Paul and Competing Mission*, p.251. Bultmann, *Second Corinthians*, p.232, translates the phrase as 'under difficult circumstances'; Barrett, *Second Corinthians*, p.321, thinks it indicates the miracles happening in the midst of Paul's distress.

33 See Chapter 2, *2.1.2*. Georgi, *Opponents*, pp.210-13; Savage, *Power through Weakness*, p.155, responds that, though the opponents might have thought *Jesus* was θεῖος ἀνήρ, it would be beyond their self-exalting tendencies to consider *themselves* as such; Theissen, *Miracle Stories*, pp.261, 264, points out that other miracle workers would not spread such narratives. J.H. Schütz, *Paul and the Anatomy of Apostolic Authority* (SNTSMS 26; Cambridge: Cambridge University Press, 1975) pp.167-68.

marginally relevant to this study.[34] It is likely (though not proven) that Paul was taunted by them about his lack of healing miracles, and in response, referred to his 'signs and wonders and mighty works' (12:12). He may well have believed that these miracles were 'signs of an apostle,' but the confession of his ability to heal seems to have been wrung out of him in the heat of defending himself against his opponents. For this reason, I would accept that the verse *does* indicate miracles performed by Paul, who uses the divine passive to show that they were accomplished through the agency of God.

1.3.5 Romans 15:18-19

> For I will not venture to speak of anything except what Christ has accomplished through me to win obedience from the Gentiles, by word and deed, by the power of signs and wonders, by the power of the Spirit of God, so that from Jerusalem and as far around as Illyricum, I have fully proclaimed the gospel of Christ.

Most workers accept this as evidence of Paul performing miracles.[35] Moo sees 'by word and deed' (v.18), as meaning all Paul's apostolic activity subsumed under the headings of speaking and doing, then detailed as proclamation and miracle-working in verse 19. Schreiber thinks that there is some evidence here of Paul accepting the idea of the legitimating function of miracles in identifying the true apostle.[36]

I would regard this verse as indicating Paul working miracles, the initiator being Christ, the power that of the Spirit. In verse 16, Paul describes himself as a servant of Christ in a (metaphorically) priestly role to the Gentiles who had received the Holy Spirit, making them an acceptable offering to God. He was writing a letter with profound theology and considerable paraenetic material to the Roman church, which he had neither set up nor visited. Although the passage is not overtly defensive, yet it seems to me likely that Paul refers to his

34 E.g. C.K. Barrett, 'Paul's Opponents in II Corinthians', *NTS* 17 (1971) 233-54; Barnett, 'Opposition', p.3; R.P. Martin, 'The Opponents of Paul in 2 Corinthians: An Old Issue Revisited', in G.F. Hawthorne and O. Betz (eds.), *Tradition and Interpretation in the New Testament* (Grand Rapids/Tübingen: Eerdmans/Mohr [Siebeck], 1987) p.285. Marshall, *Enmity in Corinth*, pp.342, 346, notes that Paul never names an enemy; 'they are damned with anonymity'.

35 E.g. J. Ziesler, *Paul's Letter to the Romans,* TPI New Testament Commentaries (London/Philadelphia: SCM/Trinity, 1989) p.342. Goulder, *Paul and Competing Mission*, p.252, points to v.18 as meaning that Christ had *not* worked words or deeds through Paul.

36 Moo, *Romans,* p.892; Schreiber, *Paulus,* p.293.

miracle working as a means of legitimating his right to teach the Roman church. He probably wrote the letter to the Romans from Corinth, so the memory of his admission of healing (2 Cor. 12:12) would have been fresh in his mind.[37]

1.3.6 Summary of Paul's Healing

A decision to be made is whether or not Paul's writing about healing is less than one would expect from the milieu in which he was working. He mentions his own miracle-healing in the authentic letters between two and five times. Sanders considers all five indicate miracles by Paul, and that they established his authority as a prophet; Nielsen accepts 1 Corinthians 2:4 and 1 Thessalonians 1:5 as Paul performing miracles; Schweizer accepts only two (2 Cor. 12:12 and Rom. 15:19), and I would agree with him, although maintaining an open mind on 1 Corinthians 2:4.[38] Even if we were to accept the five as evidence of Paul presenting evidence of himself as a miracle-worker, this *is* a small number, taking into account the relatively large volume of the letters, the climate of first-century interest in miraculous healing, and the evidence of the synoptic gospels and Acts, which purport to present the situation regarding divine healing immediately before, and contemporaneously with, Paul's mission. More importantly, it is clear that Paul does not stress the occasions when he did heal. There are *no* concrete examples in the letters, and no indication that healing was of primary importance to Paul in his proclamation of the gospel.

Scholars vary in their estimate of Paul's interest in supernatural healing. Thomas notes, 'in point of fact, "signs and wonders and mighty works" appear to have occurred with such a degree of regularity in his ministry among the Corinthians that Paul could point to them as signs of his own apostolic status (2 Cor. 12:12)'. Jervell believes that, since the greatest part of his life and work is unknown to us, his letters conceal that he lived and taught in the same way as most other church workers, with no fewer miracles than other apostles. Others regard miracles as incidental to his huge missionary endeavour, or consider that Paul did

37 A.J.M. Wedderburn, *The Reason for Romans* (Edinburgh: T. & T. Clark, 1988) p.24; D. Wenham, *Paul and Jesus. The True Story* (Grand Rapids/Cambridge: Eerdmans, 2002) p.142; Barnett, 'Opposition', p.6, considers that Paul wrote Romans soon after 2 Corinthians. Hafemann, *2 Corinthians*, p.467, considers that Paul was actually referring to 2 Cor. 12:12.

38 Sanders, *Paul,* p.24; Nielsen, *Heilung*, p.203 Schweizer, 'Mark's Theological Achievement', p.86; Jervell, *Unknown Paul,* p.91; Roetzel, *Paul,* p.164.

not minimise their importance, but never saw them as a vital activity.[39] On the other hand, Betz states that in the letters 'clear evidence that Paul performed miracles does not exist', while Broadhead notes the 'clear absence of miracle traditions in Paul'.[40] These last scholars explore neither the reason for this, nor the effects that a lack of miracles might have on Paul's mission.

Paul makes it clear that he had other 'charismatic' powers. His spiritual gifts included prophecy (inferred in 1 Cor. 13:2; 14:3), faith to 'move mountains' (inferred in 1 Cor. 13: 2) and speaking in 'tongues' (1 Cor. 13:1; 14:6, 18). He had supernatural experiences of Christ (1 Cor. 11:23; 15:3, 8), and visions (e.g. Gal. 1:16; 2:2). He mentions all these gifts in the course of issues concerned with the building up of the church (e.g. 1 Corinthians 12, 13 and 14:1-5); but does not mention his own healing gift in this connection.[41]

1.4 Paul's Comments on the Church's Gifts of Healing

In the synoptic gospels, Jesus' disciples preached and healed when they went out on mission, as did the 70(2) in the second mission in Luke's gospel. In Acts, apostles and other men in authority in the Jerusalem church also preached and healed in Jesus' name. Witherington suggests that Paul in his letters might merely have been self-forgetful of his own healing, as he was concerned with the edification of others.[42] If this were the reason for Paul's sparse references to his own healing gift, we might expect to find evidence of healing by people in the churches, so we consider the evidence for others healing.

As discussed earlier (*1.3.2*), several scholars consider that Galatians 3:5 indicates that some believers at conversion performed miracles, and I would accept this as possible. There are two letters where Paul

---

39 Thomas, *Devil, Disease*, p.39; Jervell, *Unknown Paul*, pp.9, 52; Horsley and Silberman, *Message and Kingdom*, p.157; Roetzel, *Paul*, p.164. P. Barnett, *The Message of 2 Corinthians. Power in Weakness* (Leicester: InterVarsity, 1988) p.182, thinks that at no point did Paul seek to legitimate his ministry by miracles.

40 H.D. Betz, *Der Apostel Paulus und die sokratische Tradition; eine exegetische Untersuchung zu seiner Apologie 2 Korinther 10-13* (Tübingen: Mohr [Siebeck], 1972) p.71; Broadhead, *Teaching with Authority*, pp.190-91, n.2.

41 The vision in 2 Cor. 12:1-4 is, I believe, related to Paul's views on healing (see *2.3.3*), and is not used by him to build up the church. R.F. Collins, *First Corinthians*, SacPag Series, Vol.7 (Collegeville: Liturgical Press, 1999) p.454, draws attention to the fact that Paul does *not* claim that he has the gift of healing in the same way that he claims gifts of e.g. prophecy and tongues.

42 Witherington, *Paul's Narrative*, p.242.

elaborated on members of the churches having spiritual gifts. The shorter passage (Rom. 12:6-8) comes at the beginning of Paul's ethical instruction to the Roman church, where he stressed the value of both the unity and diversity of the church 'body', and the importance of love. Healing is not mentioned there.[43]

In 1 Corinthians, Paul stated several times that all believers had been given gifts from the Holy Spirit, for instance, 'you are not lacking in any spiritual gift' (1:7), 'each one has a particular gift from God' (7:7).[44] Thiselton considers that 1 Corinthians 12:1–14:40 has as its theme, 'respect for the other', and that Paul was dealing with the Corinthians' temptation to glory because of their gifts, and Martin draws attention to the status-conferring significance that the Corinthians attached to the more spectacular spiritual gifts.[45] Paul tried to counteract this by emphasising that all spiritual gifts were valuable. He saw the test of each gift was its goal, not the status it offered. He taught that the manifestations were given by God to be utilized in building up the church (e.g. 12:7), and not for self-aggrandisement. They were apportioned according to God's purpose, and given freely; the Giver, rather than the gift, was important. The gifts of the Spirit to believers were not quantified, that is, Paul does not make clear what proportion of the church members had which gifts (e.g. 12:30, 'do all have gifts of healings?' expecting the answer 'no').

The order of listing the spiritual gifts differs in the two lists (12:8-10, 28-30), and neither list is comprehensive. Goulder suggests that the first list may be from the Corinthians' evaluation of the pneumatic traits, while the second represents the main forms of service, including more practical gifts for church life, such as teaching, almsgiving, and administration. Although Fee does not accept a ranking of the gifts or roles in either list, many commentators would accept that there is at least some order.[46] It seems to me that in both lists, the more flamboyant

---

43 Horsley, *1 Corinthians*, p.170, believes that this passage is dependent on 1 Cor. 12.

44 Sanders, *Paul and Palestinian Judaism*, p.450, considers that Paul expected all Christians to have spiritual gifts. Holmberg, *Paul and Power*, p.103, suggests that only in the Corinthian church is it expected that believers would perform miracles.

45 Thiselton, *First Corinthians*, p.900. Martin, *Corinthian Body*, pp.87-92.

46 Goulder, *Paul and Competing Mission*, p.249, considers that the second list was Paul's own list. G.D. Fee, *God's Empowering Presence. The Holy Spirit in the Letters of Paul* (Peabody: Hendrickson, 1994) p.190. Fee, *First Corinthians*, pp.590-91, 619-20, considers that Paul merely began a ranking in v. 28. Collins, *First Corinthians*, p.451, considers that the first list is in descending order of importance in Paul's estimation. So also Thiselton, *First Corinthians*, pp.1013-14; F.F. Bruce, *1 and 2 Corinthians*, NCBC (London: Marshall, Morgan & Scott, 1971) pp.119, 122.

gifts are placed lower in order, with speaking in tongues being last each time. This fits the view that Paul was attempting to dissuade the Corinthians from a triumphalist attitude to the spiritual gifts, especially when taken together with his comments about the special importance of the weaker members of the body (vv.22-25).

Within the group of gifts associated with healing, 'faith' appears on both lists, presumably referring to a special faith, rather than faith as the fruit of the Spirit given to all Christians, but it is not clear if this was a gift to believers who may require healing, or a gift to healers.[47] 'To another person were given gift*s* of healing*s*' (12:9, 30); Thomas is adamant that Paul was referring to healings of the order of those attributed to Jesus and the apostles, and not to any human skills.[48] Thiselton, however, argues that the term 'gifts of healings' (χαρίσματα ἰαμάτων) refers to different types of healing, so would not exclude 'natural' remedies, and would allow that there might be a human contribution in some of the gifts, the divine element being the Spirit's sustaining power.[49] This view allows that not all spiritual healing has to be miraculous, and it moves away from the idea that Paul considered that healing was a gift given by God to a follower for a particular occasion (that is, that the event, rather than the healer, was emphasised). Thiselton's view is important, and seems to me an acceptable reading of Paul's statements in 1 Corinthians 12.

---

47 Horsley, *1 Corinthians*, p.170, considers the 'faith in the Spirit' here overlaps with the gifts of healing and 'working powers'. W. Schrage, *Der erste Brief an die Korinther,* EKKNT, VII, Vol. 3, *1 Kor. 11,17-14,40* (Zürich/Düsseldorf: Benziger/Neukirchener, 1999) pp.150-51, believes that it is possibly of the nature of 'faith that can move mountains', as in 13:2. Fee, *First Corinthians*, p.594, considers that this was a gift of the healer. Thiselton, *First Corinthians*, pp.946-47, suggests that it might be a gift to those needing healing, but Paul might not expect that all believers who needed healing would manifest the gift of faith, so healing was not assured.

48 Thomas, *Devil, Disease*, p.39. He quotes Dunn, *Jesus and the Spirit*, p.210 (also p.254) but not Dunn's later view, *Paul and his Theology*, pp.556, 558, where Dunn considers that the gifts include more humdrum tasks, and are not always spontaneous; Dunn has modified his opinion on this point.

49 Thiselton, *First Corinthians*, pp.937, 948-51. Fee, *First Corinthians,* p.594; Telford, 'Review of "*Theios Aner*"', p.251, notes that in Old Testament scripture, since the Spirit belongs to God, it was normally given to a man for only one task or period. Holmberg, *Paul and Power*, p.103, notes that no professional healers are mentioned in the primitive church, so the gifts *would* be expected to be sporadic. Howard, *Disease and Healing*, pp.229-30, considers that the gifts of healing may not mean miraculous healing, and probably do not refer to physical healing.

The nature of the ἐνεργήματα δυνάμεων (the working of powers)[50] of verse 10 has been much debated. Witherington sees the term, pointedly separated from healings, referring to exorcisms. Holmberg considers it denotes healings and exorcisms. However, Dunn notes that Paul reports no exorcisms, and Twelftree considers that, as Christians had passed from the reign of Satan to Christ, and so were safe from evil spirits, Paul would have assumed that exorcisms would not be included in the gifts.[51] Even though Paul believed that demonic powers had lost their influence to separate believers from Christ's love (Rom. 8:38), he was very aware of the tension between the eschatological 'already' and the 'not yet,' so it is not acceptable to assume that Paul considered that Christians would not be vulnerable to demonic powers.

The χαρίσματα ἰαμάτων *are* separate from the ἐνεργήματα δυνάμεων both in verses 9-10 and again in verses 28-29 (as δυνάμεις), so this seems deliberate, but the fact that in 12:9-10 'gifts of healings' are followed by the 'workings of powers', while in 12:28-29 the order is reversed, seems to me to indicate that Paul was using both rather loosely as examples of the dramatic gifts.

Thiselton makes the important point that the 'working of powers', like the 'gifts of healing', might also include deeds other than 'supernatural' ones; he considers that assuming all the spiritual gifts were miraculous misses the collective and corporate framework Paul has built up in writing about these gifts. Thiselton writes, 'specific human agents may receive a particular gift from the Spirit to advance the gospel against oppressive forces, for the benefit of all'; and this 'accepts the utter plasticity of the created world to God'; Schrage remarks that Christianity has not asked itself up to what point the supernatural powers used the laws of human nature.[52]

Although Paul's letters indicate that he believed that God had given the church spiritual gifts, it seems significant that he never mentions specifically the church's gifts of healing elsewhere (even in 1

---

50 Thiselton, *First Corinthians*, e.g. p.953, translates as 'actively effective deeds of powers'. Fee, *First Corinthians*, p.594, regards the 'powers' as all forms of miracles. It may be that Paul means 'powers' here to include miracles of nature (as perhaps in 1 Cor. 13:2).

51 Witherington, *Conflict and Community in Corinth*, p.257. Holmberg, *Paul and Power*, p.103. Dunn, *Theology of Paul*, p.37. Brucker, 'Wunder der Apostel', p.32, also notes the absence of exorcisms from Paul's letters. G.H. Twelftree, 'Healing, Illness', in *Dictionary of Paul and his Letters*, p.380 (but see Chapter 6, *2.1*).

52 Thiselton, *First Corinthians*, pp.955-56, and n.106; Schrage, *Der erste Brief*, 3, p.151, n.102.

Corinthians 14).[53] Theissen, having pointed out that miracle-healing was less effective in higher than in lower social groups in societies (perhaps because the social and economic problems of poor health were less), yet notes that it was only to the church in Corinth (which possibly contained a significant representation of the socially established), that Paul writes of believers' spiritual gifts of healing.[54] Collins, noting that 1 Corinthians 12 is the only instance in which Paul mentions the gifts of healing in the church, suggests that the presence of a large and much-used Asclepieion in Corinth demonstrated the Corinthians' particular interest in healing.[55]

As in Paul's mentions of his own 'signs and wonders', there is no *description* of a healing performed by a believer, nor mention of any benefit of healing to a sufferer, both features in the gospel accounts of Jesus' miracles, and in Acts. Nock suggested that Paul was much more concerned with wider issues than with the individual sufferer,[56] but it is significant that his affirmation of love as the supreme mark of the Spirit (1 Corinthians 13) lies in the middle of his writing about the spiritual gifts to the church. This seems to signal his awareness that there were risks in the spiritual gifts, if they were divorced from the loving Spirit of Christ, and the fruits of the Spirit.

In summary, Paul wrote about healing by non-apostolic believers only in 1 Corinthians. His account of the church's gifts with regard to healing had the same restraint as those of his own healing gifts; he mentioned, but did not detail, them. In view of the environment in which he was working and writing, this does seem to show significant reserve about healing activities.

1.5 Reasons for the Paucity of References to Healing

We consider possible reasons for Paul's letters showing detachment about healing. These might be because of practical factors related to his

---

53 Thiselton, *First Corinthians*, p.949, and Schrage, *Der erste Brief*, 3, p.152, both note the absence of discussion of healing elsewhere in Paul's letters.

54 Theissen, *Miracle Stories,* p.249; e.g. G. Theissen, 'The Social Structure of Pauline Communities: Some Critical Remarks on J.J. Meggitt, *Paul, Poverty and Survival*', *JSNT* 84 (2001) pp.65-84; and Theissen, 'Social Conflicts in the Corinthian Community: Further Remarks on J.J. Meggitt, *Paul, Poverty and Survival*', *JSNT* 25 (2003) pp.371-91. See *2.5.1.*

55 Collins, *First Corinthians*, pp.454-55.

56 A.D. Nock, *St Paul* (London: Oxford University Press, 1938) p.241, saw this as a Jewish view, compared with the Graeco-Roman concern with the individual. Dunn, *Theology of Paul*, pp.432-33.

mission, or for personal, ethical or theological reasons, or a combination of these.

First, there may be simple reasons for the passing character of the references to healing. The nature of the letters, which were occasional, and concerned with particular questions and issues where healing may not have been raised, might be responsible. Paul might have expected his readers to take it for granted that apostles could heal, since the early church seemed to believe that Jesus' followers could and did perform miracles, in keeping with his instructions and commission to the disciples.[57] But if healing had occupied a significant part of his time, I assume that Paul would have mentioned it more often in his letters.

Another option is that Paul was not naturally interested in healing, so did not see it as a high priority in his huge task of a Gentile mission. But there is considerable evidence that the letters were basically pastoral, intended to build up the recipient churches.[58] Paul was aware of the great concern about death, illness and healing in the cities where he set up churches; for instance, he discussed the theological aspects of the deaths of members (e.g. 1 Thess. 4:13-15). Even in his more personal experience, Prisca and Aquila had been in danger of death, presumably from persecution, for Paul's sake (Rom. 16:3), and Epaphroditus had a severe illness or injury (Phil. 2:25-30), so the questions of illness and near-death were brought sharply to his attention.

Perhaps Paul did see the church using the spiritual gifts of healing and effective deeds of power in the community (1 Corinthians 12),[59] so that Gentiles, attracted to Christianity by preaching, would receive benefits of these healing powers in the church. In Corinth, where Paul wrote also of the spiritual gifts of forms of assistance and leadership (1 Cor. 12:28), he encouraged the people to make use of the gifts of Stephanas and his household (1 Cor. 16:15-18); so to include healing in the church's ministry was also feasible for the churches of Paul's mission. As Paul considered himself a pioneer of Gentile soteriology, it would have been possible for him to encourage a nucleus of believers

---

57 Meeks, *First Urban Christians*, p.138, sees this as explaining the term 'signs of an apostle' (2 Cor. 12:12). Schreiber, *Paulus*, p.270, argues that Paul's healings were so well known that his readers did not need to be told of them. Achtemeier, 'Jesus and Disciples', pp.150-51.

58 E.H. Peterson, 'Pastor Paul', in S.V. Soderlund and N.T. Wright (eds.), *Romans and the People of God* (Grand Rapids/Cambridge: Eerdmans, 1999) p.283, emphasises that Paul was a pastoral theologian. See *2.5*.

59 This takes into account the view of Thiselton, *First Corinthians*, e.g. pp.953-56, that gifts of healing may have a significant human contribution (see *1.4*).

who would preach, lead, prophesy and care for sick people, in the name of Christ. Some of those converted would have spiritual gifts of healing, and others might provide 'neighbourly' care for sick and poor people (as in Lk. 10:29-37).[60] This would build on the healing element of Jesus' ministry, which, as we have seen, occurred in the apostolic healings in Acts. But Paul never records taking the step of establishing such a nucleus, where care could be developed for those weak and ill in the community, and from which the gospel would spread, even in his absence.

There were some geographical and social factors, which theoretically might have discouraged Paul initially from such a plan in the key cities in which he planted churches. In the context of his huge mission field, a ministry that focussed, even in a relatively minor way, on healing would not have had the impact that the Galilean healings had had in Jesus' geographically–restricted mission. At least in the early part of his mission, Paul's churches comprised such a small minority of the predominantly pagan population, that the effect of sporadic healing in a city might not have produced significant religious recruitment. Paul's exposure to those sick and disabled was probably further limited by his working at tent-making (Acts 18:3) for a living. But these issues would have been temporary, at the very early stages of a successful mission, and less important in the Roman Empire, with its good communication systems, than at any other time.

To summarise, reasons for Paul mentioning healing miracles only in passing might include the nature of the letters, which were often in response to specific situations and questions. His apparent minimising of healing as an important strategy for Gentile mission might have been related to the social/geographical factors in an urban ministry in such a widespread mission field. However, it is easy to see that a model based partly on the apostolic healings in Acts could have been developed in the churches of his mission, and the reasons given above as to why Paul did not do this are recognised as being an incomplete explanation. Further issues need to be examined.

2 Factors Influencing Paul's Use of Healing in his Mission

The first consideration is how much Jesus' life and ministry, particularly his healing ministry, influenced Paul's strategy for mission.

---

60 Such a venture would be within the scriptural requirement to care for the poor (Lev. 19:10, 34), which Paul was eager to do (e.g. Gal. 2:10).

2.1 Paul's Knowledge and Use of Jesus' Healing Ministry

We have noted that Luke did not highlight Jesus' life and ministry in Acts but, instead, used the device of literary parallelism to relate apostolic healing to the healing ministry of Jesus, as well as to portray the widening of the geographical and ethnic range of the apostles' proclamation. Paul's letters also do not detail Jesus' life and ministry, and so describe nothing of Jesus' healing.[61] There is no record in the letters of Paul's preaching to his churches. The sermons in Acts are generally regarded as considerably recast by Luke, and, so, are unreliable as documentation of Paul's preaching, except perhaps to the Ephesian elders at Miletus (Acts 20:17-38).[62] Witherington, who considers that Paul's writings are notably silent on Jesus' ministry, explains this as due to Paul in his letters moving from the teachings and traditions of Jesus to specific problems in the churches; it can be argued, however, that Paul, who could not have known what had been taught to the Roman churches, gives no more detail of Jesus' life and ministry in Romans than in his other letters.[63]

There is a large body of literature in which scholars consider what Paul knew of the life and ministry of Jesus, apart from the passion story.[64] One perception is that Paul was unfamiliar with, or showed little interest in, the earthly life of Jesus.[65] The verse, 'though we once knew Christ according to the flesh, we know him no longer that way' (2 Cor. 5:16), was interpreted by Bultmann as indicating that Paul's interest was not in the historical Jesus, but only in the risen Christ while Betz suggests that Paul is rejecting the view that knowing the historical Jesus was an essential criterion of apostleship. Most scholars now believe that

---

61 Horsley and Silberman, *Message and Kingdom,* p.159, consider that there is no indication that Paul elaborated Jesus' teachings to his followers.

62 Johnson, *Acts of Apostles*, p.10, regards them as ways of recording what should have been said, i.e. like the speeches of Thucydides. J. Barclay, 'Jesus and Paul', in *Dictionary of Paul and his Letters*, p.499. Walton, *Leadership and Lifestyle,* pp.140-85.

63 Witherington, *Paul's Narrative,* p.152. V.P. Furnish, 'The Jesus-Paul Debate: From Baur to Bultmann' (orig. *BJRL* 47 [1964-5] 342-81), in Wedderburn (ed.), *Paul and Jesus*, p.46. Wenham, *Paul and Jesus,* pp.174-76, considers that in Rom. 1:2-4 Paul provided a summary of the gospel, and later in the letter alludes to different aspects of Jesus' life.

64 R.N. Longenecker, 'A Realised Hope, a New Commitment, and a Developed Proclamation: Paul and Jesus', in Longenecker (ed.), *Road from Damascus,* p.20; Witherington, *Paul's Narrative,* e.g. pp.83, 104, notes that the only incident in Jesus' life that Paul relates in any detail is the Last Supper (1 Cor. 11:23-25).

65 Theissen, *Miracle Stories,* p.295; Horsley and Silberman, *Message and Kingdom,* p.159, maintain that details of Jesus' earthly life were sketchy or unimportant to Paul.

the verse means that Paul's view of everything changed as a result of his call/conversion.[66]

More generally, most modern writers regard Paul as showing clear knowledge of the core traditions of Jesus' ministry.[67] Dunn argues that Paul would have known, before his Damascus road experience, something of Jesus' ministry, and, post-conversion, would have made it his business to learn more. Murphy-O'Connor points out that Paul, as a Pharisee, would not have persecuted the followers without finding out about Jesus, and Hawthorne believes that Paul would have researched the traditions of Jesus, spoken at length with Peter and James (Gal. 1:18-19), as well as learning from Jewish Christians in the Diaspora.[68] It seems certain that Paul would have known much of the Jesus tradition from his pre-conversion involvement in Jerusalem, and learned more from believers in Damascus, Antioch and Jerusalem.

Furnish shows that nineteenth- and early twentieth-century German theologians generally thought that Paul quoted, alluded to, and echoed Jesus' teaching and ministry.[69] There are only three direct quotations (1 Cor. 7:10; 9:14; 11:23-25) of Jesus' teaching in the letters, and scholars today vary widely in how much they find of Jesus' teaching in allusions. Both Wenham and Witherington believe that Paul did draw directly on Jesus' teaching; for instance, reflecting Jesus' refusal to produce a sign

---

66 R. Bultmann, *Faith and Understanding,* Vol. I (ET; London: SCM, 1969) pp.235-37, 277. J. Weiss, *Paul and Jesus* (ET; London/New York: Harper, 1909) pp.24, 41, 54, thought the verse indicated that Paul had actually known the historical Jesus. Betz, 'Apostle', in *ABD*, 1, p.310. Longenecker, 'Realised Hope', p.20; Dunn, *Theology of Paul,* p.184; S. Kim, 'God Reconciled His Enemy to Himself: The Origin of Paul's Concept of Reconciliation', in Longenecker (ed.), *Road from Damascus,* pp.110-11; Wolff, 'True Apostolic Knowledge', p.88, suggests that, pre-conversion, Paul believed that crucifixion indicated that Jesus had failed, and was accursed by God (as in Deut. 21:23).

67 E.g. C.F.D. Moule, 'Jesus, Judaism, and Paul', in Hawthorne and Betz (eds.), *Tradition and Interpretation,* pp.43-52; Murphy-O'Connor, *Paul*, pp.91-92; S. Kim, 'Jesus, Sayings of', in *Dictionary of Paul and his Letters*, pp.490-91; M. Thompson, *Clothed with Christ. The Example and Teaching of Jesus in Romans 12:1–15:13* (JSNTSup 59; Sheffield: Sheffield Academic Press, 1991) pp.15-76, devotes sixty pages to a consideration of Paul's knowledge of, and attitude to, the Jesus tradition, and agrees with this view.

68 Dunn, *Theology of Paul,* pp.187-88. Murphy-O'Connor, *Paul,* p.79. C.H. Dodd, *The Apostolic Preaching and its Developments* (Chicago: Willett, Clark & Co., 1937) p.17, famously noted of Gal. 1:18 that Paul would not have spent two weeks with Peter in Jerusalem 'discussing the weather'. G.F. Hawthorne, 'The Imitation of Christ: Discipleship in Philippians', in Longenecker (ed.), *Patterns of Discipleship,* p.172.

69 Furnish, 'Jesus-Paul Debate', pp.17-50, records the history in detail.

for unbelievers (1 Cor. 1:22, cf. Mk. 8:11-12, par. Lk. 11:29-30), and using the name 'Abba' for God (Gal. 4:6; Rom. 8:15). Walter (a minimalist with regard to Paul's knowledge of the earthly Jesus) considers that Paul's teachings (e.g. 1 Cor. 11:23-25; 15:3-7) probably reflect a fixed form, mediated through the catechetical and liturgical traditions of the very early church. Wedderburn, emphasising the paucity of material from Jesus' teachings, notes that Paul did not use them, even when his own authority was most threatened. Wenham points out, rightly, that Paul's silence about a subject should not be taken as ignorance of it; we know about the Lord's Supper (1 Cor. 11:23-26), only because it was being celebrated in a dysfunctional manner in Corinth.[70]

These points are relevant to Paul's theological understanding and use of Jesus' healing. If we accept that Jesus, as portrayed later by the evangelists, was known initially to the crowds largely because of his healing miracles (Chapter 1, *1.2.1*) it is certain that Paul, prior to his conversion, would have known that part of the tradition, as common early knowledge, yet Paul did not discuss Jesus' healing ministry in his letters.[71] Various reasons have been suggested; Wedderburn proposes that Paul felt that the Jerusalem 'pillars' had first-hand knowledge of Jesus' life, including his healing, and that he, Paul, was not an authority; Georgi considers that Paul's opponents in 2 Corinthians 10–13 might have brought with them to Corinth traditions of Jesus' miracles; Yeung believes that it was Paul's intention to tone down all other miracles, so as to highlight the greatest miracle, the resurrection of Christ.[72]

---

70 D. Wenham, *Paul: Follower of Jesus or Founder of Christianity?* (Grand Rapids: Eerdmans, 1995) p.353; Witherington, *Paul's Narrative*, p.152. N. Walter, 'Paul and the Early Christian Jesus-Tradition', in Wedderburn (ed.), *Paul and Jesus,* pp.60-62. Wedderburn, 'Paul and Jesus: The Problem of Continuity', in Wedderburn (ed.), *Paul and Jesus*, pp.100-101. D. Wenham, 'The Story of Jesus Known to Paul', in Green and Turner (eds.), *Jesus of Nazareth,* p.297.

71 Wenham, *Paul, Follower or Founder,* p.43; O'Neill, *Who Did Jesus Think He Was?,* p.52; Murphy-O'Connor, *Paul*, p.75. Later evidence of Jewish belief that Jesus did miracles is to be found in the Tannaitic tradition; for instance, that Jesus was executed as a magician appears in *b. Sanh.* 43a, 107b; it also appears in Josephus, *Ant.* 18:63-64. Only once did Paul use 'σωτήρ' for Christ, and then in the context of spiritual healer (Phil. 3:20).

72 Wedderburn, 'Paul and Jesus: Problem of Continuity', pp.100-101. Georgi, *Opponents*, pp.210-13, suggests that the opponents 'preaching another Jesus' (2 Cor. 11:4) may be referring to Jesus' miracle stories. M.W. Yeung, *Faith in Jesus and Paul. A Comparison, with Special Reference to 'Faith that Can Move Mountains' and 'Your Faith Has Healed/Saved You'* (Tübingen: Mohr [Siebeck], 2002) pp.282, 294.

Belleville considers that Paul's mention of Jesus' 'meekness' and 'gentleness' (2 Cor. 10:1) refers to Jesus' healing miracles, and Wenham believes the phrase, 'compassion of Christ Jesus' (Phil. 1:8), does so also.[73] These descriptions could equally well represent more generally Jesus' earthly nature; this fits with my perception that Paul did concentrate on absorbing and teaching the *character* of Jesus, rather than the actual deeds of his ministry. I am not convinced that there is clear evidence of Paul reporting instances of Jesus' healing in the letters, but I would argue that he understood and referred to the essential nature of Jesus, such as his gentleness and compassion, which were evident in Jesus' earthly ministry (perhaps particularly in healing).

2.1.1 Paul's Adaptation of Jesus' Ministry and Tradition

Paul was concerned with imitation, commonly regarded as a virtue throughout the ancient world.[74] His striving to imitate Christ seems to me to have an abstract quality, which is missed in the search for evidence of his trying to imitate the *facts* of Jesus' historical ministry; rather, he was trying to attain to something of the *essence* of Jesus' character. I believe, with Wedderburn, that Paul considered more significant than actual events of Jesus' ministry, his outlook, and Paul tried to follow that, particularly Jesus' graciousness to sinners (and sick people), so he 'translated' Jesus' openness to sinners into his own ministry to Gentiles.[75] Openness to the outsider, which was an important aspect of the nature of Jesus, was significant in Paul's ministry (see *2.5.1*), and he exhorted the church repeatedly to imitate him in living a life of godliness (e.g. 1 Cor. 11:1; Phil. 3:17; 4:9). It was not, of course, the only context of Paul's imitation of Christ; for instance, he described the importance of sharing in Christ's sufferings in relation to his death (Phil. 3:10-11).

Paul's own experience was of the risen Christ already exalted by God, and was not based on Jesus' earthly power. Living in the immediate post-Easter period, he came to recognise that Jesus'

---

73 L.J. Belleville, '"Imitate me, just as I imitate Christ": Discipleship in the Corinthian Correspondence', in Longenecker (ed.), *Patterns of Discipleship*, p.127. Wenham, *Paul, Follower or Founder,* pp.351-52, also suggests that 'faith that could move mountains' (1 Cor. 13:2) and 'fully proclaiming the Gospel of Christ' (Rom. 15:18-19) both indicate Paul referring directly to Jesus' miracles, but this seems to be stretching the meaning.

74 A.D. Clarke, '"Be Imitators of Me": Paul's Model of Leadership', *TynBul* 49 (1998) p.350. Belleville, 'Imitate Me', p.121, notes that imitation is described both in Jewish writings (e.g. 4 Maccabees, Sirach and at Qumran) and in Graeco-Roman society.

75 Wedderburn, 'Paul and Jesus: Similarity and Continuity', in Wedderburn (ed.), *Paul and Jesus*, pp.135-36, 142-43.

crucifixion was the ultimate act of love and humility, and God's power was seen supremely in Jesus' resurrection.[76] His experience of Christ and the importance of the Holy Spirit were central features of Paul's life. He chose to 'know nothing but Jesus Christ, and him crucified' (1 Cor. 2:2), and his letters demonstrate that he tried to capture in his own life and mission, whether consciously or not, the fundamental issues of Christ's passion, death and resurrection, rather than the features of Jesus' ministry, such as healing.[77]

It has been suggested that Paul interpreted his knowledge of Jesus' ministry in such a way that 'Christ became for Paul an almost abstract source of redemptive power'.[78] This coheres with my impression of the Paul who, having found out as much as possible about the historical Jesus, based his own life, theology and mission on his deep spiritual awareness of the nature of the crucified, risen Christ. Healing of illness would not be so significant to Paul's outworking of the suffering, dead and resurrected Christ, as it was in the depiction by Mark and Luke of the earthly Jesus' ministry. There, healing of body and soul was a significant way for sick people and the crowds, to whom Jesus preached, to glimpse the Kingdom of God, and for the healed to be brought back 'into the camp'. Paul's calling, having spiritualised his imitation of Christ, was to advance Jesus' mission geographically, and to bring salvation, rather than physical healing, to the Gentiles, whom he regarded as sinners (Gal. 2:15), and so excluded from the true Israel.

A metaphor is used when a literal description is not possible or adequate. Healing is often used as a metaphor for salvation, and it seems to me to be very close to describing how Paul undertook his calling to do the work of Christ as apostle to the Gentiles; it is an analogy that can be followed quite far. I am *not* suggesting that the idea of metaphorical healing was in Paul's conscious thought; there are no verbs of healing in his letters, and the metaphor he used (again, just metaphor) was that, by God's grace, he would be priest (or perhaps minister to Christ as priest), presenting the Gentiles as an acceptable sacrifice to God (Rom. 15:16).[79] However, the healing metaphor gives us a coherent idea of Paul's

---

76 Theissen and Merz, *Historical Jesus*, p.299. Kim, 'Jesus, Sayings of', p.490.

77 C. Wolff, 'Humility and Self-Denial in Jesus' Life and Message, and in the Apostolic Existence of Paul', in Wedderburn (ed.), *Paul and Jesus*, pp.159-60. Wedderburn, 'Paul and the Story of Jesus', in Wedderburn (ed.), *Paul and Jesus*, p.180, considers it likely that Paul was aware that his ministry bore a resemblance to that of Jesus.

78 Horsley and Silberman, *Message and Kingdom,* p.159.

79 C.E.B. Cranfield, *A Critical and Exegetical Commentary on the Epistle to the Romans*, ICC, Vol.2 (Edinburgh: T. & T. Clark, 1979) pp.755-56.

perception and development of the mission to the Gentiles, in response to Christ. An apocalyptic vision in the book of Revelation refers metaphorically both to individual healing (21:4), and to the healing of the nations (22:2), and the latter is what I see as best describing Paul's mission.

To summarise, it seems certain that Paul did have information about, and understood the unique nature of, Jesus' life and ministry. It further seems that he drew on the *essence* of Jesus' earthly character (e.g. Phil. 2:1-8), and concentrated on the theological significance of Jesus' death and resurrection, to develop his gospel and mission. This was a radical advance on merely recalling the events of Jesus' life, and I believe that we can understand Paul's mission and soteriology most easily as Paul extending Jesus' ministry by his metaphorical healing of Gentiles.

2.2 Events in Paul's Life, and his Reactions

Other factors might have led Paul to preach his message of salvation to the Gentiles without stressing healing. These are concerned with the events and circumstances in his life and his reaction to them, his theology and his personality.

2.2.1 Paul's Conversion

Most scholars recognise Paul's conversion/call as the important turning point in his life; for instance, Kim sees Paul's conversion as the source of his belief that the exalted Christ, the 'image of God', had retrieved and restored humanity, which had been lost in Adam.[80] Hurtado makes the point that Paul's conversion, in view of his personality and zeal, was bound to be dramatic in its effects.[81] It is accepted here that this was the origin of Paul's mission to the Gentiles.

---

80 K. Stendahl, *Paul among Jews and Gentiles* (Philadelphia: Fortress, 1976) pp.7-23, was the first to argue that Paul's Christophany should be regarded as a call rather than conversion. S. Kim, *The Origin of Paul's Gospel* (WUNT 2/4; Tübingen/Grand Rapids: Mohr [Siebeck]/Eerdmans, 1981-82) especially pp.56-66, 269-311; S. Kim, *Paul and the New Perspective. Second Thoughts on the Origin of Paul's Gospel* (WUNT 140; Grand Rapids/Tübingen: Eerdmans/Mohr [Siebeck], 2002); A.F. Segal, *Paul the Convert. The Apostolate and Apostasy of Saul the Pharisee* (New Haven/London: Yale University Press, 1990) p.6; T.L. Donaldson, 'Israelite, Convert, Apostle to the Gentiles: The Origin of Paul's Gentile Mission', in Longenecker (ed.), *Road from Damascus*, pp.62-84; Longenecker, 'Realized Hope', pp.18-41.

81 L.W. Hurtado, *Lord Jesus Christ. Devotion to Jesus in Earliest Christianity* (Grand Rapids/Cambridge: Eerdmans, 2003) pp.93-95.

His conversion gives us a point from which to follow the development of his mission, although there is no sure way of knowing how Paul's ideas of Gentile soteriology grew between then and the writing of his letters. Even details of Paul's conversion cannot be reconstructed with certainty from the autobiographical material in his letters; the Damascus road experience detailed in Acts is referred to only indirectly in Philippians 3:6, and obliquely in Galatians 1:15-16 (where he presents it as a divine call, before his birth, to minister to the Gentiles, like the prophetic call in Jer.1:5 and Isa. 49:1). It is significant that, both in the letters and in the descriptions in Acts, the specific divine command that Paul was given at the time of conversion was that of proclaiming Christ to the Gentiles; the gift of healing in Acts (9:17-18 and 22:12-13) was given to Ananias.

In summary, although his conversion was a very major event in Paul's life, it does not explain the minor part that healing played in his subsequent Gentile mission.

2.2.2 Paul's Judaism and Christianity

Paul was a Jew (e.g. 2 Cor. 11:22), ardent in his observance (Gal. 1:14), and whether or not his Judaism is regarded as continuous after his conversion, there is evidence that his background beliefs coloured his thoughts and actions.[82] He indicated his scriptural views on sickness and healing in his typology of the Exodus (e.g. Numbers 14, 16 and 20), that death might occur as a result of God's wrath (1 Cor. 10:5, 8), and that partaking unworthily in a sacred ritual (the Lord's Supper) was responsible for the illness and death of some followers (1 Cor. 11:30). More generally, he seemed to accept that illness and other afflictions might be at least partly the result of sin (Rom. 1:18-32).[83]

He is the only Pharisee (Phil. 3:5) and follower of Jesus, of whom we have first-hand information.[84] The gospels indicate that some Pharisees undertook exorcisms (e.g. Lk. 11:19), so, although they were probably

82 Dunn, 'Who Did Paul Think He Was?', p.178, points out the tension between continuity versus a clear break with Paul's Jewish past. N.T. Wright, *What Saint Paul Really Said: Was Paul of Tarsus the Real Founder of Christianity?* (Grand Rapids: Eerdmans, 1997) pp.12-20, gives a *résumé* of opinions over the twentieth century, and, p.20, concludes that almost all scholars now regard Paul as a very Jewish thinker.

83 Hafemann, *2 Corinthians*, p.34, notes that this is in contrast to the views of some of the church members in Corinth, who erroneously believed that conversion had granted them freedom from suffering.

84 J.C. Lentz, Jr., *Luke's Portrait of Paul* (SNTSMS 77; Cambridge: Cambridge University Press, 1993) pp.52-54, questions whether he was a Pharisee. Dunn, 'Who Did Paul Think he Was?', p.175.

diverse in their interest, there was no Pharisaic objection to Paul undertaking this form of healing. Rabbinic tradition was opposed to rabbis (as successors to the Pharisees) undertaking miracles, but this may have been largely in response to Christian proclamation of Jesus' miracles.[85]

Many of Paul's writings demonstrate his background in Second Temple apocalyptic Judaism. The devil, rulers of this age, elemental world spirits, principalities and powers, as well as pagan deities, were all contending for dominance of the world, against the power of the Holy Spirit, and Paul saw his contact with these 'powers' as real and insistent. Wink believes that Paul dealt with the powers by depersonalising them into abstract ideas, e.g. sin, law, flesh and death[86].

Both his Jewishness and Christianity are reflected in his theological understanding of the human body. As Christ had taken the form of flesh, then Paul would recognise that the human body could not be evil. He exhorted the Roman church to 'present your bodies as a living sacrifice' (Rom. 12:1) at the beginning of his ethical teaching in that letter, and he wrote of the church as the body of Christ (1 Cor. 12:12-27; Rom. 12:4-5), emphasising the importance of all parts of the body, and particularly, the 'weaker' parts. He warned the Corinthian church of the dangers of sinning against the body and blood of Christ in their conduct at the Lord's Supper (1 Cor. 11:27). He saw the body as the temple of the Holy Spirit (1 Cor. 3:16; 6:19), and so to be cared for (1 Cor. 3:17). He did not accept the Greek philosophical concept of dualism of body and soul, where the body was often despicable, although he did describe it as an earthly tent (2 Cor. 5:1-4) ready to be shed at death.[87] With the sense of the nearness of the Parousia, expressed in the Thessalonian letters, and the prospect of the imminent bodily resurrection of believers (1 Thess. 4:13-15), he wrestled with the form that the resurrected body would take (1 Cor. 15:42-57), but never formulated a clear answer.

---

85 B. Lindars, 'Elijah, Elisha and the Gospel Miracles', in Moule (ed.), *Miracles*, p.78, notes that rabbis tended to discountenance emphasis on miracles after the fall of Jerusalem.

86 Wink, *Naming the Powers*, p.104. Roetzel, *Letters of Paul*, p.87. W. Carr, *Principalities and Powers. The Background, Meaning and Development of the Pauline Phrase, 'hai archai kai hai exousiai'* (SNTSMS 42; Cambridge: Cambridge University Press, 1981) e.g. p.174, does not see in Paul's letters a battle between Christ and hostile powers.

87 D. Guthrie, *The Apostles* (London: Pickering & Inglis, 1975) p.213, points out that the earthen vessel description (2 Cor. 4:7) fits Paul's belief of the insignificance of what happens to his body. He yearned for his own death, so that he would be with Christ (Phil. 1:20-26).

These issues may have had some effect on his perception of the value of miracle healing of illness in this life, but, in general, his Jewishness does not seem to have been a major factor in his views on the value of healing in his mission.

2.2.3 Paul's Personality and Adaptability

It is accepted today that individuals often change attitudes and strategies according to circumstances and pressures, but ancient writers frequently assumed that people were unalterable, and so endurance was a cardinal virtue.[88] Much of the polemic in Paul's letters demonstrates a personality not prepared to compromise with the different views of other Christians (although Segal considers that this was not always true).[89] Paul frequently lists his afflictions, the 'peristasis catalogues', which give us glimpses of the extent and violence of the opposition to him.[90] Thus, although evidence of Jewish opposition to Paul (and other missionaries) is much clearer in Acts than in the letters, in one of the peristasis catalogues (2 Cor. 11:24) he demonstrates both his remarkable perseverance in attending synagogues, and the sustained Jewish anger against him.[91] The catalogues reveal Paul's literary skills; for instance, sustained sarcasm in 2 Corinthians 11:23-33 (especially vv.32-33), a counter-aretalogy intended to discredit his opponents' self-praise; and also showing his ability in rhetoric.[92] The catalogues can be accepted here as evidence of both the opposition to Paul, and his reaction to it.

---

88 Malina, *Social World of Jesus and Gospels,* p.xiii; Witherington, *Paul Quest*, pp.75-76. The stress on the value of endurance suggests that ancient people did not envisage adapting to circumstances.

89 Sanders, *Paul, the Law and the Jewish People*, p.153, refers to Paul's 'black-and-white' thinking. Segal, *Paul the Convert,* p.xii, believes that Paul matured gradually, and he sometimes gave way on his personal opinions, so that the church could progress (e.g. Phil. 1:15-18).

90 J.T. Fitzgerald, *Cracks in an Earthen Vessel: An Examination of Hardships in the Corinthian Correspondence* (SBLDS 99; Atlanta: Scholars' Press, 1988) discusses them in detail. The four main catalogues are 1 Cor. 4:9-13; 2 Cor. 4:8-9; 6:4-10; 11:23-28, but there are several others (e.g. 2 Cor. 12:10; Rom. 8:35, 38; Phil. 4:11-12).

91 Sanders, *Paul, the Law, and Jewish People*, p.179, notes that this verse suggests that Paul, at least sometimes, tried to win Jews to Christianity.

92 Meeks, *First Urban Christians,* p.118. Witherington, *Paul's Narrative,* p.238, considers that this was in mockery of the *res gestae* of the Caesars, whose mighty deeds were made public. Marshall, *Enmity in Corinth*, p.360, thinks that Paul, in ridiculing himself, is ridiculing his opponents by a carefully calculated *reductio ad absurdum.* A.D. Litfin, *St. Paul's Theology of Proclamation in 1 Corinthians 1-4 and Greco-Roman Rhetoric* (SNTSMS 79; Cambridge: Cambridge University Press, 1994) pp.138-39, discusses Paul's knowledge of rhetoric.

Opposition to Paul produced tensions within him, manifest in his letters, but it also advanced his arguments and convictions about Gentile soteriology, and this can be seen in the development of his theological thought during the sequence of the letters. Murphy-O'Connor considers that Paul functioned most effectively in reaction, rather than in progressive logic.[93] I believe that this aspect of his mind and personality was very important in relation to his theology and his attitude to healing in his mission. (See *2.4.2 and 3.*)

2.2.4 Paul's Reactions to Others' Illnesses

Christians were not exempt from illness and death in Paul's pastoral practice (e.g. 1 Cor. 15:6, 12-56; 1 Thess. 4:13). How Paul viewed the illness of others gives us first-hand information of one mid-first-century Jewish Christian's views on the subject.

We have noted that Paul accepted the view that the sins of the Israelites in the wilderness caused God's wrath, which was responsible for their illnesses and deaths (1 Cor. 10:1-14). He pointed out (10:13) that Christ would give them grace to endure (echoed in his later writing about his own illness). This pericope, about the consequences of breaking God's covenant, is followed by the first of two discussions about the Lord's Supper (10:16-22), and contains the only two verses (10:20-21) where Paul writes about demons in his letters. He uses demons in the context of covenant, adapting the scriptural ideas of both exclusivity to God, and community care for the other, in a Christological way. His train of thought seems to move from God's wrath at the breaking of the covenant in the wilderness, to the same risk which Paul saw as present in the Corinthian context of eating meals in pagan temples. There, he was aware of the danger of 'demons', which he relates to the Eucharist, but also to the effects on the 'weak' in the church community. In 1 Corinthians 11:28-31, the second discussion of the Lord's Supper, he considered that violation of the sacred incurred God's discipline, so that many Corinthians became ill, and some died,

---

93 Murphy-O'Connor, *Paul*, p.205, says 'each new problem stimulated greater profundity of thought'. Sanders, 'Paul', pp.117-19, considers that Paul did not have a single, systematic, worked-out theology. Barrett, *Paul: An Introduction*, pp.22, 44. J.D.G. Dunn, *The Theology of Paul's Letter to the Galatians* (Cambridge: Cambridge University Press, 1993) p.134, sees a moderating of Paul's attitude to the law between Galatians and Romans; Dodd, 'Mind of Paul', pp.81, 84, mentions the change in Paul's outlook to the Jewish people, which became less negative between 1 Thess. 2:16 and Rom. 11:11.

because they approached the Lord's Supper 'without discerning the body' (of Christ).[94]

In the authentic letters, there is only one named sufferer of illness, a messenger to Paul from the church in Philippi, Epaphroditus. He had a near-fatal illness or injury (Phil. 2:26-27), perhaps on his way to, perhaps while with, Paul, who was in prison. His mission was to bring the Philippians' gift (4:18), but it seems likely that he was also commissioned to minister to Paul.[95] There is scholarly argument about how Epaphroditus' illness was healed; 'God had mercy' (v.27) is taken by Fee to mean that 'God had a direct hand in his healing, most likely by "gifts of healings"' (as in 1 Cor. 12:9, 28), on the grounds that 'people of the times would rarely recover from a near-death illness otherwise'. Others consider that he probably recovered by natural means, and that there is no suggestion that Paul was divinely empowered to heal him. O'Brien considers that it is unknowable how Paul thought Epaphroditus was restored, since Paul's emphasis is on God's mercy to both Epaphroditus and himself.[96] This agnostic view seems to me to be safest.

In sending Epaphroditus back before the outcome of Paul's imprisonment was known, Paul had to support both the messenger and the church. He is profligate in his praise of Epaphroditus (2:25, 29, 30),[97] and writes that Epaphroditus 'was distressed because you (his fellow-Philippians) heard that he was ill' (v.26). This might mean that Epaphroditus wanted to spare them worry on his behalf, or that they might think that he had been unable to carry out his mission fully, especially if they thought that they had sent Paul a defective gift.[98] Epaphroditus, however, might expect to be despised because of his weakness; this would explain best why Paul stressed so strongly to the

---

94 Barrett, *First Corinthians*, p.275, relates this to the mention of demons in 1 Corinthians 10. Cheung, *Idol Food in Corinth,* p.304, points out that modern Western theologians have played down demons in the Bible, and, so, the importance of the issue in 1 Corinthians 10.

95 P.T. O'Brien, *The Epistle to the Philippians. A Commentary on the Greek Text*, NIGTC (Grand Rapids/Carlisle: Eerdmans/Paternoster, 1991) pp.332-33.

96 G.D. Fee, *Paul's Letter to the Philippians,* NICNT. (Grand Rapids: Eerdmans, 1995) p.279. Ferngren and Amundsen, 'Medicine and Christianity', p.2962; Wilkinson, *Bible and Healing,* pp.190, 192. O'Brien, *Philippians*, p.335.

97 Thomas, *Devil, Disease*, pp.75-83, noting the extravagance of Paul's praise, considers that Paul anticipated that there might be a problem with Epaphroditus' early return. This view seems justified.

98 P. Oakes, *Philippians. From People to Letter* (SNTSMS 110; Cambridge: Cambridge University Press, 2001) p.110.

Philippians that Epaphroditus' near-death experience was brought about by 'his work for Christ' (2:30), and urged them to honour workers like him. As we have seen, social and economic effects of significant illness (or injury) in the first century were enormous, but even more important were the effects of illness in reducing esteem and religious standing.[99]

In summary, Paul's conversion/call was a very major event in his life, and set him on the path to mission. His views on others' illness seem to be like many Jews of his time, that illness might be the result of sin, but he also warned of the dangers of demonic influences on the lives of Christians (that is, indirectly 'demonic', by upsetting those weak in the Christian faith); he emphasised that Epaphroditus' near-death experience had occurred because of his work for Christ. Paul's personality was such that he found it hard to accept the different views of others, and he was prepared to endure hardships himself, in the manner of the Stoics. It seems likely that he did, however, sometimes alter his judgments in response to changing circumstances, and that he developed his theology during his mission. His reactions are significant when they are applied to his illness.

2.3 Paul's 'Thorn in the Flesh'

We explore how much Paul's view of healing might have been tempered by his own experience of illness, and how this might have influenced his strategy for Gentile soteriology. Since this study is concerned with Paul's attitude to healing, his health will be considered in more detail than other factors in his life.

2.3.1 What was the Thorn?

Paul writes of his σκόλοψ τῇ σαρκί (thorn in the flesh) in 2 Corinthians 12:7-10. There has long been argument as to whether σκόλοψ (v.7), translated variously as a stake, splinter or thorn, was an illness, or represented evil, either as human opposition or as some demonic power. Thrall annotates other scholars' views that the thorn was psychological, as temptation, conscience or grief.[100] Some have regarded the thorn as a

99 Harvey, *Renewal,* pp.22-24; Edelstein and Edelstein, *Asclepius,* 2, p.175, wrote that 'the economic threat of disease to the lower and middle classes was grave, graver perhaps than at any later time'. S.J. Hafemann, 'Suffering', in *Dictionary of Paul and his Letters,* p.919. See Chapter 2, *2.2*.

100 Although he often showed his awareness of his total dependence on the grace of God (e.g. Rom. 8:31), the cry of someone in conflict with himself (Rom. 7:15-24), even if it were not Paul, demonstrates that, at the least, he recognised the pain and empathised with the sufferer. The pre-Reformation idea that it was sexual sin seems incompatible

term for Paul's enemies, or for persecution.[101] Paul had ample reason to regard the massive opposition to him as a 'thorn', but he referred to persecution in terms of the peristasis catalogues, where he underlined the saving grace of God in these troubles (e.g. Rom. 7:25; 2 Cor. 4:7; 6:4-10). Only with regard to the thorn did he describe *how* Christ's grace was given to him, so it seems that it was different from his other hardships.

From Tertullian onwards, the thorn was generally regarded as physical, that is, weakness/disease, an opinion shared by most, but not all, modern writers.[102] The thorn, as some bodily affliction, might be either naturally-occurring or as the result of severe ill treatment. In arguing for the thorn being some form of weakness or disease, I find nothing in the pericope to contradict this. Paul recorded that he prayed three times (v.8) to have it removed. Although this is usually assumed to be an allusion to Jesus praying in Gethsemane (Mk. 14:34-40), 'three times' is also used as a convention in petitionary prayers. The fact that he reported praying three times about the thorn, however, might be evidence of the severity of the illness or its *sequelae*, compared with his other sufferings, where he never recorded that he prayed for release.[103]

---

with Paul's comment in 1 Cor. 7:7. M.E. Thrall, *The Second Epistle to the Corinthians*, Vol. II., ICC (2nd ed.; London/New York: T. & T. Clark/Continuum, 2004) pp.809-18, has a detailed excursus on the nature of the thorn.

101 Murphy-O'Connor, *Paul*, pp.321-22, and in *Theology of Second Corinthians*, p.119, regards the thorn as referring to opposition to Paul's ministry. He comments that if the thorn were a form of persecution, Paul would not have prayed to be released, as persecution had brought him nearer to Christ. Twelftree, 'Healing, Illness', p.379, notes the use of σκόλοψ for enemies of Israel, found in Num. 33:55. Barnett, *Second Corinthians*, p.568, notes also this use in Ezek. 28:24.

102 Tertullian, *On Modesty* 13, thought Paul's thorn was some form of chronic pain, such as headache or earache. D.W. Amundsen, *Medicine, Society and Faith in the Ancient and Mediaeval Worlds* (Baltimore/London: Johns Hopkins University Press, 1996) p.146, notes that Tertullian had studied medicine, though Jackson, *Doctors and Diseases*, p.29, denies this and considers that he, like Celsus, wrote as a layman of things medical. Thrall, *Second Corinthians* II, pp.817-18. Wilkinson, *Bible and Healing*, p.210. S.R. Garrett, 'Paul's Thorn and Cultural Models of Affliction', in L.M. White and O.L. Yarbrough (eds.), *The Social World of the First Christians: Essays in Honor of Wayne A. Meeks* (Minneapolis: Augsburg Fortress, 1995) p.83, sees the precise identity, i.e. ailment or enemy, as unresolvable, as do C.G. Kruse, *The Second Epistle of Paul to the Corinthians* (Leicester/Grand Rapids: InterVarsity/Eerdmans, 1987) p.206, and Barnett, *Second Corinthians*, p.570.

103 Wilkinson, *Bible and Healing*, p.209, notes that, in answer to Paul's prayers for the thorn to leave him (v.8), Christ would be unlikely to respond that the thorn should remain (v.9) if it were a sin of which Paul had repented. Bultmann, *Theology of New Testament*, 1, p.128, notes that he prayed to Christ ('the Lord'); he points out that,

2.3.2 What was the Illness?

His illness was in relation to, and therefore, we can assume, began some time soon after his vision (2 Cor. 12:2-4), which was fourteen years earlier than the writing of this (part of the) letter to the Corinthians, so the illness was an acquired, not congenital, problem, and was a chronic or recurrent condition, but unrelated in time to his conversion experience.[104] It is reasonable to assume that it was the condition also mentioned in Galatians 4:13, on Paul's initial visit to Galatia, a view accepted by many, but not all, exegetes since Lightfoot.[105] We may deduce that its effects were intermittent or recurrent, and rendered Paul in some way repulsive or unsightly, at least during exacerbations.[106] Although the diagnosis of the thorn has little value compared with its theological importance, yet interest in its identification continues, and is relevant to this study because of its probable influence on Paul's attitude to, and theological insights into, illness and healing.

Many attempts at diagnosing the illness have been made over the centuries; they have neatly demonstrated changing ideas of illness during that time,[107] but have not solved the puzzle. The main diagnostic

---

outside formal liturgical worship, prayers were said directly to Christ. This is confirmed by others, e.g. Hurtado, *Lord Jesus Christ*, pp.138-40. Hughes, *Second Corinthians,* p.449. Barnett, *Second Corinthians*, p.571, points out that prayers were offered three times per day (e.g. Ps. 55:17), a convention seen in Acts 10:16. W. M. Alexander, 'St Paul's Infirmity', *ExpTim* 15 (1903-4) pp.545-6, considered that the three prayers indicated three attacks of Paul's disease.

104 Horrell, *Introduction to Paul*, p.34, notes that the letter is commonly dated to the mid-fifties. This would mean that the thorn was present throughout the period of Paul's letter-writing, and during most of his missionary journeys. (The point that 2 Corinthians 10-13 may be one of several letters encompassed by 2 Corinthians is mainly irrelevant to the discussion.) Hafemann, *2 Corinthians*, p.458, considers that the illness became manifest about AD 42–44, before his missionary journey with Barnabas (Gal. 1:21).

105 J.B. Lightfoot, *The Epistle of St. Paul to the Galatians,* Reproduced by Zondervan Commentary Series (Grand Rapids: Zondervan, 1957) pp.186-91. Dunn, *Theology of Galatians,* pp.7, 12, thinks that Gal. 4:13 demonstrates that Paul was in Galatia for the second time. T.Y. Mullins, 'Paul's Thorn in the Flesh', *JBL* 76 (1957) pp.299-303; Bruce, *Epistle of Paul to the Galatians,* p.208; Thrall, *Second Corinthians,* II, p.814; T.W. Martin, 'Whose Flesh? What Temptation? (Galatians 4:13-14),' *JSNT* 74 (1999) 65-91. Thomas, *Devil, Disease*, p.57, thinks the illness in Galatia was temporary (he offers no explanation of how he arrives at this conclusion, except that Paul eventually left Galatia), and unrelated to the thorn, as Paul did not describe the illness in Galatia as being from Satan; and, p.61, that Paul (and he) believe that it was sent by God, in order that Paul would preach in Galatia.

106 Wilkinson, *Bible and Healing*, p.212.

107 E.g. A. Schweitzer, *The Mysticism of Paul the Apostle* (ET, 2nd ed., reprint; London: A. & C. Black, 1956) pp.152-53, considers that 'Paul suffered from some kind of

contenders today are eye disease, malaria, migraine (or other recurrent severe pain), and epilepsy. That the malady was an ophthalmic disease is sometimes assumed from Galatians 4:15, where Paul wrote that the Galatians would have torn out their eyes and given them to him, and from Galatians 6:11, where he remarked on the large size of his writing, perhaps indicating poor vision.[108] Eyes were regarded metaphorically as the most valuable of organs (e.g. Deut. 32:10; Ps. 17:8; Zech. 2:8), so the Galatians' offer seems more likely to be describing a gesture of friendship than an indication of Paul having eye disease. Blindness, such a feature in the Acts accounts of Paul's Damascus road experience, seems more likely to represent Luke's theological perception of Paul's conversion, rather than a physical affliction; Luke often used sight as his metaphor for salvation (while Paul more frequently used light). Considering his missionary activities, I would regard severely damaged sight as unlikely to have been Paul's problem. Thrall comes down in favour of migraine.[109] Migraine, however, does not produce abnormal physical signs, which would be expected, as Paul was potentially unacceptable to the Galatians.

Wilkinson, summarising much of the speculation about Paul's illness, includes two views from a century ago that have stood the tests of time and changing medical fashions. Archaeologist Sir William Ramsay thought that malaria, first contracted in Pamphylia, where it was endemic, was a highly likely explanation, while Menzies Alexander, a medical theologian, suggested that Paul had chronic brucellosis.[110] Both malaria and chronic brucellosis would produce ill-health, with fevers, rigors and weakness, in recurring bouts, often over years. Malaria, especially, is an attractive option; although the symptom-complex was

---

epileptiform attacks, which does not by any means necessarily mean that he was a real epileptic'.

108 Borsch, *Power in Weakness*, p.114, and Dunn, *Commentary on Galatians*, p.236, think Paul suffered from eye disease; Hull (who became blind early in adult life) writes, *In the Beginning,* p.84, about the possibility of Paul being partially sighted. Thrall, *Second Corinthians,*II, pp.814-15, rejects ophthalmia.

109 Thrall, *Second Corinthians,* II, p.818.

110 Wilkinson, *Bible and Healing*, pp.211-26. Burke, 'Malaria in the Greco-Roman World', p.2253, points out that the epidemiological discoveries at the end of the nineteenth century about the spread of malaria led to attempts to explain much of classical history in terms of it. W.M. Ramsay, *The Church in the Roman Empire before AD 170* (2nd ed.; London: Hodder & Stoughton, 1893) p.63. Alexander, 'Paul's Infirmity', pp.469-73, and pp.545-48, especially p.547. It is not verifiable that brucellosis was present in the Roman province of Asia at the time.

known to Hippocratic medicine, no cure was known, and it was frequently fatal. Malaria is the diagnosis favoured by Wilkinson.

Epilepsy was well known in the first century.[111] Its manifestations are episodic; a fit is particularly likely to occur under stress, and would be terrifying to spectators. Epilepsy could be related to Paul's ill-treatment, as he was likely to have suffered a head injury, for instance when he was stoned (Acts 14:19; 2 Cor. 11:25). It also fulfils the criterion that it would not interfere seriously with Paul's physical stamina in his missionary activity.[112] I would regard epilepsy as a plausible explanation of the thorn.[113]

It is not clear whether the Corinthian church knew the identity of the thorn; a nineteenth-century view was that it might have been plain to Paul's contemporaries, and so he did not describe its nature.[114] More modern observations are that there is no definitive answer possible, and, indeed, the ambiguity of the illness increases its importance. Hughes writes, 'Its very anonymity has been productive of far wider blessing than if it had been possible to identify the specific nature of disability', explaining that if we knew that Paul had suffered from, say, epilepsy, then those of us who do not have the condition might ignore the lessons that Paul learned from his disease.[115]

2.3.3 Why was the Thorn so Important?

The pericope, 2 Corinthians 12:1-9, tells us a great deal about Paul. Beginning with his intention to boast in response to his opponents, he wrote of 'visions and revelations of the Lord' (v.1), but made it clear that these experiences in no way legitimated him as an apostle.[116] He

---

111 O. Temkin, *The Falling Sickness. A History of Epilepsy from the Greeks to the Beginnings of Modern Neurology* (2nd ed.; Baltimore/London: Johns Hopkins University Press, 1971) p.4.

112 Barrett, *2 Corinthians*, p.315; Barnett, *Second Corinthians*, p.568, n.19, notes that Paul 'must have had good health' to undertake the activities described in 2 Cor. 11:23-33. D. Guthrie, *New Testament Introduction* (3rd ed.; London: InterVarsity, 1970) p.390, commented that Paul must have had robust health to cope with the rigours of his mission. So also Thrall, *Second Corinthians* II, pp.817-18.

113 So also Howard, *Disease and Healing*, pp.249-51, and Twelftree, 'Healing, Illness', p.379.

114 A.P. Stanley, *The Epistles of St. Paul to the Corinthians* (4th ed.; London: J. Murray, 1876), p.210.

115 Murphy-O'Connor, *Paul*, p.162; Barnett, *Second Corinthians*, p.570; P.E. Hughes, *Paul's Second Epistle to the Corinthians,* NICNT (Grand Rapids: Eerdmans, 1962) pp.442, 446.

116 Barnett, *Second Corinthians*, p.566; Hafemann, *2 Corinthians*, p.460.

referred to himself in the third person, when, fourteen years earlier (v.2), he was caught up in the third heaven (v.3), where he heard exceptional, secret things (vv.4, 7).[117] After this elevation, he was given[118] a 'thorn in the flesh', as divine discipline, by one described as an angel from Satan,[119] to keep him from being too elated.

The ensuing insights from Christ's answer to his prayers about the thorn advance greatly our knowledge of Paul, his theology, and his mission strategy. He could not have the thorn removed, but had to endure it, and Christ gave him the grace to do so, 'My grace is sufficient for you, for power is made perfect in weakness' (v.9a). The verse is regarded as the summit of Paul's letter, the climax of his theology of weakness.[120] His weakness, and his endurance of it, showed the power of Christ, as proof of Christ's gift to him, just as much as 'signs and wonders and mighty works' (v.12).

2.3.4 Other Evidence of Illness or Disability

There is other evidence in the letters to suggest that Paul had episodes of ill-health. Dodd notes that in 1 Thessalonians (e.g. 4:17) and 1 Corinthians (e.g. 15:51) Paul expected to be alive at the Parousia, but by 2 Corinthians and Philippians, he was less sure. This could have been due, of course, to Paul's gradual recognition of a 'delay' in the Parousia, but even in Romans 9–11 (also 13:11 and 15:24) he still had a sense of

---

117 Kruse, *Second Corinthians,* p.204, considers the third person is used to distinguish Paul then, from him at the time of writing; R. Bultmann, *The Second Letter to the Corinthians* (ET; Minneapolis: Augsburg, 1985) p.220, regards it as a Jewish habit of speech. Thrall, *Second Corinthians* II, pp.782-85, considers that the date would be given to validate the truth of his boast; Barnett, *Second Corinthians*, p.562, notes that it is also so distant as not to compete with his opponents' more recent claims. Schweitzer, *Mysticism of Paul*, pp.153-54, notes that the third heaven is conceived as highest, and this is based on 1 Kgs. 8:27, 'Behold the heaven, and the heaven of heavens cannot contain [God]'; Bultmann, *Second Corinthians*, p.221, confirms this, and notes that the third heaven contains Paradise (v.4).

118 Garrett, 'Thorn', p.90, the thorn 'was given', i.e. passive, so it is ambiguous who gave it to him, though she assumes that it was God, granting authority to Satan to harass him. Barnett, *Power in Weakness*, p.178, considers that Satan acts within the limits set by God. Nielsen, *Heilung*, p.207, considers that Paul saw his illness as the work of Satan. Thomas, *Devil, Disease*, moves from, p.66, 'it appears that Paul believed that his thorn was tied to Satan himself', to, p.73, 'Paul attributes the ultimate origin of this illness to God'.

119 Garrett, 'Thorn', p.95; Bultmann, *Second Corinthians*, pp.224-25, puts it that the angel of Satan is a counterforce opposing Paul, that God is encountered in that counterforce, in the struggle with suffering.

120 E.g. Barnett, *Second Corinthians*, pp.572-75.

urgency about preparing the Gentiles for it. Dodd thinks that an episode in which Paul was in extreme danger of death led him to alter his outlook, and he regards Paul's experience described in 2 Corinthians 1:8 as causing this profound change; Dunn sees that episode as one of the transition points, which contributed to Paul's theology of suffering in 2 Corinthians, Romans and Philippians.[121] Paul's reaction, 'we do not rely on ourselves, but on God, who raises the dead' (2 Cor.1: 9) is developed later in the letter, especially in Chapter 12 (assuming that the parts of the letter follow the order in the canon).

There is no uniform agreement that the event of 2 Corinthians 1:8 refers to illness; as Thrall points out, Paul did not mention it in his later comments on his thorn, but she does not dismiss near-fatal illness. She considers in her first volume that the most likely interpretation of the 'affliction in Asia' was an experience of severe persecution, probably more recent than the episode of the 'wild beasts' of Ephesus (1 Cor. 15:31). Although 2 Corinthians 1:8-9 appears to be metaphorical, it seems that Paul was describing an experience, probably related either to 'natural' illness, or as the result of ill-treatment, and that the episode influenced radically his thinking.[122]

There are other passages, where it is not clear whether Paul was referring to illness, or to other life-threatening situations to which he was exposed. Hughes suggests that 'Satan blocked our way' (1 Thess. 2:18) indicates Paul's illness.[123] Philippians 1:20-24 is usually taken to

---

121 Dodd, 'Mind of Paul', pp.81, 84; Dunn, *Theology of Paul*, p.731.

122 M. Thrall, *A Critical and Exegetical Commentary on the Second Epistle to the Corinthians*, Vol. I (Edinburgh: T. & T. Clark, 1994) p.116, but in her discussion in the later edition (Vol. I; 2nd ed.; London/New York: T. & T. Clark/Continuum, 2004), pp.114-17, she is more positive about the possibility of the passage indicating illness. Harvey, *Renewal,* pp.112-13, notes the 'wild beasts' are metaphorical, since Paul would not survive a confrontation with wild beasts in an arena. Kruse, *Second Corinthians*, p.68, notes that θλῖψις (affliction) is an unusual word for illness. Bultmann, *Second Corinthians*, pp.27-28, considers the actual affliction is unimportant to Paul; what was important was his grasping its theological significance. Harvey, *Renewal,* p.9, notes that βαρέω is widely used e.g. in Egyptian papyri, for illness or other burdens; H. Balz, 'βαρέω', *EDNT,* 1, p.198, notes that the term is used figuratively usually. Here, it is stating the life-threatening burden, oppression or affliction in Asia. Bauer et al., *Greek-English Lexicon*, p.77, see the meaning as 'oppressed'.

123 Hughes, *Second Corinthians,* p.448. If that is so, then Paul again accepted without comment the view that Satan caused illness; the interpretation would be important, also, as possible evidence dating the illness, since 1 Thessalonians is usually regarded as the earliest letter extant. Hull, *In the Beginning*, pp.84-90, points to passages which might be interpreted as indicating Paul's poor sight (e.g. Rom. 2:19-20; 1 Cor. 13:12; 2 Cor. 4:3-4; 5:7). M. Dibelius, *Paul,* W.G. Kümmel (ed.), (ET; London/New York/Toronto:

indicate that, in prison, he was at risk of being sentenced to death, although it is not specific. 2 Corinthians 4:10, 'always carrying in the body the νέκρωσις ('death') of Jesus, so that the life of Jesus may be made visible in our bodies', might also be a reference to illness, especially as in v.16, 'our outer nature is wasting away'.[124]

In summary, I have argued that Paul had a significant illness, which influenced him during much of his adult life. The thorn probably afflicted him some years after his conversion, but near the beginning of his major missionary journeys, and during much of the time of his letter-writing. Illness may be alluded to in his letters, other than 2 Corinthians 12:7-9. My hypothesis is that his illness was a very important feature, to which he reacted in ways that influenced both his mission strategy with regard to healing, and his theology.

2.4 The Effects of Paul's Illness

Much has been written about the effect on Paul's life and ministry of his conversion/call experience (see *2.2.1*), and writers assume that his mission to the Gentiles stemmed totally from that. Also, many scholars have considered the nature of Paul's illness, but I find it strange that they have rarely commented in detail on the profound effects that probably resulted, particularly in the conduct of his mission,[125] as well as the effect on his theology. The subtle psychological effects on a person with significant chronic disability or illness are considerable. From the perspective of medicine, from my own and many other clinicians' experience of working with people who have had significant long-term, or recurrent, illness, it is certain that Paul would have been profoundly influenced, perhaps without fully realising it, by his condition, and also by the reactions of others to it.

2.4.1 Others' Response to his Illness

Comments about how others reacted to him can be found in his letters. The Galatians' response to his illness (Gal. 4:14) was that they neither

Longman, Green & Co., 1953) p.43, argues against interpreting passages to reveal traces of illness everywhere in Paul's life.

124 Bauer et al., *Greek-English Lexicon*, p.668, translates νέκρωσις as 'putting to death', so, here, as 'constant danger of death'. In modern medicine, 'necrosis' refers to death of a particular tissue in the body. Hafemann, 'Suffering', p.919, notes that it was a common Jewish notion that all suffering was part of death.

125 Hull, *In the Beginning,* is an exception in modern times; he also draws attention, p.84, to the importance of Paul's thorn to disabled people. Schweitzer, *Mysticism of Paul,* e.g. p.152, refers to Paul as a sick man throughout his mission.

despised him nor did they spit. Spitting would have been the expected reaction, partly in rejection, but also to avoid being affected by his disease, as the Galatians might have regarded his illness as demonic.[126] Instead, they accepted him with compassion, welcomed him 'as an angel', and offered him help (vv.14-15). The phrase 'as an angel of God' might be referring to Paul's divine commission, which was appreciated by the Galatians.[127] Their response to Paul's illness seems surprising, in a society where he was apparently an ill stranger, whom they might have regarded as a carrier of disease, or demon-possessed; if Paul had malaria, the Galatians might have recognised and feared it. At the very least, they would have been puzzled by the contrast between Paul's illness and their receiving, as a result of Paul's preaching, the Holy Spirit, whose gifts to them possibly included healing (Gal. 3:5).

The response of the opponents in 2 Corinthians 10–13, that is, to highlight Paul's weakness, would be much more usual. They responded to his illness by mockery, having failed to realise that tribulations were the common experience of Christians (e.g. 2 Cor. 1:4-6).[128] The proverb quoted by Jesus, 'physician, heal yourself' (Lk. 4:23) is an important indication of the contemporary atmosphere, that those who heal would be expected to be physically whole. His opponents seemed to consider that, unlike them, Paul did not heal (see *1.3.4*), and so did not prove that he was an apostle, and his own weakness may have provided them with clear evidence of this inability.

2.4.2 Paul's Illness and his Mission

The illness explains many things about Paul's dealings with the churches. Although he had sometimes concerns about his mission (e.g. Gal. 2:2), and was aware that he had not completed the task (e.g. Phil.

---

126 Dunn, *Commentary on Galatians,* p.234, says spitting may indicate disdain, or be a means of warding off the evil eye (Gal. 3:1); Elliott, 'Evil Eye', pp.62-63, also thinks there is a probable allusion to the evil eye in Gal. 3:1. Temkin, *Falling Sickness*, p.8, points out that spitting was a common Roman and Greek reaction to prevent demon possession if one witnessed an epileptic attack; Pliny, *Natural History*, 28.4.7, wrote, 'We guard against epilepsy by spitting'. M. Lattke, 'ἐκπτύω', *EDNT,* 3, p.420. Bauer *et al.*, *Greek-English Lexicon*, p.309, take the word to be figurative only, in keeping with the view of Thomas, *Devil, Disease*, p.59.

127 A.J. Goddard and S.A. Cummins, 'Ill or Ill-Treated? Conflict and Persecution as the Context of Paul's Original Ministry in Galatia (Galatians 4:12-20)', *JSNT* 52 (1993) pp.107-109. They also comment on the phrase, 'angel of Satan,' in 2 Cor. 12:7.

128 Witherington, *Conflict and Community in Corinth,* p.463. Marshall, *Enmity in Corinth*, p.153, n.110, notes that sickness/affliction was linked inversely to one's intelligence (see Chapter 2, *2.2*). Schütz, *Paul and Apostolic Authority*, p.206.

3:12-13), he considered himself generally successful in his mission (Rom. 15:19), in spite of his disability. He saw himself metaphorically as the high priest (which suggests that he was unblemished before God), presenting his Gentile churches as an acceptable sacrifice to God (Rom. 15:16), as prophesied (e.g. Isa. 60:11; Mic. 4:1-2). He wrote that his proclamation was not in eloquent wisdom (1 Cor. 1:17, 21 and 1 Cor. 2:1, 4),[129] and he confessed himself unskilled in public speaking (2 Cor. 11:6). His 'veiled gospel' was inadequate by human criteria, 'veiled to those who are perishing' (2 Cor. 4:3). In the opinion of both himself (2 Cor. 10:1) and his opponents (e.g. 2 Cor. 10:10), he lacked 'presence'.

The evidence correlates best with the view of Winter, who considers much of the opposition to Paul in 2 Corinthians 10–13 to be related to the interest in Corinth in the Sophists, intellectuals who emphasised particularly the importance of oratory. Personal appearance, natural ability in rhetoric, and physical 'presence' were preoccupations in the Second Sophistic, the term coined by Philostratus for the Greek renaissance in the Roman Empire, which was at its height in the second and early third centuries AD, but which, Winter has shown, flowered in the first century, around the time Paul was preaching.[130] It seems highly probable that Paul considered his appearance, because of his illness, might upset his audience, or cause them to despise him; he might have feared, say, having a *grand mal* fit (which would be highly likely to occur under the stress of public speaking).

The Sophists prized extempore oratory much more than the written word, which explains the comment, 'his letters are weighty and strong, his bodily presence weak and his speech contemptible' (2 Cor. 10:10). Paul had knowledge of rhetoric (see *2.2.3*) and used it in his letters; for instance, the emotional effects of Galatians 4:12-20, in the midst of a confrontational letter, would have been obvious if this had been a speech (and it probably had a similar effect on his readers). He used it again to deal with the situation of his weakness in 2 Cor. 12:7-10. His illness *may* be one reason why he wrote his detailed letters, setting out

---

129 Murphy-O'Connor, *Paul,* pp.50-51, considers that Paul was himself using a rhetorical convention here; faith was not in the wisdom of men, but in the power of God (1 Cor. 2:5).

130 Winter, *Philo and Paul,* 1st ed., pp.117-18, 204, 212 n.42; B.W. Winter, *Philo and Paul among the Sophists. Alexandrian and Corinthian Responses to a Julio-Claudian Movement* (2nd ed.; Grand Rapids/Cambridge: Eerdmans, 2002) pp.xi-xii; Witherington, *Conflict and Community in Corinth,* p.101. G.A. Kennedy, 'The Sophists as Declaimers', in G.W. Bowersock (ed.), *Approaches to the Second Sophistic* (Ephrata, Pa.: Science Press, 1974) p.18.

his theological and pastoral thoughts, as he found this to be a more satisfactory way of communicating, rather than relying solely on public speaking. We may have the thorn to thank for the insights we have into his theology.

His illness would have affected other aspects of his mission strategy. At a pragmatic level, if he had an obvious disability, he would not emphasise that he had a gift of healing, as people's expected reaction would be like those who mocked Jesus on the cross, 'He saved others, let him save himself' (Lk. 23:35); the ancient world ridiculed those who could do great things for others, but not for themselves.[131] More profoundly, although Paul's illness might not have been the only organising factor in his theological views about physical healing, he would recognise that converting the ill to physical health was not an important part of Gentile soteriology. Salvation was a spiritual result of God's grace, and Paul found that the important function of the Spirit, to transform lives, enabled even those sick and disabled (like himself) to live a life that was valuable to Christ.

2.4.3 Paul's Illness in Relation to his Theology

Paul's theological reaction to his illness is the most significant effect, although we cannot know whether his *theologia crucis* preceded the thorn, or *vice versa*. It was in response to his opponents in 2 Corinthians that Paul revealed much of what we know of his insights into theological questions of weakness and power. Paul's reaction to his critics was that he *was* weak, and his weakness emphasised to others that the power of his mission could not have come from himself, but from Christ (2 Cor. 12:10). Thus, his own weakness actually facilitated his communication of the power of the risen Christ.[132] Since that power in Paul's mission was made known to him by his own weakness, he could see that the image of Christ suffering on the cross made Christ's power clearer to all.

Another theological insight that Paul developed in his later letters was that suffering brought him nearer to Christ. For instance, in Philippians 3:10, he saw his sufferings linked with those of the crucified Christ, and saw them as positive gain. In Philippians 2:17, he saw

131 Kolenkow, 'Relationships', p.1494.

132 Schütz, *Paul and Apostolic Authority*, p.189. Dunn, *Theology of Paul,* p.438. Hafemann, *2 Corinthians*, p.34, writes that Paul believed that suffering was the revelatory vehicle through which knowledge of God was disclosed. Savage, *Power through Weakness,* p.167, goes further, believing that Paul's weakness was *the* necessary precondition for the existence of Christ's power in him.

himself as a libation poured over a Temple sacrifice.[133] Paul had inherited the tradition of the Messianic woes;[134] as the Messianic age had begun, and the Messiah, though sinless, had suffered for the non-righteous, so all his followers would expect to suffer. Christ, the Son of God, had died for his people, so the ultimate imitation of Christ for Paul was to die while doing work to further the Messiah's kingship; meanwhile, his own experience of suffering strengthened his teaching of Christ weak, dying, then raised. His illness would certainly have been a major factor in this development.

It is possible that it was his illness that caused him to explore, theologically and pastorally, in his letter to the Romans (probably written from Corinth), other positive aspects of suffering, and we may read some reflections of his illness into Romans 8; for instance, v.18, 'the sufferings of this present time'; v.26, 'the Spirit helps us in our weakness'; and v. 28, 'all things work together for good', where 'all things' may include the 'sufferings of this present time'. Romans 8:35 reflects Paul's privations described in 2 Corinthians 11:26-27 and 12:10. It is then possible to read Romans 8:38-39, his great affirmation of faith that 'neither death nor life...nor angels nor authorities...nor powers...nor anything else in all creation will be able to separate us from the love of God in Christ Jesus our Lord,' as a more specific testimony to his faith, although he was unhealed. The evil forces of illness might be the angels (since he considered in 2 Cor. 12:7 that an angel of Satan had brought the thorn); or perhaps those evil forces were either authorities[135] or powers, over which Christ's love prevailed. This is not to suggest that the passage was written *about* Paul's illness, but to demonstrate that the theological effects of his illness could easily have been a major factor in inspiring the composition.

In summary, Paul's ill-health has been explored, to see what effect it had on his ministry, particularly with regard to his interest in physical healing. Whatever the thorn was, it had a profound influence on his

---

133 Harvey, *Renewal*, pp.118-22. Hogan, *Healing*, pp.289-90, suggests that Paul's contribution to Christian healing was that he saw suffering, when it was in a spirit of union with the suffering Christ, as redemptive. E. Ferguson, 'Spiritual Sacrifice in Early Christianity and its Environment', *ANRW* II.23.2, 1980, p.1163, notes that, since Jesus' death was considered to have replaced the sacrificial system of Jewish law, Paul saw sacrifice spiritualised.

134 Kruse, *New Testament Models for Ministry*, p.113. See Chapter 2, *1.3.1*.

135 J.D.G. Dunn, *Romans 1-8*, WBC, Vol.38A (Dallas: Word, 1988) p.507, notes that only here in Romans does Paul mention angels or authorities. In the Pauline corpus, angels may be heavenly beings, *or* rulers of other nations, and he considers that in the letters, authorities meant angelic *or* demonic powers.

strategy for Gentile mission. I argue that it made him realise that restoring physical health was not an important part of his call to bring salvation to the Gentiles, as he was aware that he was given the grace of Christ to endure, unhealed, and so was able to conduct the mission given to him by God. It led him to develop an understanding of how his own weakness both brought him nearer to Christ, and facilitated his ability to communicate the power of the risen Christ, since Paul's weakness meant that the power of his message must come, not from himself, but from Christ, and Christ's power was related to his voluntary weakness for the world, at crucifixion. The thorn was probably significantly responsible for developing his emphasis on his theology of the cross.

2.5 Paul's Ethics

Although Paul's illness was, I believe, the major factor influencing his strategy of mission to the Gentiles, his ethical stance as a servant of Christ was also of prime importance to his life. Throughout his letters, he stressed that his goal was to be won in accordance with his faithfulness to Christ's humility, best expressed in Philippians 2:6-8, and based on his *theologia crucis*. He was a pastoral theologian, who had to solve major practical and theological problems. He demonstrated his pastoral care for the community of the church in tackling local issues (e.g. 1 Corinthians 5–7), and underlined his concern by further letters and visits. New religious ritual had to be capable of transcending cultural differences, and the practical aspects of these sacraments had to be regulated. [136] He had to ensure that Gentiles were acceptable to the God of Israel, and that he and other Jewish Christians were acceptable to Gentile converts, while stressing the equality of all believers.[137] Mohrlang sees that his view of Christian life as the response to God's grace was the link between his theology and his ethics.[138]

2.5.1 Examples of Paul's Ethical Teaching

Examples of his ethical teaching can be seen best in Corinth, whose social history has been most studied by New Testament scholars. The

136 Meeks, *First Urban Christians*, p.103, points out that, since the Jewish purity rules in a mixed Jew–Gentile church were dysfunctional, Paul had to redefine sacred and profane in social terms.

137 Dunn, 'Paul and Justification by Faith', in Longenecker (ed.), *Road from Damascus*, p.86.

138 R. Mohrlang, *Matthew and Paul. A Comparison of Ethical Perspectives* (SNTSMS 48; Cambridge: Cambridge University Press, 1984) p.88.

majority of people converted there were Gentiles, already heavily involved in the socio-religious life of a Roman colony in Greece, where social stratification was a particularly live issue, and was reflected within the church.[139] Although it was once believed that the church in Corinth was composed of people from only the lower social strata (1 Cor. 1:26), Judge drew attention to the probability that within the church, there was a major spread of social class, and this is now widely accepted.[140] This meant that there was a nexus of relationships, involving patron–client, honour–shame, friendship and enmity between social equals and unequals, and Theissen considers that tensions within the Corinthian church were inevitable.[141] Paul saw that the church, the body of Christ, was more important than the individual, and he taught that when one member suffered, all suffered (1 Cor. 12:26), contrary to the Graeco-Roman system of honour and shame.

Another example of Paul's ethic was that he expected that church members would work to earn a living (e.g. 1 Thess. 4:11), and he set an example by earning a livelihood in Corinth, not accepting his rightful allowance for his mission work. His working as a tent-maker[142] was counter to the expectations of the probably small but powerful group in the Corinthian church who expected to pay for his services, but it avoided Paul being a client to their patronage. He taught that, instead of being clients, church members should be benefactors to those less able than themselves.[143] The idea of people using their gifts and talents for the welfare of the whole community, without expecting personal reward

139 Horsley, *1 Corinthians*, p.52, considers that Corinth was the most status-conscious city of the Empire.

140 Deissmann, *Light from Ancient East,* p.7. E.A. Judge, *The Social Pattern of Christian Groups in the First Century: Some Prolegomena to the Study of New Testament Ideas of Social Obligation* (London: Tyndale, 1960) p.60. Clarke, *Serve the Community*, pp.174-76.

141 Marshall, *Enmity in Corinth*, e.g. pp.xi, xii; G. Theissen, 'Social Stratification in the Corinthian Community: A Contribution to the Sociology of Early Hellenistic Christianity', in Theissen, *Social Setting,* pp.69-119, notes that the church attempted social integration of people of different socio-economic levels, some with status inconsistency, into one association.

142 Murphy-O'Connor, *Theology of Second Corinthians*, p.112; Murphy-O'Connor, *Paul*, p.88, notes that the work of tent-making would upset Greek upper-class sensitivities (which regarded physical work as degrading), and would stigmatise him in the city. It also went against Christ's teaching (1 Cor. 9:14).

143 B.W. Winter, *Seek the Welfare of the City* (Grand Rapids/Carlisle: Eerdmans/Paternoster, 1994) p.60.

(often in the form of honour) was alien to Mediterranean pagans.[144] Paul taught that his churches were to signal to others a new community, where people would 'do good', without expecting reciprocity or payment. Christians were to 'bear one another's burdens, and so fulfil the law of Christ' (Gal. 6:2). He believed that this ethos, so different from Graeco-Roman culture (Rom. 12:9-21), would attract further believers, just as Jesus' healings had done.

But he taught, also, that love had to be given and expressed, not merely in 'doing' good, but in 'being' so, in care and compassion; the Kingdom of God was the norm for the Christian way of life (e.g. 1 Thess. 2:12; 1 Cor. 4:20; 6:9-10; Gal. 5:22-24; Rom. 14:17). Since Christ's death on the cross and his resurrection were the ultimate expressions of God's love for the world, Christian love was the appropriate response.[145] 'Knowledge puffs up, but love builds up' (1 Cor. 8:1); all Christians had been given the Holy Spirit, but spiritual gifts were to be exercised in love (1 Corinthians 13); love was a prominent element of the fruit of the Spirit (Gal. 5:22), Christians were to walk by the Spirit in love (Gal. 5:25–6:3), as faith works through love (Gal. 5:6). He strove both to teach, and to live his life, in accordance with these ideals.

Practical difficulties unfolded as the churches tried to live according to the precepts of the gospel.[146] Many people in the cities lived in poverty, so it is not surprising that the issue of eating meat that had been offered to pagan gods became a problem.[147] Paul's teaching on this, and related issues, was aimed at ensuring that the actions of 'strong' Christians did not become a stumbling block for the 'weak' (1 Cor. 8:1-13; 10:14–11:1). He was concerned pastorally for the welfare of the

---

144 Malina, *Social World,* p.36, notes that they believed that communal resources for welfare were strictly limited.

145 Mohrlang, *Matthew and Paul*, p.104. Walter, 'Paul and Early Christian Jesus-Tradition', p.63.

146 F.G. Downing, 'A Cynic Preparation for Paul's Gospel for Jew and Greek, Slave and Free, Male and Female', *NTS* 42 (1996) p.454, suggests that Paul's letters, often answering specific practical queries, must have been necessary because his initial proclamations had failed to explain or persuade fully. This seems unfair to Paul.

147 D.B. Martin, 'Review of J.J. Meggitt, *Paul, Poverty and Survival*', *JSNT* 84 (2001) 51-64; Theissen, 'Social Structure', pp.65-84; J.J. Meggitt, 'Response to Martin and Theissen', *JSNT* 84 (2001) 85-94. Theissen, 'Social Conflicts', pp.371-91. (See Chapter 2, *2.2*). The problem is complex; Newton, *Deity and Diet,* pp.33, 36, emphasises that religious understanding develops and changes only slowly, and that both old and new religions often co-exist.

whole church body, especially its weaker members,[148] and he demonstrated his championship of them in castigating the rich who flaunted their wealth and embarrassed the poor by their behaviour at the Lord's Supper (1 Cor. 11:17-22).

He pointed out that all spiritual gifts were for the purpose of building up the church, and, particularly, were to help the 'weak', and emphasised that gifts, such as 'tongues', used for self-aggrandisement and without love, would not do so.[149] Divine healing was likely to be particularly valued by the Corinthian church, as it featured so heavily in the stories of Jesus' ministry. I believe that Paul recognised that, even if gifts of healing and 'actively effective deeds of powers' (1 Cor. 12:9, 28-30) were envisaged as having human, fallible elements, as well as a divine component (see *1.4*), healing would interfere with the concept of equality that Paul tried to inculcate into the churches, *unless* it was accompanied by the fruits of the Spirit, especially love. Otherwise, it risked dividing churches into an elite (e.g. those who had some gift for healing), and the rest, the 'weak' (some of whom may have required healing).

In summary, Paul strove to hold his communities together in a κοινωνία based on love, with a high ethical standard of equality. He struggled to avoid any section of the community taking advantage of spiritual gifts, wealth or position, which would divide the church into an elite and the rest. He taught that, in Christ, all were equal (e.g. Gal. 3:28). He wanted no earthly symbols of power to be stumbling blocks for 'weak' believers, 'for whom Christ died' (1 Cor. 8:11; 14:15-19). This may have been another potent reason for his reluctance to consider healing as a significant feature of his mission.

---

148 The 'weak' in this context refers to the spiritually weak or insecure, in a socially divided society. In Romans, Paul saw the difficulties applying to the division between Jews and Gentiles. See, e.g., M. Reasoner, *The Strong and the Weak. Romans 14:1–15:3 in Context* (SNTSMS 103; Cambridge: Cambridge University Press, 1999). Schrage, *Der erste Brief*, 3, p.225, considers that Paul emphasises the weaker members (of the church body, 1 Cor. 12:22) as being indispensable, and regards Paul's view as inspired by his *theologia crucis*.

149 Mohrlang, *Matthew and Paul*, p.103, notes that Paul emphasised that the law of Christ (Rom. 13:8) was to love one another. Wenham, *Paul and Jesus*, p.128, suggests that those not speaking or understanding 'tongues' probably felt inferior (1 Cor. 14:26-32).

3 Conclusion

Paul's attitude in his letters to the value of healing miracles, both in his own ministry (which took place at a time and in places where people were much concerned about illness and healing), and by the people in the churches, has been considered. His view is important, as he is the only Christian writer roughly contemporary with Jesus, where we have canonical autobiographical material, written during his ministry. Looking at Paul's ministry in relation to healing is an unusual angle, and the subject is not straightforward to unravel. It is recognised that the views expressed here are derived from material from letters written for different purposes, and where healing was not the prime concern. Only once (2 Corinthians 11–12) were his healing abilities possibly challenged, and he did admit to healing then, but there is no indication that he ever adopted healing as an important part of his mission.

The references in his letters, where Paul cited himself possibly healing, have been examined, as have been his mentions of healing as gifts of the Holy Spirit to some members of the church in Corinth, the only city where healing is mentioned by Paul. Although he admitted that he himself had spiritual gifts, which included healing, all the possible references to healing are non-specific and sometimes ambiguous, with no description of anyone being healed by him, and he never stresses an ability to heal. He discouraged the Corinthian church from boasting of spiritual χαρίσματα (gifts) including healing, and using them for their own, rather than the common, good, and he stressed the importance of the fruit of the Spirit, especially love.

Although the near-certainty is that Paul knew much about Jesus' healing ministry, he was more concerned with the sufferings of Jesus, and with proclaiming the risen Christ. He related more to the 'essence' of Jesus' life, expressed, for instance, as openness, gentleness and compassion, rather than to his deeds. While Jesus' healing ministry, as portrayed by Mark and Luke, showed glimpses of the Kingdom of God to those who were sick, and allowed them, healed, to become again full members of the society of Israel, Paul's imitation of Christ was to bring spiritual salvation to the Gentiles, and so take them into the repentant remnant of 'Israel'. Paul's mission can be understood best as him having adapted the healing in Jesus' ministry to his task of incorporating the Gentile nations, 'sinners', into the true Israel. This is *not* to suggest that Paul *actually* equated his work of saving Gentiles with that of healing individuals, merely that this imagery fits the task he undertook. Looking at Paul's ministry in this way allows us to understand how he could undertake his mission to the Gentiles without emphasising physical healing.

The task was enormous; he had to advance the whole Gentile mission, while encouraging each community to unite in harmony and love. His strategy for mission was practical and pastoral, as well as theologically based; from its Jewish origins, his *kerygma* was for all nations; his imperative was to welcome Gentiles to the church on equal terms with Jewish Christians. He achieved great success in mission, and churches were planted 'from Jerusalem to Illyricum'.

He had a health problem, which remained unresolved. He reported differing reactions to his weakness; the Galatians welcomed him, while the Corinthian opponents pointed out his shortcomings in public speaking, and despised him. His experience of physical weakness taught him that, because he was unhealed, he could show Christ's power working through him more clearly; he could understand that the power of Christ was shown primarily in Christ's weakness, and he felt himself brought nearer to Christ by his illness. I believe that Paul's illness was a major life experience, one reaction to which was that physical healing did not need to be an important part of his ministry.

Probably in response to his illness, he came to the conclusion that weakness was an important attribute in spreading the gospel of Christ. His weakness was the mark of Christ, so that it was itself a great gift of grace, and it made clear that the power of his message came, not from him, but from Christ. His theology emphasised Christ weak and dying, before his risen glory, and this seems to me likely to be a consequence of an understanding resulting from his illness. Whether his *theologia crucis* began at conversion, or whether it evolved, is probably unknowable, but since I accept that both his theology and character developed in response to adversity, I favour the view that his theology of suffering developed gradually, *because* of his physical weakness, and he experienced Christ *par excellence* not in his power, but in weakness.

Finally, Paul, primarily concerned with the pastoral needs of his communities, recognised the ethical imperative of equality within them, and he strove to avoid any symbols of power (of which healing might have become one) that might destroy that equality.

Thus, Paul's emphasis on the importance of divine healing is markedly different from the portrayals by Mark and Luke of healing in Jesus' ministry, and from Luke's depiction of apostolic healing.

Chapter 6

Analysis of Healing

1 Comparison of Insights on Healing by the Biblical Writers

1.1 Overview

The main goal of the book has been to explore the attitudes of the three biblical writers, Mark, Luke and Paul, to healing, in Jesus' life and in the apostolic church, from observations on theological, historical, narrative, medical, anthropological and sociological aspects.

Chapter 1 introduces the subject, and points out some of the difficulties involved in studying ancient healing today. In particular, it draws attention to the problems now in separating what was regarded then as miracle from magic, and also the significance now of separating healing from exorcism.

Chapter 2 sets the background for Jesus' healing. In Judaism, although healing by Yahweh was fundamental, the tradition of healing by intermediaries (especially prophets and kings) in Yahweh's name was longstanding. A Messiah was awaited, who would bring radical spiritual healing to Israel. Pagan health-care in the eastern Roman Empire included religious cults where the emphasis to variable extents was on healing, Greek medicine of the Hippocratic tradition, and the services of charismatic holy men, as well as the use of magic, but there was considerable overlap between those practices, as there was in healing between Judaism and paganism by the turn of the ages. In both paganism and Second Temple Judaism, there is clear evidence of diversity of views about healing.

In Chapter 3, Mark, accepted in the study as the first gospel writer in the canon, and, therefore, the pioneer in the New Testament of the genre of theological narrative of Jesus, lays great emphasis on Jesus' healings, describing them mainly in true-to-life vignettes, in which he makes theological and ethical points. Mark has been used as the primary source for the story of Jesus' healing in the study. He is a skilful narrator, who shows the prominence of Jesus' healing, sometimes using subtle methods, such as stressing the demands that healing made upon Jesus (e.g. in 5:21-43). In the stories, the crowd recognised that Jesus healed as the bearer of numinous power, that is, Mark depicts Jesus having complete authority (from God) to heal. Mark emphasises, especially by the shape of his gospel, the balance between the power and weakness of Jesus. The climax of Jesus' ministry, for Mark, is at the cross; 'He saved others, he cannot save himself' (15:31). In the weakness of his death, Jesus was recognised by the centurion as Son of God (15:39); the two verses demonstrate Mark's contrast of healing as power and Son of Man glory, with suffering and weakness as the Son of God.

Chapter 4 describes Luke's account of Jesus' healing, using the same gospel genre as Mark. Although he emphasises Jesus' healing even more than Mark, his theological message prevails over his storytelling. Luke sees that the Messianic Spirit of prophecy included healing power, bestowed by God on Jesus at his baptism. He follows both the features and the sequence of Mark's healing stories, but he portrays Jesus' healing in a somewhat different light. Both the healed and the crowd gave thanks to *God*, not Jesus, so, to them, Jesus was the mediator of God's power, rather than the originator of healing. Luke thus highlights God's power and Jesus' perfect obedience. This difference between the accounts in Mark and Luke's gospel reflects their different theological views. It is made more obvious because of the circumstance of the abrupt end of Mark's gospel, which is accepted here as intentional, while Luke develops in his gospel the resurrection narrative, so that the glory of God's resurrection of Jesus is emphasised more than the dereliction of crucifixion, as the climax of the gospel.

The presence of the book of Acts does not settle totally the question of Luke's depiction of the source of the divine power for healing. Although it seemed probable that Luke's account of the ascension, with the ascended Christ pouring out the Holy Spirit on believers, would solve the issue, there is still a lack of clarity about the source of apostolic healing. Thus, when the apostles healed in Acts, their power was sometimes attributed to the ascended Christ, and sometimes from God. Less importantly, in his efforts to demonstrate salvation history unfolding, Luke mainly avoids portraying Jesus directly healing Gentiles in the gospel (see Chapter 4, *2.4*) in order for this to be a new development by the apostles in Acts.

Chapter 5 portrays Paul, instead of stressing the spiritual gift of healing, emphasising in his letters the fruit of the Spirit, especially love. I have argued that Paul actually plays down divine healing in his mission, and I consider that a very potent reason for his lack of emphasis on healing was his finding that he, unhealed of his 'thorn', was able to show by his very weakness that the power to spread Jesus' message came, not from himself, but from Christ, and that his weakness brought him closer to Christ. His *theologia crucis* might well have developed as a result of his 'thorn', as he recognised that it was Jesus' weakness at crucifixion, before his exaltation, that allowed him to be recognised as Messiah and Lord. Another motive in playing down physical healing might have been his ethical stance of the need for equality within the churches; it was important for the believers to live in the fellowship of equality, which would have been disrupted by members boasting of their (healing) gifts.

In these chapters, it has been demonstrated that Mark, Luke and Paul had particular perspectives on miraculous healing. In this chapter, their outlooks are compared and analysed, particularly with respect to their different theological stances.

1.2 Prolegomena in Analysis

The gospel writers studied have depicted healing as a very important factor in Jesus' ministry, and in the spread of his message. It would have been easy for Mark and Luke, writing for people aware of the Graeco-Roman enthusiasm for oratory (Chapter 5, *2.4.2*), to concentrate almost entirely on Jesus' ability as a teacher and preacher, and not on him as a healer, if Jesus' healing had been relatively insignificant to his ministry. The fact that they did not emphasises how important Jesus' healings were. Although Jesus' proclamation of God's reign is portrayed as the vital concern in the gospels, his healing is shown as a potent, and sometimes independent, activity. It is highly likely that if Jesus had not used the ability to heal, then the impact of his ministry, including his attraction of the crowds, might have been very different. Meier considers that the fact that John the Baptist did not heal probably explains why his following died out.[1]

The gospel writers also portray that healing was an *appropriate* activity for Jesus, at least for most of his ministry. It allowed him to gain the confidence of people suffering from the social consequences of various types of oppression, including illness and poverty, and allowed onlookers to witness in those healed, the love of God, as dramatic evidence of the nearness of the Kingdom of God. When Jesus came to Jerusalem in the last week of his life, and the need was for other activities, neither Mark nor Luke depicts him healing there, but, instead, they report him using his skills of teaching (Mk. 11:18 and Lk. 19:48 report the crowd spellbound by his teaching) and debating (Mk. 11:27-33; 12:13-17, 18-27; Lk. 20:21-40).

1 Meier, *Marginal Jew*, II, p.623. (See *1.3.*)

It is recognised that the evangelists (and possibly their predecessors) rearranged the order of material in their narrative for theological purposes, and perhaps used some of the detail of one healing story in another. The modern objections that have been raised to the existence of Jesus' healing miracles have been discussed in Chapter 1, and many can be rejected. For instance, the idea that the miracle stories were mainly transferred from a Hellenistic origin (Chapter 1, *1.2.1*) has to explain their existence there, and, also, why John the Baptist is not depicted as healing. Explanations of Jesus' healings as being of psychological problems only can be dismissed largely as medical fashion of the mid-twentieth century (but see Chapter 3, *1.5.2*).

Much more difficult to reject, because there is much substance in them, are the views of modern scholars who accept that Jesus healed miraculously, but believe that his healing was simply a means to an end. We have discussed the views of writers who consider that Jesus' healing was to illustrate his teaching (see Chapter 3, *1.3.2*). Others believe that Jesus' healing was only incidentally of benefit to the one healed (unlike the intentions of the pagan healing cults, e.g. of Asclepius, where the main object was cure of the suppliant's condition). Kee regards the primary significance of Jesus' healing as cosmic, or eschatological.[2] Although I agree with him that the *results* were cosmic, my unease with accepting this view totally is that Jesus, at the moment of healing, would be concentrating on the sufferer, rather than on the cosmic effects; Mark, particularly, offers the picture of Jesus' attention focussed on the suppliant.

Jesus bestowed his divine power to heal on his disciples and others (Lk. 10:1-20), and how they used it is recounted in the missions in the gospels, in parts of the narrative of Acts, and, to a tiny extent, in Paul's letters. Luke's portrayal indicates that the proclamation of the message of salvation in Acts would have been even more difficult in the cities to which the message spread, if the apostles had not been given the gift of divine healing; for instance, Paul's speech in Athens (Acts 17:16-34) had very limited success in converting people. Paul considered that he was generally successful in his Gentile mission, which was the important next stage in taking Jesus' gospel to the whole world. His

2 Kee, *Miracle in Early Christian World,* pp.87, 155. On p.146, he regards Jesus' healing as related to the dualistic world-view, that evil powers had wrested control of the universe from its creator. C.C. Grant, 'Reinterpreting the Healing Narratives', in Eiesland and Saliers (eds.), *Human Disability,* p.73, considers that the stories were not about the people healed, but were Christological, to show Jesus' divine authority and compassion.

letters demonstrate that it was possible to spread the gospel in the great cities of the eastern Roman Empire, in spite of the probability, as I have argued, that he did not exploit the gift of healing.[3]

Before the variations on the biblical writers' perception of divine healing are considered further, some preliminary points about the data available, and the structure and function of the writings, should be mentioned.

1.2.1 Literary Pitfalls in the Comparisons

In arguing that there are differences in the writers' theological perceptions of healing, one has to recognise that comparison of these documents must be cautious; some of the diversity may be more apparent than real. We have no means of knowing how much more material than we have in the canonical New Testament was available to the writers. There are extant some (perhaps most) of Paul's letters, but we have little knowledge of the selection or provenance of the material in the canonical gospels of Mark and Luke. To judge by Luke 1:1-4, the information in the gospels probably represents only a part of the Jesus tradition,[4] and miracle stories are more likely to be remembered and handed down in oral tradition than is more conceptual material.

The fact that the gospels are of a different literary genre to Paul's letters, and perhaps to Acts, may also be significant;[5] for instance, the genre of biography makes it appear that the writer is not fully aware, until the events occurred, of Jesus' death and resurrection. Again, although we accept the single authorship of Luke–Acts, the biography genre of the gospel is not totally sustained in Acts, *pace* Talbert. Many scholars consider that Acts is, rather, a historical monograph,[6] a view

3 Broadhead, *Teaching with Authority*, pp.190-91, n.2, suggests that this demonstrates the viability of a non-miraculous account of Jesus.

4 J.W. Drane, 'Patterns of Evangelization in Paul and Jesus: A Way Forward in the Jesus-Paul Debate?', in Green and Turner (eds.), *Jesus of Nazareth*, p.283.

5 Mohrlang, *Matthew and Paul*, p.130, suggests that the gospel genre may produce a restraint that Paul's letters do not have.

6 C.H. Talbert, 'The Acts of the Apostles: Monograph or "Bios"?', in B. Witherington III (ed.), *History, Literature, and Society in the Book of Acts* (Cambridge: Cambridge University Press, 1996) pp.58-72, considers that Luke-Acts is in the ancient tradition of the biography of a great man (Jesus) and his followers. W.F. Brosend II, 'The Means of Absent Ends', in Witherington (ed.), *History in Acts*, pp.356-57, points out that Acts would be an odd biography, where only half its space is devoted to its main subject, Paul, and which fails to narrate the circumstances of his death. There is, however, no concerted suggestion in the literature that Paul was the subject of the biography. J. Jervell, 'The Future of the Past', in Witherington (ed.), *History in Acts*, pp.110-11, n.13; D.W. Palmer, 'Acts and the Ancient Historical Monograph', in B.W. Winter and A.D.

that I find acceptable. Porter notes that Paul's healing miracles in Acts were relatively few compared with Jesus' in the gospel, and he suggests that this is because the proportion of narrative present is different, so the space given to describing miracles is less (see Chapter 4, *3.3.1*). He postulates further that the genre difference between Acts and the Pauline letters accounts for there being even fewer miracles in the letters, since they have the least amount of narrative.[7] I would disagree with this last statement (see Chapter 5), but appreciate that genre may influence the prominence given to healing. Genre cannot, however, be the only, or main, explanation for an area that is highly significant to a writer being omitted from his substantial writings (see Chapter 5, *1.5*), and, further, this is not merely an argument from silence; Paul does comment about illness (e.g. 2 Cor. 12:8-9), I believe in explanation of his minimising the subject of healing.

Another literary feature that is likely to affect the portrayal of healing in Luke's gospel is the existence of the sequel book of Acts. The presence of the second volume is related also to Luke's concept of salvation history (see Chapter 4, *2.1.1*), so it may be that it is the soteriological, rather than the literary, aspect that dictates Luke's accounts of healing in Galilee and in the church, as the narrative moves from John the Baptist not healing, to Jesus healing, to apostles and other Jerusalem church leaders healing. The point demonstrates the difficulties of making clearly separable distinctions between the literary and the theological in these writings.

1.2.2 Purpose and Timing of the Writings

The purpose of the writings may also influence comparisons in healing. Mark makes no explicit comment about his purpose in writing. Luke (1:1-4) notes that others, presumably including Mark, had written an orderly account of the events (of Jesus' life, where healing played a large part), and so does he, with the object of explaining these events. Many scholars regard the main purpose of Acts to be apologetic, that Luke was narrating the story of the gospel being spread throughout the

---

Clarke (eds.), *The Book of Acts in its Ancient Literary Setting* (Grand Rapids/Carlisle: Eerdmans/Paternoster, 1993) pp.1, 18, 29, accepts it as a historical monograph, where the subject is the progress of the Christian mission. Bruce, *Acts of the Apostles,* p.59, writes that Luke did not set out to write a life of Paul, but rather to portray the Jerusalem church and its leaders, as well as the Gentile mission engaged in by Paul; D.E. Aune, *The New Testament in its Literary Environment* (Philadelphia: Westminster, 1987) pp.77-78, regards Acts as difficult to classify, but does not want to detach it from its gospel.

7 Porter, *Paul of Acts*, pp.193-94.

world, at least partly to defend Christianity in the second half of the first century.[8] As part of that story, the leaders of the early church healed in Jerusalem (3:1-10), Samaria (8:6-7) then in the Gentile world, for instance, Ephesus (19:11), Troas (20:8-10) and Malta (28:8-9), that is, healing is also shown to be advancing to the 'ends of the earth'. On the other hand, Paul's letters, written mainly for pastoral purposes, were little concerned with the *evidential* value of healing.

The timing of the writings is also pertinent; in particular, Paul's letters were written in the heat of difficulties that the church faced in the middle of the first century, within two decades of the resurrection. Although the nineteenth-century Tübingen view of Acts being untrustworthy as history has been considerably refuted by recent work (which has reinstated to a large extent its historical reliability), Luke was writing a reconstruction, probably mainly for church leaders, of idealised and perhaps putative events of the earliest church, 50–60 years after its founding, when many of the earlier problems may have been resolved or forgotten.[9]

To summarise, apparent differences when miraculous healing is compared in the writings of Mark, Luke and Paul may be partly because of disparities in the nature and intentions of their works. The literary genre, the presence of Luke's two works, and the purposes and timing of the writings are factors that may have affected some of the findings, almost independently of the writers' theological views.

1.3 Comparison of Healing in Mark's and Luke's Gospels

Details of many of the differences in the healing narratives of the two gospels have been discussed in Chapter 4 (especially *2.3*), but more general findings are highlighted here.

---

8 E.g. E. Haenchen, *The Acts of the Apostles. A Commentary* (ET; Oxford: Blackwell, 1971) p.731; Bruce, *Acts*, pp.21-27; C.K. Barrett, 'How History Should be Written', in Witherington (ed.), *History in Acts*, p.37; Brosend, 'Means of Absent Ends,' pp.350-51.

9 G. Lüdemann, 'Acts of the Apostles as a Historical Source', in Neusner et al. (eds.), *Social World of Formative Christianity and Judaism,* pp.109-25, outlines the history of this view, from the time of the writings of F.C. Baur. Lüdemann himself comes down in favour of the historicity of Acts being moderately reliable. Haenchen, *Acts,* generally favours Baur's view. Barrett, *Acts*, p.xliv, notes that Baur also wrote that 'Acts is a source of the highest importance for the apostolic age'. Barrett, *Acts*, p.xl; J. Squires, 'The Plan of God in the Acts of the Apostles', in Marshall and Peterson (eds.), *Witness to the Gospel*, p.20, n.2. J. Nolland, 'Salvation-History and Eschatology', in Marshall and Peterson (eds.), *Witness to the Gospel*, p.74, n.48, however, considers that Luke idealised the early church in Acts. See also Chapter 4, *3.1*.

The two evangelists have many points in common with regard to healing. Both underline Jesus' compassion (although citing it infrequently) by their depiction of his actions. It is understood from both that Jesus healed those who came to him for help, rather than all who were sick.[10] Both depict that healing was liable to engulf Jesus' time for proclaiming the good news (Mk. 1:38; Lk. 4:43), considered by both to be a primary purpose of his ministry. Both show that Jesus' healing (as well as his teaching) was divisive in its effects, and was a significant factor in angering the religious establishment, which resulted ultimately in Jesus' death, and both realise that Jesus' followers would also suffer (e.g. Mk. 13:1-37 and Lk. 6:22-23; 11:4).

There are differences in emphasis, even within this general framework. Both indicate that Jesus' healing was related to his divinity, but they do not depict that he healed *in order to* show that he was divine, and Mark emphasises this (and, generally, Jesus' humanness) more than Luke. Achtemeier notes that in Luke's gospel, miracles validate Jesus; while Dwyer, writing of Mark's gospel, puts it, 'Humanity trembles in awe before that which is "other". The incredible thing is that the "other" has come to save and heal'.[11]

It is easier to separate Jesus' healing from his teaching in Mark, compared with Luke, but healing is even more prominent in Luke's gospel than in Mark's, both in the number of healings, and in the inclusion of Jesus' words about his healing (e.g. Lk. 10:13; 13:32). Luke, who is more concerned with demons than Mark, blurs any distinction between healing and exorcism more than Mark, but neither writer seems particularly interested in separating the two.

Although both recognise the continuum between healing sick people and social restoration, Luke stresses more than Mark the other social aspects of Jesus' ministry, by highlighting Jesus' interaction with the poor and the sinners (e.g. Lk. 7:36-50; 18:9-14; 19:1-10; 21:1-4), as well as with sick people, while Mark emphasises, rather, the way in which Jesus reintegrated the healed sick back into society (Chapter 3, *1.8.2*). Mark is explicit (6:1-6), Luke perhaps implicit (4:23-24), that Jesus could heal only a small number in his hometown, where the

---

10 Warrington, *Jesus the Healer*, p.30. Sanders, *Jesus and Judaism*, p.163, says he healed those who came to hand. M.L. Brown, *Israel's Divine Healer* (Carlisle: Paternoster, 1995) p.230, suggests that Jesus healed all who came to him in faith, and maintains, p.232, that this explains why Luke has no 'blessed are the sick' in his Beatitudes. (It seems to me likely that κλαίοντες [those weeping, Lk. 6:21] would include sick, as well as poor, people.)

11 Achtemeier, 'Lucan Perspective', p.158, especially in Lk. 7:18-23; Dwyer, 'Motif of Wonder', p.202.

majority of people failed to have faith in him. This may highlight Mark's acute awareness of the importance of the suppliant's faith (Chapter 3, *2.3*), but faith is also important in Luke's gospel,[12] so the pericope seems to demonstrate, rather, that Mark is less intent than Luke on presenting the power of Jesus, whom Luke portrays as always in control (Chapter 4, *2.3.5*).

That Jesus, by healing, was fulfilling the ancient prophecies for a Messiah is stressed in at least some of Luke's narrative depiction (especially 7:18-23), and also in references to Jesus as prophet (e.g. 13:34), but Mark's account fits poorly with the idea that a primary purpose for Jesus' healing was to fulfil prophecy, except in 7:32-37. Rather, I have argued, Mark portrays Jesus' healing in essentially realistic terms, while being well aware of the theological aspects of his healing; Jesus' touching the leper, healing Gentiles and reintegrating into society those excluded by disease, were major ways for him to cross theological boundaries that held an Israel insistent on the letter of the Law.[13]

The status of John the Baptist with regard to healing is significant. In Mark's gospel, John is depicted in terms (1:6) physically suggestive of Elijah (who did heal, 1 Kgs. 17:17-24), but there is no mention of John healing in Mark's very short description of his ministry. Mark, then, does not make a point of Jesus' healing being unprecedented. Most scholars consider that in Luke's gospel, John did not perform miraculous healing.[14] This may be because his mission was to those who did not require physical healing; he offered baptism, as a symbol of repentance and transformation, to 'sinners' of Israel (Lk. 3:11). But, more importantly, Luke, in his account of salvation history, separates the era of the Law and the Prophets, which included John's ministry (16:16), from that of Jesus; John seemed to be in prison when Jesus was baptised (3:18-22). The episode of Jesus replying to John's messengers, who asked if he were the Messiah (7:18-23), demonstrates Luke

---

12 Theissen and Merz, *Historical Jesus*, p.293, note that faith usually preceded miracles.

13 D. Senior, 'Beware of the Canaanite Woman', in M.E. Bishop (ed.), *Religion and Disability. Essays in Scripture, Theology and Ethics* (Kansas City: Sheed & Ward, 1995) p.10, draws attention to the profound crossing of boundaries by Jesus' healing, which, he considers, redefined the borders of the rule of God.

14 E.g. Aune, 'Magic' p.1542; Bock, *Luke,* 1, p.88; C.A. Evans, *Luke,* p.116; Fridrichsen, *Problem of Miracle*, p.97; Meier, *Marginal Jew*, II, pp.199-200, n.92. (Thus, incidentally, they agree with the statement in Jn. 10:41; see E. Bammel, '"John Did No Miracle": John 10:41', in Moule (ed.), *Miracles*, pp.179-202). The exception is Hull, *Hellenistic Magic,* p.105, who considers that John *did* do miracles.

delineating an era before Jesus' ministry in salvation history, when John neither healed, nor expected Jesus to heal.

The episode of the unknown exorcist healing 'in Jesus' name' (Mk. 9:38-40, par. Lk. 9:49-50), which shows that others were aware of the power of Jesus' healing, is used differently by the two evangelists. In Mark, the disciples were warned about being a stumbling-block to other followers (Mk. 9:42-48), while Luke employs the episode and its sequel (Lk. 9:51-55) to show Jesus recruiting new followers (vv.57-62), perhaps pointing to the situation in Acts, when new followers would be essential. So, at least in that section, Mark's perspective is concentrated on the 'now', Luke's more on the future.

Again, Mark portrays that the disciples on mission proclaimed repentance, cast out demons and healed (6:12-13). In Luke's gospel, the disciples were sent out to proclaim the Kingdom of God and to heal (9:2); the seventy(two) followers were instructed to heal sick people and proclaim the nearness of the Kingdom (10:9);[15] and Luke's Jesus spoke of the Kingdom immediately before he healed (Lk. 9:11), so healing and the Kingdom are closely related by Luke. Also, the parable of the Kingdom of God being like a mustard seed growing mightily (Lk. 13:18-19) follows immediately the healing of the woman with kyphosis (13:10-17), whereas Mark (4:30-32) does not associate the parable with any healing. Thus, it seems that Luke invests divine healing with more eschatological meaning than does Mark.

More generally, Tuckett considers that the concept of salvation history means that Luke sees Jesus' ministry lying in the past, where the 'today' (Lk. 4:21) is an event in a previous epoch,[16] unlike Mark's view, where the gospel preached by Jesus is the present gospel, for which followers suffer (e.g. Mk. 10:29-30). This fits with our finding of Mark's 'true-to life' descriptions of Jesus healing, compared to Luke's more theological presentations.

The most important Christological differences between the two gospel-writers are related to their portrayal of healing. Because of Mark's abrupt ending of the gospel (see Chapter 3, *1.1*), with the discovery of the empty tomb, and the women running away, the resurrection appearances are not developed, and the climax of Mark's story is the crucifixion of Jesus, desolate and forsaken, but accompanied by the tearing of the Temple veil, and the pagan centurion's recognition of Jesus as Son of God. Thus, Mark's gospel seems to be organised so that the power of Jesus' healings and the weakness of his death are

15 Meier, *Marginal Jew*, II, p.432.

16 Tuckett, *Luke*, p.35.

balanced in their importance. Remus sums it up: 'Miracles act as a counterpoise to the proclamation of a powerless, dying Saviour'.[17] We have shown (Chapter 4, e.g. *2.7*) that Luke's gospel does not use healing to contrast so sharply Jesus' power and weakness. This is partly because in Luke's gospel, rather than having the crucifixion as the climax, the power of God in raising Christ is given most prominence, with Jesus' resurrection appearances, and the story of his ascension.

The other Christological difference with regard to Jesus' healing in the two writers is that Mark sees Jesus as having complete authority from the Father to heal, while Luke, stressing that Jesus healed by the power of God (5:17), demonstrates the bystanders attributing Jesus' healing to God, to whom Jesus was totally obedient.[18] The differences can be summed up by the remark attributed to the centurion at the cross; in Mark's gospel, he recognised Jesus as Son of God, in Luke's, he considered Jesus as δίκαιος (righteous).

1.4 Comparison of Healing in Luke's Gospel and Acts

Although Luke mentions fewer healings by apostles in Acts than by Jesus in the gospel, Luke's perception that apostolic healing is a major means of spreading Jesus' message is prominent in Acts, and is presented as an important part of the advance of the church.[19]

Luke's depiction of healing in Acts paints the evidential value of the apostles' healing in a more ruthless way than the gospel account of Jesus' healing. This may be related to the different confrontational situations in which the apostles found themselves, compared with the circumstances for much of Jesus' ministry, but this seems to be only part of the explanation. Although Jesus' followers were not persecuted in the gospel, Jesus was. He warned them of coming persecution (e.g. Lk. 12:11-12; 22:31-37), and they witnessed Jesus' maltreatment and his reaction. Many of the motifs found in the gospel narratives, such as Jesus' care for sick people and 'sinners', are lost in Acts. The gospel highlights the requirement for Jesus' followers to love both their neighbours (e.g. 10:25-37) and their enemies (e.g. 6:27-36), but these aspects are less clear in Acts, where apostolic intervention might

---

17 Remus, 'Miracle', in *ABD,* 4, p.862.

18 Luke portrays the crowd recognising God, not Jesus, as the bearer of numinous power, and Jesus as the mediator of that power; see Kahl, *New Testament Miracle Stories*, pp.79-82, and Chapter 4, *2.1.4*.

19 Maddox, *Purpose of Luke-Acts*, p.132. Fiorenza, 'Miracles, Mission and Apologetics', pp.1-25, considers that healing was potent religious propaganda.

rebound on friends (e.g. 17:6-9; 18:17), as well as being disastrous to opponents of the church. Luke seems intent on portraying the advance of the church, which is assisted by the apostolic healing ministry, rather than being concerned with the treatment of the individual, a feature which is so evident in Jesus' healing in the gospels (e.g. Lk. 19:10).

Again, in the gospel descriptions of Jesus healing, faith is significant, whereas in Acts it is not depicted as so important. In two healing summaries in Acts (e.g. 5:15; 19:12, where Peter's shadow and Paul's handkerchiefs produced healing), the sufferers were distant from the healers, so it would have been difficult for any relationship, of compassion or of personal faith, to develop. These two episodes also demonstrate the difficulties of distinguishing miracle from magic, behind which, in Acts, lie important issues of legitimating the church (Chapter 4, *3.4.4*).

Miracle healing was one aspect of the authentication of the Spirit coming to the apostles (3:2-10), who were human agents of God's power. Kee considers that fulfilment of prophecy, here the prophecy of Joel, increases Christ's authority in Acts.[20] It was extended to certain non-apostolic leaders in the Jerusalem church, for instance, to Stephen and Philip, given God's blessing by the apostles' laying on of their hands, to Paul, and to Ananias in Damascus. Portraying Jesus' ascension should have allowed Luke to depict the risen Jesus as the usual channel through which the apostles could heal, but this is not always made clear, partly because the term 'Lord' in Acts is sometimes applied to God, sometimes to the risen Christ (Chapter 4, *3.4.3*).

The theme of Jesus suffering, at least partly because of his healing, is played out in the narrative of Acts, which portrays that apostolic suffering was often in relation to healing, and persecution itself led to the spread of the gospel (Chapter 4, *3.5*), so that, as in the gospel, although a triumphalist attitude in Acts is often obvious, there is, particularly in apostolic suffering, a *theologia crucis*.[21]

---

20 Kee, *Good News*, p.104, notes that this is in spite, or perhaps because, of the early church's knowledge of the rejection and death of Jesus.

21 J.B. Green, '"Salvation to the End of the Earth" (Acts 13:47): God as Saviour in the Acts of the Apostles', in Marshall and Peterson (eds.), *Witness to the Gospel,* p.100; Barrett, '*Theologia Crucis*–in Acts?', p.79, considers that Acts does contain a *theologia crucis* in this context. I.H. Marshall, 'How Does One Write on the Theology of Acts?', in Marshall and Peterson (eds.), *Witness to the Gospel,* p.12.

1.5 Comparison of Healing in Acts and Paul's Letters

Scholars have drawn attention to the internal variations within Acts. Von Harnack noted that the involvement of the supernatural was much stronger in Acts 1–15, than in the 'we' sections, and others agree, Porter pointing out that only two of the miraculous episodes of healing are found in the 'we-passages', which generally do not emphasise Paul as a miracle worker as much as the rest of Acts.[22] This difference within Acts is of minor significance, however, compared with the discrepancies that are found between the Lukan Paul and the Paul of the letters, with regard to healing. Haenchen considers that Luke portrays Paul as a great miracle-worker, while the letters do not.[23] Also, Murphy-O'Connor notes that Paul is depicted as healed in Acts,[24] whereas in the letters, he presents himself unhealed of his illness, and Paul's awareness of this, I have argued, is very important to his views on healing.

In Acts, miraculous occurrences, such as visions (e.g. Paul's encounter on the Damascus road) and ecstatic experiences, are represented as means of producing faith in Christ, and propagating the gospel (e.g. 7:56; 10:10-16), while Paul in his letters may show some reservation about their value (2 Cor. 12:1).[25] Luke in Acts depicts Paul physically healing Gentiles 'in the name of Jesus' as a means of mission (e.g. 28:8-10), while the Paul of the letters sees the grace and power of Christ as the spiritual healing agent that allows him to carry out his Gentile mission (e.g. 2 Cor. 12:9), and the church to attain to living 'in Christ' (2 Cor. 13:4-9).

---

22 A. von Harnack, *The Acts of the Apostles* (ET; London: Williams and Norgate, 1909) pp.133-61, especially 134-40. This is supported by F. Neirynck, 'The Miracle Stories in the Acts of the Apostles. An Introduction', in J. Kremer (ed.), *Les Actes des Apôtres. Traditions, Rédaction, Théologie* (BETL, XLVIII; Louvain: Leuven University Press, 1979) pp.169-213. Porter, *Paul of Acts*, pp.58-62. Barrett, *Acts,* p.xxxiv, notes that the 'we' sections tend to be about travel rather than ministry. For an account of the 'we-passages', and whether Luke could have been present at the events noted in these passages, see Bruce, *Acts*, pp.3-5, 46-59.

23 Haenchen, *Acts*, p.113, quotes as evidence Acts 13:6-12; 14:8-10, 19-20; 19:12; 20:7-12; 28:3-6, whereas he considers that Paul's activities in Corinth were so undramatic that his opponents denied his ability to perform miracles (2 Cor. 12:12). Lentz, *Luke's Portrait of Paul,* p.2, considers that Paul is presented in Acts as always in control, and, p.171, that he appears 'too good to be true'.

24 Murphy-O'Connor, *Paul*, p.161, points out that, whereas Paul's recovery from spiritual blindness is emphasised in Acts, his illness (2 Cor. 12:7) is glossed over (e.g. Acts 14:12).

25 Dunn, *Unity and Diversity*, p.181.

Perhaps the greatest difference between Acts and the letters, which impinges on their authors' views on healing, is in Christology, apparent in their different emphases on Jesus' crucifixion and resurrection. In Acts, only in 20:28 does Luke suggest that Christ's death is in atonement for the sins of the world; otherwise, the soteriological significance of the cross, *because* it is substitutionary in character, is missing; Conzelmann considers that Luke's understanding in relation to the meaning of Christ's death does not develop.[26] Luke seems to portray the developing church concentrating on the glory of the resurrection and ascension, and the power of God in raising Jesus from death (Acts 7:55). Jesus' passion and death are mentioned in Acts mainly to show that apostles and followers would also suffer persecution in order to spread the gospel. The stress on Christ's resurrection, as a symbol of the believer's hope, and of the glory of God, is paralleled in Luke's positive approach to apostolic miracle healing. In his letters, Paul, who sees physical healing as of minor importance, regards the death of Jesus in weakness as of prime theological significance (e.g. Rom. 3:25; 4:25; 1 Cor. 1:23; 2:2; 15:3; 2 Cor. 5:14-21; Gal. 3:1; Phil. 2:6-8); it was at his death for sinful humanity that his glory became apparent. Dunn suggests that it is mainly in the kerygmatic and liturgical formulae passed on by Paul that there is material about the resurrection of Jesus.[27] This highlights the major difference in the Christologies of Luke and Paul, which, I argue, can be found in their attitudes to healing.

Lastly, there is a perception of there being little ethical teaching in Acts, except a general appeal in the speeches (e.g. 2:38; 3:19; 17:30; 26:20), although the ethical effects of the Holy Spirit are described (e.g. 2:41-47; 4:32-37; 9:31; 11:23-24; 15:32-33). Turner considers that the Spirit of prophecy in Acts, based on Joel 2:28-29, was not merely for empowering for mission, but had an important function in the spiritual life of the individual believer and that of his community.[28] Although Paul's speeches in Acts are often considered to reflect mainly Luke's, rather than Paul's, understanding, Walton notes that the only suggestion in Acts that the converts should imitate the apostles, as they strove to

26 Conzelmann, *Acts,* pp.xlv-xlvii. B. Gärtner, 'To suffer', in C. Brown (ed.), *NIDNTT,* 3 (Exeter: Paternoster, 1976) pp.723-24.

27 Dunn, *Unity and Diversity*, p.22. (e.g. Rom. 1:3-4; 4:24-25; 8:34; 1 Cor. 15:3-11; Phil. 2:9-11; 1 Thess. 1:10).

28 Turner, *Power from on High*, pp.351-55, 359. Barrett, in *Acts*, pp.lxxiii-iv, and in '*Imitatio Christi*', p.253, considers that Luke does not mention the Spirit's work as the *moral* renovation of human life (although he may have assumed it) in Acts. Maddox, *Purpose of Luke-Acts*, p.131, noting that very little of Jesus' ethical teaching is included, considers that this is because Luke's subject-matter is the church's new experience.

imitate Jesus, occurs in Paul's farewell address to the elders at Miletus (20:18-35); there, they were exhorted to work, as Paul had, to help the weak.[29]

Paul recognises the need to build up the lives of believers, whom he considers were transformed by conversion (e.g. Rom. 12:2), although they were not perfect (e.g. 1 Cor. 6:9-11). He offers them much ethical teaching, and emphasises the value of imitation (e.g. 1 Cor. 4:16; 11:1). Perhaps Paul's letters expose the problems in the churches, 'warts and all', while Luke's presentation is more idealised, so that ethical issues did not need to be stressed so much in Acts.

The ethical teaching issue becomes important when we consider briefly healing in the later New Testament letters.

1.6 Conclusions on Healing in Mark, Luke and Paul

Healing miracles are central to the story in both gospels and Acts. Jesus' healing activities caused the members of the Jewish religious establishment to be opposed to him, and healing was an important factor in bringing about his death.[30] Apostolic healing in Acts is depicted as a very significant factor in facilitating the mission to spread Jesus' gospel to both Jews and Gentiles, but again it was a major cause of persecution by the establishment, especially the Jewish religious authorities. Although Paul accepts healing as one manifestation of the Holy Spirit's gift, he exercises restraint in the emphasis that he places on his own and others' gifts of healing.

Mark and Paul share the same view, that the theological highpoint was Jesus' death in weakness, in substitution for the world's sin. Although they have very different emphases on healing in their writings, I consider that both reach a *theologia crucis*, perhaps based on, but at least related to, their perceptions of healing. Mark sees healing as the other side of the coin in Jesus' life, where it served to emphasise the enormity of Jesus' rejection and death, while Paul builds on his understanding of Jesus' death, and the consequent requirement of the Christian to share in Christ's sufferings (e.g. Phil. 3:10-11), to find a

29 Walton, *Leadership and Lifestyle*, e.g. pp.13, 140-85, considers that this speech is close in thought to Paul's early letters. Porter, *Paul of Acts*, p.125, considers it highly debatable whether we have direct access to the historical Paul as a speechmaker in Acts.

30 J.G. Williams, *Bible, Violence and the Sacred. Liberation from the Myth of Sanctioned Violence.* (San Francisco/New York: HarperSanFrancisco, 1991) p.218, suggests that this was due to envy in Jesus winning the favour of the people (e.g. Lk. 11:32; 15:10).

theology of suffering, and he plays down the significance of physical healing.

Vulnerability is an especially important feature to both Mark and Paul; Mark emphasises Jesus' vulnerability on the cross and in one healing (8:22-25); Paul perceives that the vulnerability that resulted from his own weakness (2 Cor. 12:9) allows him to spread the gospel, at the heart of which is the cross, where God's love is made visible in Christ's weakness.[31] Luke in his gospel sees divine healing as major evidence of God's power, working through Jesus, a power that is seen exquisitely in Jesus' resurrection by God; and in Acts, healing is powerful propaganda, while vulnerability is demonstrated mainly in relation to the persecution of apostles.

Both Mark and Paul see faith given to Jesus' followers as an important gift, which can produce miracles (e.g. Mk. 11:22).[32] Paul emphasises that faith 'that can move mountains' requires also love, in order to be effective in spreading the message of the Kingdom (1 Cor. 13:2); love/compassion is largely not cited, but is present, in Jesus' healing in the gospels. Faith, although important in Luke's gospel, seems less so in Acts, at least in relation to healing, and love seems to be less vital to Acts than to either the gospels or Paul's letters.

There are significant differences in how the ancient writers view miraculous healing, both in Jesus' life, and in the apostolic church. Mark and Luke both give Jesus' healing high prominence, but whereas Mark uses it to demonstrate the contrast with Jesus' death in weakness, Luke considers it as evidence of God's power, and consistent with God's glory in Jesus' resurrection. In Acts, Luke seems still more aware that healing was an essential tool to spread the gospel, even when, or perhaps because, it was associated with persecution of apostles. Paul appears to be reticent about miracle healing, both by himself and by his church. Rather, as a pastor he emphasises the importance of the weak.

To summarise, we have compared how Mark, Luke and Paul regard divine healing, and how their views are influenced by their theological understanding (as well as by factors such as the purpose and genre of their writings). Luke refers most often to healing, sees it as evidence of God's power, and a potent way of spreading the gospel, while Mark

---

31 Mohrlang, *Matthew and Paul*, p.102, puts it that Christ's death is the supreme expression of God's love for the world. S. Horne, '"Those who are Blind See": Some New Testament Uses of Impairment, Inability and Paradox', in Eiesland and Saliers (eds.), *Human Disability*, p.98.

32 Dunn, *Jesus Remembered*, p.692, believes that synergism between the faith of the suppliant and Jesus' healing power was envisaged.

(who also emphasises divine healing) and Paul (who does not) are more aware than Luke of the religious power of suffering and vulnerability, seen at its most stark at Jesus' crucifixion. Luke uses healing in Acts for its evidential value, as an important way of spreading the gospel, and as evidence of a *theologia gloriae*, but also he depicts healing as one reason for the persecution of Christ's followers, like the consequences of Jesus' healing in his gospel, and sees apostolic suffering as significant for the gospel's spread, so there is evidence also of a *theologia crucis*. Paul and Mark have similar views on Christology, and, from very different writings with regard to healing, their *theologia crucis* is clear.

2 The Legacy of Jesus' Healing

The influence that Jesus' healing ministry had on early Christianity is considered briefly here. An important aspect is whether or not our biblical writers anticipated that Jesus' healing would extend beyond the apostolic period. We will consider first what they believed about the uniqueness of Jesus' healing, and the destruction of Satan (and so, perhaps, of the power of sickness). Since Jesus preached the importance of caring for the marginalised, we will then examine the evidence for implementation of this part of his healing legacy in the early church.

The early church made a rapid transition in understanding that Jesus was not only a healer and prophet, but was their Lord; 'Maranatha', a transliteration of Aramaic, 'Our Lord, come' (1 Cor. 16:22), referring to Jesus as Lord, had been accepted as a standard liturgical formula, even before Paul's letters.[33] At least by the time of the writing of Colossians 1:15-20, and perhaps as early as 1 Corinthians 8:6, and Romans 8:31-39, Christ was regarded as part of the Godhead. The awareness of Christ's divinity must have influenced greatly the early church's thought about the uniqueness of Jesus' healing. Some modern views on Jesus' uniqueness in healing are summarised here as a footnote.[34]

---

33 L. Hurtado, 'Lord', in *Dictionary of Paul and his Letters*, pp.562-63. Savage, *Power Through Weakness,* p.153, suggests that Paul saw that it was by dying on a cross for humanity's sins, that Christ had shown that he was, indeed, Lord.

34 K. Ward, 'Miracles', in Walker (ed.), *Different Gospels*, p.54, believes that Jesus' healing miracles were not unique in type; Kee, *Miracle in Early Christian World,* p.170, considers that probably they were not; Warrington, *Jesus the Healer*, e.g. p.1, believes that Jesus' healing *ministry* was unique. E.P. Sanders, *The Historical Figure of Jesus* (Harmondsworth: Penguin, 1993) pp.167-70, considers that the miracles have an eschatological significance, which was unique to Jesus. Meier, *Marginal Jew,* II, pp.624-25, discusses the issue and views of others. See Chapter 3, *2.1*.

It is accepted that concentrating only on healing skews, and so grossly underestimates, Jesus' uniqueness in his whole ministry. We have suggested that both Mark and Luke consider that Jesus' healing was unique in its effects, though perhaps not in its methods (see Chapter 3, *1.7.1,* Chapter 4, *3.4.2*). Paul in the seven undisputed letters makes no comment on this.

2.1 Healing and the Overthrow of Satan

It might be possible to deduce whether Mark, Luke and Paul expect that divine healing would continue, by considering what they saw as the fate of Satan.

Demons and evil spirits are mentioned frequently, as part of a great group (e.g. Mk. 1:24; 5:9-10) under the control of Satan.[35] Danker suggests that evil is most threatened in the presence of the holy, and that seems to be a likely explanation of why the struggle between God and Satan, recognised by the gospel-writers, was so prominent in the ministry of Jesus.[36] They regard Satan, as the power involved in evil, standing in an ambiguous relationship to God, seeking to lead people away from God.[37]

Satan's role in the New Testament writings studied is seen clearly in relation to sickness and healing; he is regarded as causing at least some illnesses by all our biblical writers.[38] Luke held Satan responsible for the kyphotic woman's state (Lk. 13:10), Paul saw his own illness as being brought by an angel of Satan (2 Cor. 12:7), and the disciples, sent out to

---

35 Carr, *Angels and Principalities,* especially pp.174-77, insists that there is no evidence for belief in demonic forces until the end of the second century. That does not fit with the language of the New Testament, and Wink, *Naming the Powers*, pp.23, 26, refutes Carr's argument vigorously.

36 Danker, *Jesus and the New Age*, p.100. Lane Fox, *Pagans and Christians*, p.327, asserts that pagans believed that Christians exaggerated the power of Satan, and then claimed that they could defeat that power.

37 Wink, *Naming the Powers*, p.105, includes evils such as idolatry, injustice and inhumanity. Meeks, *First Urban Christians*, p.189, points out that Paul writes of evil either as a force smaller than the political realm (e.g. immorality, weakness or fear), or as something much broader (e.g. Satan); Garrett, 'Thorn', p.88, n.19, p.90.

38 This statement is in contradiction to the view of Thomas, *Devil, Disease*, e.g. p.301, who considers that, of our three writers, only Luke attributes an affliction (what Thomas calls 'infirmity') to the devil; he does admit that Mark (9:17) mentions a 'dumb' spirit, and Paul mentions Satan with respect to his thorn, although God is the thorn's ultimate origin. Hogan, *Healing*, p.248, notes that Luke, who summarises Jesus' ministry as 'doing good, and healing all who were oppressed by the devil' (Acts 10:38), is especially clear about the role of Satan in illness.

preach and heal, had power over demons (Mk. 6:7; Lk. 9:1; 10:17). Healing implied control over the forces that caused illness, and Jesus' healing activity is depicted as a battlefield, where his power was opposed to Satan's.[39] In the Beelzebub controversy (Mk. 3:22, par. Lk. 11:15), the accusation against Jesus was that Satan was the source of his power in casting out demons (hostility was often expressed by 'demonising' the miracle maker) but Luke portrays that Jesus' power from God released the victim from the grip of Satan (Lk. 11:14), as it was greater than the power of possessing demons.

Healing in the gospels demonstrates the tension between the 'already' and the 'not yet' with regard to Satan's defeat, and the Kingdom of God; the Kingdom was already glimpsed when Jesus healed, but Satan was not yet defeated. Satan's overthrow (Lk. 11:21-22) is depicted as only part of the restoration of the demonised man (11:24-26), who still required the Holy Spirit to come to him, that is, the Kingdom of God to break in to his life. Twelftree thinks the gospel belief was that Satan was defeated in two stages; the Kingdom of God was arriving in healing (and exorcism), but Satan's activity would continue until the final judgment.[40] A common Jewish apocalyptic expectation was that there would be an interregnum between the old world and the new age, the age which would bring destruction to the demonic world; Paul sees that interval as between Christ's resurrection and his Parousia, during which Satan would still be active. According to Lane Fox, the pagan world thought that Christians saw the church as a sinless body, set apart from the demonic world, but this is not confirmed in Paul's letters (e.g. 1 Cor. 5:5; 7:5; 2 Cor. 2:11). The time of Satan's final destruction remains vague in the New Testament material studied here.[41]

---

39 Malina, *Social World of Jesus,* p.93; Wink, *Naming the Powers*, p.26. In n.42, p.26, he notes that Jesus saw his exorcisms and healings as an assault on the Kingdom of Satan, by the breaking-in of the Kingdom of God. It would be more accurate to say that this is what the evangelists *portray* as Jesus' opinion.

40 Twelftree, 'ΕΚΒΑΛΛΩ ΤΑ ΔΑΙΜΟΝΙΑ', pp.390, 392, describes the healed person as 'the Kingdom of God in microcosm'. Cotter, *Miracles,* p.125, notes that exorcism was only the beginning of Satan's end. Maddox, *Purpose of Luke-Acts*, p.143, writes that Luke does not aim for chronological consistency in the defeat of Satan

41 Lane Fox, *Pagans and Christians*, p.328. Bultmann, *Jesus Christ and Mythology,* p.33. Cotter, *Miracles,* p.119, notes that, as early as 1 En. 55:4, there was a belief that in the Messianic age the demons would be destroyed. Wink, *Naming the Powers*, p.33. Witherington, *Paul's Narrative Thought World*, p.19, considers that Paul was aware that Satan was not finally defeated. For instance, Rom. 16:20, 'the God of peace will shortly crush Satan under your feet'; 1 Cor. 15:24, 'then comes the end, when [Christ] hands over the kingdom to God the Father, after he has destroyed every ruler and every authority and power'.

Satan is also found as a healer. Luke 4:4-12 suggests that miracles could be performed on orders from the devil, and Mark, Luke and Paul were all aware of his healing activities; demonic false Christs and false prophets are mentioned as doing 'signs and wonders', with the intention of leading the elect astray (Mk. 13:22; Lk. 6:46; 13:26). Simon Magus' power of healing (Acts 8:9) is regarded as demonic (Chapter 4, *3.3.2*). Paul saw Satan disguised as an angel of light, teaching falsely and possibly healing (2 Cor. 11:14), and, as the lawless one, doing 'signs and wonders and mighty works' (2 Thess. 2:9). These examples serve to show the ease with which healing might become a demonic power.

We see that Satan is depicted as important as a cause of illness and misery, in direct confrontation with Jesus healing (and exorcising), but is also portrayed occasionally as a demonic healer. Significantly, none of the biblical writers studied consider Satan as having been totally defeated, so how Jesus' divine healing legacy would continue would be at least a theoretical issue for them.

2.1.1 Who Would Heal in the Post-Apostolic Church?

The question of how the three writers portray Jesus' legacy of healing continuing after the end of the apostolic age has to be considered. Some help in this may be obtained from considering who Mark, Luke and Paul depict as healing 'in the name of Jesus' in the early church. It is true that for all the writers, the coming and presence of the Holy Spirit may be taken as evidence that they believed that Jesus' healing would continue in some form in the church.[42]

In Mark's gospel, Jesus' twelve disciples, whom he sent on mission, healed with his authority (although no specific healings by disciples are recorded in the gospels), but only in the 'longer ending' of the gospel (16:17-18) were miraculous signs to be performed by later followers. The story of the 'unknown exorcist', found in both gospels (Mk. 9:38-40, par. Lk. 9:49-50) indicates that healing done in Jesus' name, even when the healer was not his immediate disciple, was acceptable to him, and this might be of importance in the post-apostolic church. In the second mission in Luke's gospel (10:1-21), the seventy also healed, perhaps presaging the events in Acts (see Chapter 4, *2.6.1*). In Acts, the apostles, and the church leaders commissioned by them, healed in the name of Jesus, but there is no suggestion there that 'ordinary' Christians

42 C. Brown, *Miracles and the Critical Mind* (Grand Rapids/Exeter: Eerdmans/Paternoster, 1984) p.325, considers that much Christian thought has related the miracles to the exclusive personal action of Jesus, and has isolated them from the activity of Father and Spirit.

might also have healed. Even on the day of Pentecost, the main indication of the Spirit's presence among new converts was inspired speech, and this continued to be its manifestation for 'ordinary' converts (e.g. 2:4, 33; 4:8, 25, 31; 10:45-46; 19:6).[43] Paul, although putting much less emphasis than Luke on healing, sees the church as the community of the Spirit (1 Cor. 3:16), where not only apostles and prophets, but also other believers might heal, as a manifestation of the Holy Spirit, (1 Corinthians 12, and, probably, Gal. 3:5; see Chapter 5, *1.3.2*), so, unlike the situation in Acts, ordinary church members might have the spiritual gift of healing.

The literary techniques of all the writers leave the question of healing in the post-apostolic church open. Mark's gospel ends abruptly, and Paul's letters are by their nature open-ended. Healing in Luke's account is shown as an important way of advancing the church in Acts, but even he offers no clear signpost as to the way healing would develop beyond the period he portrays.

Thus, there is no clear lead from any of the writers as to how the legacy of Jesus' healing would continue in post-apostolic times.

2.2 *Miraculous Healing and Human Care of Sick/Weak People*

In the Old Testament, descriptions of the relationship between Yahweh and his chosen people frequently contain expressions of Yahweh's compassion, steadfast love, and mercy (e.g. Isa. 54:10). The compassion of Yahweh is depicted as the basis for him doing good for his people, and in return, the ordinary people of Israel were commanded to look after those who were sick (see Chapter 2, *1.3.2*).[44] Jesus' healing and his ethical teaching, built on this Jewish tradition, might be expected to set an important example for care in the early church.

2.2.1 Sociological Aspects of Healing

Sociological considerations may reveal some clues about how, or whether, Jesus' healing might continue. There has been much interest,

43 See Chapter 4, *3.3.1*. Barrett, *Acts*, pp.liii-liv, sees the Holy Spirit in Acts as the founding gift, with the characteristic mark of its presence among new converts in Acts being speech, as glossolalia, prophecy, or proclamation. Possession of this gift by Gentiles was proof that they were rightly included (e.g. 10:44, 45, 47; 11:15, 16; 15:8).

44 E.g. Deut. 13:17, 'Yahweh will multiply his people'; Ps. 103:3-4, 'He heals their diseases'. Borsch, *Power in Weakness*, p.118, points out that such caring was costly to Yahweh (e.g. Isa. 46:4). Oepke, 'νόσος', *TDNT*, 4, p.1094. Hull, *In the Beginning*, p.107, notes the high ethic of the teaching of 2 Esdras 2:21, that they were not to ridicule lame people, and those who were blind were to have a vision of Yahweh's splendour.

since sociology began to be applied to New Testament study, in the disturbing aspects of miracles. Theissen points out that miracles occur particularly in subject cultures, as one of the few ways by which power can be exerted. Miracles are a potentially dangerous power, in that they may wreck the established order.[45] In particular, we often underestimate the sociologically disruptive effects of Jesus' miraculous healing on the Jewish religious establishment, which was, until then, exclusively responsible for both excluding and reinstating to normal social life, people with certain illnesses; it is not surprising that Jesus was attacked for healing. Jesus is also portrayed in the gospels as 'healing' the rift in the social body of Israel, by associating with outcasts, sick and marginalized people to bring them back into the fold, and this caused deep offence to the Jewish religious establishment. He had to exert authority in undertaking this 'social restoration with disruption' to establish a pure Israel, and part of that power came from his miracle healing.

The conditions changed rapidly from this situation in Jesus' lifetime, so we would expect that the pattern of healing would change when the prime requirement was for unity in the early church.[46] Internal integrity of the mystery cults was important in their success within the main stream of Graeco-Roman society, but monotheism meant exclusion from all other religious connections.[47] Sociologically, making a culture unique gives the group cohesion, and cohesion is the resultant of all the forces acting on members to remain in the group. Values and behaviour that do not facilitate group integrity are regarded negatively; Sanders notes that it was inevitable that a 'high tolerance for sinners was not a characteristic of the early church', unlike the situation in Jesus' ministry.[48]

The sociological pressures on the embryonic church can be seen most clearly in Paul's letters. To make the life of his communities attract others required agreement and 'purity' within, along with openness to outsiders, but with strength to deal with threats. The human body, which is a model for any system with boundaries, was Paul's image of society

---

45 Theissen, *Miracles Stories*, p.257. Cairns, *Faith that Rebels*, p.31, believes that the danger of miracles was a view from the social world of eighteenth-century England. However, it would be true of any society where there were gross inequalities of power.

46 Crossan, *Birth of Christianity,* p.414, points out that the Palestinian countryside disappeared completely from all New Testament sources; Remus, *Jesus as Healer*, p.115.

47 Betz, 'Magic and Mystery', e.g. p.253. Meeks, *First Urban Christians,* p.159.

48 Meeks, *First Urban Christians*, p.85; Malina, *Social World*, p.43. Sanders, *Jesus and Judaism*, p.174.

(e.g. 1 Cor. 12:12-30), and he recognised the need to build up the church as the body of Christ, in order to effect Gentile salvation.[49] Care of the weak by 'strong' members was an important way of maintaining group cohesion; miraculous healing would add to the power of the 'strong', at the expense of the 'weak'.

Thus, sociological reflection on Jesus' healing legacy leads us to believe that 'neighbourly' human care of the weak and ill would be more likely to hold the church body together, rather than miracle healing.

2.2.2 Love/Compassion in Jesus' Healing

The Synoptic writers depict that Jesus healed sick people unconditionally, without questioning the theological cause of their illness. We have noted that both Mark and Luke portray Jesus' love/compassion in his healing, although they rarely remark upon this. For instance, both highlight Jesus' healing on the Sabbath, and, although they portray it as demonstrating that Jesus was 'Lord of the Sabbath', indicating his power, they recognise it also as Jesus exercising love in 'doing good', as the correct interpretation of Torah (e.g. Mk. 3:4-5, par. Lk. 6:8-10). Similarly, Jesus touching the sick person is depicted as important in his healing; touching the leper (Mk. 1:41) was a gesture of solidarity between the leper and the healer (although it also defied the Jewish purity laws). 'Mercy', requested by suppliants such as Bartimaeus (Mk. 10:47), suggests the relationship of a superior to an inferior, while 'love' is unconditional, and 'compassion' introduces an element of the struggle required in a healing relationship based on love. Paul, who, we have suggested (Chapter 5, *2.1.1*), made use of the 'essence' rather than the detail of Jesus' life, referred to Christ's σπλάγχνον (compassion) in Philippians 1:8 and 2:1.[50]

To the gospel writers, Jesus' healing was a manifestation of the power of God, which was an important part of the concept of 'Kingdom of God', but Fridrichsen stresses that Jesus' miracles are depicted, not only as signs of the coming Kingdom, but also as evidence of his

49 Douglas, *Purity and Danger*, p.115; Meeks, *First Urban Christians*, p.87, remarks that Paul uses the language of belonging, e.g. 'brothers', more often than other early Christian writers.

50 Bauer et al., *Greek–English Lexicon*, p.938, render the term 'love'. The Latin-derived word 'compassion', 'suffering with,' is a definition of the emotion in relation to healing, which has important connotations of weakness of the healer (compared with Stoic endurance, which emphasises self-sufficiency or self-mastery); the Greek σπλάγχνον conveys the gut-wrenching nature of the emotion that may be involved in the relationship between a physician and a seriously ill sufferer.

concern and love for the sick people, and we have emphasised that this personal aspect of Jesus' healing is to be found clearly in the gospels, particularly in Mark. The Benedictine scholar, Jean Leclerq, said that the healing ministry of Jesus was one of the best evidences of the love of God that he knew.[51]

Mark and Luke emphasise Jesus' teaching that believers must care for one another (e.g. Mk. 12:31; Lk. 6:31); in the Pauline letters, the community of the church is called to do so (e.g. 1 Cor. 12:25; Rom. 12:10, 13), and Paul writes that love and compassion in his churches made his joy complete (Phil. 2:1-2). The gospel writers depict that Jesus stressed the need to care especially for those who were marginalised by society (e.g. Mk. 9:36-37; Lk. 21:1-4), who certainly included sick people. Paul teaches of the importance of caring for those who were socially, physically and spiritually weak (e.g. 1 Cor. 8:7-13; 1 Thess. 5:14; Rom. 14:1-2; 15:1), just as Jesus had, and practical care for the disadvantaged in Acts is described (4:32-37; 6:1-6). Theissen believes that the early Christian communities understood the miracle stories as imposing an obligation on followers to provide for sick people.[52] The tradition of Jesus' parable of the Good Samaritan, with its elements of a person neither of the religious leadership nor of ethnic Israel, who had compassion, who treated the wounds of the robbed stranger, and paid for his further care, must also have been a powerful influence.[53]

Jesus' miracles are rarely mentioned in the New Testament outside the gospels, although Fridrichsen considers that they were recollected vividly (e.g. Heb. 2:4).[54] Divine healing seems to move in prominence from near-centre stage in the synoptic gospels and Acts, through being an occasional manifestation of the Holy Spirit in Paul's letters, to there being little substantive reference to it in the other pages of the New Testament (Rev. 22:2 is assumed to be metaphorical), although it is recognised that the power of Satan (and, therefore, of disease, *pace*

---

51 Leclerq, in a conversation with Kelsey, *Healing and Christianity,* p.70. Fridrichsen, *Problem of Miracle*, p.73.

52 Theissen, *Miracle Stories*, pp.251-52, 302; Marshall, *Faith as Theme*, p.64, considers that the Kingdom of God was seen as a protest against suffering, and imposed obligations of care on followers.

53 Remus, *Jesus as Healer*, p.113, suggests that the parable of the Good Samaritan may have been responsible for the eventual setting up of Christian hostels for strangers. It also offers us useful information on 'ordinary' folk-healing methods at the time; oil and wine were applied locally. The use of oil is mentioned in Mk. 6:13, where the disciples used oil in healing, but its purpose is not stated. In Isa. 1:6, oil was used to soften scars of wounds.

54 Fridrichsen, *Problem of Miracle*, pp.33, 58.

Thomas) had not been completely overcome.[55] The recipients of the other letters of the New Testament are frequently exhorted to show kindness and compassion to one another (e.g. Eph. 4:32; Col. 3:12; 1 Pet. 3:8); and the teaching of ethics, and of the necessity for followers to suffer for the gospel (e.g. 2 Tim. 1:8; 1 Pet. 1:6-7; 2:21) is also found throughout these letters. It is notable that Jesus' followers in these New Testament letters continued his ministry of preaching and teaching, but seemed not to emulate his healing miracles, or, at least, do not refer to doing so in these letters.

This dichotomy may be related partly to the 'high' Christology (for instance, Col. 1:15-20) that developed rapidly after the resurrection, so that Jesus' healings were regarded as unique, certainly in their power and effects; but this does not totally explain it. An unsuitable genre would also be a simple explanation for the lack of references to healing, but, as has been mentioned previously, a writer would be unlikely to omit completely a subject that was important to him. It may be that the later letters were canonised *because* they emphasised a particular view. It has to be admitted that the omission of mention of divine healing has been highlighted because of this book's focus on healing, but it may repay further study.

There is also very little material about health, or healing of sick people, in the later letters. Trophimus is reported to be ill in Miletus (2 Tim. 4:19), but there is no comment about his care; a little wine for Timothy's ailments is suggested by the letter-writer (1 Tim. 5:23), while other references to ill-health are clearly metaphorical.[56]

The reference in James 5:14-16 to the care of sick people in the church 'in the name of the Lord' is the only recorded example in a non-Pauline New Testament letter, where procedure to be followed is described. It is generally accepted that 'someone weak' (v.14) refers to a person who is physically ill.[57] Dibelius considered that the passage referred to supernatural healing (as exorcism), and believed that the elders were appointed *because* they had divine healing powers,

---

55 Thomas, *Devil, Disease*, e.g. p.297.

56 The only reference to good health is in the opening blessing in 3 Jn. 2. The lame people being healed (Heb. 12:13), and 'by his wounds you are healed' (1 Pet. 2:24) are metaphorical. See D.W. Amundsen and G.B. Ferngren, 'The Perception of Disease and Disease Causality in the New Testament', *ANRW* II.37.3 (1996) p.2946.

57 Adamson, *Epistle of James*, pp.198-99, thinks the sickness was physical; so also Thomas, *Devil, Disease*, p.20, and D.P. Nystrom, *James*, NIV Application Commentary (Grand Rapids: Zondervan, 1997) p.304. Ferngren and Amundsen, 'Medicine and Christianity', p.2961, present the pros and cons of the controversy over both the nature and treatment of the 'weak' person.

'miracle-workers rather than elderly patriarchs'.[58] The prayer of faith, and the anointing with oil in the name of the Lord, both suggest that this was a sacred rite, and might represent care by members of the church who were 'ordained', πρεσβυτέροι (elders), but with no particular healing abilities.[59] If this interpretation is correct, then it is the only recorded instance in the non-Pauline New Testament letters of how Jesus' exhortations to care for the weak was being followed in the church, continuing the Old Testament understanding that prayers for sick people (e.g. Ps. 107:17-20), now mediated through Christ, would be answered.

2.2.3 Healing in the Church after New Testament Times

In an effort to decide whether miraculous healing persisted in the church, and whether human care for sick people developed further, the period beyond the New Testament is considered very briefly. If healing were not found then, it would be reasonable to conclude, from the findings in the non-Pauline New Testament letters, that the legacy of Jesus' miracle healing, as a unique phenomenon, lasted only until the end of the apostolic era, and that awareness of the 'essence' of his healing, as concern and compassion in the care of the weak and sick, had also died out. A likely corollary of the view of those writers who consider that Jesus' miracles were *primarily* pedagogical or revelatory (for instance, to demonstrate the power of the Kingdom of God, see Chapter 3, *1.3.2*), would be that miraculous healing would cease when the need for such revelation was assumed to have passed, the basis of dispensationalism.[60] If either or both types of healing (miraculous or 'ordinary') flourished, it would suggest that the paucity of references to healing in the later letters is due to some oddity in them.

---

58 M. Dibelius, *James. A Commentary on the Epistle of James* (revised by H. Greeven; Philadelphia: Fortress, 1976) pp.252-53. Adamson, *Epistle of James*, p.207, sees the elders as having 'spiritual competence', rather than that there was one elder who was the conduit for divine healing.

59 Thiselton, *First Corinthians*, p.947, connects the 'prayer of faith' with the gift of faith of 1 Cor. 12:9a. Nystrom, *James*, pp.305-306, considers the prayer is not that God will heal, but that he will use the sick person to bring about his purpose. Thomas, *Devil, Disease*, p.36, believes James assumes that the prayer *would* result in healing, and critiques Turner, *Holy Spirit and Gifts*, pp.253-54, who considers that the outcome was not totally certain. Thomas, pp.26-28, assumes that the oil was not used for its physical properties, but as a sign to the church that God was able to heal.

60 Kelsey, *Healing and Christianity*, pp.17-19. Dispensationalism is the view that God gave a special dispensation for miracles only for a particular period and purpose, for instance, to allow the church to be established.

Continuation of miraculous healing seems to have been accepted; for instance, both Justin and Origen considered that healing miracles were being performed in their contemporary church life. Remus believes that early Christians saw Jesus' miracle healing as something that continued after the period of the New Testament.[61]

Many circumstances affected post-apostolic Christianity; for instance, intermittent Roman persecutions encouraged the growth of ideals of asceticism and martyrdom, so that interest in healing might be expected to be less prominent. Another development was the proliferation of increasingly magical miracle stories performed by disciples and followers in the Christian apocryphal literature, especially the apocryphal Acts, from the early second century. These works of imagination may have been attempts to show that Christian apostles out-performed their opponents.[62] Perhaps in an effort to keep Jesus' healings immune from accusations of magic, second-century apologists tried to distance Christian miracles from pagan magic.[63] The church also considered pagan religious healing, for instance the healing cult of Asclepius, demonic.[64]

With regard to Hippocratic medicine (which was religiously neutral), Nutton draws attention to the dangers of generalisation in discussing it in ancient Graeco-Roman culture, and this applies particularly to its place in early Christianity.[65] In the second-century church, Jesus was

61 Justin, *Apologies* 2.6; Origen, *Contra Celsum* 1.25. Remus, *Jesus as Healer*, p.95. We noted, Chapter 1, *1.3.2*, the employment of an official exorcist in the church at least until the late twentieth century; so the idea of divine healing has continued to be accepted.

62 Schneemelcher (ed.), *New Testament Apocrypha*, 2. *Writings Related to the Apostles, Apocalypses, and Related Subjects*, e.g. pp.214, 235. Achtemeier, 'Jesus and Disciples', p.161; Fridrichsen, *Problem of Miracle*, p.85; R.J. Bauckham, 'Apocryphal and Pseudoepigraphical Writings', in Martin and Davids (eds.), *Dictionary of the Later New Testament and its Developments*, pp.70-72, notes that the mystery is the rather minor increase in the miracles of the adult Jesus (in spite of Jn. 20:30; 21:25), compared with the huge increase in miracles reported as performed by the apostles.

63 Origen, *Contra Celsum* 6.41; 7.4, noted that the educated and affluent associated magical practices with the uneducated and poor.

64 Wells, *Greek Language of Healing*, p.14, and Remus, *Jesus as Healer*, p.9, have both regarded it as a major rival to Christianity. (See Chapter 2, *2.2.2*); Justin, *Apologies* 1.54.10; *Dialogue with. Trypho* 69.3; and Origen, *Contra Celsum* 3.25, all referred to Asclepius as demonic. D.W. Amundsen, *Medicine, Society and Faith in the Ancient and Mediaeval Worlds* (Baltimore: Johns Hopkins University Press, 1996) p.148, discusses their views.

65 V. Nutton, 'Healers in the Medical Market Place. Towards a Social History of Graeco-Roman Medicine', in A. Wear (ed.), *Medicine in Society. Historical Essays*

often given the metaphorical title of *Christus medicus*, the healer of souls diseased by sin. Although the term was used in the eschatological sense, many Christians saw Christ as the only physician, and were hesitant about, or actively opposed to,[66] the use of physicians and medicines, but there was also a positive side to the argument.[67] The apologists were mainly in favour of medicine (though Tatian despised physicians); Origen saw that medicine might be beneficial to mankind, so 'inferior' (i.e. ordinary) Christians might accept treatment from physicians, but 'superior' (i.e. ordained) Christians should not.[68]

In spite of these different views, it seems that ordinary human care for the poor and ill became eventually an important part of the church's work.[69] Organised systems of care for sick people developed, including hospices for the poor and ill. During a devastating epidemic in the eastern Roman Empire in AD 165-180, when, it was estimated, one-

---

(Cambridge: Cambridge University Press, 1992) p.57. Amundsen, *Medicine, Society and Faith*, p.152; Ferngren and Amundsen, 'Medicine and Christianity', p.2960, consider that the views of some dominant individuals were (and are) likely to be accepted as the norm there.

66 E.g. Clement, *Recognitions of Clement* 10:70; Remus, *Jesus as Healer*, p.15, objects that in the early church, Jesus is a healer, *not* a physician. Ferngren and Amundsen, 'Medicine and Christianity', p.2965, Temkin, *Hippocrates,* p114, note that there *were* physicians in early Christianity; for instance, Alexander was the first Christian physician known to have been martyred (in AD 187). Lane Fox, *Pagans and Christians*, p.329, notes the view of Alexander's contemporaries that he was 'not without a share of the charisma of the apostles', presumably in having miraculous healing powers. Van der Loos, *Miracles*, p.83. Brown, *Israel's Divine Healer*, pp.63-66, believes that many in early Christianity disdained physicians. Christian piety often combined with the ideas of Stoicism to prevent sick people from seeking the help of physicians, as this would call into question their faith in Christ.

67 Ferngren and Amundsen, 'Medicine and Christianity', p.2964, assert that Christians were mainly positive about medicine by the second century; they believe, p.2977, that Christians adopted Greek medicine very early, so there was little tension between divine healing and Hippocratic medicine. They also consider, p.2979, that medicine eventually integrated with Christianity.

68 Tatian, *Oration to the Greeks* 17-18. Origen, *Contra Celsum* 3.12. Amundsen, *Medicine, Society and Faith*, pp.146-48. S.J. Melcher, 'Visualising the Perfect Cult: The Priestly Rationale for Exclusion', in Eiesland and Saliers (eds.), *Human Disability*, p.56, notes that Origen's view fits with the Levitical norms of purity laid down for the people (Leviticus 12–15), with higher standards for priests (Leviticus 21–22).

69 Ferngren and Amundsen, 'Medicine and Christianity', p.2976, suggest that this was a major reason for the spread of Christianity before Constantine. Avalos, *Health Care and Christianity*, pp.4-5, points to the rapid rise in urban populations, the resulting overwhelming of health-care in cities, resulting in repeated epidemics at the time that Christianity was spreading, as factors which led to developments in Christian health-care.

quarter to one-third of the population of the Roman Empire died, the selfless care by Christians for their sick brethren resulted in a lower death rate among them, was probably a factor in increasing the proportion of Christians, and also won them the admiration of pagans. By the third century, in a time of 'plague', Christian communities were caring for ill pagans.[70]

This very brief outline of the times beyond the New Testament suggests that healing remained a vital part of the church, and was responsible, at least in part, for the church flourishing. The different views noted above underline the significance of Avalos' comment on the lack of dialogue between New Testament scholars and historians of medicine in a significant field of study.[71] Importantly, Jesus' healing legacy did survive, and grew in the post-apostolic centuries.

2.3 Conclusions on Jesus' Legacy of Healing

Although the gospel writers considered Jesus' healing to be unique in its effects, they also stressed that it demonstrated (unspoken) his love/compassion for the weak, and Paul recognised that this was a very significant element of Jesus' whole ministry. The biblical writers' awareness that Satan had not yet been destroyed must have meant that they accepted implicitly that healing would be ongoing. The sociological imperative for the early church was for unity, which included care for one another, and especially for the weak, rather than miracle healing.

The paucity of references in the later New Testament letters makes it difficult to predict whether divine healing would, in fact, develop or disappear in the post-apostolic church, and whether ordinary human care of sick people would remain important as a religious duty. The rapid recognition of Jesus as the Son of God may be partly responsible for believers in the later New Testament letters apparently not trying to emulate Jesus' miracle healing. Specific advice on caring for the ill and weak, an activity that Jesus and all the New Testament writers

70 R. Stark, *The Rise of Christianity. A Sociologist Reconsiders History* (Princeton: University of Princeton Press, 1996) pp.73-83. He, pp.83-85, notes that the apostate Emperor Julian launched a campaign for pagan charities to emulate those of the 'impious Galileans'. Ferngren and Amundsen, 'Medicine and Christianity', p.2972.

71 Avalos, *Health Care and Rise of Christianity*, p.6, draws attention to the lack of response from New Testament scholars to a comment by Amundsen, *Medicine, Society and Faith*, p.9, that the role of healing miracles in the Roman Empire in the second and third centuries was negligible. Avalos, trained in both anthropology and biblical studies, considers that this represents poor cross-fertilisation by these disciplines.

repeatedly charged Christians to do, is described only once in the non-Pauline letters of the New Testament (Jas. 5:14-16).

Although the many influences on Christian life after the period of the New Testament militate against distinguishing any consistent pattern of the development of healing then, miracle healing was reported, and human care of sick people, eventually including care of both Christians and pagans, became important. Therefore, until the coming of an age when sickness disappears completely, we expect the heart of Jesus' healing to remain, a legacy where compassion is the 'essence'.

3 Healing, Power and Risk

The language of power is pervasive in the New Testament, although often imprecise and unsystematic. People had a rich and subtle awareness of the various forms that power might take in the ancient world, where military force, words and healing were all important.[72] Rhetoric and medicine, as related τέχναι (vocations), with a common Greek origin in the fifth century BC, flourished during the Second Sophistic,[73] and it has been noted (Chapter 5, *2.4.2*) that many saw rhetoric as a tool of power politics. In the Roman Empire, the successful wielded power, often as a military general or a rhetor,[74] but there was also a strong correlation between commanding the world and healing sick people; for instance, the power and credibility of emperor Vespasian had to be proved at the beginning of his reign (and dynasty) by his healing in public (Chapter 2, *2.2.2*); miracles were important in the political and religious imagination of the Graeco-Roman world.[75]

72 Wink, *Naming the Powers*, pp.3, 6-7, considers that power was understood as composed of both spiritual and material factors, and, p.101, notes that today we are reductionist, considering only the material elements of power. Remus, *Jesus as Healer*, p.16.

73 L.T. Pearcy, 'Medicine and Rhetoric in the Period of the Second Sophistic', *ANRW* II.37.1 (1996) pp.445, 456, notes that Plato used medicine as a pattern for rhetoric. Litfin, *Paul's Theology of Proclamation,* p.256, describing Paul's struggle with the Corinthians, notes that medicine was used at that time as an analogy of rhetoric.

74 H.D. Betz, 'In Defence of the Spirit: Paul's Letter to the Galatians as a Document of Early Christian Apologetics', in Fiorenza (ed.), *Aspects of Religious Propaganda*, p.100. Winter, *Philo and Paul*, 2nd ed., p.207, notes that ability as an orator was a correlate of power. C. Gempf, 'Public Speaking and Published Accounts', in Winter and Clarke (eds.), *Acts in Ancient Literary Setting,* p.260, notes that 'you force them or convince them'.

75 Suetonius, *Lives of the Caesars: Divus Vespasian* 7.2; Tacitus, *The Histories* 4.81-83, notes that Vespasian first obtained a medical opinion that healing of a blind man was possible, before his attempt to heal him in Alexandria, under the instructions of the god

The areas of the New Testament studied depict miracle healing as a risky pursuit, especially in raising the opposition of the religious establishment, but there were other possible pitfalls related to healing in the early church. Healing could easily have become for the church its main power, and the mark of its success, and the church could have developed into a competitor to the healing cults, such as that of Asclepius, in what was an important area of life in the first century. It would then have been liable to die out, when another cult superseded it. But the writers, particularly Mark and Paul, point to such a development as not being the example of Jesus. To them, Jesus dying violently, in weakness, as substitution for humanity's sins, was the high point in demonstrating God's love.

Another risk of healing is identified by Hull, who considers that the Bible was written by healthy people, who (especially in the stories of Jesus healing) saw that the solution to disability was restoration to health.[76] There is a distinct danger, particularly in relation to faith-healing in the church, that Jesus' healing narratives might be used to reinforce the idea that those not healed have insufficient faith. More generally, churches through the ages have often not refuted the suspicion of there being some moral imperfection in the ill or disabled; Moltmann considers that the ancient dictum, 'what is not accepted is also not healed', applies to the attitude that many healthy people in the church have had towards those with disability.[77] Jesus, by his preaching, his healing miracles, and his association, care and compassion for the marginalised, demonstrated that the powerless were important to him. It has been suggested that in Christianity those who are sick or weak have had a preferential position;[78] Jesus refers to the Kingdom of God as belonging to the weak (e.g. Mk. 10:14; Lk. 6:20-21); Paul notes that 'the wisdom of the wise is to be destroyed' (1 Cor. 1:19), and chides the strong about the weak 'for whom Christ died' (1 Cor. 8:11).

The world's interest, perhaps especially in the first century, was in the power of the healer. Bolt has drawn attention to the likelihood that

---

Serapis; healing was seen as a risky business, even for an Emperor. Betz, 'Magic and Mystery', p.245. Borg, *Conflict, Holiness and Politics*, p.73.

76 Hull, *In the Beginning*, p.67. Grant, 'Reinterpreting Healing Narratives', pp.77-78, believes that those healed in the gospels were, and still are, considered in terms that are appropriate to those fit in mind and body. (It is, however, clear that Mark was at pains to point out that Bartimaeus, physically blind, 'saw' accurately who Jesus was.)

77 Grant, 'Reinterpreting Healing Narratives', p.73. J. Moltmann, 'Liberate Yourselves by Accepting One Another', in Eiesland and Saliers (eds.), *Human Disability*, p.116.

78 Tuckett, *Luke*, p.107, notes that this changed radically the Greek honour system. Ferngren and Amundsen, 'Medicine and Christianity', p.2976.

the early hearers of the healing stories in the gospels would have been interested in the suppliants, with whom they could identify; the humble, the poor and the ill had no power, and were often despised (the prevalence of magical practices bears witness to their problems).[79] The story of Jesus suffering and dying on the cross, then being raised from death, must have been seen by these believers as the supreme healing miracle, bringing Jesus as victim close to their own experience. No miracle had saved from death the powerful healer, but, although there were differences between the resurrection and the stories of Jesus' healing miracles (e.g. Jesus' resurrection was by God, it was apparent only to those with faith, and Jesus was not raised to his earthly body, as Jairus' daughter had been), suffering believers would be more ready to accept the fact of a suffering, risen Christ. We have noted that the recognition of Christ and his resurrection in glory, and the acceptance of him as Lord and part of the Godhead, followed rapidly after the crucifixion; identification with his suffering may partly explain why the exalted Christ became so quickly accepted. The resurrection was not accessible to intellect, but was clear only to those who believed, or came to believe, in Christ, and that belief required that followers understood and identified with his suffering for the world, rather than with his healing power.[80] Mark and Paul both recognise the theological importance of suffering, as does Luke, at least in his depiction of Jesus' and apostolic suffering, which was important in spreading the gospel.

Healing *is* important, and the ancient writers, in different ways, have demonstrated this. Disease is a threat, and thus has power, over the people afflicted, or afraid of it. It is also a spur, forcing others to try to heal or control it, even when this is dangerous (e.g. Herakles, Asclepius, Jesus, but also carers during epidemics). The main danger to healers, however, is that healing is among the group of human activities where arrogance is rampant; it should vanish when the large element of mystery involved in healing is recognised, mystery inherent in the nature of God and his works.

Because of their need, sick people have always moved others to heal or to care. This inherent power of those who are sick, demanding care, and relief of distress, is an important force. It has been latent in some eras, for instance, in the first-century Roman Empire, when power

---

79 Bolt, *Jesus' Defeat of Death,* draws attention to this throughout his book, but especially in pp.272-73. Rutgers, *Jews in Late Ancient Rome*, p.227; Ferngren and Amundsen, 'Medicine and Christianity', p.2958.

80 Borsch, *Power in Weakness*, p.106, says that if it were by intellect that we could comprehend God, it would be *our* image of God.

resided in the elite (and healthy), and healing was seen as an attribute of the powerful. Then, Jesus showed the power of the weak, both in the compassion of his ministry and, supremely, by his death. The power of the Kingdom of God is that of suffering love. O'Neill writes that God does not see human suffering from a position of supreme power.[81] This agrees with Bonhoeffer's comment, 'Man in his distress looks to the power of God in the world; the Bible directs us to God's powerlessness and suffering'.[82] It is at the cross, the icon of domination of a subject people, the place of most abject weakness, that divine power is seen in its most striking manifestation.

4 Conclusion

The ancient writers' views on healing have been compared, and significant differences in how they viewed miraculous healing in Jesus' life and in the apostolic church have been demonstrated.

The question of the continuance of Jesus' healing gift to the church has been considered. Both the persistence of Satan, and the emphasis on the Holy Spirit in the writings, would suggest that Mark, Luke and Paul saw divine healing continuing in the post-apostolic era, but they did not make it clear how. All the writers studied stressed that one of Jesus' important gifts was implicit in his command that his followers should care for one another, following the compassion that is obvious, though often unremarked upon, in the healing narratives in the gospels. This paradigm is spelled out in the parable of the Good Samaritan, and exhortations to care for each other, and particularly for the weak, are found throughout the non-Pauline letters of the New Testament. There are no accounts of miraculous healing there, and very little comment on practical care of sick people in the church (except in Jas. 5:14-16). Yet, in the first centuries of the post-New-Testament church, miraculous healing was considered to continue, while ordinary human care for sick people increased, and was a significant factor in Christianity flourishing.

---

81 O'Neill, *Who Did Jesus Think He Was?,* p.189. Wenham, *Paul: Follower or Founder,* p.353, sees the cross as the supreme evidence that weakness is a way of God exercising his saving power. Marshall, *Faith as Theme*, p.68; Borsch, *Power in Weakness*, pp.122, 125, notes that the power of God's Kingdom does not result in control of others, but, rather, offers *them* empowerment.

82 D. Bonhoeffer, *Letters and Papers from Prison* (3rd ed; London: SCM, 1971) p.361. W. Wink, *Unmasking the Powers. The Invisible Forces that Determine Human Existence* (Philadelphia: Fortress, 1986) p.56, writes that we encounter God in the darkness.

Jesus' healing ministry occurred in a world aware of the value that people put on healing, sophisticated enough to have several systems of healing in the pagan world, and to have differing views about healing (which impinged on the relationship between God and man) in Judaism. Power and healing in the first century have been considered, and it is concluded that Jesus' ministry drew attention to the importance of weakness, in a world where power was assumed to be the prerogative of the great.

5 Findings

In considering the findings reached in this monograph, it has to be emphasised again that, as healing has been detached from most of the other parts of the Jesus tradition, an atypical view of the overall picture of the gospels, Acts and Pauline letters, is presented.[83] It is biased further by my interest in medicine, but both features allow an unusual aspect of the ancient writers' views to emerge. Some of the points are already established consensus, some are points demonstrated or emphasised.

The main finding, as expected, in keeping with the variety of ideas about healing in Second Temple Judaism and paganism, and also with the diversity in many other aspects of the church from the earliest period, is how diverse are the views about healing of the biblical authors studied. It has been shown that the two gospel writers studied, although both emphasise the importance of Jesus' healing, have appreciably different theological views about it, and this is at least partly related to the relative significance that they put on Jesus' suffering, death and resurrection. Mark has a *theologia crucis*, which he demonstrates by the shape of his gospel in relation to Jesus' divine healing and his passion, and by the gospel's ending available to us. Luke sees healing as a weapon of divine power, where the power is God's, with Jesus subordinate, until, at his ascension, Jesus usually (but not invariably) has power to mediate the healing works of the apostles. Luke's *theologia gloriae* is finely balanced by a *theologia crucis;* apostolic suffering in Acts, partly as a result of their healing, brings into focus Luke's awareness of a *theologia crucis.*

It has also been demonstrated that Luke and Paul have very different outlooks on divine healing in the apostolic church, related to their views on the Christological and soteriological purposes of healing, as well as to its missionary implications. The views of Mark and Paul, dependent

83 Remus, *Jesus as Healer*, p.27, comments that Jesus as *only* a miracle worker takes him out of context, and misunderstands him.

on a *theologia crucis*, are similar in their understanding about divine healing, although very different in their emphasis on healing.

Study of the descriptions by Mark of Jesus' healing produces evidence of areas not usually noted, such as the precision of Mark's characterisation in the healing narratives, his consciousness of the pressures on Jesus which result from his healing gift, his awareness of Jesus rehabilitating the healed person (and family) into normal society, and his sensitive depiction of the crowd reactions. Comparison of the Markan narrative with that of Luke shows that Luke is not such a precise observer of human nature in healing situations as Mark, being more concerned to make theological points from the narratives.

I have argued that Luke is unlikely to have been (or to have written as) a physician of the Hippocratic tradition, where accuracy of the observed evidence would have taken precedence over all other considerations. For instance, Luke's theological awareness of God's right hand being the metaphor for power dulls his appreciation of how difficult it would be for a right-handed swordsman to damage an opposing subject's right ear. This is 'new' evidence against Luke being a physician, and incidentally allows us to study his understanding of divine healing, without having to take into account that he may have been influenced by Hippocratic concern, where careful observation is the key.

Another previously poorly-emphasised finding in relation to healing in the early church concerns Paul's mission and theology. I have argued that Paul's 'thorn' was probably the prime reason for him not stressing miracle-healing, and minimising its significance in his mission, and that Paul reached his theological understanding of suffering largely because of his illness. Further, his illness would have sensitised his ethical awareness of the risk that miracle healing by some believers in the churches might interfere with the equality of the strong and weak in their communities.

The question about why teaching and preaching of Jesus' message continued in the non-Pauline letters of the New Testament, while miracle-healing apparently did not (or, at least, was not mentioned), remains a mystery. These letters give very limited indication that care of sick people was being provided, but even a brief consideration of healing in the church after the New Testament demonstrates that probably divine healing, and certainly ordinary care of sick people, flourished.

Drawing attention to miracle healing in the New Testament, an important area of life, is not popular with most modern scholars.

Demonstrating the fundamental differences in both emphases and theological significance of healing in the three New Testament writers shows, however, by implication, how profound was the theological diversity which existed in the very earliest churches.

Healing in Matthew's gospel, and in the gospel of John (where the healing stories are more obviously used as 'set pieces' in John's theology) has not been studied. These two gospels would be likely to yield more information on how great were the differences, even within the canon, of the theological understanding of Jesus' healing in the early church. It would be interesting also to examine the apparent dichotomy in the later New Testament between the plethora of material emulating Jesus' teaching of the gospel, and the dearth of miraculous healing, to see if this was related to the choice of writers whose letters were canonised (i.e. those with a particular interest in kerygma and ethical teaching), or was a significant alteration from the areas of the New Testament which have been studied here.

Bibliography

Primary Sources

Aretaeus. *The Extant Works of Aretaeus the Cappadocian.* Francis Adams (ed.), London: Sydenham Society Publications, 1856.

Aristides, Aelius. *Herakles. The Complete Works.* Charles A. Behr (ed.), Leiden: Brill, 1981.

Asclepius. *A Collection and Interpretation of the Testimonies.* Emma J. and Ludwig Edelstein. 2 Vols. Baltimore: Johns Hopkins University Press, 1945.

Celsus, Aulus Cornelius. *De Medicina.* 3 Vols. W.G. Spencer (ed.); LCL; London/Cambridge, MA: Heinemann/Harvard University Press, 1935-38.

Cicero. *De Oratore.* H. Rackham (ed.), LCL; London/Cambridge, MA: Heinemann/Harvard University Press, 1942.

– *Orations.* R. Gardner (ed.), 2 Vols. LCL; London/Cambridge, MA: Heinemann/Harvard University Press, 1958.

Clement. *Recognitions of Clement*, in Alexander Roberts and James Donaldson (eds.), *The Ante-Nicene Fathers.* Vol.8. *Second and Third Century Acts of the Apostles.* Grand Rapids/Edinburgh: Eerdmans/T. & T. Clark, 1989.

Diogenes Laertius. *The Lives of Eminent Philosophers; Empedocles; Pythagoras.* R.D. Hicks, (ed.), 2 Vols. LCL; London/New York: Heinemann/ Putnam's Sons, 1925.

Eliezer ben Hyrcanus. *The Tradition and the Man.* Jacob Neusner (ed.), *Studies in Judaism in Late Antiquity.* 3 Vols. Leiden: Brill, 1973.

Empedocles. *The Extant Fragments.* M.R. Wright (ed.), New Haven/London: Yale University Press, 1981.

Euripides. *Alcestis.* D.J. Conacher. (ed.), Warminster: Aris & Phillips, 1988.

Galen. *On the Natural Faculties,* in Robert M. Hutchins (ed.), Vol.10, *Hippocrates and Galen.* Chicago/London/Toronto: Encyclopaedia Britannica, 1952, pp.167-215.

– *Galen of Pergamon.* George Sarton (ed.), Lawrence, Kansas: University of Kansas Press, 1954.

– *On Anatomical Procedures.* Charles Singer, ET; London: Wellcome Museum of History of Medicine Press, 1956.

Hippocrates. *Epidemics I*, in *The Genuine Works of Hippocrates,* Vol.1, Francis Adams; London: Sydenham Society, 1859.

– *Airs, Waters, Places; Prognostics; On Wounds of the Head.* 4 Vols., William H.S. Jones (ed.), LCL; London/New York: Heinemann/Putnam's Sons, 1923-31.

– *On Fractures; Epidemics I,* in *Hippocrates and Galen*, Vol.10. Robert M. Hutchins (ed.), Chicago/London/Toronto: Encyclopaedia Britannica, 1952, pp.1-160.

Josephus. *Jewish Antiquities.* Henry St. J. Thackeray and Ralph Marcus (eds.), 10 Vols. LCL; London/Cambridge, MA: Heinemann/Harvard University Press, 1926-65.

Justin. *The Apologies of Justin Martyr.* A.W.F. Blunt (ed.), Cambridge: Cambridge University Press, 1911.

– *Dialogue with Trypho.* Alexander Roberts and James Donaldson (eds.), *The Ante-Nicene Fathers.* Vol.1. *The Apostolic Fathers.* Edinburgh/Grand Rapids: T. & T. Clark/Eerdmans, 1989.

Origen. *Contra Celsum. English Translation, Introduction and Notes.* Henry Chadwick (ed.). Cambridge: Cambridge University Press, 1953.

Philo. *On Giants .On the Contemplative Life. On the Life of Moses. On the Special Laws I.* C.D. Yonge, new ed.; Peabody: Hendrickson, 1997.

Philostratus. *The Life of Apollonius.* F.C. Conybeare (ed.), 2 Vols. LCL; London/Cambridge, MA: Heinemann/Harvard University Press, 1912, 1950.

Plato. *The Republic*, Vol.1. James Adam (ed.), 2nd ed.; Cambridge: Cambridge University Press, 1963.

Pliny. *Natural History.* H. Rackham, William H.S. Jones et al. (eds.), 10 Vols. LCL; London/Cambridge, MA: Heinemann/Harvard University Press, 1938-1969.

Plutarch. *Moralia.* Frank C. Babbit et al. (eds.), 16 Vols. LCL; London/Cambridge, MA: Heinemann/Harvard University Press, 1927-2004.

– *Lives; Pyrrhus; Solon.* Bernadotte Perrin (ed.), 11 Vols. LCL; London/Cambridge, MA: Heinemann/Harvard University Press, 1914-26.

– *On Isis and Osiris.* J. Gwyn Griffiths. Cardiff: University of Wales Press, 1970.

Porphyry. *Life of Pythagoras.* Kenneth S. Guthrie (ed.), Michigan: Phanes, 1987.

Suetonius. *Divus Claudius.* Donna W. Hurley, (ed.), Cambridge: Cambridge University Press, 2001.

– *The Lives of the Caesars; Divus Vespasian*. John C. Rolfe (ed.), 2 Vols. LCL; London/Cambridge, MA: Heinemann/Harvard University Press, 1914.

Tacitus. *The Histories*. 3 Vols. Clifford H. Moore (ed.), LCL; London/New York: Heinemann/Putnam's Sons, 1925-31.

– *The Annals*. 2 Vols. John Jackson (ed.), LCL; London/New York: Heinemann/Putnam's Sons, 1931.

Tatian. *Oration to the Greeks*. Alexander Roberts and James Donaldson (eds.), *The Ante-Nicene Fathers*, Vol.2. *Fathers of the Second Century*. Edinburgh/Grand Rapids: T. & T. Clark/Eerdmans, 1989.

Tertullian. *On Modesty*. Alexander Roberts and James Donaldson (eds.), *The Ante-Nicene Fathers*. Vol.4. Edinburgh/Grand Rapids: T. & T. Clark/Eerdmans, 1989.

– *Apology*. T.R Glover and Gerald H. Rendall (eds.), LCL; London/Cambridge, MA: Heinemann/Harvard University Press, 1931.

Secondary Sources

Aageson, James W. '"Control" in Pauline Language and Culture. A Study of Romans 6', *NTS* 42 (1996) 75-89.

Achtemeier, Paul J. 'Miracles and the Historical Jesus: A Study of Mark 9:14-29', *CBQ* 37 (1975) 471-91.

– 'Jesus and the Disciples as Miracle Workers in the Apocryphal New Testament', in Elisabeth S. Fiorenza (ed.), *Aspects of Religious Propaganda in Judaism and Early Christianity*. Notre Dame: University of Notre Dame Press, 1976, pp.149-86.

– 'The Lucan Perspective on the Miracles of Jesus: A Preliminary Sketch', in Charles H. Talbert, (ed.), *Perspectives on Luke-Acts*. Edinburgh: T. & T. Clark, 1978, pp.153-67.

– *The Quest for Unity in the New Testament Church*. Philadelphia: Fortress, 1987.

Adamson, James B. *The Epistle of James*. NICNT. Grand Rapids: Eerdmans, 1976.

Aland, Barbara; Kurt Aland; Johannes Karavidopoulos; Carlo M. Martini; and Bruce M. Metzger (eds.), *Novum Testamentum Graece*. 27th ed.; Stuttgart: Deutsche Bibelgesellschaft, 1993.

– *The Greek New Testament*. 4th rev. ed.; Stuttgart: Deutsche Bibelgesellschaft, 1994.

Alexander, Loveday C. 'Paul and the Hellenistic Schools: The Evidence of Galen', in Troels Engberg-Pedersen (ed.), *Paul in his Hellenistic*

Context. Studies of the New Testament and its World. Edinburgh: T. & T. Clark, 1994.

Alexander, W. Menzies. 'St Paul's Infirmity', *ExpTim* 15 (1903-04), Part I, pp.469-73, Part II, pp.545-48.

Amundsen, Darrel W. *Medicine, Society and Faith in the Ancient and Medieval Worlds.* Baltimore/London: Johns Hopkins University Press, 1996.

– and Gary B. Ferngren, 'The Perception of Disease and Disease Causality in the New Testament', in Wolfgang Haase (ed.), *Aufstieg und Niedergang der Römischen Welt* II.37.3. Berlin/New York: de Gruyter, 1996, pp.2934-56.

Anderson, Hugh. 'Jesus: Aspects of the Question of his Authority', in Jacob Neusner, Peder Borgen, Ernest S. Frerichs and Richard Horsley (eds.), *The Social World of Formative Christianity and Judaism.* Philadelphia: Fortress, 1988, pp.290-310.

Arnold, Clinton E. *Ephesians: Power and Magic. The Concept of Power in Ephesians in Light of its Historical Setting.* SNTSMS 63; Cambridge: Cambridge University Press, 1989.

Aune, David E. 'Magic in Early Christianity', in Wolfgang Haase (ed.), *Aufstieg und Niedergang der Römischen Welt* II.23.2. Berlin: de Gruyter, 1980, pp.1507-57.

– *Prophecy in Early Christianity and the Ancient Mediterranean World.* Grand Rapids: Eerdmans, 1983.

– *The New Testament in its Literary Environment.* Philadelphia: Westminster, 1987.

– 'Christian Prophecy and the Messianic Status of Jesus', in James H. Charlesworth (ed.), *The Messiah. Developments in Earliest Judaism and Christianity.* Minneapolis: Fortress, 1992, pp.404-22.

Avalos, Hector. *Illness and Health Care in the Ancient Near East. The Role of the Temple in Greece, Mesopotamia and Israel.* HSM 54; Atlanta: Scholars Press, 1995.

– 'Disability and Liturgy in Ancient and Modern Religious Traditions', in Nancy L. Eiesland and Don E. Saliers (eds.), *Human Disability and the Service of God. Reassessing Religious Practice.* Nashville: Abingdon, 1998, pp.35-54.

– *Health Care and the Rise of Christianity.* Peabody: Hendrickson, 1999.

Balz, Horst, 'Βαρέω', in H. Balz and G. Schneider (eds.), *Exegetical Dictionary of the New Testament.* Vol.1; ET; Edinburgh: T. & T. Clark, 1990, p.198.

Bammel, Ernst. '"John Did No Miracle": John 10:41', in Charles F.D. Moule (ed.), *Miracles. Cambridge Studies in Their Philosophy and History.* London: Mowbray, 1965, pp.179-202.

Barclay, John M.G. 'Jesus and Paul', in Ralph P. Martin and Peter H. Davids (eds.), *Dictionary of Later New Testament and its Developments.* Downers Grove/Leicester: InterVarsity Press, 1997, pp.492-503.

– 'Poverty in Pauline Studies: A Response to Steven Friesen', *JSNT* 26 (2004) 363-66.

Barnett, Paul W. 'Opposition in Corinth', *JSNT* 22 (1984) 3-17.

– *The Message of 2 Corinthians. Power in Weakness.* Leicester: InterVarsity Press, 1988.

– *The Second Epistle to the Corinthians.* NICNT. Grand Rapids/Cambridge: Eerdmans, 1997.

Barrett, Charles K. *The Holy Spirit and the Gospel Tradition.* New ed.; Philadelphia: Fortress, 1965.

– *A Commentary on the Second Epistle to the Corinthians.* BNTC. London: A. & C. Black, 1973.

– 'Theologia Crucis–in Acts?', in C. Andresen and G. Klein (eds.), *Theologia Crucis–Signum Crucis (Festschrift für Erich Dinkler).* Tübingen: Mohr (Siebeck), 1979, pp.73-84.

– *Essays on Paul.* London: SPCK, 1982.

– 'How History Should Be Written', in Ben Witherington, III (ed.), *History, Literature, and Society in the Book of Acts.* Cambridge: Cambridge University Press, 1992, pp.33-57.

– *Paul. An Introduction to his Thought.* Louisville: Westminster John Knox, 1994.

– '*Imitatio Christi* in Acts', in Joel B. Green and Max Turner (eds.), *Jesus of Nazareth: Lord and Christ. Essays on the Historical Jesus and New Testament Christology.* Grand Rapids/Carlisle: Eerdmans/Paternoster, 1994, pp.251-62.

– *The Acts of the Apostles. A Shorter Commentary.* Edinburgh/New York: T. & T. Clark, 2002.

Bartsch, Hans-Werner, (ed.), *Kerygma and Myth. A Theological Debate,* Vol.1. ET; London: SPCK, 1972.

Bauckham, Richard J. 'Apocryphal and Pseudoepigraphical Writings', in Ralph P. Martin and Peter H. Davids (eds.), *Dictionary of the Later New Testament and its Developments.* Downers Grove/Leicester: InterVarsity Press, 1997, pp.68-72.

Bauer, Walter; Frederick W. Danker; William F. Arndt; and F. Wilbur Gingrich (eds.), *A Greek-English Lexicon of the New Testament and*

Other Early Christian Literature. 3rd ed.; Chicago: University of Chicago Press, 2000.

Beckwith, Francis J. 'History and Miracles', in R. Douglas Geivett and Gary R. Habermas (eds.), *In Defence of Miracles. A Comprehensive Case for God's Action in History.* Leicester: Apollos, 1997, pp.86-98.

Beker, J. Christiaan. 'Christologies and Anthropologies of Paul, Luke–Acts and Marcion', in Martinus C. de Boer (ed.), *From Jesus to John. Essays on Jesus and New Testament Christology in Honour of Marinus de Jonge.* JSNTSup 84; Sheffield: Sheffield Academic Press, 1993, pp.174-82.

Belleville, Linda J. '"Imitate Me, Just as I Imitate Christ": Discipleship in the Corinthian Correspondence', in Richard N. Longenecker (ed.), *Patterns of Discipleship in the New Testament.* Grand Rapids: Eerdmans, 1996, pp.120-42.

Bennett, Risdon. *The Diseases of the Bible.* London: The Religious Tract Society, 1887.

Berry, Richard J. 'Miracles: Scepticism, Credulity or Reality?', in Andrew Walker (ed.), *Different Gospels. Christian Orthodoxy and Modern Theologies.* 2nd ed.; London: SPCK, 1993, pp.67-73.

Best, Ernest. *Mark. The Gospel as Story.* Studies of the New Testament and its World Series. Edinburgh: T. & T. Clark, 1983.

Betz, Hans Dieter. *Der Apostel Paulus und die sokratische Tradition; eine exegetische Untersuchung zu seiner Apologie 2 Korinther 10–13.* Tübingen: Mohr (Siebeck), 1972.

– 'In Defence of the Spirit: Paul's Letter to the Galatians as a Document of Early Christian Apologetics', in Elisabeth S. Fiorenza (ed.), *Aspects of Religious Propaganda in Judaism and Early Christianity.* Notre Dame: University of Notre Dame Press, 1976, pp.99-114.

– *The Greek Magical Papyri in Translation, Including the Demotic Spells*, Vol.1. *Texts*. Chicago: University of Chicago Press, 1986.

– 'Apostle', in David N. Freedman (ed.), *Anchor Bible Dictionary*, Vol.1. New York: Doubleday, 1992, pp.309-11.

– 'Magic and Mystery in the Greek Magical Papyri', in Christopher A. Faraone and Dirk Obbink (eds.), *Magika Hiera: Ancient Greek Magic and Religion.* Oxford: Oxford University Press, 1997, pp.244-59.

Betz, Otto. 'The Concept of the So-Called "Divine Man" in Mark's Christology', in David E. Aune (ed.), *Studies in New Testament and Early Christian Literature. Essays in Honor of Allen P. Wikgren.* NovTSup 33; Leiden: Brill, 1972, pp.229-40.

Black, C. Clifton. 'Christ Crucified in Paul and Mark: Reflections on an Intracanonical Conversation', in Eugene H. Lovering, Jr. and Jerry L.

Sumney, (eds.), *Theology and Ethics in Paul and his Interpreters.* Nashville: Abingdon, 1996, pp.184-206.

Blackburn, Barry L. '"Miracle Working Theioi Andres" in Hellenism (and Hellenistic Judaism)', in David Wenham and Craig Blomberg (eds.), *Gospel Perspectives*, Vol.6. *The Miracles of Jesus.* Sheffield: JSOT Press, 1986, pp.185-218.

– *Theios Anēr and the Markan Miracle Traditions. A Critique of the Theios Anēr Concept as an Interpretative Background of the Miracle Traditions Used by Mark.* WUNT 2/40; Tübingen: Mohr (Siebeck), 1991.

– 'The Miracles of Jesus', in Bruce Chilton and Craig A. Evans (eds.), *Studying the Historical Jesus. Evaluations of the State of Current Research.* NTTS 19; Leiden: Brill, 1994, pp.353-94.

Blomberg, Craig L. 'The Miracles as Parables', in David Wenham and Craig Blomberg (eds.), *Gospel Perspectives.* Vol.6. *The Miracles of Jesus.* Sheffield: JSOT Press, 1986, pp.327-59.

– 'Concluding Reflections on Miracles and Gospel Perspectives', in David Wenham and Craig Blomberg (eds.), *Gospel Perspectives.* Vol.6. *The Miracles of Jesus.* Sheffield: JSOT Press, 1986, pp.443-57.

– '"Your Faith has Made you Whole": The Evangelical Liberation Theology of Jesus', in Joel B. Green and Max Turner (eds.), *Jesus of Nazareth: Lord and Christ.* Grand Rapids/Carlisle: Eerdmans/Paternoster, 1994, pp.75-93.

Bock, Darrell L. *Luke.* Vol. 1, *1:1–9:50.* BECNT. Grand Rapids: Baker Books, 1994.

– *Luke.* Vol. 2, *9:51–24:53.* BECNT. Grand Rapids: Baker Books, 1996.

Bockmuehl, Markus. 'Halakhah and Ethics in the Jesus Tradition', in John Barclay and John Sweet (eds.), *Early Christian Thought in its Jewish Context.* Cambridge: Cambridge University Press, 1996, pp.264-78.

Bolt, Peter G. 'Life, Death, and the Afterlife in the Greco-Roman World', in Richard N. Longenecker (ed.), *Life in the Face of Death. The Resurrection Message of the New Testament.* Grand Rapids/Cambridge: Eerdmans, 1998, pp.51-79.

– *Jesus' Defeat of Death. Persuading Mark's Early Readers.* SNTSMS 125; Cambridge: Cambridge University Press, 2003.

Bonhoeffer, Dietrich. *Letters and Papers from Prison.* 3rd ed.; London: SCM, 1971.

Borg, Marcus J. *Conflict, Holiness and Politics in the Teachings of Jesus*. New York: Mellen, 1984.

– *Jesus. A New Vision. Spirit, Culture and the Life of Discipleship*. New York: Harper & Row, 1987.

– and N. Thomas Wright. *The Meaning of Jesus*. New York/San Francisco: HarperSanFrancisco, 1999.

Boring, M. Eugene. 'Markan Christology. God-Language for Jesus?', *NTS* 45 (1999) 451-71.

Borsch, Frederick Houk. *Power in Weakness. New Hearing for Gospel Stories of Healing and Discipleship*. Philadelphia: Fortress, 1983.

Bowersock, George W. (ed.), *Approaches to the Second Sophistic*. Papers presented at the 105th Annual Meeting of the American Philological Association. Ephrata: Science Press, 1974.

Brenk, Frederick E. 'In the Light of the Moon: Demonology in the Early Imperial Period', in Wolfgang Haase (ed.), *Aufstieg und Niedergang der Römischen Welt* II.16.3. Berlin/New York: de Gruyter, 1986, pp.2068-145.

Broadhead, Edwin K. *Teaching with Authority. Miracles and Christology in the Gospel of Mark*. JSNTSup.74; Sheffield: JSOT Press, 1992.

Brosend, William F., II. 'The Means of Absent Ends', in Ben Witherington, III (ed.), *History, Literature and Society in the Book of Acts*. Cambridge: Cambridge University Press, 1996, pp.348-62.

Brown, Colin. *Miracles and the Critical Mind*. Grand Rapids/Exeter: Eerdmans/Paternoster, 1984.

Brown, Michael L. *Israel's Divine Healer*. Carlisle: Paternoster, 1995.

Brown, Peter R.L. 'The Rise and Function of the Holy Man in Late Antiquity', *JRS* 61 (1971) 80-101.

– *The World of Late Antiquity from Marcus Aurelius to Muhammad*. London: Thames & Hudson, 1971.

Bruce, Frederick F. *1 and 2 Corinthians*. NCBC. London: Marshall, Morgan & Scott, 1971.

– *The Epistle of Paul to the Galatians*. NIGTC. Exeter: Paternoster, 1982.

– *The Acts of the Apostles. The Greek Text with Introduction and Commentary*. 3rd ed.; Grand Rapids/Leicester: Eerdmans/Apollos, 1990.

Brucker, Ralph. 'Die Wunder der Apostel Kontroverse Wunder in frühen Christentum–Wirklichkeit oder Propaganda?', *ZNT* 7.4 (2001) 32-45.

Bultmann, Rudolf. *Theology of the New Testament,* Vol.1. ET; London: SCM, 1952.

– *Jesus Christ and Mythology.* Brit. ed.; London: SCM, 1960.

– *The History of the Synoptic Tradition.* ET; 2nd ed.; Oxford: Blackwell, 1968.

– *Faith and Understanding.* Vol.I. ET; London: SCM, 1969.

– 'New Testament and Mythology', in Hans-Werner Bartsch (ed.), *Kerygma and Myth. A Theological Debate.* Vol.1. ET; London: SPCK, 1972, pp.1-44.

– *The Second Letter to the Corinthians.* ET; Minneapolis: Augsburg, 1985.

Burke, Paul F. 'Malaria in the Greco-Roman World: A Historical and Epidemiological Survey', in Wolfgang Haase (ed.), *Aufstieg und Niedergang der Römischen Welt* II.37.3. Berlin/New York: de Gruyter,1996, pp.2252-79.

Burridge, Richard A. *What Are the Gospels? A Comparison with Graeco-Roman Biography.* SNTSMS 70; Cambridge: Cambridge University Press, 1992.

Cadbury, Henry J. *The Style and Literary Method of Luke.* Vol.1. HTS 6; Cambridge, MA: Harvard University Press, 1919.

– *The Making of Luke-Acts.* London: MacMillan & Co., 1927.

– *The Peril of Modernizing Jesus.* (Orig. 1937); London: SPCK, 1962.

Cairns, David S. *The Faith That Rebels.* London: SCM, 1928.

Caragounis, Chrys C. 'Kingdom of God, Son of Man, and Jesus' Self-Understanding', Part 2, *TynBul* 40 (1989) 223-38.

Carr, Wesley. *Angels and Principalities. The Background, Meaning and Development of the Pauline Phrase 'hai archai kai hai exousiai'.* SNTSMS 42; Cambridge: Cambridge University Press, 1981.

Carroll, John T. 'Sickness and Healing in the New Testament Gospels', *Int* 49 (1995) 130-42.

Cassidy, Richard J. *Paul in Chains. Roman Imprisonment and the Letters of St. Paul.* New York: Crossroad, 2001.

Catchpole, David R. 'Mark', in John Barclay and John Sweet (eds.), *Early Christian Thought in its Jewish Context.* Cambridge: Cambridge University Press, 1996, pp.70-83.

Charles, R.H. (ed.), *The Book of Jubilees.* London: A. & C. Black, 1902.

Charlesworth, James H. (ed.), *The Old Testament Pseudepigrapha.* 2 Vols. London: Darton, Longman and Todd, 1983, 1985.

– 'From Messianology to Christology: Problems and Prospects', in J.H. Charlesworth (ed.), *The Messiah. Developments in Earliest Judaism and Christianity.* Minneapolis, Fortress, 1992, pp.3-35.

Chester, Andrew. 'The Jews of Judea and Galilee', in John M.G. Barclay and John P.M. Sweet, (eds.), *Early Christian Thought in its Jewish Context.* Cambridge: Cambridge University Press, 1996, pp.9-26.

Cheung, Alex T. *Idol Food in Corinth.* JSNTSup176; Sheffield, Sheffield Academic Press, 1999.

Chilton, Bruce D. 'Exorcism and History: Mark 1:21-28', in David Wenham and Craig Blomberg (eds.), *Gospel Perspectives*, Vol.6. *The Miracles of Jesus.* Sheffield: JSOT Press, 1986, pp.253-71.

– *Jesus' Baptism and Jesus' Healing.* Harrisburg: Trinity, 1998.

– 'An Exorcism of History: Mark 1:21-28', in Bruce Chilton and Craig A. Evans (eds.), *Authenticating the Activities of Jesus.* Leiden: Brill, 1999, pp.215-45.

Clarke, Andrew D. *Secular and Christian Leadership in Corinth.* Leiden: Brill, 1993.

– '"Be Imitators of Me"; Paul's Model of Leadership,' *TynBul* 49 (1998) 329-60.

– *Serve the Community of the Church.* Grand Rapids/Cambridge: Eerdmans, 2000.

Collins, Raymond F. *First Corinthians.* SacPag Series, Vol.7. Collegeville: Liturgical Press, 1999.

Conzelmann, Hans. *The Theology of St. Luke.* (Orig. *Die Mitte der Zeit,* 1925). ET; London: Faber & Faber, 1960.

– *A Commentary on the Acts of the Apostles.* Hermeneia Series. ET; Philadelphia: Fortress, 1987.

Cook, John G. 'In Defence of Ambiguity: Is There a Hidden Demon in Mark 1:29-31?', *NTS* 43 (1997) 184-208.

Corrington, Gail P. *The 'Divine Man': His Origin and Function in Hellenistic Popular Religion.* New York: Lang, 1986.

Cotter, Wendy. *Miracles in Greco-Roman Antiquity.* London: Routledge, 1999.

Craig, William L. 'The Problem of Miracles: A Historical and Philosophical Perspective', in David Wenham and Craig Blomberg (eds.), *Gospel Perspectives,* Vol.6. *The Miracles of Jesus.* Sheffield: JSOT Press, 1986, pp.9-48.

Cranfield, Charles E.B. *A Critical and Exegetical Commentary on the Epistle to the Romans.* ICC. Vol.2. Edinburgh: T. & T. Clark, 1979.

Crossan, John Dominic. *The Birth of Christianity. Discovering What Happened in the Years Immediately after the Execution of Jesus.* New York/San Francisco: HarperSanFrancisco, 1998.

Croy, N. Clayton. *Endurance in Suffering. Hebrews 12:1-13 in its Rhetorical, Religious and Philosophical Context.* SNTSMS 98; Cambridge: Cambridge University Press, 1998.

Dahl, N.A. 'The Purpose of Mark's Gospel', in Christopher M. Tuckett (ed.), *The Messianic Secret.* Philadelphia: Fortress, 1983, pp.29-34.

Danby, Herbert. *The Mishnah.* Oxford: Clarendon, 1933.

Danker, Frederick W. *Benefactor: Epigraphic Study of a Graeco-Roman and New Testament Semantic Field.* St. Louis: Clayton, 1982.

– *Jesus and the New Age. A Commentary on St. Luke's Gospel.* Philadelphia: Fortress, 1988.

Davids, Peter H. 'Signs and Wonders', in Ralph P. Martin and Peter H. Davids (eds.), *Dictionary of the Later New Testament and its Developments.* Downers Grove/Leicester: InterVarsity Press, 1997, pp.1093-95.

Davies, Stevan L. *Jesus the Healer. Possession, Trance, and the Origins of Christianity.* London: SCM, 1995.

Davis, Eli. 'The Illness of Miriam, Sister of Moses', 2nd International Symposium on Medicine in Bible and Talmud, Jerusalem, 1984, J.O. Leibowitz, (ed.), *Koroth* 9.1-2 (1985) 99-100.

Deissmann, Adolph. *Light from the Ancient East. The New Testament Illustrated by Recently Discovered Texts of the Graeco-Roman World.* ET; London: Hodder & Stoughton, 1910.

De Jonge, Marinus. 'Monotheism and Christology', in John Barclay and John Sweet (eds.), *Early Christian Thought in its Jewish Context.* Cambridge: Cambridge University Press, 1996, pp.225-37.

Delling, Gerhard. 'σκόλοψ', in Gerhard Kittel and Gerhard Friedrich (eds.), *Theological Dictionary of the New Testament,* Vol.7, 1971, pp.409-13.

Derrett, J. Duncan M. 'Mark's Technique: The Haemorrhaging Woman and Jairus' Daughter', *Bib* 63 (1982) 474-505.

Dibelius, Martin. *From Tradition to Gospel.* (Orig. 1919). ET; New York: Scribner's Sons, 1935.

– *Paul.* Edited and completed by Werner G. Kümmel. ET; London/New York/Toronto: Longmans, Green and Co., 1953.

– *James. A Commentary on the Epistle of James* (revised by H. Greeven). Hermeneia. Philadelphia: Fortress, 1976.

Dodd, Charles H. *The Apostolic Preaching and its Developments.* (Orig. 1937). 3rd ed.; London: Hodder & Stoughton, 1970.

– 'The Mind of Paul: II', (orig. 1934), reproduced in C.H. Dodd, *New Testament Studies.* Manchester: Manchester University Press, 1953, pp.83-128.

Donahue, John R. and Daniel J Harrington. *The Gospel of Mark*. SacPag Series, Vol.2. Collegeville: Liturgical Press, 2002.

Donaldson, Terence L. *Paul and the Gentiles.* Minneapolis: Fortress, 1997.

– 'Israelite, Convert, Apostle to the Gentiles: The Origin of Paul's Gentile Mission', in Richard N. Longenecker (ed.), *The Road from Damascus. The Impact of Paul's Conversion on his Life, Thought and Ministry.* Grand Rapids: Eerdmans, 1997, pp.62-84.

Douglas, Mary. *Purity and Danger. An Analysis of the Concepts of Pollution and Taboo.* London/New York: Routledge, 1966, reprint 1993.

Downing, F. Gerald. 'A Cynic Preparation for Paul's Gospel for Jew and Greek, Slave and Free, Male and Female', *NTS* 42 (1996) 454-62.

Drane, John W. 'Patterns of Evangelization in Paul and Jesus: A Way Forward in the Jesus–Paul Debate?', in Joel B. Green and Max Turner (eds.), *Jesus of Nazareth: Lord and Christ.* Grand Rapids/Carlisle: Eerdmans/Paternoster, 1994, pp.281-96.

Dunn, James D.G. *Jesus and the Spirit.* Philadelphia: Westminster, 1975.

– *Unity and Diversity in the New Testament. An Inquiry into the Character of Earliest Christianity.* London: SCM, 1977.

– 'Pharisees, Sinners, and Jesus', in Jacob Neusner; Peder Borgen; Ernest S. Frerichs and Richard Horsley (eds.), *The Social World of Formative Christianity and Judaism.* Philadelphia: Fortress, 1988, pp.264-89.

– *Romans 1-8.* WBC, Vol.38A. Dallas: Word Books, 1988.

– *Christology in the Making.* 2nd ed.; London: SCM, 1989.

– *Jesus, Paul and the Law. Studies in Mark and Galatians.* London: SPCK, 1990.

– 'Messianic Ideas and their Influence on the Jesus of History', in James H. Charlesworth (ed.), *The Messiah. Developments in Earliest Judaism and Christianity.* Minneapolis: Fortress, 1992, pp.365-81.

– 'The New Testament as History', in Andrew Walker (ed.), *Different Gospels. Christian Orthodoxy and Modern Theologies.* 2nd ed.; London: SPCK, 1993, pp.43-53.

– *A Commentary on the Epistle to the Galatians*. BNTC. London: A. & C. Black, 1993.

– *The Theology of Paul's Letter to the Galatians.* Cambridge: Cambridge University Press, 1993.

– *The Acts of the Apostles.* Epworth Commentaries. Peterborough: Epworth, 1996.

– *The Theology of Paul the Apostle*. Grand Rapids/Cambridge: Eerdmans, 1998.
– 'Who Did Paul Think He Was? A Study of Jewish–Christian Identity', *NTS* 45 (1999) 174-93.
– *Christianity in the Making*. Vol.1. *Jesus Remembered*. Grand Rapids/Cambridge: Eerdmans, 2003.
– 'Altering the Default Setting: Re-Envisaging the Early Transmission of the Jesus Tradition', *NTS* 49 (2003) 139-75.
Dwyer, Timothy. 'The Motif of Wonder in the Gospel of Mark', *JSNT* 57 (1995) 49-59.
Edwards, James R. 'The Gospel of the Ebionites and the Gospel of Luke', *NTS* 48 (2002) 568-86.
– *The Gospel According to Mark*. PNTC. Grand Rapids/Cambridge: Eerdmans, 2002.
Elliott, John H. *What is Social-Scientific Criticism?* Minneapolis: Fortress, 1993.
– 'The Evil Eye and the Sermon on the Mount', *Bib Int* 2 (1994) 51-84.
Engberg-Pedersen, Troels. *Paul in his Hellenistic Context. Studies of the New Testament and its World*. Edinburgh: T. & T. Clark, 1994
– *Paul and the Stoics*. Edinburgh: T. & T. Clark, 2000.
Epstein, Isodore. (ed.), *The Babylonian Talmud*. 20 Vols. London: Soncino, 1933–1959.
Evans, Craig A. *Luke*. NIBC. Peabody: Hendrickson, 1990.
– 'Authenticating the Activities of Jesus', in Bruce Chilton and Craig A. Evans (eds.), *Authenticating the Activities of Jesus*. Leiden: Brill, 1999, pp.3-29.
Evans, Christopher F. *Saint Luke*. TPI New Testament Commentaries. London/Philadelphia: SCM/Trinity, 1990.
Eve, Eric. *The Jewish Context of Jesus' Miracles*. JSNTSup 231; Sheffield: Sheffield Academic Press, 2002.
Faraone, Christopher A. 'The Agonistic Context of Early Greek Binding Spells', in C.A. Faraone and Dirk Obbink (eds.), *Magika Hiera: Ancient Greek Magic and Religion*. Oxford: Oxford University Press, 1991, paperback 1997, pp.3-32.
Fee, Gordon D. *The First Epistle to the Corinthians*. NICNT. Grand Rapids: Eerdmans, 1987.
– 'Gifts of the Spirit', in Gerald F. Hawthorne, Ralph P. Martin and Daniel G. Reid (eds.), *Dictionary of Paul and his Letters*. Downers Grove/Leicester: InterVarsity Press, 1993, pp.339-47.
– *God's Empowering Presence: The Holy Spirit in the Letters of Paul*. Peabody: Hendrickson, 1994.

– *Paul's Letter to the Philippians.* NICNT. Grand Rapids: Eerdmans, 1995.

Ferguson, Everett. 'Spiritual Sacrifice in Early Christianity and its Environment', in Wolfgang Haase (ed.), *Aufstieg und Niedergang der Römischen Welt* II.23.2. Berlin: de Gruyter, 1980, pp.1151-89.

– *Demonology of the Early Christian World.* Symposium Series. Vol.12; New York/Toronto: Mellen, 1984.

– *Backgrounds of Early Christianity.* 2nd ed.; Grand Rapids: Eerdmans, 1993.

Ferngren, Gary B. and Darrel W. Amundsen, 'Medicine and Christianity in the Roman Empire: Compatibilities and Tensions', in Wolfgang Haase (ed.), *Aufstieg und Niedergang der Römischen Welt* II.37.3. Berlin/New York: de Gruyter, 1996, pp.2957-80.

Fiorenza, Elisabeth Schüssler. 'Miracles, Mission and Apologetics: An Introduction', in Elisabeth S. Fiorenza (ed.), *Aspects of Religious Propaganda in Judaism and Early Christianity.* Notre Dame: University of Notre Dame Press, 1976, pp.1-25.

Fitzgerald, John T. *Cracks in an Earthen Vessel: An Examination of the Catalogues of Hardships in the Corinthian Correspondence.* SBLDS 99; Atlanta: Scholars Press, 1988.

Fitzmyer, Joseph A. *The Gospel According to Luke (I–IX).* AB, Vol.28. New York: Doubleday, 1981.

– *The Gospel According to Luke (X–XXIV).* AB, Vol.28A. New York: Doubleday, 1985.

– *Paul and His Theology. A Brief Sketch.* 2nd ed.; Englewood Cliffs, NJ: Prentice Hall, 1989.

– *The Acts of the Apostles. A New Translation with Introduction and Commentary.* AB. New York: Doubleday, 1997.

Fletcher-Louis, Crispin H.T. *Luke-Acts: Angels, Christology and Soteriology.* WUNT 2/94; Tübingen: Mohr (Siebeck), 1997.

Fohrer, Georg, and Werner Foerster. 'σῴζω', in Gerhard Kittel and Gerhard Friedrich (eds.), *Theological Dictionary of the New Testament,* Vol.7, 1971, pp.965-1024.

Forbes, Christopher. 'Comparison, Self-Praise and Irony: Paul's Boasting and the Conventions of Hellenistic Rhetoric', *NTS* 32 (1986) 1-30.

France, Richard T. *The Gospel of Mark. A Commentary on the Greek Text.* NIGTC. Grand Rapids/Carlisle: Eerdmans/Paternoster, 2002.

Fridrichsen, Anton. *The Problem of Miracle in Primitive Christianity.* (Orig. 1925). ET; Minneapolis: Augsburg, 1972.

Friesen, Steven J. 'Poverty in Pauline Studies: Beyond the So-Called New Consensus', *JSNT* 26 (2004) 323-61.

Fuller, Reginald H. *The Foundations of New Testament Christology.* New York: Scribner's Sons, 1965.

– *Interpreting the Miracles.* (Orig. 1963); London: SCM, 1971.

Funk, Robert W. and the Jesus Seminar. *The Acts of Jesus.* New York: HarperCollins, 1998.

Furnish, Victor Paul. *II Corinthians.* AB, Vol.32A. New York: Doubleday, 1984.

– 'The Jesus–Paul Debate: From Baur to Bultmann', (orig. 1964-65) in Alexander J.M. Wedderburn (ed.), *Paul and Jesus. Collected Essays.* JSNTSup 37; Sheffield: JSOT Press, 1989, pp.17-50.

Gallagher, Eugene V. *Divine Man or Magician? Celsus and Origen on Jesus.* SBLDS 64; Chico: Scholars Press, 1982.

Garrett, Susan R. *The Demise of the Devil. Magic and the Demonic in Luke's Writings.* Minneapolis: Fortress, 1989.

– 'Light on a Dark Subject and vice versa: Magic and Magicians in the New Testament', in Jacob Neusner, Ernest S. Frerichs and Paul V.McC. Flesher (eds.), *Religion, Science and Magic. In Concert and in Conflict.* Oxford: Oxford University Press, 1989, pp.142-63.

– 'Paul's Thorn and Cultural Models of Affliction', in L. Michael White and O. Larry Yarbrough (eds.), *The Social World of the First Christians. Essays in Honor of Wayne A. Meeks.* Minneapolis: Augsburg Fortress, 1995, pp.82-99.

Gärtner, Burkhard. 'To suffer', in Colin Brown (ed.), *NIDNTT*, Vol.3. Exeter: Paternoster, 1978, pp.719-26.

Gaventa, Beverly Roberts. *First and Second Thessalonians. Interpretation. A Bible Commentary for Teaching and Preaching.* Louisville: John Knox, 1998.

Geivett, R. Douglas and Gary R. Habermas, 'Introduction', in R.D. Geivett and G.R. Habermas (eds.), *In Defence of Miracles. A Comprehensive Case for God's Action in History.* Leicester: Apollos/InterVarsity Press, 1997, pp.9-26.

Gempf, Conrad. 'Public Speaking and Published Accounts', in Bruce W. Winter and Andrew D. Clarke (eds.), *The Book of Acts in its Ancient Literary Setting,* Vol.1 *The Book of Acts in its First Century Setting*, Grand Rapids/Carlisle: Eerdmans/Paternoster, 1993, pp.259-303.

Georgi, Dieter. 'Socioeconomic Reasons for the "Divine Man" as a Propagandist Pattern', in Elisabeth S. Fiorenza (ed.), *Aspects of*

Religious Propaganda in Judaism and Early Christianity. Notre Dame: University of Notre Dame Press, 1976, pp.27-42.
– *The Opponents of Paul in Second Corinthians.* ET; Edinburgh: T. & T. Clark, 1987.
Goddard, A.J. and S.A. Cummins, 'Ill or Ill-Treated? Conflict and Persecution as the Context of Paul's Original Ministry in Galatia (Galatians 4:12-20)', *JSNT* 52 (1993) 93-126.
Goldin, Judah. 'The Magic of Magic and Superstition', in Elisabeth S. Fiorenza (ed.), *Aspects of Religious Propaganda in Judaism and Early Christianity.* Notre Dame: University of Notre Dame Press, 1976, pp.115-47.
Goulder, Michael D. *Paul and the Competing Mission in Corinth.* Peabody: Hendrickson, 2001.
Graf, Fritz. 'Prayer in Magic and Religious Ritual', in Christopher A. Faraone and Dirk Obbink (eds.), *Magika Hiera: Ancient Greek Magic and Religion.* Oxford: Oxford University Press, 1991, pp.188-213.
Grant, Colleen C. 'Reinterpreting the Healing Narratives', in Nancy L. Eiesland and Don E. Saliers (eds.), *Disability in the Service of God. Reassessing Religious Practice.* Nashville: Abingdon, 1998, pp.72-87.
Green, Joel B. 'Good News to Whom? Jesus and the "Poor" in the Gospel of Luke', in Joel B. Green and Max Turner (eds.), *Jesus of Nazareth: Lord and Christ.* Grand Rapids/Carlisle: Eerdmans/Paternoster, 1994, pp.59-74.
– *The Gospel of Luke.* NICNT. Grand Rapids: Eerdmans, 1997.
– '"Salvation to the End of the Earth" (Acts 13:47): God as Saviour in the Acts of the Apostles', in I. Howard Marshall and David Peterson (eds.), *Witness to the Gospel. The Theology of Acts.* Grand Rapids/Cambridge: Eerdmans, 1998, pp.83-106.
– 'The Death of Jesus and the Ways of God', *Int* 52 (1998) 24-37.
Grundmann, Walter. 'δύναμαι/δύναμις', in Gerhard Kittel and Gerhard Friedrich (eds.), *Theological Dictionary of the New Testament,* Vol.2, 1965, pp.284-317.
Guelich, Robert A. *Mark 1–8:26.* WBC, Vol.34A. Dallas: Word Books, 1989.
Gundry, Robert H. *Mark. A Commentary on his Apology for the Cross.* Grand Rapids: Eerdmans, 1993.
Guthrie, Donald. *New Testament Introduction.* 3rd ed.; London: InterVarsity Press, 1970.
– *The Apostles.* London: Pickering & Inglis, 1975.

Guthrie, Douglas. *A History of Medicine*. London: Nelson & Sons, 1945.

Habermas, Gary R. 'Did Jesus Perform Miracles?', in Michael J. Wilkins and James P. Moreland (eds.), *Jesus Under Fire*. Carlisle: Paternoster, 1996, pp.117-40.

Haenchen, Ernst. *The Acts of the Apostles. A Commentary*. ET; Oxford: Blackwell, 1971.

Hafemann, Scott J., 'Suffering', in Gerald F. Hawthorne, Ralph P. Martin, and Daniel G. Reid (eds.), *Dictionary of Paul and his Letters*, Downers Grove/Leicester: InterVarsity Press, 1993, pp.919-21.

– *2 Corinthians*. The NIV Application Commentary. Grand Rapids: Zondervan, 2000.

Hahn, F., 'υἱός θεοῦ', in H. Balz and G. Schneider (eds.), *Exegetical Dictionary of the New Testament,* Vol.3, ET; Edinburgh: T. & T. Clark, 1990, p.384.

Hamm, Dennis. 'Paul's Blindness and its Healing: Clues to Symbolic Intent (Acts 9, 22 and 26)', *Bib* 71 (1990) 63-72.

Von Harnack, Adolf. *What is Christianity?* ET; New York: Putnam, 1901.

– *Luke the Physician. The Author of the Third Gospel and the Acts of the Apostles.* ET; London: Williams and Norgate, 1907.

– *The Acts of the Apostles*. ET; London: Williams and Norgate, 1909.

Harris, Murray J. '"The Dead are Restored to Life": Miracles of Revivification in the Gospels', in David Wenham and Craig Blomberg (eds.), *Gospel Perspectives*, Vol.6. *The Miracles of Jesus.* Sheffield: JSOT Press, 1986, pp.295-326.

Harrisville, Roy A. *1 Corinthians*. ACNT. Minneapolis: Augsburg, 1987.

Hartman, Louis F. and Alexander A. Di Lella, 'Daniel', in Raymond E. Brown, Joseph E. Fitzmyer; and Roland E. Murphy (eds.), *The New Jerome Biblical Commentary*. 2nd ed.; London: Chapman, 1997, pp.406-20.

Harvey, A.E. *Jesus and the Constraints of History*. Bampton Lectures, 1980; London: Duckworth & Co., 1982.

– *Renewal through Suffering. A Study of 2 Corinthians*. Edinburgh: T. & T. Clark, 1996.

Hawthorne, Gerald F. 'The Imitation of Christ: Discipleship in Philippians', in Richard N. Longenecker (ed.), *Patterns of Discipleship in the New Testament.* Grand Rapids: Eerdmans, 1996, pp.163-79.

Hays, Richard B. *The Faith of Jesus Christ. An Investigation of the Narrative Substructure of Galatians 3:1–4:11.* SBLDS 56; Chico: Scholars Press, 1983.

Hemer, Colin J. 'Medicine in the New Testament World', in Bernard Palmer (ed.), *Medicine and the Bible.* Exeter: Paternoster, 1986, pp.43-83.

– *The Book of Acts in the Setting of Hellenistic History.* Conrad H. Gempf (ed.), WUNT 49; Tübingen: Mohr (Siebeck), 1989.

Hengel, Martin. *Judaism and Hellenism.* Vol.1. ET; London: SCM, 1974.

– *Christ and Power.* ET; Philadelphia: Fortress, 1977.

– *The Charismatic Leader and his Followers.* ET; Edinburgh: T. & T. Clark, 1981.

– *Between Jesus and Paul.* London: SCM, 1983.

– and Anna Maria Schwemer, *Paul between Damascus and Antioch.* ET; London: SCM, 1997.

Hobart, William Kirk. *The Medical Language of St. Luke: A Proof from Internal Evidence that 'The Gospel According to St Luke' and 'The Acts of the Apostles' were Written by the Same Person, and that the Writer was a Medical Man.* Dublin: Hodges, Figgis and Co., 1882.

Hogan, Larry P. *Healing in the Second Tempel* (sic) *Period.* Freiburg/Göttingen: Universitätsverlag/Vandenhoeck & Ruprecht, 1992.

Holladay, Carl. *Theios Aner in Hellenistic-Judaism: A Critique of the Use of this Category in New Testament Christology.* SBLDS 40; Missoula: Scholars Press, 1977.

Holmberg, Bengt. *Paul and Power: The Structure of Authority in the Primitive Church as Reflected in the Pauline Epistles.* ConBNT Series 11; Lund: Gleerup, 1978.

Hooker, Morna D. *The Gospel According to St Mark.* BNTC. London: Black, 1991.

– *The Signs of a Prophet. The Prophetic Actions of Jesus.* Harrisburg: Trinity, 1997.

Hopkins, Keith. *Death and Renewal. Sociological Studies in Roman History*, Vol.2. Cambridge: Cambridge University Press, 1983.

– *A World Full of Gods. Pagans, Jews and Christians in the Roman Empire.* London: Phoenix/Weidenfeld & Nicolson, 1999.

– (with Melinda Letts). 'Death in Rome', in K. Hopkins, *Death and Renewal,* Vol.2. Cambridge: Cambridge University Press, 1983, pp.201-56.

Horbury, William. *Jewish Messianism and the Cult of Christ.* London: SCM, 1998.

Horrell, David G. *The Social Ethos of the Corinthian Correspondence. Interests and Ideology from 1 Corinthians to 1 Clement.* Edinburgh: T. & T. Clark, 1996.

– *An Introduction to the Study of Paul.* London/New York: Continuum, 2000.

Horsley, Richard A. *1 Corinthians.* ANTC. Nashville: Abingdon, 1998.

– and Neil Asher Silberman. *The Message and the Kingdom. How Jesus and Paul Ignited a Revolution and Transformed the Ancient World.* New York: Grosset/Putnam, 1997.

Howard, J. Keir. *Disease and Healing in the New Testament: An Analysis and Interpretation.* New York/Oxford: University of America Press, 2001.

Hughes, Philip Edgcumbe. *Paul's Second Epistle to the Corinthians.* NICNT. Grand Rapids: Eerdmans, 1962.

Hull, John M. *Hellenistic Magic and the Synoptic Tradition.* London: SCM, 1974.

– *In the Beginning there was Darkness. A Blind Person's Conversations with the Bible.* London: SCM, 2001.

Hume, David. 'Of Miracles', in *Philosophical Essays Concerning the Human Understanding.* (Orig. 1748); reprinted in R. Douglas Geivett and Gary R. Habermas (eds.), *In Defence of Miracles. A Comprehensive Case for God's Action in History.* Leicester: Apollos, 1997, pp.29-44.

Hurtado, Larry W. *One God, One Lord. Early Christian Devotion and Ancient Jewish Monotheism.* Philadelphia: Fortress, 1988.

– *Mark.* NIBC. Peabody: Hendrickson, 1989.

– 'Lord', in Gerald F. Hawthorne, Ralph P. Martin, and Daniel G. Reid (eds.), *Dictionary of Paul and his Letters.* Downers Grove/Leicester; InterVarsity Press, 1993, pp.560-69.

– *Lord Jesus Christ. Devotion to Jesus in Earliest Christianity.* Grand Rapids/Cambridge: Eerdmans, 2003.

Inwood, Brad. *The Poem of Empedocles.* ET, rev. ed.; Toronto: University of Toronto Press, 2001.

Isaac, E. '1 Enoch', in James H. Charlesworth (ed.), *The Old Testament Pseudepigrapha*, Vol.1. London: Darton, Longman and Todd, 1983, pp.5-89.

Jackson, Ralph. *Doctors and Diseases in the Roman Empire.* London: British Museum Pub., 1988.

Jervell, Jacob. *The Unknown Paul. Essays on Luke-Acts and Early Christian History*. Minneapolis: Augsburg, 1984.

– 'The Future of the Past: Luke's Vision of Salvation History and its Bearing on his Writing of History', in Ben Witherington, III (ed.), *History, Literature and Society in the Book of Acts*. Cambridge: Cambridge University Press, 1996, pp.104-26.

– *The Theology of the Acts of the Apostles*. Cambridge: Cambridge University Press, 1996.

– *Die Apostelgeschichte*. KEK. Göttingen: Vandenhoeck & Ruprecht, 1998.

Jervis, L. Ann. 'Becoming like God through Christ: Discipleship in Romans', in Richard N. Longenecker (ed.), *Patterns of Discipleship in the New Testament*. Grand Rapids: Eerdmans, 1996, pp.143-62.

Johnson, Luke Timothy. *The Gospel of Luke*. SacPag Series, Vol.3. Collegeville: Liturgical, 1991.

– *The Acts of the Apostles*. SacPag Series, Vol.5. Collegeville: Liturgical, 1992.

– *The Writings of the New Testament. An Interpretation*. Rev. ed.; London: SCM, 1999.

Johnston, T.B. and J. Whillis (eds.), *Gray's Anatomy. Descriptive and Applied.* 30th ed.; London/New York: Longmans, Green & Co., 1949.

Judge, Edwin A. *The Social Pattern of Christian Groups in the First Century: Some Prolegomena to the Study of New Testament Ideas of Social Obligation*. London: Tyndale, 1960.

Kahl, Werner. *New Testament Miracle Stories in their Religious–Historical Setting: A religionsgeschichtliche Comparison from a Structural Perspective*. Göttingen: Vandenhoeck & Ruprecht, 1994.

Kähler, Martin. *The So-Called Historical Jesus and the Historic, Biblical Christ*. (Orig. 1892). ET; Philadelphia: Fortress, 1964.

Kee, Howard Clark. *The Origins of Christianity. Sources and Documents*. Englewood Cliffs: Prentice Hall, 1973.

– *Community of the New Age. Studies in Mark's Gospel*. NTL Series. London: SCM, 1977.

– *Miracle in the Early Christian World. A Study in Sociohistorical Method*. New Haven/London: Yale University Press, 1983.

– 'Testaments of the Twelve Patriarchs', in James H. Charlesworth (ed.), *Old Testament Pseudepigrapha*, Vol.1. London: Darton, Longman and Todd, 1983, pp.775-828.

– *Medicine, Miracle and Magic in New Testament Times*. SNTSMS 55; Cambridge: Cambridge University Press, 1986.

– 'Magic and Messiah', in Jacob Neusner, Ernest S. Frerichs and Paul V.McC. Flesher (eds.), *Religion, Science and Magic in Concert and in Conflict.* Oxford: Oxford University Press, 1989, pp.121-41.

– *Good News to the Ends of the Earth. The Theology of Acts.* London: SCM, 1990.

– 'Medicine and Healing', in *Anchor Bible Dictionary*, Vol.4 (1992) pp.659-64.

– *To Every Nation under Heaven. The Acts of the Apostles.* The New Testament in Context Series. Harrisburg: Trinity, 1997.

Kelsey, Morton. *Healing and Christianity: A Classic Study.* 2nd ed.; Minneapolis: Augsburg Fortress, 1995.

Kennedy, George A. 'The Sophists as Declaimers', in George W. Bowersock (ed.), *Approaches to the Second Sophistic.* Ephrata: Science Press, 1974, pp.17-22.

Kim, Seyoon. *The Origin of Paul's Gospel.* WUNT 2/4; Tübingen/Grand Rapids: Mohr (Siebeck)/Eerdmans, 1981-82.

– 'Jesus, Sayings of', in Gerald F. Hawthorne, Ralph P. Martin, and Daniel G. Reid (eds.), *Dictionary of Paul and his Letters.* Downers Grove/Leicester; InterVarsity Press, 1993, pp.474-92.

– 'God Reconciled his Enemy to Himself: The Origin of Paul's Concept of Reconciliation', in Richard N. Longenecker (ed.), *The Road from Damascus. The Impact of Paul's Conversion on his Life, Thought and Ministry.* Grand Rapids: Eerdmans, 1997, pp.102-24.

– *Paul and the New Perspective. Second Thoughts on the Origin of Paul's Gospel.* WUNT 140; Tübingen/Grand Rapids: Mohr (Siebeck)/Eerdmans, 2002.

Kingsbury, Jack Dean. 'The "Divine Man" as the Key to Mark's Christology: The End of an Era?', *Int* 35 (1981) 243-56.

– *The Christology of Mark's Gospel.* Philadelphia: Fortress, 1983.

Klauck, Hans-Josef. *The Religious Context of Early Christianity. A Guide to Graeco-Roman Religions.* Edinburgh: T. & T. Clark, 2000.

– *Magic and Paganism in Early Christianity. The World of the Acts of the Apostles.* ET; Edinburgh: T. & T. Clark, 2000.

Kleinman, Arthur. *Patients and Healers in the Context of Culture. An Exploration of the Borderland between Anthropology, Medicine and Psychiatry.* Berkeley & Los Angeles: University of California Press, 1980.

Kolenkow, Anitra Bingham. 'Relationships between Miracle and Prophecy in the Greco-Roman World and Early Christianity', in Wolfgang Haase (ed.), *Aufstieg und Niedergang der Römischen Welt* II.23.2. Berlin: de Gruyter, 1980, pp.1470-506.

– 'Paul and his Opponents in 2 Corinthians 10-13, *Theioi Andres* and Spiritual Guides', in Lukas Bormann, Kelly del Tredici, and Angela Standhartinger (eds.), *Religious Propaganda and Missionary Competition in the New Testament World.* NovTSup 74; Leiden: Brill, 1994, pp.351-74.

Kotansky, Roy. 'Incantations and Prayers for Salvation on Inscribed Greek Amulets', in Christopher A. Faraone and Dirk Obbink (eds.), *Magika Hiera: Ancient Greek Magic and Religion.* Oxford: Oxford University Press, 1991, pp.107-37.

Kruse, Colin G. *New Testament Models for Ministry. Jesus and Paul.* London: Marshall, Morgan & Scott, 1983.

– *The Second Epistle of Paul to the Corinthians.* TynNTC. Leicester/Grand Rapids: InterVarsity Press/Eerdmans, 1987.

Lalleman, Pieter J. 'Healing by a Mere Touch as a Christian Concept', *TynBul* 48 (1997) 355-61.

Lampe, George W.H. 'Miracles in the Acts of the Apostles', in C.F.D. Moule (ed.), *Miracles. Cambridge Studies in Their Philosophy and History.* London: Mowbray, 1965, pp.163-78.

– 'Miracles and Early Christian Apologetic', in C.F.D. Moule (ed.), *Miracles. Cambridge Studies in their Philosophy and History.* London: Mowbray, 1965, pp.205-18.

Lane Fox, Robin. *Pagans and Christians.* London: Viking, 1986.

Lattke, M. 'ἐκπτύω', in H. Balz and G. Schneider (eds.), *Exegetical Dictionary of the New Testament.* Vol.1, ET; Edinburgh: T. & T. Clark, 1990, p.420.

Lentz, John Clayton Jr, *Luke's Portrait of Paul.* SNTSMS 77; Cambridge: Cambridge University Press, 1993.

Lewis, Clive S. *Mere Christianity.* London: Collins, 1956.

Lewis, Gilbert. 'Cultural Influences on Illness Behavior: A Medical Anthropological Approach', in Leon Eisenberg and Arthur Kleinman (eds.), *The Relevance of Social Science for Medicine.* Dordrecht, Holland: Reidel, 1981, pp.151-96.

Lightfoot, Joseph B. *The Epistle of St. Paul to the Galatians.* Reproduced by Zondervan Commentary Series. Grand Rapids: Zondervan, 1957.

Lindars, Barnabas. 'Elijah, Elisha and the Gospel Miracles', in C.F.D. Moule (ed.), *Miracles. Cambridge Studies in their Philosophy and History.* London: Mowbray, 1965, pp.63-79.

Litfin, A. Duane. *St Paul's Theology of Proclamation, 1 Corinthians 1–4 and Graeco-Roman Rhetoric.* SNTSMS 79; Cambridge: Cambridge University Press, 1994.

Loader, William. 'Challenged at the Boundaries: A Conservative Jesus in Mark's Tradition', *JSNT* 63 (1996) 45-61.

Longenecker, Richard N. (ed.), *Patterns of Discipleship in the New Testament.* Grand Rapids: Eerdmans, 1996.

– 'A Realized Hope, a New Commitment, and a Developed Proclamation: Paul and Jesus', in Richard N. Longenecker (ed.), *The Road from Damascus. The Impact of Paul's Conversion on his Life, Thought and Ministry.* Grand Rapids: Eerdmans, 1997, pp.18-42.

– *Life in the Face of Death. The Resurrection Message of the New Testament.* Grand Rapids/Cambridge: Eerdmans, 1998.

Van der Loos, H. *The Miracles of Jesus.* NovTSup 9; Leiden: Brill, 1965.

Lüdemann, Gerd. 'Acts of the Apostles as a Historical Source', in Jacob Neusner, Peder Borgen, Ernest S. Frerichs and Richard Horsley (eds.), *The Social World of Formative Christianity and Judaism.* Philadelphia: Fortress, 1988, pp.109-25.

Mack, Burton L. *A Myth of Innocence: Mark and Christian Origins.* Philadelphia: Fortress, 1988.

MacMullen, Ramsay. *Roman Social Relations 50 BC to AD 284.* New Haven/London: Yale University Press, 1974.

– *Paganism in the Roman Empire.* New Haven/London: Yale University Press, 1981.

Maddox, Robert. *The Purpose of Luke–Acts.* Göttingen: Vandenhoeck & Ruprecht, 1982.

Malherbe, Abraham J. *Social Aspects of Early Christianity.* Baton Rouge: Louisiana State University Press, 1977.

Malina, Bruce J. 'Reading Theory Perspective: Reading Luke-Acts', in Jerome H. Neyrey (ed.), *The Social World of Luke-Acts: Models for Interpretation.* Peabody: Hendrickson, 1991, pp.3-23.

– *The Social World of Jesus and the Gospels.* New York/London: Routledge, 1996.

– *The Social Gospel of Jesus. The Kingdom of God in Mediterranean Perspective.* Minneapolis: Fortress, 2001.

– and Jerome H. Neyrey, 'Honor and Shame in Luke-Acts: Pivotal Values of the Mediterranean World', in J.H. Neyrey (ed.), *The Social World of Luke-Acts: Models for Interpretation.* Peabody: Hendrickson, 1991, pp.25-65.

– and Jerome H. Neyrey, 'First-Century Personality: Dyadic, Not Individual', in J.H. Neyrey (ed.), *The Social World of Luke-Acts: Models for Interpretation.* Peabody: Hendrickson, 1991, pp.67-96.

– and Jerome H. Neyrey, *Portraits of Paul. An Archaeology of Ancient Personality*. Louisville: Westminster/John Knox, 1996.

Marcus, Joel. 'Mark–Interpreter of Paul', *NTS* 46 (2000) 473-87.

Margalioth, Mordecai A. (ed.), *Sepher-ha-Razim: The Book of Mysteries*. (Orig. 1966). ET; SBLTT 25; Atlanta: Scholars Press, 1983.

Marshall, Christopher D. *Faith as a Theme in Mark's Narrative*. SNTSMS 64; Cambridge: Cambridge University Press, 1989.

Marshall, I. Howard. *Luke. Historian and Theologian*. Exeter: Paternoster, 1970.

– 'Palestinian and Hellenistic Christianity: Some Critical Comments', *NTS* 19 (1973) 271-87.

– *The Gospel of Luke. A Commentary on the Greek Text*. NIGTC. Exeter: Paternoster, 1978.

– *The Acts of the Apostles. An Introduction and Commentary*. Leicester/Grand Rapids: InterVarsity Press/Eerdmans, 1980.

– 'A New Understanding of the Present and the Future: Paul and Eschatology', in Richard N. Longenecker (ed.), *The Road From Damascus. The Impact of Paul's Conversion on his Life, Thought and Ministry*. Grand Rapids: Eerdmans, 1997, pp.43-61.

Marshall, Peter. *Enmity in Corinth: Social Conventions in Paul's Relations with the Corinthians*. WUNT 2/23; Tübingen: Mohr (Siebeck), 1987.

Martin, Dale B. *The Corinthian Body*. New Haven: Yale University Press, 1995.

– 'Review of Justin J. Meggitt, *Paul, Poverty and Survival*, 1998', *JSNT* 84 (2001) 51-64.

Martin, Ralph P. *Mark: Evangelist and Theologian*. Grand Rapids: Zondervan, 1973.

– *2 Corinthians*. WBC, Vol.40. Waco: Word Books, 1986.

– 'The Opponents of Paul in 2 Corinthians: An Old Issue Revisited', in Gerald F. Hawthorne and Otto Betz (eds.), *Tradition and Interpretation in the New Testament. Essays in Honor of E. Earle Ellis*. Grand Rapids/Tübingen: Eerdmans/Mohr (Siebeck), 1987, pp.279-89.

Martin, Troy W. 'Whose Flesh? What Temptation? (Galatians 4:13-14)', *JSNT* 74 (1999) 65-91.

Martínez, Florentino García. *The Dead Sea Scrolls Translated. The Qumran Texts in English*. 2nd ed.; Leiden/Grand Rapids: Brill/Eerdmans, 1996.

Von Martitz, W. 'υἱός' κτλ., in Gerhard Kittel and Gerhard Friedrich (eds.), *Theological Dictionary of the New Testament,* Vol.8, 1972, pp.334-40.

Matera, Frank J. '"He Saved Others; He Cannot Save Himself". A Literary-Critical Perspective on the Markan Miracles', *Int* 47 (1993) 15-28.

Meeks, Wayne A. *The Prophet–King. Moses Traditions and the Johannine Christology*. Leiden: Brill, 1967.

– *The First Urban Christians: The Social World of the Apostle Paul.* New Haven: Yale University Press, 1983.

Meggitt, Justin J. *Paul, Poverty and Survival.* Edinburgh: T. & T. Clark, 1998.

– 'Response to Martin and Theissen', *JSNT* 84 (2001) 85-94.

Meier, John P. *A Marginal Jew. Rethinking the Historical Jesus.* Vol.II. *Mentor, Message and Miracles.* New York: Doubleday, 1994.

Melcher, Sarah J. 'Visualising the Perfect Cult: The Priestly Rationale for Exclusion', in Nancy L. Eiesland and Don E. Saliers (eds.), *Human Disability and the Service of God. Reassessing Religious Practice.* Nashville: Abingdon, 1998, pp.55-71.

Menken, M.J.J. 'The Position of Σπλαγχνίζεσθαι and Σπλάγχνα in the Gospel of Luke', *NovT* 30 (1988) 107-114.

Menzies, Robert P. *Empowered for Witness. The Spirit in Luke-Acts.* JPTSup 6; Sheffield: Sheffield Academic Press, 1994.

Metzger, Bruce M. 'The Fourth Book of Ezra', in James H. Charlesworth (ed.), *The Old Testament Pseudepigrapha,* Vol.1. London: Darton, Longman and Todd, 1983, pp.517-59.

Minear, Paul S. *To Heal and to Reveal. The Prophetic Vocation According to Luke.* New York: Seabury, 1976.

Moessner, David P. '"The Christ Must Suffer": New Light on the Jesus–Peter, Stephen, Paul Parallels in Luke-Acts', *NovT* 28 (1986) 220-56.

Mohrlang, Roger. *Matthew and Paul. A Comparison of Ethical Perspectives.* SNTSMS 48; Cambridge: Cambridge University Press, 1984.

Moltmann, Jürgen. 'Liberate Yourselves by Accepting one Another', in Nancy L. Eiesland and Don L. Saliers (eds.), *Human Disability and the Service of God. Reassessing Religious Practice.* Nashville: Abingdon, 1998, pp.105-22.

Moo, Douglas J. *The Epistle to the Romans.* NICNT. Grand Rapids/Cambridge: Eerdmans, 1996.

Moule, Charles F.D. 'Jesus, Judaism and Paul', in Gerald F. Hawthorne and Otto Betz (eds.), *Tradition and Interpretation in the New*

Testament. Essays in Honor of E. Earle Ellis. Grand Rapids/Tübingen: Eerdmans/Mohr (Siebeck), 1987, pp.43-52.

Mullins, T.Y. 'Paul's Thorn in the Flesh', *JBL* 76 (1957) 299-303.

Murphy-O'Connor, Jerome. *The Theology of the Second Letter to the Corinthians.* Cambridge: Cambridge University Press, 1991, reprint 1996.

– *Paul. A Critical Life.* Oxford: Clarendon, 1996.

Myers, Charles. *Binding the Strong Man. A Political Reading of Mark's Story of Jesus.* Maryknoll: Orbis, 1988.

Neirynck, Franz. 'The Miracle Stories in the Acts of the Apostles. An Introduction', in Jacob Kremer (ed.), *Les Actes des Apôtres. Traditions, Rédaction, Théologie.* BETL 48; Louvain: Leuven University Press, 1979, pp.169-213.

Neusner, Jacob, (ed.), *The Modern Study of the Mishnah.* Leiden: Brill, 1973.

– *Eliezer ben Hyrcanus. The Tradition and the Man.* Studies in Judaism in Late Antiquity, Vol.1. Leiden: Brill, 1973.

– 'Science and Magic, Miracle and Magic in Formative Judaism', in Jacob Neusner, Ernest S. Frerichs, Peder Borgen and Richard Horsley (eds.), *The Social World of Formative Christianity and Judaism.* Philadelphia: Fortress, 1988, pp.61-81.

Newton, Derek. *Deity and Diet. The Dilemma of Sacrificial Food at Corinth.* JSNTSup 169; Sheffield: Sheffield Academic Press, 1998.

Neyrey, Jerome H. 'The Absence of Jesus' Emotions–The Lucan Redaction of Luke 22:39-46', *Bib* 61 (1980) 153-71.

– *Paul, in Other Words: A Cultural Reading of his Letters.* Louisville: Westminster John Knox, 1990.

Nickelsburg, George W.E. *1 Enoch 1. A Commentary on the Book of 1 Enoch, Chapters 1-36; 81-108.* Hermeneia Series. Minneapolis: Augsburg Fortress, 2001.

Nielsen, Helge Kjær. *Heilung und Verkündigung. Das Verständnis der Heilung und ihres Verhältnisses zur Verkündigung bei Jesus und in der ältesten Kirche.* Leiden/New York/Köln: Brill, 1987.

– 'Review of S. Schreiber, *Paulus als Wündertater,* 1996', *JTS* 48 (1997) 596-98.

Nock, Arthur Darby. 'Paul and the Magus', in F.J. Foakes Jackson and Kirsopp Lake (eds.), *The Beginnings of Christianity,* Vol.5. Part 1. *The Acts of the Apostles.* London: MacMillan, 1933, pp.164-88.

– *St. Paul.* London: Oxford University Press, 1938, revised 1948.

– 'Religious Symbols and Symbolism I', (orig. 1955; republished in Zeph. Stewart (ed.), *Essays on Religion and the Ancient World,* Vol.2. Oxford: Clarendon, 1972, pp.877-94.

Nolland, John. *Luke 1–9:20.* WBC, Vol.35A. Dallas: Word Books, 1989.

– *Luke 18:35–24:53.* WBC, Vol.35C. Dallas: Word Books, 1993.

– 'Salvation-History and Eschatology', in I. Howard Marshall and David Peterson (eds.), *Witness to the Gospel. The Theology of Acts.* Grand Rapids/Cambridge: Eerdmans, 1998, pp.63-81.

Nutton, Vivian. 'Healers in the Medical Market-Place: Towards a Social History of Graeco-Roman Medicine', in Andrew Wear (ed.), *Medicine in Society. Historical Essays.* Cambridge: Cambridge University Press, 1992, pp.15-58.

Nystrom, David P. *James.* The NIV Application Commentary. Grand Rapids: Zondervan, 1997.

Oakes, Peter. *Philippians. From People to Letter.* SNTSMS 110. Cambridge: Cambridge University Press, 2001.

– 'Constructing Poverty Scales for Graeco-Roman Society', *JSNT* 26 (2004) 367-71.

O'Brien, Peter T. *The Epistle to the Philippians. A Commentary on the Greek Text.* NIGTC. Grand Rapids/Carlisle: Eerdmans/Paternoster, 1991.

Oepke, Albrecht. 'ἰάομαι', in Gerhard Kittel and Gerhard Friedrich (eds.), *Theological Dictionary of the New Testament,* Vol.3, 1967, pp.194-215.

– 'νόσος', in Gerhard Kittel and Gerhard Friedrich (eds.), *Theological Dictionary of the New Testament,* Vol.4, 1967, pp.1091-98.

O'Neill, John C. *Who Did Jesus Think He Was?* Leiden: Brill, 1995.

Palmer, Darryl W. 'Acts and the Ancient Historical Monograph', in Bruce W. Winter and Andrew D. Clarke (eds.), *The Book of Acts in its Ancient Literary Setting.* Vol.1. *The Book of Acts in its first Century Setting.* Grand Rapids/Carlisle: Eerdmans/Paternoster, 1993, pp.1-29.

Parsons, Mikeal C. *The Departure of Jesus in Luke-Acts. The Ascension Narratives in Context.* JSNTSup 21; Sheffield: Sheffield Academic Press, 1987.

Pearcy, Lee T. 'Medicine and Rhetoric in the Period of the Second Sophistic', in Wolfgang Haase (ed.), *Aufstieg und Niedergang der Römischen Welt* II. 37.1. Berlin/New York: de Gruyter, 1996, pp.445-56.

Perrin, Norman. 'The Christology of Mark. A Study in Methodology', in William R. Telford (ed.), *The Interpretation of Mark.* 2nd ed.; Edinburgh: T. & T. Clark, 1995, pp.125-40.

Peterson, Eugene H. 'Pastor Paul', in Sven K. Soderlund and N. Thomas Wright (eds.), *Romans and the People of God.* Grand Rapids/Cambridge: Eerdmans, 1999, pp.283-94.

Phillips, C.R., III. '"*Nullum Crimen sine Lege*": Socioreligious Sanctions on Magic', in Christopher A. Faraone and Dirk Obbink (eds.), *Magika Hiera. Ancient Greek Magic and Religion.* Oxford: Oxford University Press, 1991, pp.260-76.

Pilch, John J. 'Understanding Biblical Healing: Selecting the Appropriate Model', *BTB* 18 (1988) 60-66.

– 'Sickness and Healing in Luke-Acts', in Jerome H. Neyrey (ed.), *The Social World of Luke-Acts: Models for Interpretation.* Peabody: Hendrickson, 1991, pp.181-209.

Polaski, Sandra Hack. *Paul and the Discourse of Power.* Sheffield: Sheffield Academic Press, 1999.

Porter, Stanley E. *The Paul of Acts. Essays in Literary Criticism, Rhetoric, and Theology.* WUNT 115; Tübingen: Mohr (Siebeck), 1999.

Räisänen, Heikki. *The 'Messianic Secret' in Mark.* ET; Edinburgh: T. & T. Clark, 1990.

Ramsay, William M. *The Church in the Roman Empire before AD 170.* 2nd ed.; London: Hodder & Stoughton, 1893.

– *A Historical Commentary on St. Paul's Epistle to the Galatians.* London: Hodder & Stoughton, 1899.

Reasoner, Mark. *The Strong and the Weak. Romans 14:1–15:13 in Context.* SNTSMS 103; Cambridge: Cambridge University Press, 1999.

Reimer, Andy M. *Miracle and Magic. A Study in the Acts of the Apostles and the Life of Apollonius of Tyana.* JSNTSup 235; London: Sheffield Academic Press, 2002.

Remus, Harold. 'Miracle' (New Testament), in *Anchor Bible Dictionary* Vol.4 (1992) pp.856-69.

– *Jesus as Healer.* Cambridge: Cambridge University Press, 1997.

Rengstorf, Karl Heinrich. 'σημεῖον', in Gerhard Kittel and Gerhard Friedrich (eds.), *Theological Dictionary of the New Testament*, Vol.7, 1971, pp.200-69.

Rhoads, David and Donald Michie. *Mark as Story. An Introduction to the Narrative of a Gospel.* Philadelphia: Fortress, 1982.

Robbins, Vernon K. 'The Woman who Touched Jesus' Garment: Socio-Rhetorical Analysis of the Synoptic Accounts', *NTS* 33 (1987) 502-15.

Roberts, Alexander and James Donaldson (eds.), *The Ante-Nicene Fathers. The Writings of the Fathers.* 10 Vols. 2nd ed.; Edinburgh/Grand Rapids: T. & T. Clark/Eerdmans, 1986-90.

Robinson, James M. and Helmut Koester. *Trajectories Through Early Christianity.* Philadelphia: Fortress, 1971.

Roetzel, Calvin J. *The Letters of Paul.* 2nd ed.; Atlanta: John Knox, 1982; Brit. ed.; London: SCM, 1983.

– *The World that Shaped the New Testament.* Atlanta: John Knox, 1985.

– *Paul: The Man and the Myth.* Edinburgh: T. & T. Clark, 1999.

Ross, J.P. 'Some Notes on Miracle in the Old Testament', in C.F.D. Moule (ed.), *Miracles. Cambridge Studies in their Philosophy and History.* London: Mowbray, 1965, pp.43-60.

Rutgers, Leonard Victor. *The Jews in Late Ancient Rome.* Leiden: Brill, 1995.

Sanders, Ed. P. *The Tendencies of the Synoptic Tradition.* SNTSMS 9; Cambridge: Cambridge University Press, 1969.

– *Paul and Palestinian Judaism: A Comparison of Patterns of Religion.* London: SCM, 1977.

– *Paul, the Law, and the Jewish People.* Philadelphia: Fortress, 1983.

– *Jesus and Judaism.* London: SCM, 1985.

– *Paul.* Oxford: Oxford University Press, 1991.

– *The Historical Figure of Jesus.* Harmondsworth: Penguin, 1993.

– 'Paul', in John Barclay and John Sweet (eds.), *Early Christian Thought in its Jewish Context.* Cambridge: Cambridge University Press, 1996, pp.112-29.

– and Margaret Davies. *Studying the Synoptic Gospels.* London/Philadelphia: SCM/Trinity, 1989.

Savage, Timothy B. *Power through Weakness. Paul's Understanding of the Christian Ministry in 2 Corinthians.* SNTSMS 86; Cambridge: Cambridge University Press, 1996.

Scarborough, John. 'The Pharmacology of Sacred Plants, Herbs and Roots', in Christopher A. Faraone and Dirk Obbink (eds.), *Magika Hiera: Ancient Greek Magic and Religion.* Oxford: Oxford University Press, 1991, pp.138-74.

Schacter, Daniel L. 'Memory Distortion: History and Current Status', in D.L. Schacter (ed.), *Memory Distortion. How Minds, Brains and Societies Reconstruct the Past.* Cambridge, MA/London: Harvard University Press, 1995, pp.1-43.

Schneemelcher, Wilhelm (ed.). *New Testament Apocrypha.* Vol.1. *Gospel and Related Writings.* ET, 2nd ed.; Cambridge/Louisville: Clarke & Co./Westminster John Knox, 1991.

– *New Testament Apocrypha.* Vol.2. *Writings Related to the Apostles, Apocalypses, and Related Subjects.* ET, 2nd ed.; Cambridge/ Louisville: Clarke & Co./Westminster John Knox, 1992.

Schrage, Wolfgang. *Der erste Brief an die Korinther.* EKKNT; VII.3. 1 Kor. 11,17–14,40. Zürich/Düsseldorf: Benziger/Neukirchener, 1999.

Schreiber, Stefan. *Paulus als Wundertäter: Redaktionschlichtliche Untersuchungen zur Apostelgeschichte und den authentischen Paulusbriefen.* BZNW 79; Berlin/New York: de Gruyter, 1996.

Schütz, John Howard. *Paul and the Anatomy of Apostolic Authority.* SNTSMS 26; Cambridge: Cambridge University Press, 1975.

Schweitzer, Albert. *The Mysticism of Paul the Apostle.* ET; 2nd ed., reprint; London: A. & C. Black, 1956.

Schweizer, Eduard. *The Good News According to Mark.* ET; Atlanta: John Knox, 1970.

– 'Mark's Theological Achievement', in William R. Telford (ed.), *The Interpretation of Mark.* 2nd ed.; Edinburgh: T. & T. Clark, 1995, pp.63-87.

Segal, Alan F. 'Hellenistic Magic: Some Questions of Definition', in R. van den Broek and Maarten J. Vermaseren (eds.), *Studies in Gnosticism and Hellenistic Religions. Festschrift für G. Quispel.* EPRO 91; Leiden: Brill, 1981, pp.349-75.

– *Paul the Convert. The Apostolate and Apostasy of Saul the Pharisee.* New Haven/London: Yale University Press, 1990.

– 'On the Nature of Magic: A Report on a Dialogue between a Historian and a Sociologist', in L. Michael White and O. Larry Yarbrough (eds.), *The Social World of the First Christians: Essays in Honour of Wayne A. Meeks.* Minneapolis: Augsburg Fortress, 1995, pp.275-92.

Senior, Donald, 'Beware of the Canaanite Woman', in Marilyn E. Bishop (ed.), *Religion and Disability. Essays in Scripture, Theology and Ethics.* Kansas City: Sheed & Ward, 1995, pp.1-26.

Shelton, James B. *Mighty in Word and Deed. The Role of the Holy Spirit in Luke-Acts.* Peabody: Hendrickson, 1991.

Shepherd, William H., Jr. *The Narrative Function of the Holy Spirit as a Character in Luke–Acts.* SBLDS 147: Atlanta: Scholars Press, 1994.

Singer, Charles J. and Abraham Wasserstein. 'Medicine', in Nicholas G.L. Hammond and Howard H. Scullard (eds.), *OCD,* 2nd ed.; Oxford: Oxford University Press, 1970, pp.660-64.

Smith, Jonathan Z. 'Towards Interpreting Demonic Powers in Hellenistic and Roman Antiquity', in Wolfgang Haase (ed.), *Aufstieg und Niedergang der Römischen Welt* II.16.1. Berlin: de Gruyter,1978, pp.425-39.

Smith, Morton. 'Prolegomena to a Discussion of Aretalogies, Divine Men, the Gospels and Jesus', *JBL* 90 (1971) 174-99.

– *Jesus the Magician.* London: Gollancz, 1978.

Squires, John T. *The Plan of God in Luke-Acts.* SNTSMS 76; Cambridge: Cambridge University Press, 1993.

– 'The Plan of God in the Acts of the Apostles', in I. Howard Marshall and David Peterson (eds.), *Witness to the Gospel. The Theology of Acts.* Grand Rapids/Cambridge: Eerdmans, 1998, pp.19-39.

Stanley, A.P. *The Epistles of St. Paul to the Corinthians.* 4th ed.; London: J. Murray, 1876.

Stanton, Graham N. 'Jesus of Nazareth: A Magician and False Prophet who Deceived God's People?', in Joel B. Green and Max Turner (eds.), *Jesus of Nazareth: Lord and Christ.* Grand Rapids/Carlisle: Eerdmans/Paternoster, 1994, pp.164-80.

Stark, Rodney. *The Rise of Christianity. A Sociologist Reconsiders History.* Princeton: University of Princeton Press, 1996.

Stein, Robert H. *Luke.* The New American Commentary, Vol.24. Nashville: Broadman Press, 1992.

Stendahl, Krister. 'Biblical Theology, Contemporary', in G. A. Buttrick et al. (eds.), *IDB*, Vol.1. New York/Nashville: Abingdon, 1962, pp.418-32.

– *Paul among Jews and Gentiles.* Philadelphia: Fortress, 1976.

Strange, W.A. 'The Jesus Tradition in Acts', *NTS* 46 (2000) 59-74.

Strecker, Christian. 'Jesus and the Demoniacs', in Wolfgang Stegemann, Bruce J. Malina and Gerd Theissen (eds.), *The Social Setting of Jesus and the Gospels.* Minneapolis: Fortress, 2002, pp.117-33.

Sumney, Jerry L. *Identifying Paul's Opponents. The Question of Method in 2 Corinthians.* JSNTSup 40; Sheffield: Sheffield Academic Press, 1990.

– 'Paul's "Weakness": An Integral Part of his Apostleship', *JSNT* 52 (1993) 71-91.

Sussman, Max. 'Sickness and Disease', *Anchor Bible Dictionary,* Vol.6 (1992) pp.6-15.

Sweet, John P.M. 'The Theory of Miracles in the Wisdom of Solomon', in C.F.D. Moule (ed.), *Miracles. Cambridge Studies in their Philosophy and History.* London: Mowbray, 1965, pp.113-26.

Talbert, Charles H. 'The Acts of the Apostles: Monograph or "Bios"?', in Ben Witherington, III (ed.), *History, Literature, and Society in the Book of Acts*. Cambridge: Cambridge University Press, 1996, pp.58-72.

– *Reading Acts. A Literary and Theological Commentary on the Acts of the Apostles*. New York: Crossroad, 1997.

Tannehill, Robert C. *The Narrative Unity of Luke–Acts. A Literary Interpretation*. Vol.1. *The Gospel According to Luke*. Philadelphia: Fortress, 1986.

– *The Narrative Unity of Luke–Acts. A Literary Interpretation*. Vol.2. *The Acts of the Apostles*. Minneapolis: Fortress, 1990.

– *Luke*. ANTC. Nashville: Abingdon, 1996.

Telford, William R. 'Book Review of Carl H. Holladay, *"Theios Aner" in Hellenistic Judaism: A Critique of the Use of this Category in New Testament Christology* (1977)', *JTS* 30 (1979) 246-52.

– *Mark*. Sheffield: Sheffield Academic Press, 1995, reprint 1997.

– *The Theology of the Gospel of Mark*. Cambridge: Cambridge University Press, 1999.

Temkin, Owsei. *The Falling Sickness. A History of Epilepsy from the Greeks to the Beginnings of Modern Neurology*. 2nd ed.; Baltimore/London: Johns Hopkins University Press, 1971.

– *Hippocrates in a World of Pagans and Christians*. Baltimore/London: Johns Hopkins University Press, 1991.

Theissen, Gerd. 'Social Stratification in the Corinthian Community: A Contribution to the Sociology of Early Hellenistic Christianity' in John H. Schütz (ed. and ET), of G. Theissen, *The Social Setting of Pauline Christianity: Essays on Corinth*. ET; Edinburgh: T. & T. Clark, 1982, pp.69-119.

– *The Miracle Stories of the Early Christian Tradition*. ET; Edinburgh: T. &. T. Clark, 1983.

– *The Gospels in Context. Social and Political History in the Synoptic Tradition*. ET; Edinburgh: T. & T. Clark, 1992.

– 'The Social Structure of Pauline Communities: Some Critical Remarks on J.J. Meggitt, *Paul, Poverty and Survival*', *JSNT* 84 (2001) 65-85.

– 'Social Conflicts in the Corinthian Community: Further Remarks on J.J. Meggitt, *Paul, Poverty and Survival*', *JSNT* 25 n.s.3 (2003) 371-91.

– and Annette Merz. *The Historical Jesus. A Comprehensive Guide*. ET; London: SCM, 1998.

Thiselton, Anthony C. *The First Epistle to the Corinthians. A Commentary on the Greek Text.* NIGTC. Grand Rapids/Carlisle: Eerdmans/Paternoster, 2000.

Thomas, John Christopher. *The Devil, Disease and Deliverance. Origins of Illness in New Testament Thought.* JPTSup 13; Sheffield: Sheffield Academic Press, 1998, reprint 2002.

Thompson, Michael. *Clothed with Christ. The Example and Teaching of Jesus in Romans 12:1–15:13.* JSNTSup 59; Sheffield: JSOT Press, 1991.

Thrall, Margaret E. *A Critical and Exegetical Commentary on the Second Epistle to the Corinthians.* ICC, Vol.I. Edinburgh: T. & T. Clark, 1994.

– *A Critical and Exegetical Commentary on the Second Epistle to the Corinthians*, ICC, 2 Vols. 2nd ed.; London/New York: T. & T. Clark/Continuum, 2004.

Tiede, David L. *The Charismatic Figure as Miracle Worker.* SBLDS 1; Missoula: University of Montana Press, 1972.

– *Prophecy and History in Luke–Acts.* Philadelphia: Fortress, 1980.

– 'Aretalogy', in *Anchor Bible Dictionary,* Vol.1 (1992) pp.372-73.

Tuckett, Christopher M. (ed.), *The Messianic Secret.* Philadelphia: Fortress, 1983.

– *Luke.* New Testament Guides. Sheffield: Sheffield Academic Press, 1996.

– *Christology and the New Testament. Jesus and his Earliest Followers.* Louisville: Westminster/John Knox, 2001.

Turner, Max. 'The Spirit and the Power of Jesus' Miracles in the Lucan Conception', *NovT* 35 (1991) 124-52.

– *Power from on High: The Spirit in Israel's Restoration and Witness in Luke–Acts.* JPTSup 9; Sheffield: Sheffield Academic Press, 1996.

– *The Holy Spirit and Spiritual Gifts Then and Now.* Carlisle: Paternoster, 1996.

Twaddle, A.C. 'Sickness and the Sickness Career: Some Implications', in Leon Eisenberg and Arthur Kleinman (eds.), *The Relevance of Social Science for Medicine* (Dordrecht: Reidel, 1981) pp.111-33.

Twelftree, Graham H. 'ΕΙ ΔΕ — ΕΓΩ ΕΚΒΑΛΛΩ ΤΑ ΔΑΙΜΟΝΙΑ', in David Wenham and Craig Blomberg (eds.), *Gospel Perspectives*, Vol.6. *The Miracles of Jesus* (Sheffield: JSOT Press, 1986) pp.361-400.

– *Jesus the Exorcist: A Contribution to the Study of the Historical Jesus.* WUNT 2/54; Tübingen: Mohr (Siebeck), 1993.

VanderKam, James C. *The Book of Jubilees. Guides to Apocrypha and Pseudepigrapha.* Sheffield: Sheffield Academic Press, 2001.

Vawter, Bruce. 'Introduction to Prophetic Literature', in Raymond E. Brown, Joseph E. Fitzmyer; and Roland E. Murphy (eds.), *The New Jerome Biblical Commentary.* 2nd ed.; London: Chapman, 1997, pp.186-200.

Vermes, Geza. *Jesus the Jew. A Historian's Reading of the Gospels.* London: Collins, 1973.

De Vos, Craig S. 'Finding a Charge that Fits: The Accusation against Paul and Silas at Philippi (Acts 16:19-21)', *JSNT* 74 (1999) 51-63.

Walter, Nikolaus. 'Paul and the Early Christian Jesus-Tradition', in Alexander J.M. Wedderburn (ed.), *Paul and Jesus. Collected Essays.* JSNTSup 37; Sheffield: JSOT Press, 1989, pp.51-80.

Walton, Steve. *Leadership and Lifestyle. The Portrait of Paul in the Miletus Speech and 1 Thessalonians.* SNTSMS 108; Cambridge: Cambridge University Press, 2000.

Wanamaker, Charles A. *The Epistles to the Thessalonians. A Commentary on the Greek Text.* NIGTC. Grand Rapids/Exeter: Eerdmans/Paternoster, 1990.

Ward, Keith. 'Miracles', in Andrew Walker (ed.), *Different Gospels. Christian Orthodoxy and Modern Theologies.* 2nd ed.; London: SPCK, 1993, pp.54-66.

Warrington, Keith. *Jesus the Healer. Paradigm or Unique Phenomenon?* Carlisle/Waynesboro: Paternoster, 2000.

Weatherhead, Leslie D. *Psychology, Religion and Healing.* London: Hodder & Stoughton, 1951.

Wedderburn, Alexander J.M. *The Reason for Romans.* Edinburgh: T. & T. Clark, 1988.

– 'Introduction', pp.11-15; 'Paul and Jesus. The Problem of Continuity', pp.99-115; 'Paul and Jesus. Similarity and Continuity', pp.117-43; 'Paul and the Story of Jesus', pp.161-89, 'Postscript', pp.191-95, in *Paul and Jesus. Collected Essays.* JSNTSup 37; Sheffield: Sheffield Academic Press, 1989.

Weeden, Theodore J. 'The Heresy that Necessitated Mark's Gospel,' (orig. *ZNW* 59 (1968) 145-58) in William R. Telford (ed.), *The Interpretation of Mark.* 2nd ed.; Edinburgh: T. & T. Clark, 1995, pp.89-104.

– *Mark: Traditions in Conflict.* Philadelphia: Fortress, 1971.

Weiss, Johannes. *Paul and Jesus.* ET; London/New York: Harper & Bros., 1909.

Wells, Louise. *The Greek Language of Healing from Homer to New Testament Times*. BZNW 83; Berlin/New York: de Gruyter, 1998.

Wenham, David. *Paul: Follower of Jesus or Founder of Christianity?* Grand Rapids: Eerdmans, 1995.

– 'The Story of Jesus Known to Paul', in Joel B. Green and Max Turner (eds.), *Jesus of Nazareth: Lord and Christ*. Grand Rapids/Carlisle: Eerdmans/Paternoster, 1994, pp.297-311.

– *Paul and Jesus. The True Story*. Grand Rapids/Cambridge: Eerdmans, 2002.

– and Steve Walton. *Exploring the New Testament*. Vol.1. *A Guide to the Gospels and Acts*. London: SPCK, 2001.

Wenham, Gordon J. 'Christ's Healing Ministry and his Attitude to the Law', in Harold H. Rowdon (ed.), *Christ the Lord*. Leicester: InterVarsity Press, 1982, pp.115-26.

Wilkinson, John. *The Bible and Healing. A Medical and Theological Commentary*. Edinburgh/Grand Rapids: Handsel/Eerdmans, 1998.

Williams, James G. *The Bible, Violence and the Sacred. Liberation from the Myth of Sanctioned Violence*. San Francisco/New York: HarperSanFrancisco, 1991.

Williams, Sam K. 'The Hearing of Faith: Ἀκοή Πίστεως in Galatians 3', *NTS* 35 (1989) 82-93.

Wink, Walter. 'Mark 2:1-12', *Int* 36 (1982) 63-67.

– *Naming the Powers. The Language of Power in the New Testament. The Powers*, Vol.1. Philadelphia: Fortress, 1984.

– *Unmasking the Powers. The Invisible Forces that Determine Human Existence. The Powers*, Vol.2. Philadelphia: Fortress, 1986.

Winter, Bruce W. *Seek the Welfare of the City. Christians as Benefactors and Citizens*. Grand Rapids/Carlisle: Eerdmans/Paternoster, 1994.

– *Philo and Paul among the Sophists*. SNTSMS 96; Cambridge: Cambridge University Press, 1997.

– *After Paul Left Corinth. The Influence of Secular Ethics and Social Change*. Grand Rapids/Cambridge: Eerdmans, 2001.

– *Philo and Paul among the Sophists. Alexandrian and Corinthian Responses to a Julio-Claudian Movement*. 2nd ed.; Grand Rapids/Cambridge, 2002.

- and Clarke, Andrew D. (eds.), *The Book of Acts in its Ancient Literary Setting*. Grand Rapids/Carlisle: Eerdmans/Paternoster, 1993.

Wiseman, Donald J. 'Medicine in the Old Testament World', in Bernard Palmer (ed.), *Medicine and the Bible*. Exeter: Paternoster, 1986, pp.13-42.

Witherington, Ben, III. *The Christology of Jesus*. Minneapolis: Fortress, 1990.

– *Paul's Narrative Thought World: The Tapestry of Tragedy and Triumph*. Louisville: Westminster/John Knox, 1994.

– *Conflict and Community in Corinth: A Socio-Rhetorical Commentary on 1 and 2 Corinthians*. Grand Rapids: Eerdmans, 1995.

– *The Paul Quest. The Renewed Search for the Jew of Tarsus*. Leicester: InterVarsity Press, 1998.

– *The Acts of the Apostles: A Socio-Rhetorical Commentary*. Grand Rapids/Cambridge: Eerdmans, 1998.

– *Grace in Galatia. A Commentary on Paul's Letter to the Galatians*. Grand Rapids: Eerdmans, 1998.

– 'Salvation and Health in Christian Antiquity: The Soteriology of Luke-Acts in its First-Century Setting', in I. Howard Marshall and David Peterson (eds.), *Witness to the Gospel. The Theology of Acts*. Grand Rapids/Cambridge: Eerdmans, 1998, pp.145-66.

– *The Gospel of Mark. A Socio-Rhetorical Commentary*. Grand Rapids/Cambridge: Eerdmans, 2001.

Wolff, Christian. 'True Apostolic Knowledge of Christ: Exegetical Reflections on 2 Corinthians 5:14 ff.', in Alexander J.M. Wedderburn (ed.), *Paul and Jesus. Collected Essays*. JSNTSup 37; Sheffield: Sheffield Academic Press, 1989, pp.81-98.

– 'Humility and Self-Denial in Jesus' Life and in the Apostolic Existence of Paul', in Alexander J.M. Wedderburn (ed.), *Paul and Jesus. Collected Essays*. JSNTSup 37; Sheffield: Sheffield Academic Press, 1989, pp.145-60.

Wrede, W. *The Messianic Secret*. (orig. 1901). ET; Cambridge/London: J. Clarke & Co. 1971.

Wright, N. Thomas. *The Climax of the Covenant. Christ and the Law in Pauline Theology*. Minneapolis: Fortress, 1992.

– *Jesus and the Victory of God*. London: SPCK, 1996.

– 'Jesus', in John Barclay and John Sweet (eds.), *Early Christian Thought in its Jewish Context*. Cambridge: Cambridge University Press, 1996, pp.43-58.

– *What Saint Paul Really Said: Was Paul of Tarsus the Real Founder of Christianity?* Grand Rapids: Eerdmans, 1997.

Wright, R.B. 'Psalms of Solomon', in James H. Charlesworth (ed.), *Old Testament Pseudepigrapha*, Vol.2. London: Darton, Longman and Todd, 1985, pp.638-70.

Yamauchi, Edwin M. 'Magic or Miracle? Diseases, Demons and Exorcisms', in David Wenham and Craig Blomberg (eds.), *Gospel*

Perspectives, Vol.6: *The Miracles of Jesus.* Sheffield: JSOT Press, 1986, pp.89-183.

Yeung, Maureen W-S. *Faith in Jesus and Paul. A Comparison with Special Reference to 'Faith that can Remove Mountains' and 'Your Faith has Healed/Saved You'.* Tübingen: Mohr (Siebeck), 2002.

Ziesler, John. *Paul's Letter to the Romans.* TPI New Testament Commentaries. London/Philadelphia: SCM/Trinity, 1989.

Select Author Index

Index of Biblical References

Paternoster Biblical Monographs

(All titles uniform with this volume)
Dates in bold are of projected publication

Joseph Abraham
Eve: Accused or Acquitted?
A Reconsideration of Feminist Readings of the Creation Narrative Texts in Genesis 1–3

Two contrary views dominate contemporary feminist biblical scholarship. One finds in the Bible an unequivocal equality between the sexes from the very creation of humanity, whilst the other sees the biblical text as irredeemably patriarchal and androcentric. Dr Abraham enters into dialogue with both camps as well as introducing his own method of approach. An invaluable tool for any one who is interested in this contemporary debate.

2002 / 0-85364-971-5 / xxiv + 272pp

Octavian D. Baban
Mimesis and Luke's on the Road Encounters in Luke-Acts
Luke's Theology of the Way and its Literary Representation

The book argues on theological and literary (mimetic) grounds that Luke's on-the-road encounters, especially those belonging to the post-Easter period, are part of his complex theology of the Way. Jesus' teaching and that of the apostles is presented by Luke as a challenging answer to the Hellenistic reader's thirst for adventure, good literature, and existential paradigms.

2005 */ 1-84227-253-5 / approx. 374pp*

Paul Barker
The Triumph of Grace in Deuteronomy

This book is a textual and theological analysis of the interaction between the sin and faithlessness of Israel and the grace of Yahweh in response, looking especially at Deuteronomy chapters 1–3, 8–10 and 29–30. The author argues that the grace of Yahweh is determinative for the ongoing relationship between Yahweh and Israel and that Deuteronomy anticipates and fully expects Israel to be faithless.

2004 / 1-84227-226-8 / xxii + 270pp

Jonathan F. Bayes
The Weakness of the Law
God's Law and the Christian in New Testament Perspective

A study of the four New Testament books which refer to the law as weak (Acts, Romans, Galatians, Hebrews) leads to a defence of the third use in the Reformed debate about the law in the life of the believer.

2000 / 0-85364-957-X / xii + 244pp

July 2005

Andrew D. Clarke

Secular and Christian Leadership in Corinth

A Socio-Historical and Exegetical Study of 1 Corinthians 1–6

This volume is an investigation into the leadership structures and dynamics of first-century Roman Corinth. These are compared with the practice of leadership in the Corinthian Christian community which are reflected in 1 Corinthians 1–6, and contrasted with Paul's own principles of Christian leadership.

***2005** / 1-84227-229-2 / 200pp*

Stephen Finamore

God, Order and Chaos

René Girard and the Apocalypse

Readers are often disturbed by the images of destruction in the book of Revelation and unsure why they are unleashed after the exaltation of Jesus. This book examines past approaches to these texts and uses René Girard's theories to revive some old ideas and propose some new ones.

***2005** / 1-84227-197-0 / approx. 344pp*

David G. Firth

Surrendering Retribution in the Psalms

Responses to Violence in the Individual Complaints

In *Surrendering Retribution in the Psalms*, David Firth examines the ways in which the book of Psalms inculcates a model response to violence through the repetition of standard patterns of prayer. Rather than seeking justification for retributive violence, Psalms encourages not only a surrender of the right of retribution to Yahweh, but also sets limits on the retribution that can be sought in imprecations. Arising initially from the author's experience in South Africa, the possibilities of this model to a particular context of violence is then briefly explored.

***2005** / 1-84227-337-X / xviii + 154pp*

Scott J. Hafemann

Suffering and Ministry in the Spirit

Paul's Defence of His Ministry in II Corinthians 2:14–3:3

Shedding new light on the way Paul defended his apostleship, the author offers a careful, detailed study of 2 Corinthians 2:14–3:3 linked with other key passages throughout 1 and 2 Corinthians. Demonstrating the unity and coherence of Paul's argument in this passage, the author shows that Paul's suffering served as the vehicle for revealing God's power and glory through the Spirit.

2000 / 0-85364-967-7 / xiv + 262pp

July 2005

Scott J. Hafemann
Paul, Moses and the History of Israel
The Letter/Spirit Contrast and the Argument from Scripture in 2 Corinthians 3
An exegetical study of the call of Moses, the second giving of the Law (Exodus 32–34), the new covenant, and the prophetic understanding of the history of Israel in 2 Corinthians 3. Hafemann's work demonstrates Paul's contextual use of the Old Testament and the essential unity between the Law and the Gospel within the context of the distinctive ministries of Moses and Paul.
2005 / 1-84227-317-5 / xii + 498pp

Douglas S. McComiskey
Lukan Theology in the Light of the Gospel's Literary Structure
Luke's Gospel was purposefully written with theology embedded in its patterned literary structure. A critical analysis of this cyclical structure provides new windows into Luke's interpretation of the individual pericopes comprising the Gospel and illuminates several of his theological interests.
2004 / 1-84227-148-2 / xviii + 388pp

Stephen Motyer
Your Father the Devil?
A New Approach to John and 'The Jews'
Who are 'the Jews' in John's Gospel? Defending John against the charge of antisemitism, Motyer argues that, far from demonising the Jews, the Gospel seeks to present Jesus as 'Good News for Jews' in a late first century setting.
1997 / 0-85364-832-8 / xiv + 260pp

Esther Ng
Reconstructing Christian Origins?
The Feminist Theology of Elizabeth Schüssler Fiorenza: An Evaluation
In a detailed evaluation, the author challenges Elizabeth Schüssler Fiorenza's reconstruction of early Christian origins and her underlying presuppositions. The author also presents her own views on women's roles both then and now.
2002 / 1-84227-055-9 / xxiv + 468pp

July 2005

Robin Parry

Old Testament Story and Christian Ethics

The Rape of Dinah as a Case Study

What is the role of story in ethics and, more particularly, what is the role of Old Testament story in Christian ethics? This book, drawing on the work of contemporary philosophers, argues that narrative is crucial in the ethical shaping of people and, drawing on the work of contemporary Old Testament scholars, that story plays a key role in Old Testament ethics. Parry then argues that when situated in canonical context Old Testament stories can be reappropriated by Christian readers in their own ethical formation. The shocking story of the rape of Dinah and the massacre of the Shechemites provides a fascinating case study for exploring the parameters within which Christian ethical appropriations of Old Testament stories can live.

2004 / 1-84227-210-1 / xx + 350pp

Ian Paul

Power to See the World Anew

The Value of Paul Ricoeur's Hermeneutic of Metaphor in Interpreting the Symbolism of Revelation 12 and 13

This book is a study of the hermeneutics of metaphor of Paul Ricoeur, one of the most important writers on hermeneutics and metaphor of the last century. It sets out the key points of his theory, important criticisms of his work, and how his approach, modified in the light of these criticisms, offers a methodological framework for reading apocalyptic texts.

2006 */ 1-84227-056-7 / approx. 350pp*

Robert L. Plummer

Paul's Understanding of the Church's Mission

Did the Apostle Paul Expect the Early Christian Communities to Evangelize?

This book engages in a careful study of Paul's letters to determine if the apostle expected the communities to which he wrote to engage in missionary activity. It helpfully summarizes the discussion on this debated issue, judiciously handling contested texts, and provides a way forward in addressing this critical question. While admitting that Paul rarely explicitly commands the communities he founded to evangelize, Plummer amasses significant incidental data to provide a convincing case that Paul did indeed expect his churches to engage in mission activity. Throughout the study, Plummer progressively builds a theological basis for the church's mission that is both distinctively Pauline and compelling.

2006 */ 1-84227-333-7 / approx. 324pp*

July 2005

David Powys

'Hell': A Hard Look at a Hard Question

The Fate of the Unrighteous in New Testament Thought

This comprehensive treatment seeks to unlock the original meaning of terms and phrases long thought to support the traditional doctrine of hell. It concludes that there is an alternative—one which is more biblical, and which can positively revive the rationale for Christian mission.

1997 / 0-85364-831-X / xxii + 478pp

Sorin Sabou

Between Horror and Hope

Paul's Metaphorical Language of Death in Romans 6.1-11

This book argues that Paul's metaphorical language of death in Romans 6.1-11 conveys two aspects: horror and hope. The 'horror' aspect is conveyed by the 'crucifixion' language, and the 'hope' aspect by 'burial' language. The life of the Christian believer is understood, as relationship with sin is concerned ('death to sin'), between these two realities: horror and hope.

***2005** / 1-84227-322-1 / approx. 224pp*

Rosalind Selby

The Comical Doctrine

The Epistemology of New Testament Hermeneutics

This book argues that the gospel breaks through postmodernity's critique of truth and the referential possibilities of textuality with its gift of grace. With a rigorous, philosophical challenge to modernist and postmodernist assumptions, Selby offers an alternative epistemology to all who would still read with faith *and* with academic credibility.

***2005** / 1-84227-212-8 / approx. 350pp*

Kiwoong Son

Zion Symbolism in Hebrews

Hebrews 12.18-24 as a Hermeneutical Key to the Epistle

This book challenges the general tendency of understanding the Epistle to the Hebrews against a Hellenistic background and suggests that the Epistle should be understood in the light of the Jewish apocalyptic tradition. The author especially argues for the importance of the theological symbolism of Sinai and Zion (Heb. 12:18-24) as it provides the Epistle's theological background as well as the rhetorical basis of the superiority motif of Jesus throughout the Epistle.

***2005** / 1-84227-368-X / approx. 280pp*

July 2005

Paternoster Theological Monographs

(All titles uniform with this volume)

Dates in bold are of projected publication

Emil Bartos

Deification in Eastern Orthodox Theology

An Evaluation and Critique of the Theology of Dumitru Staniloae

Bartos studies a fundamental yet neglected aspect of Orthodox theology: deification. By examining the doctrines of anthropology, christology, soteriology and ecclesiology as they relate to deification, he provides an important contribution to contemporary dialogue between Eastern and Western theologians.

1999 / 0-85364-956-1 / xii + 370pp

Graham Buxton

The Trinity, Creation and Pastoral Ministry

Imaging the Perichoretic God

In this book the author proposes a three-way conversation between theology, science and pastoral ministry. His approach draws on a Trinitarian understanding of God as a relational being of love, whose life 'spills over' into all created reality, human and non-human. By locating human meaning and purpose within God's 'creation-community' this book offers the possibility of a transforming engagement between those in pastoral ministry and the scientific community.

***2005** / 1-84227-369-8 / approx. 380 pp*

Iain D. Campbell

Fixing the Indemnity

The Life and Work of George Adam Smith

When Old Testament scholar George Adam Smith (1856–1942) delivered the Lyman Beecher lectures at Yale University in 1899, he confidently declared that 'modern criticism has won its war against traditional theories. It only remains to fix the amount of the indemnity.' In this biography, Iain D. Campbell assesses Smith's critical approach to the Old Testament and evaluates its consequences, showing that Smith's life and work still raises questions about the relationship between biblical scholarship and evangelical faith.

2004 / 1-84227-228-4 / xx + 256pp

July 2005

Tim Chester

Mission and the Coming of God

Eschatology, the Trinity and Mission in the Theology of Jürgen Moltmann

This book explores the theology and missiology of the influential contemporary theologian, Jürgen Moltmann. It highlights the important contribution Moltmann has made while offering a critique of his thought from an evangelical perspective. In so doing, it touches on pertinent issues for evangelical missiology. The conclusion takes Calvin as a starting point, proposing 'an eschatology of the cross' which offers a critique of the over-realised eschatologies in liberation theology and certain forms of evangelicalism.

***2006** / 1-84227-320-5 / approx. 224pp*

Sylvia Wilkey Collinson

Making Disciples

The Significance of Jesus' Educational Strategy for Today's Church

This study examines the biblical practice of discipling, formulates a definition, and makes comparisons with modern models of education. A recommendation is made for greater attention to its practice today.

2004 / 1-84227-116-4 / xiv + 278pp

Darrell Cosden

A Theology of Work

Work and the New Creation

Through dialogue with Moltmann, Pope John Paul II and others, this book develops a genitive 'theology of work', presenting a theological definition of work and a model for a theological ethics of work that shows work's nature, value and meaning now and eschatologically. Work is shown to be a transformative activity consisting of three dynamically inter-related dimensions: the instrumental, relational and ontological.

2005 / 1-84227-332-9 / xvi + 208pp

Stephen M. Dunning

The Crisis and the Quest

A Kierkegaardian Reading of Charles Williams

Employing Kierkegaardian categories and analysis, this study investigates both the central crisis in Charles Williams's authorship between hermetism and Christianity (Kierkegaard's Religions A and B), and the quest to resolve this crisis, a quest that ultimately presses the bounds of orthodoxy.

2000 / 0-85364-985-5 / xxiv + 254pp

Keith Ferdinando

The Triumph of Christ in African Perspective

A Study of Demonology and Redemption in the African Context

The book explores the implications of the gospel for traditional African fears of occult aggression. It analyses such traditional approaches to suffering and biblical responses to fears of demonic evil, concluding with an evaluation of African beliefs from the perspective of the gospel.

1999 / 0-85364-830-1 / xviii + 450pp

Andrew Goddard

Living the Word, Resisting the World

The Life and Thought of Jacques Ellul

This work offers a definitive study of both the life and thought of the French Reformed thinker Jacques Ellul (1912-1994). It will prove an indispensable resource for those interested in this influential theologian and sociologist and for Christian ethics and political thought generally.

2002 / 1-84227-053-2 / xxiv + 378pp

David Hilborn

The Words of our Lips

Language-Use in Free Church Worship

Studies of liturgical language have tended to focus on the written canons of Roman Catholic and Anglican communities. By contrast, David Hilborn analyses the more extemporary approach of English Nonconformity. Drawing on recent developments in linguistic pragmatics, he explores similarities and differences between 'fixed' and 'free' worship, and argues for the interdependence of each.

***2006** / 0-85364-977-4 / approx. 350pp*

Roger Hitching

The Church and Deaf People

A Study of Identity, Communication and Relationships with Special Reference to the Ecclesiology of Jürgen Moltmann

In *The Church and Deaf People* Roger Hitching sensitively examines the history and present experience of deaf people and finds similarities between aspects of sign language and Moltmann's theological method that 'open up' new ways of understanding theological concepts.

2003 / 1-84227-222-5 / xxii + 236pp

John G. Kelly

One God, One People

The Differentiated Unity of the People of God in the Theology of Jürgen Moltmann

The author expounds and critiques Moltmann's doctrine of God and highlights the systematic connections between it and Moltmann's influential discussion of Israel. He then proposes a fresh approach to Jewish–Christian relations building on Moltmann's work using insights from Habermas and Rawls.

2005 */ 0-85346-969-3 / approx. 350pp*

Mark F.W. Lovatt

Confronting the Will-to-Power

A Reconsideration of the Theology of Reinhold Niebuhr

Confronting the Will-to-Power is an analysis of the theology of Reinhold Niebuhr, arguing that his work is an attempt to identify, and provide a practical theological answer to, the existence and nature of human evil.

2001 / 1-84227-054-0 / xviii + 216pp

Neil B. MacDonald

Karl Barth and the Strange New World within the Bible

Barth, Wittgenstein, and the Metadilemmas of the Enlightenment

Barth's discovery of the strange new world within the Bible is examined in the context of Kant, Hume, Overbeck, and, most importantly, Wittgenstein. MacDonald covers some fundamental issues in theology today: epistemology, the final form of the text and biblical truth-claims.

2000 / 0-85364-970-7 / xxvi + 374pp

Keith A. Mascord

Alvin Plantinga and Christian Apologetics

This book draws together the contributions of the philosopher Alvin Plantinga to the major contemporary challenges to Christian belief, highlighting in particular his ground-breaking work in epistemology and the problem of evil. Plantinga's theory that both theistic and Christian belief is warrantedly basic is explored and critiqued, and an assessment offered as to the significance of his work for apologetic theory and practice.

2005 */ 1-84227-256-X / approx. 304pp*

July 2005

Gillian McCulloch

The Deconstruction of Dualism in Theology

With Reference to Ecofeminist Theology and New Age Spirituality

This book challenges eco-theological anti-dualism in Christian theology, arguing that dualism has a twofold function in Christian religious discourse. Firstly, it enables us to express the discontinuities and divisions that are part of the process of reality. Secondly, dualistic language allows us to express the mysteries of divine transcendence/immanence and the survival of the soul without collapsing into monism and materialism, both of which are problematic for Christian epistemology.

2002 / 1-84227-044-3 / xii + 282pp

Leslie McCurdy

Attributes and Atonement

The Holy Love of God in the Theology of P.T. Forsyth

Attributes and Atonement is an intriguing full-length study of P.T. Forsyth's doctrine of the cross as it relates particularly to God's holy love. It includes an unparalleled bibliography of both primary and secondary material relating to Forsyth.

1999 / 0-85364-833-6 / xiv + 328pp

Nozomu Miyahira

Towards a Theology of the Concord of God

A Japanese Perspective on the Trinity

This book introduces a new Japanese theology and a unique Trinitarian formula based on the Japanese intellectual climate: three betweennesses and one concord. It also presents a new interpretation of the Trinity, a co-subordinationism, which is in line with orthodox Trinitarianism; each single person of the Trinity is eternally and equally subordinate (or serviceable) to the other persons, so that they retain the mutual dynamic equality.

2000 / 0-85364-863-8 / xiv + 256pp

Eddy José Muskus

The Origins and Early Development of Liberation Theology in Latin America

With Particular Reference to Gustavo Gutiérrez

This work challenges the fundamental premise of Liberation Theology, 'opting for the poor', and its claim that Christ is found in them. It also argues that Liberation Theology emerged as a direct result of the failure of the Roman Catholic Church in Latin America.

2002 / 0-85364-974-X / xiv + 296pp

Jim Purves

The Triune God and the Charismatic Movement

A Critical Appraisal from a Scottish Perspective

All emotion and no theology? Or a fundamental challenge to reappraise and realign our trinitarian theology in the light of Christian experience? This study of charismatic renewal as it found expression within Scotland at the end of the twentieth century evaluates the use of Patristic, Reformed and contemporary models of the Trinity in explaining the workings of the Holy Spirit.

2004 / 1-84227-321-3 / xxiv + 246pp

Anna Robbins

Methods in the Madness

Diversity in Twentieth-Century Christian Social Ethics

The author compares the ethical methods of Walter Rauschenbusch, Reinhold Niebuhr and others. She argues that unless Christians are clear about the ways that theology and philosophy are expressed practically they may lose the ability to discuss social ethics across contexts, let alone reach effective agreements.

2004 / 1-84227-211-X / xx + 294pp

Ed Rybarczyk

Beyond Salvation

Eastern Orthodoxy and Classical Pentecostalism on Becoming Like Christ

At first glance eastern Orthodoxy and classical Pentecostalism seem quite distinct. This ground-breaking study shows they share much in common, especially as it concerns the experiential elements of following Christ. Both traditions assert that authentic Christianity transcends the wooden categories of modernism.

2004 / 1-84227-144-X / xii + 356pp

Signe Sandsmark

Is World View Neutral Education Possible and Desirable?

A Christian Response to Liberal Arguments

(Published jointly with The Stapleford Centre)

This book discusses reasons for belief in world view neutrality, and argues that 'neutral' education will have a hidden, but strong world view influence. It discusses the place for Christian education in the common school.

2000 / 0-85364-973-1 / xiv + 182pp

Hazel Sherman

Reading Zechariah

The Allegorical Tradition of Biblical Interpretation through the Commentary of Didymus the Blind and Theodore of Mopsuestia

A close reading of the commentary on Zechariah by Didymus the Blind alongside that of Theodore of Mopsuestia suggests that popular categorising of Antiochene and Alexandrian biblical exegesis as 'historical' or 'allegorical' is inadequate and misleading.

2005 */ 1-84227-213-6 / approx. 280pp*

Andrew Sloane

On Being a Christian in the Academy

Nicholas Wolterstorff and the Practice of Christian Scholarship

An exposition and critical appraisal of Nicholas Wolterstorff's epistemology in the light of the philosophy of science, and an application of his thought to the practice of Christian scholarship.

2003 / 1-84227-058-3 / xvi + 274pp

Damon W.K. So

Jesus' Revelation of His Father

A Narrative-Conceptual Study of the Trinity with Special Reference to Karl Barth

This book explores the trinitarian dynamics in the context of Jesus' revelation of his Father in his earthly ministry with references to key passages in Matthew's Gospel. It develops from the exegeses of these passages a non-linear concept of revelation which links Jesus' communion with his Father to his revelatory words and actions through a nuanced understanding of the Holy Spirit, with references to K. Barth, G.W.H. Lampe, J.D.G. Dunn and E. Irving.

2005 */ 1-84227-323-X / approx. 380pp*

Daniel Strange

The Possibility of Salvation Among the Unevangelised

An Analysis of Inclusivism in Recent Evangelical Theology

For evangelical theologians the 'fate of the unevangelised' impinges upon fundamental tenets of evangelical identity. The position known as 'inclusivism', defined by the belief that the unevangelised can be ontologically saved by Christ whilst being epistemologically unaware of him, has been defended most vigorously by the Canadian evangelical Clark H. Pinnock. Through a detailed analysis and critique of Pinnock's work, this book examines a cluster of issues surrounding the unevangelised and its implications for christology, soteriology and the doctrine of revelation.

2002 / 1-84227-047-8 / xviii + 362pp

Scott Swain

God According to the Gospel

Biblical Narrative and the Identity of God in the Theology of Robert W. Jenson

Robert W. Jenson is one of the leading voices in contemporary Trinitarian theology. His boldest contribution in this area concerns his use of biblical narrative both to ground and explicate the Christian doctrine of God. *God According to the Gospel* critically examines Jenson's proposal and suggests an alternative way of reading the biblical portrayal of the triune God.

***2006** / 1-84227-258-6 / approx. 180pp*

Justyn Terry

The Justifying Judgement of God

A Reassessment of the Place of Judgement in the Saving Work of Christ

The argument of this book is that judgement, understood as the whole process of bringing justice, is the primary metaphor of atonement, with others, such as victory, redemption and sacrifice, subordinate to it. Judgement also provides the proper context for understanding penal substitution and the call to repentance, baptism, eucharist and holiness.

***2005** / 1-84227-370-1 / approx. 274 pp*

Graham Tomlin

The Power of the Cross

Theology and the Death of Christ in Paul, Luther and Pascal

This book explores the theology of the cross in St Paul, Luther and Pascal. It offers new perspectives on the theology of each, and some implications for the nature of power, apologetics, theology and church life in a postmodern context.

1999 / 0-85364-984-7 / xiv + 344pp

Adonis Vidu

Postliberal Theological Method

A Critical Study

The postliberal theology of Hans Frei, George Lindbeck, Ronald Thiemann, John Milbank and others is one of the more influential contemporary options. This book focuses on several aspects pertaining to its theological method, specifically its understanding of background, hermeneutics, epistemic justification, ontology, the nature of doctrine and, finally, Christological method.

***2005** / 1-84227-395-7 / approx. 324pp*

July 2005

Graham J. Watts

Revelation and the Spirit

A Comparative Study of the Relationship between the Doctrine of Revelation and Pneumatology in the Theology of Eberhard Jüngel and of Wolfhart Pannenberg

The relationship between revelation and pneumatology is relatively unexplored. This approach offers a fresh angle on two important twentieth century theologians and raises pneumatological questions which are theologically crucial and relevant to mission in a postmodern culture.

2005 */ 1-84227-104-0 / xxii + 232pp*

Nigel G. Wright

Disavowing Constantine

Mission, Church and the Social Order in the Theologies of John Howard Yoder and Jürgen Moltmann

This book is a timely restatement of a radical theology of church and state in the Anabaptist and Baptist tradition. Dr Wright constructs his argument in dialogue and debate with Yoder and Moltmann, major contributors to a free church perspective.

2000 / 0-85364-978-2 / xvi + 252pp

Paternoster: thinking faith

Paternoster
9 Holdom Avenue,
Bletchley,
Milton Keynes MK1 1QR,
United Kingdom
Web: www.authenticmedia.co.uk/paternoster

July 2005